WHEN THE STARS ARE RIGHT

When the Stars Are Right

H. P. Lovecraft and Astronomy

Edward Guimont and Horace A. Smith

Hippocampus Press

New York

Copyright © 2023 by Edward Guimont and Horace A. Smith.

Published by Hippocampus Press
P.O. Box 641, New York, NY 10156.
www.hippocampuspress.com

All rights reserved.
No part of this work may be reproduced in any form or by any means without the written permission of the publisher.

Cover by Daniel V. Sauer, dansauerdesign.com
Hippocampus Press logo designed by Anastasia Damianakos.

First Edition
1 3 5 7 9 8 6 4 2

ISBN 978-1-61498-407-8 (paperback)
ISBN 978-1-61498-420-7 (e-book)

Dedication

Horace A. Smith dedicates this work to Deborah Benedict, who put up with all the piles of books.

Edward Guimont dedicates this work to Jessica Rivas, who was indulgent of all the pilgrimages to Providence.

Contents

Acknowledgments 9
Abbreviations 11
Chapter 1. My Gaze Was Ever Upward 13
Chapter 2. Ladd Observatory and Three Whom Lovecraft Pestered 52
Chapter 3. A Rooftop of Lovecraft's Astronomy 76
Chapter 4. Lovecraft Seeks the Garden of Eratosthenes 90
Chapter 5. Lovecraft's Lunar Cycle 112
Chapter 6. Stop the Presses—Venus in the West! 147
Chapter 7. Lovecraft Ventures to Venus 163
Chapter 8. In the Two-Corona Class 211
Chapter 9. At the Mountains of Mars 227
Chapter 10. Yuggoth's Environs 265
Chapter 11. The Great Enveloping Cosmic Dark 305
Chapter 12. Astronomy at the End 334
Appendix I. A Partial Timeline of Lovecraft and Astronomy 347
Appendix II. Lovecraft Dabbles in Astrophotography 351
Appendix III. Astronomy with Lovecraft's First Telescope 362
Bibliography 373
Index 399

Acknowledgments

The authors would like to thank Martin Andersson, Bill Black, Bobby Derie, Cian Gill, David J. Halperin, S. T. Joshi, Justin Mullis, Michael Umbricht, and David Zeppieri for their suggestions, comments, and help in answering questions. Jordan Goffin of the Providence Public Library and Stephanie Ovoian of the Providence Athenæum helped with inquiries into publications to which Lovecraft might have had access at those institutions. Matt Testa and the Arthur Friedheim Library Archives of the Peabody Institute at the Johns Hopkins University graciously provided access to their Garrett P. Serviss materials. Richard Bleiler, Donovan Reinwald, and the other staff of the University of Connecticut Homer Babbidge Library provided access to research materials without which, particularly during the coronavirus pandemic, this project could not have been completed. Raymond Butti, Heather Cole, and Laurie Rossi at the John Hay Library also were invaluable in helping us access materials related to Lovecraft and the Ladd Observatory. S. T. Joshi's *I Am Providence: The Life and Times of H. P. Lovecraft* was our go-to book for information concerning Lovecraft's all-too-brief life.

Although many works are explicitly cited in the text, we also benefited from the background information provided by several web-based collections of material relevant to Lovecraft, including *The H. P. Lovecraft Archive* (Donovan K. Loucks), *Tentaclii* (David Haden), *Lovecraftian Science* (Fred S. Lubnow), and *H. P. Lovecraft and His Legacy* (Chris Perridas). David Haden and Justin Mullis read drafts of several chapters and provided suggestions which led to significant improvements. Of course, any mistakes remaining in the text must be blamed on the authors.

Figure credits accompany each illustration, but we here give a general thank you to the Brown University Library, the California Museum of Photography, University of California, Riverside, the Digital Library at Villanova University, Michael Foight, Leigh Gleason, Heather Cole, and Russell J. Hawley for assisting with permissions to reproduce figures.

Finally, we acknowledge those Lovecraftian scholars who led the way on looking at Lovecraft's relations to astronomy and interplanetary fiction: Gavin Callaghan, Fritz Leiber, T. R. Livesey, and Fred S. Lubnow.

Abbreviations

HPL   H. P. Lovecraft

Hippocampus Press
AG   *Letters to Alfred Galpin and Others*
AT   *The Ancient Track*
CE   *Collected Essays* 1–5
CF   *Collected Fiction* 1–4
CLM   *Letters to C. L. Moore and Others*
DPO   "Dispatches from the Providence Observatory" (Livesey, *LA* 2)
DS   *Dawnward Spire, Lonely Hill* (letters of HPL and Clark Ashton Smith)
DW   *Letters with Donald and Howard Wandrei and to Emil Petaja*
EHP   *Letters to E. Hoffmann Price and Richard F. Searight*
ES   *Essential Solitude* (letters of HPL and August Derleth)
ET   *Letters to Elizabeth Toldridge and Anne Tillery Renshaw*
FLB   *Letters to F. Lee Baldwin, Duane W. Rimel, and Nils Frome*
IAP   *I Am Providence* (Joshi)
JFM   *Letters to James F. Morton*
JVS   *Letters to J. Vernon Shea, Carl F. Strauch, and Lee McBride White*
LA   *Lovecraft Annual* 1–15
LFF   *Letters to Family and Family Friends*
LL   *Lovecraft's Library*, 4th edition
LSS   "The Lovecraftian Solar System" (Lubnow, *LA* 13)
MF   *A Means to Freedom* (letters of HPL and Robert E. Howard)
Misc   *Miscellaneous Letters*
MWM   *Letters to Maurice W. Moe and Others*
RB   *Letters to Robert Bloch and Others*
RK   *Letters to Rheinhart Kleiner and Others*
WBT   *Letters to Wilfred B. Talman and Helen V. and Genevieve Sully*
WH   *Letters to Woodburn Harris and Others*

Non–Hippocampus Press publications
ECM   *Edison's Conquest of Mars* (Garrett P. Serviss)
LOP   "Lovecraft's Other Planets" (Joshi, *Crypt of Cthulhu* 4)
OFF   *O Fortunate Floridian* (Lovecraft, letters to R. H. Barlow)
WW   *The War of the Worlds* (Wells)

Chapter 1
My Gaze Was Ever Upward

Before there was Cthulhu, before there was the Dunwich Horror, before there was the *Necronomicon,* there was astronomy. This book explores Howard Phillips Lovecraft's lifelong engagement with that subject. It became the chief scientific enthusiasm of his youth. It was the subject of his first substantial published work. It is reflected in and influenced his fiction and his philosophy. And it was one of the subjects of a letter left unfinished on his desk at his death.

To explore our topic, we need to look closely at Lovecraft's life, examining the actions and the writing most associated with, and revealing of, his astronomical interests. In doing this, we have found it helpful to divide the chapters of this book into two main types. Chapters 1–4, 6, 8, and 12 have a biographical focus. Chapters 5, 7, and 9–11 focus on Lovecraft's fiction, those who influenced it, and those who were influenced by it. There is some overlap in material between chapters to permit each chapter to be more easily understood if read on its own. Additional material relevant to Lovecraft's involvement with astronomy, but outside the flow of the main narrative, has been placed in appendices. Appendix I, a timeline of Lovecraft's astronomical endeavors, will assist as a quick reference. In this initial chapter, we look at the early years of Lovecraft's love of astronomy, beginning with its childhood origin and ending with the crash of his dreams of a career in that science.

In some ways astronomy is a safe subject in the discussion of Lovecraft. Astronomy is largely divorced from the questions of racism that dog aspects of his life. As a science, astronomy in the first decades of the twentieth century was dominated by Europeans (who were most important to theoretical astrophysics) and by Americans (who had the largest telescopes). Lovecraft would read of the ancient, classical, and Islamic roots of astronomy, but rarely did that reading challenge his prejudices. In fact, the teenage Lovecraft was quite willing to credit the ancient

Chaldeans, Egyptians, Chinese, and Indians with important contributions to astronomy, while he recognized no similar contribution from his beloved ancient Rome (*Rhode Island Journal of Astronomy*, 9 July 1905).

An Old Book and a New Book

Howard Phillips Lovecraft was born on 20 August 1890. Following the commitment of his father (Winfield Scott Lovecraft) to Butler Hospital in 1893, Howard and his mother (Sarah Susan Phillips) lived with his maternal grandparents in Providence, Rhode Island, the city he would always regard as home. It was at that home, at 454 Angell Street, that Lovecraft awakened to astronomy. Lovecraft's reminiscences of that awakening highlight, not the glorious night sky, but books.

Lovecraft was not the first of the family to fall under astronomy's spell. Lovecraft's maternal grandmother, Robie Alzada (Place) Phillips (1827–1896), was an astronomy enthusiast long before her grandson was born. Lovecraft wrote that

> My maternal grandmother, who died when I was six, was a devoted lover of astronomy, having made that a specialty at Lapham Seminary,[1] where she was educated; and though she never personally showed me the beauties of the skies, it is to her excellent but somewhat obsolete collection of astronomical books that I owe my affection for celestial science. Her copy of Burritt's Geography of the Heavens is today the most prized volume in my library. (Letter to Maurice W. Moe, 1 January 1915; *MWM* 44–45)

The "prized volume" inherited from his grandmother was already out of date when it came into his hands. Science had marched on since Elijah Hinsdale Burritt (1794–1838) published the first edition of *Geography of the Heavens* in 1833. Nonetheless, its descriptions of basic astronomical phenomena, accompanied by numerous classical allusions, remained solid. Burritt's popular introduction to astronomy went through many editions in the nineteenth century and was revised by others after his death. Lovecraft owned an 1853 edition, as well as the accompanying *Atlas*, with its illustrations of constellations (*LL* 153).[2]

---

1. A Freewill Baptist institution, the school was initially named Smithville Seminary, which later became the Lapham Institute. HPL was only five years old when his maternal grandmother died on 26 January 1896.

2. We make use of the important resource *Lovecraft's Library: A Catalogue* (*LL*), which summarizes what is known of books in HPL's collection. The

1. My Gaze Was Ever Upward

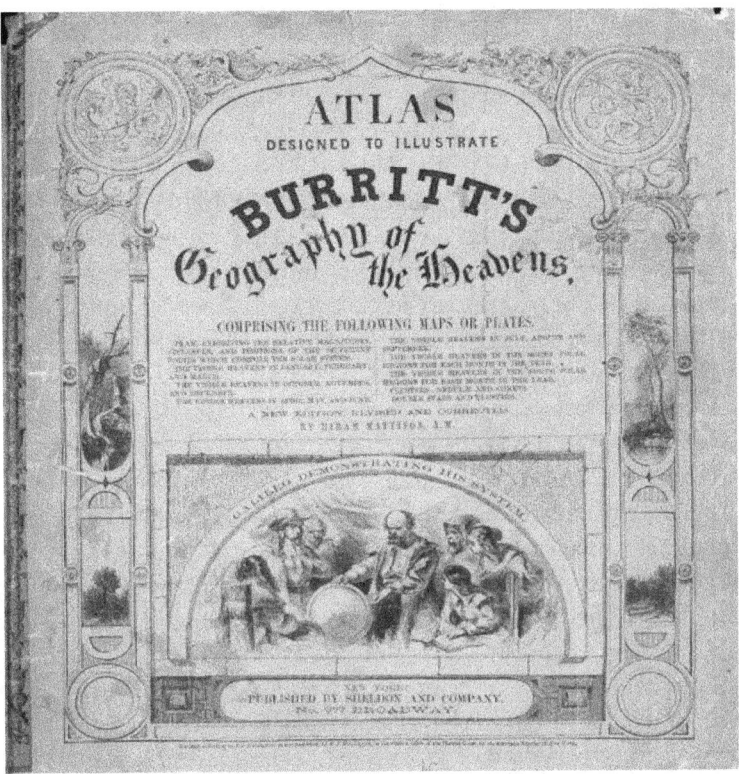

Cover of the 1856 edition of the star atlas accompanying Burritt's *Geography of the Heavens*. Lovecraft lost his 1853 *Atlas* in a move but replaced it with an 1856 edition in 1931 (*LFF* 949). Library of Congress.

Lovecraft's statement that "it is to her excellent but somewhat obsolete collection of astronomy books that I owe my affection for celestial science" indicates that he inherited more than just Burritt's book from his grandmother. What were the other books? We do not know for sure. In the *Annals of the Providence Observatory,* a work Lovecraft wrote in 1904, he listed eleven books in his astronomical library, dating most of them: the *American Ephemeris* for 1904, *The Knowledge Diary* for 1904, an 1853 edition of Burritt's *Geography of the Heavens,* Gall's *Easy Guide to the Constellations* (1895),[3] Young's *Lessons in Astronomy* (1892), *Astronomy* by

---

most recent edition, by S. T. Joshi and David E. Schultz, is listed in the bibliography.

3. *LL* lists a 1903 edition (361).

Sharpless and Phillips (1882), an 1846 edition of Dick's *Practical Astronomer*, Proctor's *Other Worlds Than Ours* (1870), Loomis's *Progress in Astronomy* (1853), Norton's *Astronomy* (1859), and *The Moon* by Nasmyth and Carpenter (undated by Lovecraft, but *Lovecraft's Library* lists a 4th edition of 1903). A few of the older volumes may have been inherited, but which? Lovecraft was already expanding his library through purchases, so that publication date alone is not a sure guide. Nevertheless, even if Lovecraft did receive more than one astronomy book from his grandmother's library, Burritt's book was dearest to him.

A second book might have helped to lure Lovecraft to science, if not astronomy (Haden "Lovecraft and Webster's"; de Camp 34). That book was *Webster's International Dictionary*, which Lovecraft came across in childhood. He wrote that "I became utterly infatuated with the pages of illustrations of 'Philosophic and Scientific Instruments' in the back of Webster's unabridged of 1864"[4] (letter to Bernard Austin Dwyer, 3 March 1927; *MWM* 431). The dictionary's illustrations of astronomical telescopes probably caught young Lovecraft's attention. However, the continuation of the letter to Dwyer appears to associate the *Webster's* illustrations, not with astronomy, but with Lovecraft's establishment of a basement chemistry laboratory in 1898–99. A letter to Alfred Galpin (29 August 1918; *AG* 210–11) also associates the illustrations with chemistry, making it doubtful whether those illustrations played an important role in attracting Lovecraft to astronomy in particular.

Chemistry was Lovecraft's first scientific love, as witness his laboratory, but astronomy moved to the fore in 1902 and 1903. At the age of twelve Lovecraft's enthusiasm for astronomy was fired by the acquisition of another book:

> Incidentally—it was this very day of 1903—Feb'y 12th—(which fell, however, on *Thursday*) that I bought the very first *new* book on *astronomy* that I ever owned. It was Young's "Lessons in Astronomy", & I got it at the R.I. News Co., for $1.25.[5] Previously I had had only Grandma's copy

---

4. Haden ("Lovecraft and Webster's") wondered whether HPL had seen an edition with updated illustrations. *Lovecraft's Library* includes the 1864 edition, but notes HPL's confusing mention of an 1873 supplement.

5. Attempts at transforming prices to modern equivalents are fraught with difficulties, but can nonetheless be instructive. Treated as a commodity price, HPL's $1.25 would be equivalent to about $40 in 2022. In this book we will use commodity price indices in converting old to 2022 prices, but

of Burritt's "Geography of the Heavens". As I returned in the evening darkness on the rear platform of an Elmgrove Ave. car—415, I think it was; one of the graceful J. M. Jones cars—I looked over the pictures & chapter headings with perhaps the most delightful sense of breathless anticipation I have ever known. Most literally, a strange cosmos of new worlds lay before me![6] (Letter to Lillian D. Clark, 12 February 1926; *LFF* 551)

The author of Lovecraft's find, Charles Augustus Young (1834–1908), was a professor at Dartmouth and, later, Princeton, and a pioneer of the developing science of astronomical spectroscopy, especially as applied to the study of the sun. His astronomy textbooks were widely used in the United States at the time that Lovecraft purchased his. *Lessons in Astronomy* was a mostly non-mathematical introduction to the subject, aimed at high schools. Lovecraft had a good memory, but, as Livesey noted (DPO 6), his recollection of this event is remarkably vivid considering that it occurred more than two decades before Lovecraft wrote his letter. Clearly, the discovery of Young's book marked an important point in Lovecraft's intellectual life, and he was primed to delight in it. Somewhat neglecting chemistry, he later proclaimed that "astronomy has always been my favourite science, followed assiduously since I was twelve years old" (letter to Clark Ashton Smith, 25 March 1923; *DS* 48).

Hoff (250) called attention to a difference between the two treasured books that introduced Lovecraft to astronomy. Whereas Burritt's *Geography of the Heavens* often takes a practical and observational approach to its subject, Young's textbook presents a more rigorous development of the principles of astronomy. Many twentieth-century textbooks on astronomy would follow the approach of Young rather than Burritt. Despite their different approaches, both books enthralled young Lovecraft.

---

other alternatives exist.

6. Joshi thought that HPL probably purchased the 1903 edition of Young's book (*IAP* 80), although HPL also owned an 1893 edition (*LL* 170). The entry in the *Annals of the Providence Observatory,* noting an 1892 but not a 1903 edition, surprisingly indicates that it may have been the earlier book that he bought. However, that would pose a problem. An 1895 edition of Young's book had also been published, and republished in 1898. It would thus have been odd for the 1892 edition still to have been sold as new in 1903. Young's preface to the 1903 edition is dated January 1903, and that edition lists copyright dates of 1895 and 1903, but not 1892.

Astronomy in the Time of Lovecraft

When Lovecraft rode home on the streetcar, clasping Young's book, the science of astronomy was making important strides and changing the contents of its toolkit. Bigger telescopes were a part of these advances. The 36-inch refracting telescope of the Lick Observatory had gone into operation on Mt. Hamilton in California in 1888, two years before Lovecraft was born.[7] The 40-inch refracting telescope at the Yerkes Observatory in Wisconsin followed in 1897. In 1908, a 60-inch reflecting telescope went into operation on Mt. Wilson under clear Californian skies, to be followed by the Mt. Wilson 100-inch reflecting telescope in 1917. The 40-, 60-, and 100-inch telescopes were brain-children of the enterprising American astronomer George Ellery Hale (1868–1938), and they helped the United States take the lead in many branches of observational astronomy. Hale would orchestrate the construction of one more telescope of record-breaking size, the 200-inch Palomar telescope. It would not be dedicated until 1948, after the deaths of both Hale and Lovecraft.

Larger and larger telescopes were not the only things moving observational astronomy forward. From the inception of astronomy, the human eye, either alone or at the eyepiece, had been the means by which the cosmos was witnessed. However, as the twentieth century dawned, photographic plates replaced the eye as the means by which the secrets of the universe were revealed. The switch from visual to photographic observations, begun in the middle of the nineteenth century, took hold worldwide as the century ended. By the 1890s, Harvard College Observatory operated stations in Massachusetts and Peru that regularly photographed both the northern and southern celestial hemispheres (Sobel; Jones and Boyd). Nearer to Lovecraft's home, Brown University's Ladd Observatory employed photography for studies of novae, meteors, and solar eclipses. Ladd Observatory's photographic endeavors would certainly have come to Lovecraft's attention once he began to visit that observa-

---

7. The size of a telescope is usually specified by the diameter of its objective lens or mirror. We will retain the imperial units that would have been used by HPL, rather than their metric equivalents. Lord Rosse's large 72-inch speculum mirror telescope in Ireland, completed in 1845, still existed when the Lick telescope saw first light, as did the Melbourne 48-inch reflecting telescope. However, both were obsolete in design when the Lick telescope was fabricated. HPL would note the "final disposition" of Lord Rosse's telescope in his *Evening News* article for 1 April 1915.

tory in 1903. In a few years he would be making his own celestial photographs (Appendix II).

Charles A. Young's specialty, spectroscopy, had become an important astronomical tool in the second half of the nineteenth century. Spectroscopes spread the light of sun, stars, nebulae, and planets by wavelength, producing spectra that extend from blue (shorter wavelength) to red (longer wavelength) colors. Spectra can be used to determine the line-of-sight motions, chemical compositions, and physical conditions of celestial objects. Schemes were developed for systematically placing stars into various pigeonholes based on the appearance of their spectra, the most successful classification system being one developed at the Harvard College Observatory around 1910. Harvard astronomer Annie Jump Cannon (1863–1941) would classify photographic spectra of hundreds of thousands of stars for the Henry Draper Catalogue (Sobel 247). Although the study of celestial spectra began in the nineteenth century, full exploitation of astronomical spectroscopy waited on developments in physics that did not come until the twentieth century.

Charles Augustus Young wrote the book that introduced Lovecraft to modern astronomy. Public domain; Wikimedia Commons.

Despite progress in many areas of astronomy, an astonishing amount remained undiscovered when the twelve-year-old Lovecraft became captivated by the subject. The lives of the stars, their elemental abundances, and their sources of energy had yet to be unraveled. No one had a clue as to what really caused new stars (novae) to blaze forth temporarily in the heavens. The shape of our own Milky Way galaxy was known to be flattened, but that was all. Whether the Milky Way was alone or one of many galaxies was open to debate. The vastness of time and space was increasingly evident, but the scale of the universe in size and age remained poorly known.

Ignorance concerning large-scale features of the universe is obvious in a perusal of Young's book. The 1903 edition of *Lessons in Astronomy* has twelve chapters and two appendices. Only part of a single chapter is devoted to the large-scale structure of the universe, including the nature of our galaxy. Stars of the Milky Way are therein described as forming either a flattened disk or perhaps a ring, with a diameter of 20,000 or 30,000 light years. The sun is stated to be close to the center of the Milky Way. It was a picture soon to be overthrown. By 1918, Harlow Shapley's investigations would increase the diameter of the Milky Way and displace the sun from its center to the galactic suburbs. Around 1930, astronomers realized that interstellar dust hid the heart of the Milky Way from view in visible light.

Young's book mentions the possibility that there might be other star systems like the Milky Way, but only briefly and without conviction. The Andromeda galaxy, now known to be larger than the Milky Way galaxy and some 2.5 million light years distant, is called only the "Andromeda nebula," its nature still unknown. Edwin Hubble would provide strong evidence that the Andromeda nebula was, in fact, a galaxy external to our own, but not until 1924. Dark matter and dark energy, which so perplex modern astronomers, make no appearance in Young's book; they would not be discovered for decades.

Turning to the solar system, we find that astronomers of the early twentieth century were stymied in resolving many questions of planetary astronomy, a field in which photography had not yet completely supplanted visual observations. Percival Lowell and others sketched fine lines stretching over the Martian surface. Lowell interpreted those lines as canals, which he proposed to be constructions of intelligent beings who dwelt on the Red Planet. He did not persuade most of his colleagues of that conclusion, Charles A. Young being one of the skeptics. Venus, its surface hidden beneath clouds, was still more of an enigma. Even the length of its day was unknown, an uncertainty to which Young called attention. On the solar system's largest planet, Jupiter's Great Red Spot had brightened to prominence in 1879. Astronomers kept watch and argued its nature in the ensuing decades. Fleeting comets dazzled watchers, but what were they? The dirty-snowball model of their composition lay decades in the future. Following the discovery of Neptune in 1846, astronomers hunted for a ninth planet of the solar system. None had been found as the twentieth century dawned, but hope was not lost. There was indeed much about the solar system to attract a lad who loved the mysterious, and Lovecraft willingly yielded to that temptation. As a young amateur astronomer, he relished observing the moon, planets, and comets. Decades later, his fiction would show familiarity with now long-discarded hypotheses that sought to explain the origin and evolution of the sun and its planetary retinue (see, for example, chapter 7). Scientific curiosity may even have dissuaded Lovecraft from contemplating suicide in 1904, when he was depressed after his grandfather's death and the disruption of his home life (*IAP* 97–99).

Amateur Astronomer and Science Writer

Lovecraft loved books and delighted in reading about the heavens, but he was no armchair astronomer. If he were not already doing so before 1903, that year saw him spending clear nights watching the sky over Providence. While some family member may have pointed out prominent star patterns such as the Big Dipper or Orion to a very young Lovecraft, he names no stargazing mentor. Modern-day star parties, at which enthusiasts gather with their telescopes, were still in the future and provided no help to a Lovecraft eager to study the heavens. Nor was the projection planetarium yet in existence to aid his education.

Across the Atlantic, the British Astronomical Association had been founded in the year of Lovecraft's birth. Its sections collected and analyzed observations of the moon, planets, meteors, and stars made by amateur astronomers and provided guidance on observing methods. In the early 1900s there was no comparable organization for amateurs in the United States, although one was developing in Canada and American professional astronomers had recently organized.[8]

Popular Astronomy magazine began publication in 1893 and eventually encouraged the formation of citizen-science groups in the United States. Most notable of these would be the American Association of Variable Star Observers,[9] founded in 1911 and still doing good science today (Williams and Saladyga). However, its formation was still eight years in the future when Lovecraft turned to astronomy. There was not even a local astronomy club in Providence in 1903. A Providence association of amateur astronomers, the Skyscrapers (still going strong as of 2022), would eventually be formed, but not until 1932. Lovecraft was largely on his own when learning to observe, although, as we shall see in

---

8. The Royal Astronomical Society of Canada was granted that name in 1903. What would become the American Astronomical Society, formed in 1899, consisted mainly, although not exclusively, of professional astronomers.

9. Variable stars are stars that change in brightness.

chapter 2, he did become acquainted with the astronomers of Brown University's Ladd Observatory.

Once Lovecraft turned his eyes to the sky, it was not long before the constellations and stars were his familiar friends. Books and maps helped him learn the patterns of the stars. Lovecraft developed a particular fondness for rotating planispheres,[10] which show the starry sky as a function of date and hour. He acquired a Whittaker's planisphere, followed by a Barritt–Serviss planet finder and planisphere. The latter he would keep for three decades, until his death in 1937. In the 28 May 1905 issue of

One of the inexpensive pocket planispheres that won Lovecraft's favorable mention. Courtesy of David Kolb.

---

10. More information about planispheres can be found in "The Planisphere: a brief historical review" by David W. Hughes and Carole Stott, *Journal of the British Astronomical Association* 105 (1995): 35–39 and *Card Planispheres: A Collector's Guide* by Peter Grimwood (Orreries UK, 2018).

1. My Gaze Was Ever Upward

his self-published *Rhode Island Journal of Astronomy*, he favorably reviewed a 15-cent pocket planisphere produced by the Educational Novelty Company of Worcester, Massachusetts. In later years, he would recommend planispheres to acquaintances and fellow writers. With the aid of such devices, his own knowledge of the heavens, and various almanacs, Lovecraft would take pains to make his fictional descriptions of the sky realistic (DPO 31–36; chapter 12).

Early in 1903, Lovecraft's mother presented him with an Excelsior spyglass sold by the New York mail-order firm of Kirtland Bros. and Co. for the grand sum of 99 cents (about $32 in 2022). He soon acquired a better telescope: "In the summer of 1903 my mother presented me with a 2¼″ astronomical telescope, and thenceforward my gaze was ever upward at night" (letter to Rheinhart Kleiner, 16 November 1916; *RK* 71). That telescope, like the Excelsior, was purchased from Kirtland Brothers and Company, but for the considerably higher price of $16.50 (about $500 in 2022). Lovecraft set it atop a tripod purchased for $8.00 from Reuben L. Allen, a Providence purveyor of optical goods.

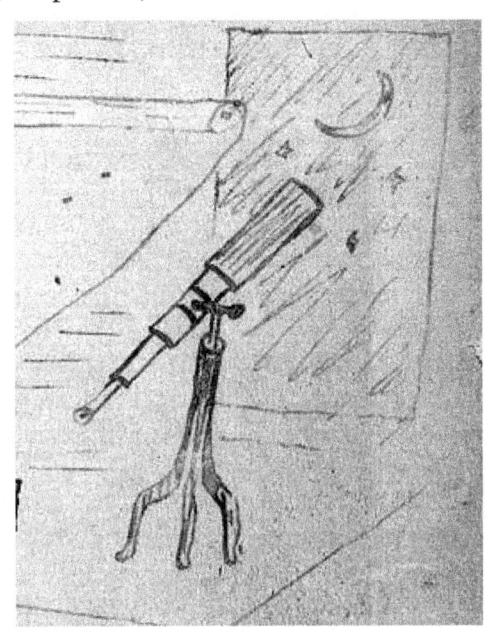

This telescope on the cover of the January 1906 issue of the *Rhode Island Journal of Astronomy* may be intended to represent Lovecraft's 2¼-inch telescope. Howard P. Lovecraft Collection, Ms. Lovecraft, Brown University Library.

It would be his main telescope until September 1906, when he purchased a 3-inch Bardou & Son telescope[11] from Montgomery Ward for $50.00 (a remarkable $1,500 in

---

11. His 3-inch telescope is sometimes mistakenly referred to as a "Bardon" or "Bardore" telescope because of understandable misreading of the handwriting in HPL's *Astronomical Notebook* (*CE* 3.332).

2022; see chapters 3 and 4, and Appendix III, for more about Lovecraft's telescopes).

The apertures of Lovecraft's telescopes will seem small to today's amateur astronomers, who often employ telescopes with objectives 6, 8, 12, or more inches in diameter. However, astronomical telescopes were very expensive in the early 1900s, and most amateur astronomers had to content themselves with smaller instruments. The 1911 catalogue of the highly regarded John A. Brashear Company offered an equatorially mounted 5-inch refracting telescope for $500 ($15,000 in 2022), approaching the annual wages of an ordinary laborer, and far beyond the price-range possible for Lovecraft, even with his mother's indulgence.[12] In the 1920s, Russell W. Porter (1871–1949) began to encourage American amateurs to make their own telescopes, usually reflecting telescopes with objective mirrors rather than lenses. The consequent growth in amateur telescope-making came after the time of Lovecraft's youthful enthusiasm. When the teenage Lovecraft looked skyward, guidebooks for amateur astronomers often told readers to strive for a refracting telescope of 3 inches aperture. One book that the teenage Lovecraft owned, Richard A. Proctor's *Half-Hours with the Telescope,* advised readers that "a well-constructed achromatic [telescope] of two or three inches in aperture will not merely supply amusement and instruction, it may be made to do useful work" (Proctor 1). When Lovecraft wrote his astronomy column for the 17 May 1915 issue of the *Asheville Gazette-News,* he stated that "a three-inch instrument magnifying from 50 to 150 times [was] an ideal outfit for the beginner in astronomy" (*CE* 3.316).

Lovecraft's homes at 454 Angell Street and, after his grandfather's death in 1904, 598 Angell Street were in a residential part of Providence, east of Brown University. Cities today are associated with light pollution: the glare from a myriad artificial lights scatters into the night sky so as to drown from view all but the brightest stars and planets. Problems were already arising in the early twentieth century. Gaslights had illuminated some Providence streets before the Civil War, and the city's first electric streetlights, harsh arc-lamps, were installed in 1882. By the

---

12. In Robert Frost's poem "The Star-Splitter," published in 1923, a philosophical astronomy enthusiast burns his house to buy a telescope with the insurance payment. A "good glass" cost the astronomically minded arsonist $600.

early 1900s, Providence had a few thousand streetlights of various types, while in the city's industrial areas stars competed with smoke from coal-burning furnaces. In 1914, Frank Seagrave would give up on the city and move his private astronomical observatory from its original location at 119 Benefit Street[13] to the darker and clearer skies of North Scituate, Rhode Island. Nevertheless, Providence's light pollution in the late nineteenth and early twentieth centuries was much less than is the case today, and that was particularly true outside of the business district.

In 1891, Brown University's Ladd Observatory would open on Doyle Avenue, about a mile from Lovecraft's residences. As recounted in chapter 2, Ladd Observatory would welcome Lovecraft beginning in 1903, becoming the scene of his introduction to academic astronomy. Proximity to the university was no doubt one motivation for its siting, but light pollution was apparently still low enough when the observatory was built that its location was regarded as suitable for astronomical observations. The same held true for the areas around Lovecraft's Angell Street homes, although Lovecraft occasionally complained of smoky skies.

The apparent brightness of a star is commonly denoted by its visual magnitude; brighter stars have smaller magnitudes. The very bright stars Vega and Arcturus have apparent visual magnitudes of 0. Stars of the Big Dipper—or the Plough as Lovecraft termed it, following British practice—are about magnitude 2, save for fainter Megrez, which is of the third magnitude. Lovecraft does not specify the faintest star that he could see with the unaided eye, but a few of his drawings of constellations suggest that he could see stars to at least the fifth magnitude. An observer at a moonless, clear, rural location would be able to see still fainter stars—perhaps to magnitude 6.2. However, even with a fifth-magnitude limit, Lovecraft would have been able to see not just the brightest stars but the array of fainter stars important to constellation identification. He would probably be disappointed to discover that light pollution has worsened, and that stars fainter than magnitude 4.5 are beyond naked eye visibility at Ladd Observatory in the early twenty-first

---

13. This was not far from the location of the house that would be the model for the "Shunned House." HPL considered moving into an apartment in Seagrave's old house in 1933. The opening of Seagrave's observatory at its new location was noted by HPL in his *Evening News* column for 1 September 1914.

century.[14] Given a limiting magnitude of 4.5, a naked-eye observer might see about 500 stars at any one time, but with a limiting magnitude of 6.0 that total grows to 2400. Of course, with binoculars or a telescope, even fainter stars can be brought into view. The limiting visual magnitudes for Lovecraft's Excelsior, 2¼-inch, and 3-inch telescopes, assuming a moderately dark sky, would have been about 8.5, 10.5, and 11.0, respectively.

On the first day of 1915, Lovecraft recounted his early astronomical endeavors in a letter to his friend Maurice W. Moe:

> In January, 1903, astronomy began to engross me completely. I procured a small telescope, and surveyed the heavens constantly. Not one clear night passed without long observation on my part, and the practical, first-hand knowledge thus acquired has ever since been of the highest utility to me in my astronomical writing. (*MWM* 45–46)

In 1899, even before he succumbed to astronomy, Lovecraft had begun to write and disseminate handwritten and hectographed science magazines, surviving numbers of which can be accessed through the Brown Digital Repository. The first of these, the *Scientific Gazette,* was commenced before his ninth birthday. Chemistry and volcanoes were among the first topics considered. When Lovecraft's interest turned to astronomy, so did his writing.

Beginning in the summer of 1903, several of his publications—if one can generously use that word in connection with these homemade items—dealt with astronomy, including *Astronomy: A Journal of Current Phenomena, The Planet, Annals of the Providence Observatory, The Science Library,* and the *Rhode Island Journal of Science and Astronomy.* Often these titles were short-lived, sometimes not going beyond a single issue. However, the *Rhode Island Journal of Astronomy,* begun with the issue of 2 August 1903, proved to be long-lasting and rich in detailing Lovecraft's astronomical pursuits. At first weekly, then (irregularly) fortnightly, and finally monthly, the magazine would, with some lapses, be issued until April 1907, with incomplete attempts at revival in January and February 1909. Sixty-nine issues are known to exist and a few issues may have been lost. Because of these publications we can not only follow Lovecraft's enthusiasm for astronomy, but see how his skills matured as he developed into an experienced astronomical observer.

---

14. According to the observatory's curator Michael Umbricht, fornaxchimiae.blogspot.com/search/label/Astronomy.

The first issues of the *Rhode Island Journal of Astronomy* show Lovecraft having fun with astronomy. He delighted in observing solar system objects: Venus, Mars, Jupiter, Saturn, passing comets, the sun, and, especially, the moon. Objects beyond the solar system, including double stars, star clusters, and nebulae, were not entirely neglected, but were less often featured in the pages of the *Journal*.

While Lovecraft was clearly having fun at the telescope, fun was not his only goal. His observing had a serious side. When he pointed his new 2¼-inch telescope at Venus and the moon in 1903, Lovecraft sought not merely to observe for his own amusement, but also to carry out ambitious if unrealistic research programs to unravel their mysteries. In this first flower of observing enthusiasm, he attempted to tackle problems that resisted professional astronomers with much larger instruments. What was the rotation period of Venus? Did features on the moon change? His research efforts are the subject of chapter 4. Here it is sufficient to note that, within a few years, Lovecraft would learn to look more realistically at the capabilities of his modest telescopes. One can smile at his initial overreach, but one can also admire his desire to join the ranks of astronomical discoverers.

By 1905, the *Rhode Island Journal of Astronomy* was being reproduced by the hectograph process. Lovecraft recalled that 15 to 25 hectographed copies were made of each issue (*IAP* 84). These publications were not always gratis. For example, in 1906, when the *Journal* was published monthly, advertisements within offered it for 3 cents a copy or 25 cents for a year. We do not know how many readers were paying customers. In fact, we do not know who read the *Journal* or Lovecraft's other juvenile science magazines. Presumably they were seen by some of Lovecraft's family and friends, but did they see any wider distribution— perhaps to staff of Ladd Observatory?[15] Without subscriber lists or any statement by Lovecraft, we don't really know. In the issue for January 1907, Lovecraft reported that a reader corrected an error he had made in describing the planned Mt. Wilson 100-inch telescope. Someone on the Ladd staff would have had the knowledge to make that correction, but a careful reader of newspapers would, too. The 8 October 1905 issue stated: "Subscribers residing outside of Providence will receive their papers in

---

15. No copies are listed in the Ladd Observatory library's records of acquisitions, nor (as of May 2022) have any been found by the authors in the observatory's materials in the John Hay Library.

a bunch once a month by mail." Joshi suspected that Lovecraft's aunt Annie Phillips Gamwell, who was then living in Cambridge, Massachusetts, with her husband, may have been such a distant subscriber (*IAP* 103).

The *Rhode Island Journal of Astronomy* underwent changes of emphasis during its lifespan as Lovecraft progressed through his teenage years. When the *Journal* began in 1903, his new-born enthusiasm for observing was conspicuous. Issues contained numerous reports of Lovecraft's astronomical observations and of his own efforts to employ those observations for research. However, the *Journal* also contained astronomical news, book notices, educational notes, and even advertisements for optical purveyors R. L. Allen and Kirkland Brothers and Company. Whether those concerns actually paid for those advertisements is perhaps doubtful, but, as we have seen, both were businesses Lovecraft had patronized. Perhaps some informal arrangements were made, at least with Allen, who was located within Providence.

When the *Journal* resumed in April 1905, after a lapse in publication since 31 January 1904, it contained a wider array of advertisements. His own enterprises were commonly noticed. The 16 April 1905 issue called on readers to "Hire the Blackstone Orchestra—Fine Music Cheap—H. P. Lovecraft C. P. Munroe Leaders." The 7 May 1905 issue called attention to the Providence Detective Agency ("All civil or criminal cases quickly attended to at low prices"). Lovecraft and his friend Chester Pierce Munroe were the intrepid chief detectives. One wonders whether they ever tracked down any despicable villains.[16] The March 1906 issue proclaimed "ATTENTION!!!!! Is called to great improvement in our paper since February." However, astronomy remained the heart of the publication. Lovecraft regarded the early issues of the *Journal* to be more like a newspaper, while the longer but more infrequent later issues he considered more like a magazine (*Journal,* August 1906). Gradually, Lovecraft's own observations made up less of the content. Essays on astronomical topics, sometimes extending over more than a single issue, became common. Those essays would sometimes have a new life in his newspaper columns once those began in the summer of 1906.

---

16. Alas, the villains appear to have been mainly fictional (letter to Alfred Galpin, 27 May 1918; *AG* 191). One doubts that there was ever an alternative life-path in which HPL became a private eye of the film-noir type! However, imagination can take a different view, vide S. T. Joshi's novel *Honeymoon in Jail.*

As noted, early issues of the *Rhode Island Journal of Astronomy* are particularly revealing of Lovecraft's youthful intoxication with observing. If it was a clear evening, Lovecraft was watching the skies. The 18 October 1903 *Journal* rejoiced: "EXTRA!!!! 8^h30^m!!! CLEAR WEATHER." Lovecraft took advantage of that particular opportunity to observe Jupiter and Saturn. The 1 November 1903 issue saw Lovecraft reporting with satisfaction that the "past week has been remarkable for it's [*sic*] clear nights, every one being suited to astronomical pursuits."

Lovecraft's juvenile publications emphasize scientific aspects of his astronomical observations. We generally have to turn to later correspondence to see that he also appreciated the beauty of the night sky. In a letter to Clark Ashton Smith dated 25 March 1923 (*DS* 48–49), Lovecraft picturesquely recalled heady nights at the telescope: "I have seen the ringed Saturn through my own telescope, (a Bardou instrument with 3″ object-glass and eyepieces up to 150 diameters) and have gazed upon the moon's frightful abysses where no diffusing air softens the nighted blackness of distorted shadows."

Despite Lovecraft's assiduous observing, a few celestial wonders are missing from the *Journal*. Given their rarity at a particular location, it is not surprising that Lovecraft had to wait until 1925 to witness a total solar eclipse (see chapter 8). More surprising, perhaps, is that he seems not to have seen a good showing of the aurora borealis, or northern lights. In 1926, Lovecraft lamented to his aunt Lillian Clark: "As for the Aurora—too bad I always miss it! I have never seen a decent display" (*LFF* 562).

Appearances of the aurora borealis wax and wane with the 11-year solar cycle. Solar cycle 14, which peaked early in 1906, was weak, reducing his opportunities for seeing the aurora when his penchant for observing was at its peak, although he apparently did miss a nice auroral display on 21 August 1903. The following solar cycle produced spectacular northern lights over New England on the night of 7 March 1918 (Duncan, "Bright Aurora"). Chris Perridas ("The Aurora Borealis in 'Polaris'") noted that the circumstances of the aurora mentioned in Lovecraft's short story "Polaris" matched those of that auroral display.[17] "Polaris" is believed to have been written in the spring or summer of 1918 (*IAP* 255–57), so a connection with the March aurora is plausible.

---

17. A bright but less spectacular aurora followed on 5 April 1918, one solar rotation later. Perridas considers this a possible but less likely alternative inspiration for "Polaris."

By this time, however, Lovecraft no longer wrote the *Rhode Island Journal of Astronomy*, and even his later personal astronomical notebook had ended, so that we are less aware of what he himself observed. If we take Lovecraft's 1926 letter at face value, then the statement by the protagonist of "Polaris" that "Well do I remember the night of the great Aurora, when over the swamp played the shocking coruscations of the daemon-light" (*CF* 1.66) cannot be autobiographical. Lovecraft mentions no aurora in his letter to Maurice W. Moe of 15 May 1918 (*MWM* 70–71) describing a dream that has been regarded as an inspiration for "Polaris."

The reader may wish to know whether Lovecraft reported seeing anything resembling the unidentified flying objects (unidentified aerial phenomena, if you prefer) that would be widely reported in 1947 and subsequent years. The answer is no. However, in 1909, amidst a flurry of newspaper accounts of mysterious airships over New England, Lovecraft was able to inform a roadside group that what they saw was no airship but actually the planet Venus (see chapters 6 and 7)!

Besides his journals, the young Lovecraft attempted monographs on various astronomical topics, some of which appear to have progressed to numerous pages. In 1935, Lovecraft informed his friend James F. Morton (letter of 2 April 1935; *JFM* 363) that

> In the course of my exhumations . . . I came upon the remains of old composition books which I used in 1905 and 1906. One of them (according to the cover) contain'd a story (which I've completely forgotten) called "Gone, But Whither?" I'll bet it was a hellraiser . . . Another book was "A Brief Course in Astronomy; Descriptive, Practical, & Observational; For Beginners & General Readers" (1906). That got as far as the typed stage—tho' all manuscripts are long ago thrown away!

Given his weakness in high school algebra, it is interesting that one of Lovecraft's treatises was not on astronomy, but was a 34-page account of *Practical Geometry* (*Rhode Island Journal of Astronomy*, 20 September 1903).

One of Lovecraft's productions, dated July 1907, was "Celestial Objects for All: An Easy Guide to Astronomical Observations with Opera, and Field Glasses" (*CE* 3.89–99), much of which was apparently also included in his lost "A Brief Course in Astronomy." Perhaps inspired by Garrett P. Serviss's *Astronomy with an Opera-Glass*, which Lovecraft recommended as good supplementary reading (along with Burritt's *Geography of the Heavens* and E. Walter Maunder's *Astronomy without a Telescope*), "Celestial Objects for All" is probably based on Lovecraft's own observations. The entry on the moon is far longer than any other within this guide, and Lovecraft notes that "the study of the moon has few equals, no matter what instrument is used."

In later years, Lovecraft sometimes looked askance at these juvenilia. He reflected on them in a letter of November 1933 to Robert Bloch, then only sixteen years old (*RB* 88): "Just to give you a laugh at the old man I'll enclose (please return) a couple issues of my pompous *R. I. Journal of Astronomy* . . . Pretty kiddish stuff, even for 15." The issues are, of course, not what a mature Lovecraft would have written, but they nonetheless played their role in his education as a writer and are invaluable to all who wish to learn how Lovecraft became a skilled amateur astronomer. Near the end of his life, Lovecraft recalled that he "was always overwhelmingly grateful for any recognition accorded my little R. I. Journal of Astronomy" (letter to Wilson Shepherd, 17 February 1937; *RB* 370). Alas, we do not know who gave Lovecraft that early encouragement. Kind words from anyone on the Ladd Observatory staff would undoubtedly have particularly heartened Lovecraft.

Lovecraft is occasionally accused of misogyny, accusations that S. T. Joshi has disputed (Joshi, *Recognition* 308–9). Lovecraft's juvenile science magazines add little to the arguments on this subject, but their treatment of women astronomers deserves brief mention. Astronomy in the early 1900s was, unsurprisingly, a male-dominated profession, but in the *Rhode Island Journal of Astronomy* Lovecraft did not neglect astronomical work by women. Within its issues for 1906, we find notices of the retirement of Professor Mary Byrd (identified as the author of the *Laboratory Manual of Astronomy,* a book Lovecraft owned), of Williamina Fleming's discovery of an eclipsing star, of Dorothea Klumpke's study of photographs of nebulae, and of Henrietta Leavitt's discovery of twenty-five variable stars. Although the subject is not explicitly addressed, there is no indication that Lovecraft thought women inferior to men in ability to make astronomical discoveries.

Lovecraft's entrepreneurial spirit—perhaps more pronounced at this time than when he was an adult—occasionally reveals itself in his science publications. His card printing business was advertised in several of them: 5 cents for a dozen cards. He announced the creation of the Phase Machine, a pasteboard device he built for predicting the zodiacal sign in which the moon was located and the phase of the moon (*Rhode Island Journal of Astronomy,* 6 December 1903; August 1906, *Scientific Gazette,* 6 December 1903). Copies of the Phase Machine, by then renamed the Improved Zodiacal Machine, were hawked for 25 cents ($8.00 in 2022) in the October 1906 issue of the *Rhode Island Journal of Astronomy*. The price fell to 15 cents by the following issue. One wonders whether he had any buyers.

Lovecraft occasionally reported astronomical discoveries in the *Rhode Island Journal of Astronomy*. One item noted the identification of new variable stars by Henrietta Swan Leavitt (1868–1921), shown here at her desk in the Harvard College Observatory. Public domain.

Almost everything that we know about Lovecraft's astronomical observing we know either from his self-published journals or from letters he wrote years later, but there is one exception. A contemporary and neighbor of Lovecraft's during his youth, Clara Hess, left us a brief recollection of Lovecraft at the telescope around 1904:

> Howard used to go out into the fields in back of my home to study the stars. One early fall evening several of the children in the vicinity assembled to watch him from a distance. Feeling sorry for his loneliness I went up to him and asked him about his telescope and was permitted to look through it. But his language was so technical that I could not understand it and I returned to my group and left him to his lonely study of the heavens. (*IAP* 95)

1. My Gaze Was Ever Upward

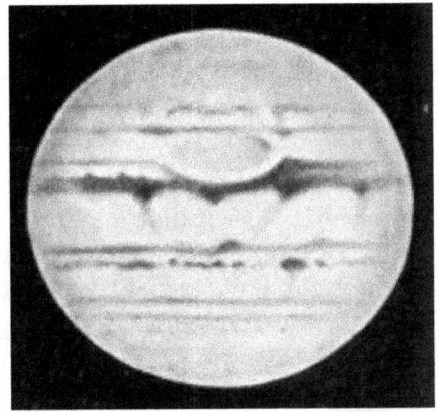

Lovecraft's drawing of Jupiter (south at top) is from the 6 September 1903 *Rhode Island Journal of Astronomy*. He reported the Great Red Spot (presumably the oval) to have been faintly visible in his 2¼-inch telescope, while the south equatorial belt was at the time more prominent than its northern counterpart. Howard P. Lovecraft Collection, Ms. Lovecraft, Brown University Library.

Lovecraft's sketch can be compared with this drawing of Jupiter made by E. M. Antoniadi on 29 August 1903 (also with south at the top). Antoniadi used an 8.5-inch telescope, much larger than Lovecraft's. *Memoirs of the British Astronomical Society*, vol. XIII, 1906, Plate 1.

Lovecraft's Phase Machine, as depicted in the *Scientific Gazette,* appears to be a sort of simple lunar volvelle. The half white-half black disk represents the Moon, half sunlit and half shadowed. Howard P. Lovecraft Collection, Ms. Lovecraft, Brown University Library.

Hess portrays a Lovecraft unable or unwilling to explain his astronomical work to a young acquaintance unfamiliar with the subject. However, we should perhaps not make too much of this. We have other evidence that Lovecraft did desire to spread the word about astronomy, although he may have wished to avoid anything resembling a dumbing-down of his beloved science. This is apparent through his juvenile publications, through his creation of the Providence Astronomical Society (see below), through newspaper columns he began to write in 1906, and also through his willingness to lecture on the subject.

His astronomical lectures began late in 1903. The *Rhode Island Journal of Astronomy* of 27 December 1903 reported: "For the past few nights a course of lectures has been given by this office on the solar system. It was illustrated by a dozen lantern slides made by Mr. Edwards of the Ladd Observatory . . . The lectures are given at the office of this paper and the admission is free." That "office" was located in his grandfather's Angell Street home, and his audience would probably have been family members and friends. John Edwards, a member of the Ladd Observatory staff, assisted several of Lovecraft's astronomical endeavors and is introduced in more detail in chapter 2. Lovecraft lists the subjects of the slides: (1) the solar system, (2) sun-spots, (3) a total solar eclipse, (4) two views of Venus, (5) the full moon, (6) the gibbous moon (alas, this slide was defective), (7) Mars, (8) Jupiter, (9) Saturn, (10) the comet of 1811, (11) an aerolite falling, and (12) lunar scenery. A similar lecturer today might choose many of the same subjects, but of course taking advantage of the wonderful images from space probes.

Two and a half years later, the June 1906 issue of the *Rhode Island Journal of Astronomy* announces that Lovecraft has resumed lecturing, speaking on the sun to the East Side Historical Club on 9 May. This was followed on 7 December 1906 by a second lecture to the East Side Historical Club, this time on the solar system and illustrated by 15 slides (*Rhode Island Journal of Astronomy,* January 1907). The talk must have been well received, because Lovecraft returned a month later on 4 January to give the club a lecture on the "entire science" of astronomy, illustrated by 50 slides (*Rhode Island Journal of Astronomy,* January 1907). That would have been no short talk! Lest we imagine a group of stuffed-shirt adults paying heed to Lovecraft's words, we need to note that Joshi (*IAP* 109) believes that the East Side Historical Club consisted of Lovecraft's high school friends.

1. My Gaze Was Ever Upward 35

Lovecraft's magic lantern projects an image of the moon (*Rhode Island Journal of Astronomy*, 27 December 1903). A hand, perhaps Lovecraft's, holds the pointer. Howard P. Lovecraft Collection, Ms. Lovecraft, Brown University Library.

The January 1907 issue of the *Journal* also carries an intriguing advertisement: "Providence Laboratory (physical and chemical) Announces a course of illustrated lectures on ASTRONOMY—New Slides—New + Improved Lantern," as well as "PRIVATE LESSONS IN ASTRONOMY PHYSICS CHEMISTRY." Lovecraft was, of course, the person behind the Providence Laboratory.

Probably few, if any, took up Lovecraft's offer of lessons, but his talks for the East Side Historical Club (or the newspaper columns he had written since the summer of 1906) may have led to him addressing a less familiar group. Notice of his lecture on 25 January to the Boys Club of the First Baptist Church appeared in the February 1907 issue of the *Rhode Island Journal of Astronomy*, just before the journal ceased regular publication. Lovecraft had at one time attended Sunday school at the church, and his mother remained on the church rolls. One imagines that Lovecraft drew upon the material prepared for his East Side Historical Club lectures, but the occasion shows his willingness to address a group that probably included strangers—and, of course, such a lecture required self-confidence, since a group of boys can be a tough audience. We have no review of Lovecraft's presentations from any in his audience. One trusts that he was able to explain his subject to better advantage on these planned occasions than he apparently did in his impromptu encounter with Clara Hess.

Another intriguing aspect of Lovecraft's astronomical outreach at this time is the Providence Astronomical Society, which he promoted and presumably created. It is first mentioned in the June 1906 issue of the *Rhode Island Journal of Astronomy*, but a printed announcement accompanying the April 1907[18] issue put its founding in 1904. The organization of the Providence Astronomical Society does not appear to have been an attempt to form a general astronomy club for the city. So far as we are aware, communications to members of the Providence Astronomical Society were limited to announcements in the *Rhode Island Journal of Astronomy*. Probably the society consisted of a small number of Lovecraft's friends. Chester and Harold Munroe, who were involved in several of his endeavors, may be likely participants. However, Love-

> **PROV. ASTRONOMICAL SCY.**
> ESTAB. 1904 ; H. P. LOVECRAFT, PRES'T.
> An organisation designed to encourage the study of the heavens.
> All persons interested in Astronomy should at once join, as this society affords valuable instruction and cooperation. All business transacted by mail, so those far from Providence may join. Persons unfamiliar with the science are taught. Members are required only to send in monthly reports. ALL FREE
> **Write for directions and membership certificate NOW**
> 598, Angell St., Providence, R.I., U.S.A.

Lovecraft's notice of the Providence Astronomical Society. Joshi (*IAP* 108) believes that Lovecraft printed the notice on his own press. Howard P. Lovecraft Collection, Brown University Library.

---

18. Whether the notice originally accompanied that issue of the *Journal* or whether it was attached later is unclear.

craft remained very much in charge. The *Journal* provided society members with instructions for observing various astronomical phenomena. We do not know how many members followed Lovecraft's instructions and reported their observations to him, but mentions of the Providence Astronomical Society continued to appear until the November 1906 issue of the *Journal*. One suspects that few members diligently carried out all the various observations that Lovecraft proposed.

The spring and summer of 1906 saw Lovecraft's byline appear for the first time in commercial publications. As July turned into August, he commenced columns on astronomy for two Rhode Island newspapers, the Providence *Tribune* and the *Pawtuxet Valley Gleaner*. The former would continue until June 1908, the latter until the *Gleaner* folded, probably also in 1908. Considering that these newspaper series began before Lovecraft reached his sixteenth birthday, they are a remarkable achievement. In the summer of 1906, Lovecraft could still regard himself as something of a prodigy. His newspaper articles are the subject of chapter 6, so we postpone a more extensive discussion until then.

As he began to write about astronomy for the public, Lovecraft delved more deeply into the technical side of the subject. The July 1906 *Rhode Island Journal of Astronomy* reported his acquisition of Charles A. Young's *Elements of Astronomy*. Like Young's *Lessons in Astronomy,* which introduced Lovecraft to modern astronomy, this was a textbook. However, *Elements* included more mathematics, to the level of algebra and trigonometry but not calculus. Given the difficulty that mathematics would soon present to Lovecraft's hopes for an astronomical career, it is interesting that Lovecraft began to look into the mathematical side of the science at this time.

A sideline of Lovecraft's astronomy-related activities deserves brief mention at this point. An interest in almanacs was sparked by inherited copies of the *Old Farmer's Almanack,* an almanac begun by Robert B. Thomas in 1792 and still published. The earliest of Lovecraft's almanacs were collected by his great-great-grandfather, Stephen Place, Sr. (Faig, "Lovecraft's Travelogues" 80). Published annually, they contained astronomical data for the year of the almanac, but also weather forecasts, advice for farmers, short essays, miscellaneous information, advertisements, and various pleasantries. Lovecraft's interest in old almanacs was more antiquarian than astronomical in nature. In later years he would strive to complete his collection of the *Old Farmer's Almanac,* especially seeking copies of the rare early editions (Haden, "Almanacs").

Spectroscopy had become an important tool in both chemistry and astronomy before the twentieth century dawned. In "The Colour out of Space" (1927), Lovecraft described the puzzlement of nineteenth-century scientists when they examined the spectrum of a strange meteorite that fell upon Nahum Gardner's farm: "upon heating before the spectroscope it displayed shining bands unlike any known colours of the normal spectrum" (*CF* 2.372). In his high-school years, Lovecraft possessed two spectroscopes of his own. The first is mentioned in his *Third Annual Report of the Providence Meteorological Station* (16 January 1907; *CE* 3.84–88): "On Dec. 24, 1906 . . . the Prov. Meteo. Station procured a diffraction spectroscope by Ives." A dozen years after its purchase (perhaps it was a Christmas present?), Lovecraft recalled the Ives spectroscope in a letter to Alfred Galpin (*AG* 211): "I still have my spectroscope—a rather low-priced diffraction instrument costing $15.00." Soon after its purchase, on 11 January 1907, we find Lovecraft borrowing *How to Work with the Spectroscope* from the Ladd Observatory library, a volume he did not return until 11 June.[19] As far as we can tell, Lovecraft used his Ives spectroscope for meteorology (and possibly chemistry) rather than astronomy. He examined "rain-bands" produced by water vapor in the atmosphere, a project perhaps encouraged by Ladd Observatory director Winslow Upton. Shortly after assuming his professorship at Brown University, Upton published a paper on such rain-bands (Upton, "Use of the Spectroscope"), which appear as dark features when one observes the spectrum of the daytime sky. Lovecraft's Ives spectroscope was not well suited for astronomical spectroscopy (aside from the solar spectrum), being too big to use in conjunction with his small telescopes, which in any case gathered too little light to observe spectra of anything but the brightest objects. Although Lovecraft called his Ives spectroscope "low-priced," the $15 spent on it illustrates Lovecraft's (or his mother's) continued free spending as 1906 ended. This was not an insignificant expenditure when wages were often less than 30 cents an hour; in 2022, its equivalent cost would be about $450.

---

19. John Browning's pamphlet includes some practical advice, as well as a listing of spectroscopes and other optical equipment that his company sold. Borrowers of books from the Ladd library, and the books they borrowed, are listed in *Ladd Observatory Books Loaned*, archived at the John Hay Library (Department of Astronomy papers, Box 2, MS-1ZAS-1). HPL is noted as borrowing only three books.

Lovecraft's letter to Galpin went on to note: "I have also a still cheaper pocket spectroscope, which was the delight of my fellow students at H.S.H.S. [Hope Street High School]. It is unbelievably tiny—will go into a vest pocket without making much of a bulge—yet gives a neat, bright little spectrum, with clear Frauenhofer lines when directed at sunlight." Frauenhofer, or Fraunhofer, lines are dark lines seen in the solar spectrum, named after Joseph von Fraunhofer (1787–1826). Fraunhofer lines in the solar spectrum reveal the presence of various chemical elements within the sun.

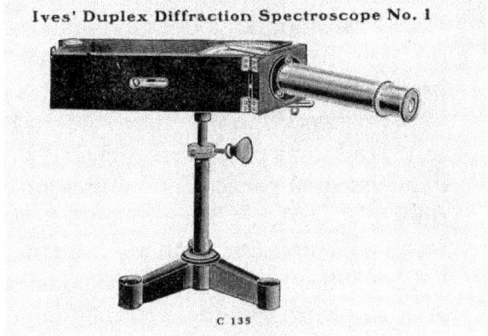

This spectroscope, sold for $15 in a July 1906 catalogue by the Scientific Shop in Chicago, may be similar if not identical to the Ives spectroscope Lovecraft bought later that year.

A Universe Immense in Time and Space

As Lovecraft's knowledge of astronomy grew, it began to shape a philosophy of cosmicism, in which humanity is insignificant on the scale of the universe. When Lovecraft wrote his juvenile science magazines, he was well aware that science had demoted Earth from any special place in the cosmos. The Copernican revolution had removed the Earth from the center of the cosmos and made it only one of several planets orbiting the sun. The sun, heart of that solar system, was by 1900 known to be only one of hundreds of millions of stars, extending to incredibly vast distances. True, it was not known whether many of those suns were accompanied by planets, nor did astronomers yet know whether there were galaxies other than our own. However, the role of Earth in the universe was looking pretty small.

In 1922 the *Liberal*[20] published Lovecraft's "A Confession of Unfaith." In it, Lovecraft stated that

> The most poignant sensations of my existence are those of 1896, when I discovered the Hellenic world, and of 1902, when I discovered the

---

20. Paul J. Campbell's amateur journal. HPL's full essay is available in the Brown Digital Repository and in *CE* 5.145–48.

myriad suns and worlds of infinite space. Sometimes I think the latter event the greater, for the grandeur of that growing conception of the universe still excites a thrill hardly to be duplicated. I made of astronomy my principal scientific study, obtaining larger and larger telescopes, collecting astronomical books to the number of 61,[21] and writing copiously on the subject in the form of special and monthly articles in the local press. By my thirteenth birthday I was thoroughly impressed with man's impermanence and insignificance, and by my seventeenth, about which time I did some particularly detailed writing on the subject, I had formed in all essential particulars my present pessimistic cosmic views. The futility of all existence began to impress and oppress me; and my references to human progress, formerly hopeful, began to decline in enthusiasm. . . . My attitude has always been cosmic, and I looked on man as if from another planet. He was merely an interesting species presented for study and classification.

The concept of the immensity of space is present in the first astronomy book read by Lovecraft, Elijah Burritt's *Geography of the Heavens*. Burritt included a picturesque illustration of the vastness of the universe, one that he took (with credit) from Thomas Dick's *Christian Philosopher*. It involves a seraph, a high-ranking angelic being in Judeo-Christian theology. Burritt pictured a seraph flying across God's creation:

Suppose that one of the highest order of intelligences is endowed with a power of rapid motion superior to that of light, and with a corresponding degree of intellectual energy; that he has been flying without intermission, from one province of creation to another, for six thousand years,[22] and will continue the same rapid course for a thousand millions of years to come; it is highly probable, if not absolutely certain, that, at the end of this vast tour, he would have advanced no farther than the suburbs of creation,—and that all the magnificent systems of material and intellectual beings he had surveyed, during his rapid flight, and for such a length of ages, bear no more proportion to the whole Empire of Omnipotence, than the smallest grain of sand does to all the particles of matter of the same size contained in ten thousand worlds. Were a seraph, in prosecuting the tour of creation in the manner now stated, ever to

---

21. Joshi states that, of the 61 astronomy books HPL apparently owned in 1921, only about 35 were in his library when it was catalogued after his death (*IAP* 80).

22. Presumably in concordance with the timeline for the age of creation devised by Bishop James Ussher (1581–1656).

arrive at a limit beyond which no farther displays of the Divinity could be perceived, the thought would overwhelm his faculties with unutterable emotions; he would feel that he had now, in some measure, comprehended all the plans and operations of Omnipotence, and that no farther manifestation of the Divine glory remained to be explored. But we may rest assured that this can never happen in the case of any created intelligence. (Burritt, *Geography of the Heavens,* 1853 ed., 159)

A very young Lovecraft, encountering this passage in his grandmother's book, might have been set to pondering the vastness of the universe compared to the tiny dimensions of the Earth. One may also wonder whether this description of a seraph flying through space had an influence on the mode of locomotion of Lovecraft's later creations. Seraphim are usually described as winged beings. In the King James Bible, Isaiah 6: 1–3 states "In the year that king Uzziah died I saw also the Lord sitting upon a throne, high and lifted up, and his train filled the temple. Above it stood the seraphims: each one had six wings; with twain he covered his face, and with twain he covered his feet, and with twain he did fly." Lovecraft would imagine his own beings who winged their way through the ether between the stars. In "The Whisperer in Darkness" (written in 1930; *CF* 2), the clawed Mi-Go from Yuggoth have wings. In his correspondence with Albert Wilmarth, Henry Akeley wrote of the Mi-Go that the *"things come from another planet, being able to live in interstellar space and fly through it* on clumsy, powerful wings which have a way of resisting the ether but which are too poor at steering to be of much use in helping them about on earth" (*CF* 2.477). Of Outer Beings in general, Akeley remarked, "Only a few species have the ether-resisting wings characteristic of the Vermont variety" (*CF* 2.502). We will return to this subject in chapter seven.

In any case, Lovecraft's growing awareness of the immense scale of the universe directed his thinking along certain lines. In 1917, he wrote:

> [. . .] a mere knowledge of the approximate dimensions of the visible universe is enough to destroy forever the notion of a personal godhead whose whole care is expended upon puny mankind, and whose only genuine and original Messiah was dispatched to save the insignificant vermin, or men, who inhabit this one relatively microscopic globe. Not that science positively refutes religion—it merely makes religion seem so monstrously improbable that a large majority of men can no longer believe in it. (*Misc* 59)

Joshi ("Time, Space, and Natural Law" 175–76) commented that, while the mere size of the universe would not necessarily mean that humanity was insignificant, Lovecraft's more telling argument was that there was no reason for a divinity to give particular attention to our tiny portion of the universe.

The influence of the vastness of the cosmos on Lovecraft's outlook would be long-lasting. As 1929 ended, he restated its importance in a letter to Elizabeth Toldridge (20 December 1929):

> To my mind an elementary knowledge of the nature & workings of the universe is a really essential part of any artist's or thinker's background. It is the greatest clarifier of perspective I know of, & is a whole imaginative education in itself because of the stupendous magnitudes & distances it brings up for attention. But all the distances described in the two books I lent you are as nothing compared with the nearly unthinkable chasms envisaged by modern astronomy. (*ET* 117)

Stories Read and Written

At the time that Lovecraft discovered astronomy and its wonders in his science books, he was also encountering astronomy in the stories he read. By his teenage years, Lovecraft had read works by writers who are regarded as pioneers of speculative and science fiction, including Edgar Allan Poe (1809–1849), Jules Verne (1828–1905), and H. G. Wells (1866–1946). All three wrote stories that incorporated astronomical elements, and their influences upon Lovecraft's writing are discussed, along with other literary influences, in chapters 5, 7, and 9–11.

Lovecraft himself was trying his hand at fiction by 1897, although many of his juvenile stories do not survive. Perhaps surprisingly, few of these early stories appear to have had a strong scientific foundation. "The Alchemist," written in 1908 (an important year for Lovecraft, as we shall see), takes little from his youthful interest in chemistry. Nor is any surviving early tale based on astronomy. There was, however, a lost story with an astronomical basis. Lovecraft wrote a letter to Rheinhart Kleiner in which he remarked:

> I wrote one story about that side of the moon which is forever turned away from us—using, for fictional purposes, the [Peter Andreas] Hansen theory that air and water still exist there as the result of an abnormal centre of gravity in the Moon. I hardly need add that the theory is really exploded—I was even aware of that fact at the time—but I desired to compose a "thriller". (20 January 1916; *RK* 49–50)

Breakdown

Until 1908, Lovecraft's trajectory in astronomy, with some lapses, was upward. He became a skilled amateur astronomer. His self-published magazines had become more and more sophisticated. He began and maintained his association with Ladd Observatory. His newspaper columns on astronomy commenced and introduced him to the reading public. He lectured on astronomy to family and friends and, in the case of the Boys Club, probably to strangers. Prospects of a career in astronomy, if by no means assured, remained open. Pretty good going for a seventeen-year-old! However, as 1908 arrived, Lovecraft's life and his astronomical ambitions were about to crash.

All had apparently gone well in school as regards Lovecraft's ability to master the material until he arrived at Hope Street High School in the fall of 1904. Hope Street High School was a respectable institution. It was one of the schools approved by the New England College Entrance Certificate Board. That Board represented a number of colleges, including Brown University, that accepted students who graduated with high enough grades (certificate grades) from approved schools. Upon successful attainment of certificate grades in appropriate high school courses, and with the high school principal's signature of approval, students would be eligible for acceptance into college "by certificate," requiring no entrance examinations (New England College Entrance Certificate Board 1907).

Joshi (*IAP* 100–101) reviewed Lovecraft's grades for the three years he attended high school (the 1904–05, 1906–07, and 1907–08 school years). At Hope Street, a 70 was a passing grade, whereas an 80 was a higher certificate grade. Lovecraft's grades for 1904–05 are not bad, but not spectacular, either. An 87 in Latin, an 82 in Ancient History, and an 85 in Botany achieved certificate level, but his 77 in English and 74 in Elementary Algebra did not. A "near-breakdown" caused him to miss most of the 1905–06 school year. When Lovecraft returned to high school for the 1906–07 year, he managed certificate grades in seven of the eight subjects he took. His 95 in Physics was outstanding. The one weak point was a grade of 75 in Intermediate Algebra, although he received a 92 in his other mathematics course, Plane Geometry.

The 1907–08 school year found Lovecraft attempting only three courses, achieving certificate grades in all three. His grades of 95 in Chemistry and Physics reveal mastery of those subjects. His 85 in his third course, a 10-week repeat of Intermediate Algebra, showed improvement. Joshi (*IAP* 80) notes that Lovecraft never took an astronomy course in high school, although some were offered. That is curious, but perhaps they were too elementary for him or rarely offered, or perhaps he would have taken astronomy had he completed four full years of high school courses. As it happened, by the end of the 1907–08 year Lovecraft had not accrued enough credits to graduate from Hope Street High School. He would not return in 1908–09 to complete a high school degree.

Many students would, of course, be pleased to obtain grades as high as Lovecraft achieved in those high school classes he did complete. Instead, Lovecraft, always sensitive to what he perceived as his own failings, was dismayed. His discouragement centered on algebra, and is worth discussion because it would be this weakness in mathematics that Lovecraft believed crushed his hopes of a career in astronomy. In 1933 Lovecraft recalled:

> In studies I was not bad—except for mathematics, which repelled and exhausted me. I passed in these subjects—but just about that. Or rather, it was algebra which formed the bugbear. Geometry was not so bad. But the whole thing disappointed me bitterly, for I was then intending to pursue astronomy as a career, and of course advanced astronomy is simply a mass of mathematics. That was the first major set-back I ever received—the first time I was ever brought up short against a consciousness of my own limitations. It was clear to me that I hadn't brains enough to be an astronomer—and that was a pill I couldn't swallow with equanimity. (Letter to Robert E. Howard, 29 March 1933; *MF* 583)

Dreams of attending Brown University and becoming himself a professor of astronomy were dashed when the hitherto precocious Lovecraft was unable even to graduate from high school. He would withdraw into an isolation from which he would not emerge for six years. This was a pivotal point in his life, and in his relationship to astronomy.

What mathematics courses would Lovecraft have faced, had he been able to graduate from high school and get into Brown University? Today undergraduate students interested in astronomy as a career need a heavy dose of mathematics and physics. That was true in 1910 as well, although some institutions emphasized more the mathematics side and some more the physics side. The *Brown University Catalogue* and its *Announcement of Courses* for the 1910–11 academic year tell us about the mathematics that a student at Brown would have taken. All students were required to complete mathematics to the level of solid geometry and trigonometry, but more was expected of astronomy students. A Bachelor of Science degree required mathematics courses including differential and integral calculus. Spherical trigonometry would also be vital in astronomy, while an understanding of differential equations would be necessary for many physics courses. That would be just for an undergraduate degree. By 1910 most college faculty positions in astronomy (and such positions were always few in number) would have required a master's degree if not a doctorate. Probably Lovecraft was right that he would have found slogging through the required mathematics heavy going, perhaps impossibly so.

However, we may ask why losing an astronomical career meant the end of Lovecraft's college hopes. Many astronomy enthusiasts today find the mathematical sections of the science uncongenial and regretfully give up dreams of becoming professional astronomers. That does not necessarily mean that they abandon college. Could not Lovecraft have returned to finish his high school degree and attempted college in another field? True, astronomy had been his love, but his interests were far from narrow and a college degree would help secure his gentlemanly status while opening other career opportunities.

Admission to Brown University could be through entrance exams or "presentation of a certificate signed by the principal of any school which has the privilege of issuing certificates to Brown University." As we saw above, Hope Street High School had such a privilege. Assuming that a certificate grade of 80 was the minimum grade to which students hoping for college need aspire, we find that Lovecraft's grades in 13 of the 16 courses he took at Hope Street exceeded that requirement.[23] Had Lovecraft been able to finish high school with grades comparable to those he achieved in the classes he did take, entry into Brown University would not have been out of the question. Even with the abbreviated course load he had taken, Lovecraft was already close to completing Brown University's requirements for admission to the Bachelor of Arts

---

23. In the letter to Alfred Galpin mentioned below, HPL states only that he was certified in physics and chemistry, subjects in which he had scored particularly highly.

degree program. That is particularly true since students with some deficiencies could be admitted to the university "with conditions."[24]

There was of course the problem of money. The 1909–1910 *Catalogue of Brown University* estimated tuition and fees to amount to $105 a year, with incidental expenses of another $48. There would also be expenses for books, room, and board. The *Catalogue* estimated that a student sharing a dorm room with a roommate might get by with an annual outlay of $403 ($13,000 in 2022). Since Lovecraft was already living in Providence, his additional expenses while attending college would likely have been less. However, these costs, while they might seem modest today, were not negligible at the time.

The estate of Lovecraft's father was valued as $10,000 at his death in 1898 ($350,000 in 2022). Lovecraft and his mother received a modest inheritance when his grandfather Whipple Phillips died in 1904 ($2500 for Lovecraft, and $5000 for his mother; $81,000 and $162,000, respectively, in 2022). However, Lovecraft's uncle Edwin Phillips apparently lost an unknown but significant amount of that money in 1911 (Faig, *Lovecraftian Voyages* 22–23). Around 1909, shortly before that loss, Lovecraft (or his mother) spent $161 on a correspondence course in chemistry (*IAP* 128–29), an expense that would have no practical return. Money spent on college might easily have been reckoned a better investment. There would also have been the possibility of part-time employment to help with costs. The *Brown University Catalogue* noted that "Students who need to earn money find in the city numerous opportunities for doing so by giving private instruction, by

---

24. For certificate admission to the Bachelor of Arts degree program at Brown University (*Catalogue* 1909) evidence of accomplishment had to be presented in English, plane geometry, and Greek and Roman history. In addition, at least six points were needed from Latin (3 points), elementary Greek (2 points), advanced Greek (1 point), elementary French (1 point), advanced French (1 point), elementary German (1 point), or advanced German (1 point). Finally, one subject needed to be presented from solid geometry and plane trigonometry, medieval and modern history, English history, American history, physics, or chemistry. A letter of certification from the high school principal was also necessary. Admission by examination required satisfactory grades in a similar array of subjects. Not all applicants completed satisfactory grades in all required subjects. Applicants who did not succeed in all requirements could be admitted "with conditions." A substantial fraction of Brown's freshman class fell into that category.

teaching in evening schools, and in various other ways." There is, however, no evidence that Lovecraft entertained the possibility of a return to high school or attendance at college without astronomy.

Did Lovecraft approach anyone for advice before deciding to forego college? His mother may have lacked the judgment to guide her son on the issue, but what about Ladd Observatory's director? With the experience of a quarter-century of teaching, Professor Upton undoubtedly had faced similar questions before. Joshi (*IAP* 110) noted that Dr. Franklin Chase Clark, Brown University graduate and husband of his aunt Lillian Phillips, became something of a father figure to the young Lovecraft. He would seem to be another person from whom Lovecraft might have sought guidance. However, we have no evidence that the dismayed Lovecraft asked anyone for advice about either high school or college.

Instead, the summer of 1908 saw Lovecraft collapse in the worst breakdown of his life. The breakdown may have been so severe as to preclude even the possibility of serious schoolwork, at least on any subject he found uncongenial. Writing to Alfred Galpin in 1918 (*AG* 210), Lovecraft stated that "I left high school certified in physics & chemistry, & intended to specialise in those subjects in college; but just then my nervous system went all to pieces, & I was forced to relinquish all thought of activity." In recalling his attempts to study chemistry from 1909 to 1912 through the home study course mentioned above, Lovecraft reported mastering the sections on inorganic chemistry and qualitative analysis, while the complications of organic chemistry left him with debilitating headaches (*RK* 61; *IAP* 129). The intense studying needed to finish high school and attempt college may have formed an impossible and humiliating barrier to him, an obstacle he could not imagine overcoming.

Joshi (*IAP* 126–28) associated the 1908 breakdown with Lovecraft's shattering realization that his weakness in mathematics meant that careers in astronomy or even chemistry would not be possible. Joshi considered, however, that there might have been more to the breakdown than the dashing of Lovecraft's career goal. When weighing possible contributory factors, both psychological and physical, Joshi was forced to conclude that much about this devastating breakdown remains in the realm of conjecture. Livesey (*DPO* 75–76) suggested that the transformation of the science of observational astronomy away from the romantic days when discoveries were made at the telescope eyepiece and toward the detailed analysis of photographs, may also have discouraged

Lovecraft. One wonders, however, how much of the possible tedium of photographic investigations was apparent to Lovecraft in 1908 (although he had dabbled in astrophotography; see Appendix II). Moreover, positional astronomy of the nineteenth century already involved many tedious calculations, even though the observations themselves were made at the eyepiece.

A downward trend in the level of Lovecraft's astronomical endeavors is evident even before 1908. The *Rhode Island Journal of Astronomy* ceased to be issued after April 1907. Moreover, as we saw, Lovecraft attempted only three classes in high school during the 1907–08 school year before permanently withdrawing. Lovecraft's newspaper columns lasted somewhat longer, but both were done by sometime in 1908.

Whatever its cause, and, given Lovecraft's statement, Joshi is very likely right that the collapse of his career dreams played an important part in it, the breakdown of 1908 began an extended low in Lovecraft's life. In 1934, Lovecraft wrote to R. H. Barlow that

> Many times in my youth I was so exhausted by the sheer burden of consciousness & mental & physical activity that I had to drop out of school for a greater or lesser period & take a complete rest free from all responsibilities; & when I was 18 I suffered such a breakdown that I had to forego college. In those days I could hardly bear to see or speak to anyone, & liked to shut out the world by pulling down dark shades & using artificial light. (*OFF* 125)

Half a decade of relative isolation ensued. However, even during this period, Lovecraft did not abandon astronomy. Aside from a couple of failed attempts to revive the *Rhode Island Journal of Astronomy* early in 1909, there were no more self-published astronomical journals. Nor, for some years, would his byline appear on astronomical newspaper columns. However, Lovecraft began a personal *Astronomical Notebook* in 1909.[25] In it, he would record observations intermittently until 1914.[26] Long-lost to the general public, save for a few excerpts recorded—not always correctly—by David H. Keller, this notebook has recently resurfaced. As of this writing, it is online courtesy of Villanova University's Falvey Memorial Library.

---

25. We follow Joshi (*CE* 3.332) in adopting this title for the notebook. Its cover merely states "Astronomical Observations Made by H. P. Lovecraft."

26. The cover of the notebook lists the years 1909 through 1915, but no observations dated 1915 are contained within.

Lovecraft's observations recorded in this notebook are the work of no novice, but show him to be an experienced and knowledgeable amateur astronomer. The notebook opens with observations of an occultation of Mars by the moon on 1 September 1909.[27] Telescopic observations of Mars, then at a close opposition, and the moon follow on the next night. There are no other entries until Lovecraft's observation of Halley's comet on the evening of 26 May 1910, the highlight of the notebook.[28] Although the notebook outlined an ambitious list of observing goals, the long gap in time between the 1909 and 1910 entries indicates that actual observations were few. No observations at all are recorded for the years 1911 and 1913. The wonderful but lone observation of Halley's comet emphasizes the change in Lovecraft's observing habits. The Lovecraft of 1903 would surely have seen and described this famous celestial visitor on more than a single night. Observing did pick up somewhat in 1914, a year when Lovecraft was coming out of his isolation. Lovecraft's notebook concludes with a list of the astronomical equipment he then possessed, including his 3-inch Bardou telescope, prism binoculars, and his Whittaker and Barritt-Serviss planispheres (the name Serviss being inscribed with the long ſ of colonial days).

Only after years of isolation and stagnation did Lovecraft emerge from the collapse of 1908 to resume his newspaper writing on astronomy and to venture into the world of amateur journalism. By 1914, childhood precocity and dreams of professorial employment in astronomy were long behind him. However, that year would see Lovecraft inaugurate a new newspaper column on astronomy in the Providence *Evening News*. In the following year there was a second series of astronomy articles, this time for a paper in distant North Carolina (see chapter 6).

Astronomy would never again occupy Lovecraft's daily life to the extent that it did in the first flowering of enthusiasm from 1903 to 1907.

---

27. There is a brief mention of a lunar eclipse in June, but the notebook itself is stated as beginning in September 1909, so the eclipse entry may have been added after the event.

28. Newspapers reported that Providence's parks thronged with comet watchers that night. HPL writes that he observed from a point on the Providence–Taunton Pike, whence he was able to trace about 30 degrees of the tail of Halley's comet. HPL was seriously ill with the measles early in 1910 and so missed the bright January comet of that year (letter to R. H. Barlow, 23 July 1936; *OFF* 356).

Nevertheless, astronomy would be a part of his life until its end. When he returned to fiction in the late 1910s, astronomy would not be left behind. We need only note that astronomy figured importantly in "Polaris," written in 1918, and "Beyond the Wall of Sleep," written in 1919.[29] As L. Sprague de Camp remarked in *Lovecraft: A Biography,* and as S. T. Joshi remarked in *Lovecraft and a World in Transition,* perhaps Lovecraft's failure to follow the astronomical career he so wanted had its fortunate side. We have his unique fiction, rather than the solid but unexceptional astronomy books that Professor Lovecraft might have written. While his readers may take satisfaction in that outcome, to the Lovecraft of 1908 the situation was more bleak. Long years would pass before Lovecraft himself could regard the loss of college and a profession in astronomy with anything approaching equanimity.

---

29. We may note, also, David Haden's astronomical interpretation of HPL's 1919 poem "The City" (*Tentaclii,* 31 October 2019).

1. My Gaze Was Ever Upward

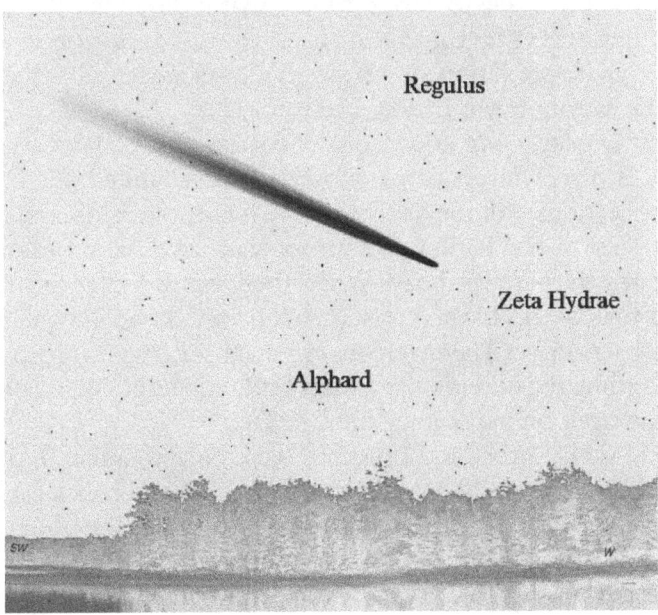

Lovecraft's drawing of Comet Halley on the evening of 26 May 1910 (top). Its accuracy is indicated by the simulation (bottom) that shows the apparent position of Comet Halley on that evening (Starry Nights software). H. P. Lovecraft Collection. Digital Library@Villanova University.

Chapter 2
Ladd Observatory and
Three Whom Lovecraft Pestered

When young Howard Phillips Lovecraft was awakening to astronomy, he learned by reading and by observing with his own telescopes. However, he was not entirely on his own. He did have at hand an introduction to the world of professional astronomy. That was Brown University's Ladd Observatory and its staff of three: Winslow Upton, Frederick Slocum, and John Edwards. Any understanding of how astronomy grew to have the place that it did in his life, and of how he was devastated by the end of his dream of an astronomical career, requires an appreciation of Lovecraft's association with the world of academic astronomy at Ladd Observatory.

Unfortunately, our knowledge of the interactions between Lovecraft and the Brown University astronomers is very limited. He has left us a few recollections, but they are brief. We have no reminiscences of Lovecraft by any of the Ladd Observatory staff, two of whom died before Lovecraft's thirtieth birthday. What, then, can we infer from the information that we do have? We start with some basic information about Ladd Observatory. Then we consider such statements as Lovecraft left us concerning the observatory and its staff, remembering that those were sometimes put on paper long after the fact.

Ladd Observatory and Lovecraft were born together in time. Lovecraft's birth came on 20 August 1890; ground was broken for Ladd Observatory in May of the same year. The birthing of the observatory was an extended process, the completed building not being dedicated until 21 October 1891, when it was formally presented to Brown University by its donor, Governor Herbert W. Ladd. A drawing and plan of the new observatory were included in the 19 July 1890 issue of the *American Architect and Building News,* showcasing the design of the Stone, Carpenter, and Willson architectural firm.

2. Ladd Observatory and Three Whom Lovecraft Pestered 53

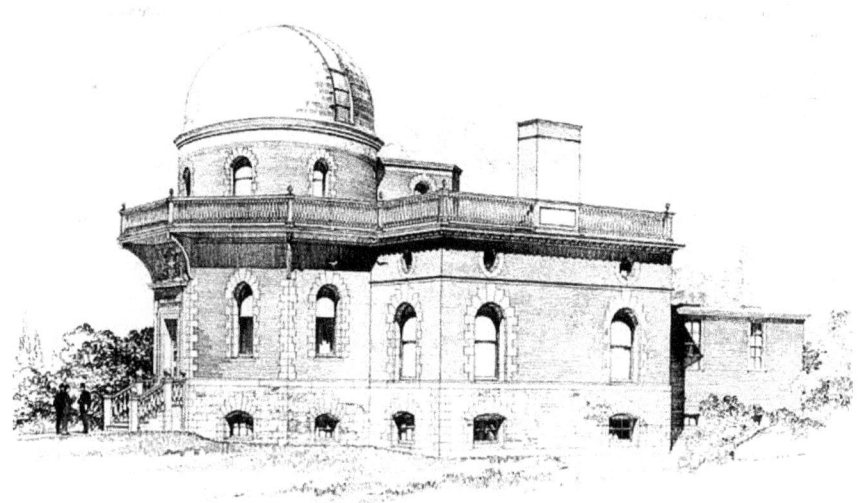

Sketch of the planned Ladd Observatory from the *American Architect and Building News* No. 760 (19 July 1890).

The observatory of which its first director, Professor Winslow Upton, took charge is still in existence. Upton described the new observatory in a paper published in the *Sidereal Messenger* magazine in 1891, shortly after its dedication:

> It is situated on the summit of a hill in a sparsely settled part of the city of Providence, and is 200 feet above sea level. It is one mile north of the other college buildings. The building is constructed of brick with stone trimmings, except the ell for the transit instruments, which is of wood. The tower is octagonal up to the second floor, and cylindrical from that floor to the revolving dome. . . . The central part of the main building is a broad corridor running to the transit ell, which is separated from it by a small hall containing two side entrances. On the south of the corridor is one large room for the library, and on the north, a smaller room for a study and computing room . . . The roof is flat and surrounded by a railing; a balcony extends around the equatorial room. The revolving dome is made of copper and has a slit covered by two shutters which move sideways in either direction giving an opening of four feet. The chief instrument of the Observatory is an equatorial telescope of 12.2 inches aperture and 15 feet focal length. The instrument was made by G. N. Saegmuller, the objective constructed by J. A. Brashear. . . . The other instruments are a 3-inch portable transit, by Saegmuller; a smaller transit for students' use; a chronograph, by Warner & Swasey; several

chronometers and sextants, a barograph, thermograph and recording hygrometer by Richard Frères; a recording rain and snow gauge, by Ferguson, and ordinary meteorological instruments.

The location was only about a mile from places where Lovecraft lived in the early 1900s, a distance the young Lovecraft could easily traverse by bicycle or on foot.

A 12-inch telescope was a respectable instrument in 1891, but, even at the time of its dedication, it was by no means one of the world's largest telescopes. The Lick Observatory in California had since 1888 been home to a refracting telescope with a lens three times the diameter of the Ladd Observatory instrument. However, Ladd Observatory had no rival in Rhode Island. Providence did have Frank Seagrave's private observatory, then located at 119 Benefit Street, but it housed a smaller Alvan Clark refractor of 8¼-inches aperture.[1]

As Upton noted, Ladd Observatory held transit telescopes as well as the 12-inch main telescope. These could be used to note when stars crossed the meridian, a north-south line in the sky. Those observations could be used to calculate the local time and, for some years, the Ladd Observatory provided the correct time to subscribing businesses. This time service was inaugurated in September 1893, with the observatory sending the exact time to the Providence Electric Protective Company, which apparently did the actual distribution to individual subscribers.[2] David Haden has pointed out that one of the clocks for precision timekeeping at the observatory was, appropriately enough, a "Howard Astronomical Regulator"[3] (Haden, "Stars and Time"). Director Upton noted that "The clock is connected with the bell-ringer's room, so that now the college bell will be rung at exactly the right time."[4]

---

1. Seagrave's observatory, chased outside of Providence in 1914 by light pollution and smoke, is today owned by the Skyscrapers astronomy club. There is no evidence that HPL met Seagrave or that he visited his observatory. Alvan Clark and Sons were renowned makers of astronomical telescopes.

2. *Jewelers' Circular and Horological Review* for 27 September 1893. Telegraphic time services by observatories are the subject of Ian R. Bartky's book *Selling the True Time*.

3. A regulator clock could be adjusted to keep accurate time, and provided a standard against which other clocks could be tested.

4. *Brown Daily Herald* (30 September 1895). Michael L. Umbricht has written an excellent account of the Ladd Observatory's timekeeping:

2. Ladd Observatory and Three Whom Lovecraft Pestered

Ladd Observatory's astronomical library would prove at least as important as its telescopes for the young Lovecraft. There, perhaps beneath the large lithograph of Saturn hanging over the fireplace and surrounded by books and journals, he could spend hours delving into publications unavailable to him at home or in the public library. Those included technical publications aimed at professional astronomers.

As 1902 turned to 1903 and Lovecraft's interest in astronomy blossomed, he was fortunate to have this real astronomical observatory not far from his home. He was more fortunate still to have a relative who was able to introduce him to the director of that observatory, winning Lovecraft access to its facilities. In later years Lovecraft recalled his relationship to the Ladd Observatory and its staff in several letters:

> In the summer of 1903 my mother presented me with a 2¼″ astronomical telescope, and thenceforward my gaze was ever upward at night. The late Prof. Upton of Brown, a friend of the family, gave me the freedom of the college observatory, & I came & went there at will on my bicycle. Ladd Observatory tops a considerable eminence about a mile from the house. I used to walk up Doyle Avenue hill with my wheel, but when returning would have a glorious coast down it. So constant were my observations, that my neck became much affected by the strain of peering at a difficult angle. It gave me much pain, & resulted in a permanent curvature perceptible today to a close observer. (Letter to Rheinhart Kleiner, 16 November 1916; *RK* 71)

> From 1906 to 1918 I contributed monthly articles on astronomical phenomena to one of the lesser Providence dailies.[5] One thing that helped me greatly was the free access which I had to the Ladd Observatory of Brown University—an unusual privilege for a kid, but made possible because Prof. Upton—head of the college astronomical department and director of the observatory—was a friend of the family. I suppose I pestered the people at the observatory half to death, but they were very kind about it. I had a chance to see all the standard modern equipment of an observatory (including a 12″ telescope) in action, and read endlessly in the observatory library. The professors and their humbler assistant—an affable little cockney from England named John Edwards—often helped me pick up equipment, and Edwards made me some magnificent pho-

---

blogs.brown.edu/ladd/2018/11/27/clock-vaults/#more-1082.

5. Actually, HPL at different times contributed astronomical articles to four newspapers, as recounted in chapter 6.

tographic lantern-slides (from illustrations in books) which I used in giving illustrated astronomical lectures before clubs. (Letter to Duane W. Rimel, 29 March 1934; *FLB* 157)

Ladd Observatory was featured on several early postcards of Providence. Could the bicycle in shadow, leaning on the steps in the lower postcard, be the one Lovecraft rode from his home to the observatory? H. Smith collection.

2. Ladd Observatory and Three Whom Lovecraft Pestered

Last night I had an interesting view of Peltier's comet through the 12″ telescope of Ladd Observatory (of Brown U) a mile north of here. I used to haunt this observatory 30 years ago—the director and his two assistants (all dead now—save one asst. now at Wesleyan U. in Middletown, Conn.) being infinitely tolerant of a pompous juvenile ass with grandiose astronomical ambitions! (Letter to R. H. Barlow, 23 July 1936; *OFF* 356)

As a boy I used to haunt the Ladd Observatory of Brown University—looking through the 12-inch refractor now & then, reading the books in the library, & probably making an unmitigated nuisance of myself through my incessant questioning of everybody present. Curiously enough, the assistant there was one of your grandfather's humbler compatriots—a Cornishman named John Edwards, whose capacity for misplacing h's was limitless. Scarcely less limited was his mechanical skill, & in his infinite kindness he fixed me up all sorts of devices (a long focus celestial camera, a set of celestial lantern slides, a diagonal eyepiece for my telescope, etc. etc.) at no more than cost price. I still have the slides somewhere—as well as lunar and other photographs I took with the camera. He is dead now—as is Prof. Upton, the director in those days, our acquaintance with whom gave me my passport to that dark-domed enchanted castle. My third victim there—Associate Prof. Slocum—is now head of the observatory at Wesleyan U. in Middletown, Conn. I would have carried astronomy further but for the mathematics—but I hadn't quite the right stuff in me. (Letter to Jonquil Leiber, 29 November 1936; *CLM* 289–90)

Beyond the names, who were these Ladd Observatory astronomers whom Lovecraft claims to have plagued?

Winslow Upton

Most important, especially at the beginning, was the first director of Ladd Observatory, Professor Winslow Upton, for it was he who provided Lovecraft's entrée to his enchanted astronomical castle. Upton was born in 1853 in Salem, Massachusetts, a city that is the real-life counterpart, to the limited extent that there is one, to Lovecraft's legend-haunted Arkham.[6] It was not clear at first that astronomy would be Upton's profession. His father was a musician and, after he graduated high

---

6. Obituaries for Professor Upton may be found in the *Brown Daily Herald* for 9 January 1914, in the *Brown Alumni Monthly* 14, No. 7 (1914), in *Science,* New Series 39, No. 997 (6 February 1914): 202–04 (by R. C. Archibald), and in *Popular Astronomy* 22 (April 1914): 208 (by Frederick

school, the son briefly studied music. When Upton entered Brown University in 1871 music gave way to science, and he graduated as valedictorian of his class in 1875.

Today, the Ph.D. degree or its equivalent is usually required for entry to a career in academic astronomy. That was not the case in the 1870s. Instead, Upton served as a journeyman astronomer at the University of Cincinnati, earning an A.M. degree there in 1877 before spending time at the Harvard College Observatory, the U.S. Lake Survey, and the U.S. Naval Observatory. He also studied meteorology with the U.S. Signal Service. Upton may have lacked a Ph.D., but he completed a thorough internship at several astronomical institutions.

Nor did Upton desert music when he turned to astronomy. He is credited with writing the Gilbert and Sullivan parody, the *Observatory Pinafore,* in 1878 during his stay at the Harvard College Observatory, although the work would not be staged until a meeting of the American Astronomical Society in 1929 (Sobel 226–27). A few lines suffice to illustrate the good-natured fun of the spoof:

> I'm called an astronomer, skillful astronomer,
>   Though I could never tell why;
> But yet an astronomer, happy astronomer,
>   Modest astronomer, I.
> I read the thermometers, break the photometers,
> Mend them with paper and wax;
> I often lament that so seldom is spent
> A fair evening on star parallax.
> I write many letters, give aid to my betters,
>   And often sit up late o' nights
> To catch a few glimpses of the many eclipses
>   of Jupiter's bright satellites.[7]

Upton's musical interests continued until the end of his life. He directed his church choir's Christmas music shortly before his death on 8 January 1914.

Slocum). See also Martha Mitchell's article on Upton in the *Encyclopedia Brunoniana* (1993).

7. As of 2022, the complete lyrics of the *Observatory Pinafore* are online at hea-www.harvard.edu/~jcm/html/play.html. Several of the research programs of the Harvard College Observatory find mention in these lines.

2. Ladd Observatory and Three Whom Lovecraft Pestered 59

Winslow Upton in the Ladd Observatory. The counterweight behind him helped lift the observer's chair and table to a convenient height for reaching the telescope eyepiece. Courtesy of the Brown University Library.

Upton married Cornelia Augusta Babcock in 1882 and returned to Brown University in 1883 to take up an appointment as professor of astronomy. At Brown, Upton published a number of astronomical and meteorological papers as well as a star atlas, a copy of which Lovecraft purchased in 1906. Upton carried a considerable teaching load at Brown University and was also a supporter of, and teacher in, the associated Woman's College. Remarks at Upton's funeral by Brown University president William Faunce are revealing of his personality:

> For one year he was Dean, and I was brought into contact with him more than ever. But his nervous system was too delicately organized for the position and at the end of the year he wished to give it up. The burden of every man was his burden, the disappointments of others were his disappointments. The tenderness of his heart was something which only those who came into close touch with him can know. ("Death of Professor Upton" 171)

When Upton was appointed professor, Brown had no observatory. Upton wanted one and eventually threatened to leave the university unless progress was made toward acquiring such a facility. Governor Herbert W. Ladd stepped in to provide funds, and planning for the new facility was placed in Upton's hands. When it opened in 1891, Upton was the obvious person to be its first director. He would remain director until his death at the age of sixty. Under Upton's direction, Ladd Observatory was used for teaching, for timekeeping, and for studies of the sun, meteors, novae, and occultations of stars by the moon.[8] It was to this college observatory, modest in size but unmatched by anything in his city, that Lovecraft came, beginning in 1903.

As we have seen, Lovecraft wrote that it was a family friendship with Upton that opened the doors of the observatory for him, but he does not tell us specifics of how that came about. We do not know whether Lovecraft asked a family member to intervene on his behalf or whether it was the family member who, seeing Lovecraft's burgeoning interest in astronomy, took the initiative. Chris Perridas suggests that Upton's friendship with Lovecraft's family may have meant that Upton was already acquainted with Lovecraft before the two met at the observatory.[9] However, a letter Lovecraft wrote to his aunt Lillian Clark (12 February 1926; *LFF* 551) implies that Lovecraft did not know Upton before he visited the observatory: "The worst cold I ever had came in late April & early May of 1903, & was so bad that it prevented my going to the Ladd Observatory on May 4th, though you and Dr. Clark had made an appointment for me with Prof. Upton." That letter provides support for S. T. Joshi's suggestion that it was the husband of Lovecraft's aunt Lillian, Franklin Chase Clark, who provided the link with Upton (*IAP* 85). In any case, whatever the family connection, one doubts whether Lovecraft was given a permanent welcome to the observatory until Upton had had a chance to judge the lad's interest and decorum. Upton's impression of Lovecraft must have been favorable, for the observatory door remained open to the youngster.

Ladd Observatory entered Lovecraft's life at a time when other things were about to leave it. His maternal grandfather, Whipple Phillips, died on 28 March 1904, forcing Lovecraft and his mother to move from the house Lovecraft considered his ancestral home at 454 Angell

---

8. Nova Persei 1901, which figures in HPL's story "Beyond the Wall of Sleep," was observed at the Ladd Observatory (see chapter 11).

9. Chris Perridas, chrisperridas.blogspot.com/2006/04/lovecraft-winslow-upton-ladd.html

Street. Ladd Observatory provided one source of continuity at this troubled time—a place linked to the Brown University academic world that the teenage Lovecraft could enter, and to which he might aspire to belong as a student or faculty member. The crash would thus be all the more complete a few years later when Lovecraft realized that a career in professional astronomy was beyond his reach. Any sense of belonging to the gentleman's club of academic astronomy would then abruptly vanish.

Upton maintained an interest in meteorology as well as astronomy, keeping a weather station at the observatory, and publishing papers on New England storms. Lovecraft's juvenile science writings reveal that he too was very interested in meteorology, and that he set up his own weather instruments and made his own weather forecasts. It is quite possible that the Ladd Observatory weather station, and perhaps Upton's encouragement, inspired that interest. Threatening storms would be featured in several of Lovecraft's stories, but are, of course, a far from uncommon feature in tales of gothic literature.

The Ladd Observatory library c. 1900, a likely refuge for the young Lovecraft. Note the model of a reed boat before the fireplace and Saturn over the mantel. The drawing of Saturn is a signed and numbered chromolithograph produced by Étienne Trouvelot.[10] Courtesy of the Brown University Library.

---

10. Michael L. Umbricht, personal communication.

It is sometimes stated that Lovecraft frequently observed with the Ladd Observatory telescope. In fact, his letter to Kleiner, quoted above, suggests as much. However, one should perhaps be cautious on this point. Many of the limited supply of clear nights must have been given over to the Ladd astronomers themselves or to Brown University students. Still, if Lovecraft did have the freedom to use the observatory's main instrument when it was not in demand for classes, that would imply very great confidence indeed by the director in the teenager's maturity and competence. We know that Lovecraft did look through the telescope on occasion, but, as we have argued (Smith, "Eratosthenes" and also chapter 4), it is probably an exaggeration to imagine the teenage Lovecraft as a nightly figure in the dome. We might, however, picture him regularly visiting the observatory library, reading astronomical journals, and plying with questions staff members who wandered nearby. It was presumably Upton who gave Lovecraft the privilege of borrowing books from the Ladd library, and we find him availing himself of that privilege on three occasions, as recorded in the *Ladd Observatory Books Loaned* record book (John Hay Library). Besides the pamphlet on spectroscopes mentioned in chapter 1, Lovecraft borrowed *Laboratory Astronomy* by Robert Wheeler Willson (borrowed 27 October 1906 and returned 24 November) and *The Planet Mars* by William H. Pickering (borrowed 11 June 1907 and returned 25 July). The last is a bit puzzling because, while Pickering did issue a book of his collected papers on Mars, it was not published until 1921. Perhaps Lovecraft borrowed a reprint of Pickering's translation of Giovanni Schiaparelli's book on Mars. The translation was originally published in 1894 in several issues of the journal *Astronomy and Astro-physics*.[11] Most of the volumes in the Ladd Observatory library were probably intended to be consulted on the premises, and Lovecraft undoubtedly read many more publications than he borrowed.

Early in 1907, Upton introduced Lovecraft to Percival Lowell, who was at Brown University to lecture about Mars: "[Lowell] lectured in this city in 1907, when I was writing for the Tribune, and Prof. Upton of Brown introduced me to him before the lecture in Sayles' Hall" (letter to Rheinhart Kleiner, 19 February 1916; *RK* 53). Recall that by 1907 Lovecraft had been frequenting Ladd Observatory for more than three years.

---

11. The issues are not listed in the Ladd Observatory library acquisitions manifest in the John Hay Library, but the record does not seem to include journals.

2. Ladd Observatory and Three Whom Lovecraft Pestered 63

While Upton may not have considered Lovecraft a protégé, he apparently did regard him as someone sufficiently presentable to be introduced to the well-known astronomer who championed intelligent life on the Red Planet (see chapter 9). Upton would certainly have had ample time by this point to have withdrawn from any association with the lad had Lovecraft proved himself untrustworthy or foolish. He was perhaps not the pompous ass that he remembered himself being.

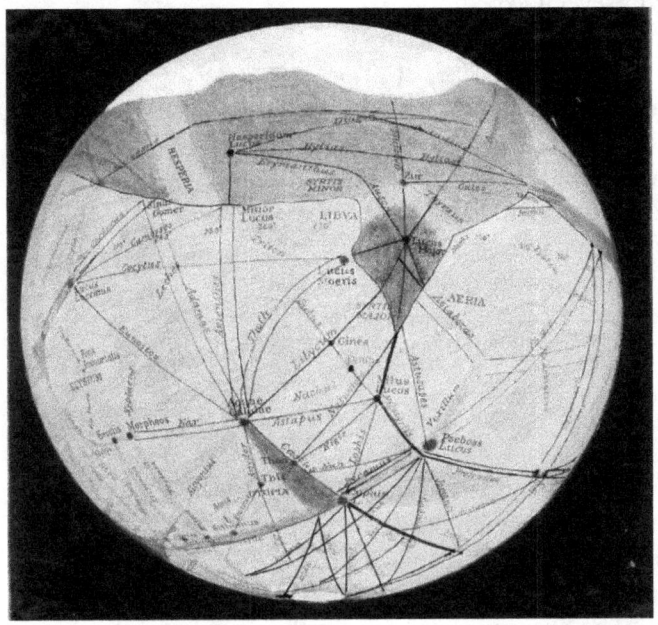

Percival Lowell made this drawing of Mars two years before Lovecraft met him. The fine canals drawn by Lowell, keys to his belief in intelligent Martians, do not actually exist.

When Lovecraft knew him, Upton was writing a monthly astronomy column that was published in the Providence *Journal* and the Boston *Evening Transcript*.[12] Lovecraft thus emulated the Brown professor when he began his own newspaper astronomy columns in the summer of 1906. Lovecraft's monthly articles in the Providence *Tribune* generally follow the model set by Upton's articles in describing phenomena in the heavens during the upcoming month. Lovecraft showed greater daring in his

---

12. Professor Upton began his newspaper column about 1893 and continued it until his death.

weekly articles in the *Pawtuxet Valley Gleaner,* venturing into such questions as whether there was life on the moon or Mars (chapters 4 and 6).

Upton was an occasionally adventurous astronomer, engaging in several expeditions to distant lands, often to see eclipses of the sun. That leads to a speculative though ultimately doubtful link between Upton and Lovecraft's fiction that is still worth mention. Before he took up his professorship, Upton went to Caroline Island in the Pacific to observe the solar eclipse of 6 May 1883 (*Report of the Eclipse Expedition,* 1884). We are reminded that Cthulhu's stone city of R'lyeh lies in the Pacific and that Ponape (now written Pohnpei), with its ancient stone ruins, is an island in the Caroline group. Ponape appears in "The Shadow over Innsmouth," in "Out of the Aeons" by Lovecraft and Hazel Heald, and perhaps is also an inspiration for "The Call of Cthulhu" and "Dagon," in which Cyclopean stones on Pacific islands are mentioned. Could those settings be an Upton influence?[13]

Ladd Observatory director Winslow Upton, in a photograph published after his death in the *Brown Alumni Monthly* for February 1914.

We do not know whether, two decades after the 1883 eclipse, Upton regaled the young Lovecraft with tales of his exploits on this or other voyages. If he did, Lovecraft does not tell us so. However, a photograph of the Ladd Observatory library, taken around the beginning of the twentieth century, shows a model reed boat in front of the fireplace, perhaps a

---

13. One of the less scientific fruits of the expedition was Upton's genial opera commemorating the undertaking. Upton also stopped at Hawaii during this trip, writing an account of his visit to the Kilauea volcano (*Hawaiian Journal of History* 29 [1995]: 75–82).

memento of Upton's visit to Lake Titicaca during his 1896–97 sabbatical at the Harvard observing station in Arequipa, Peru. Had Lovecraft seen the boat and asked after its provenance, it might have served as an opening for the director to recount stories of his far-flung travels. Was, then, Upton's eclipse expedition an inspiration for Lovecraft the writer?

Alas for this idea, the Caroline Island (or Caroline Atoll) that Upton visited belongs to the Line Islands, some 1500 kilometers south of Hawaii, not to the Caroline Island group that includes Ponape, which lies northeast of New Guinea. Moreover, other sources, such as A. Merritt's "The Moon Pool"—a story appreciated by Lovecraft as early as its 1918 appearance in *All-Story Weekly*—provide very plausible inspirations for the Pacific locations in Lovecraft's stories. Still, one wonders whether Lovecraft knew of Upton's eclipse excursion in 1883.

Characters named Daniel and Edward Derby Upton appear in "The Thing on the Doorstep." Upton is also the middle name of Richard Upton Pickman in "Pickman's Model." None of these characters appears to be modeled after Winslow Upton in anything but name, although Daniel Upton, who narrates "The Thing on the Doorstep," grew up in Arkham as Winslow Upton did in Salem. There is a Professor Upham rather than Upton in "The Dreams in the Witch House." However, Lovecraft's boyhood friend Ronald Upham is a more likely source for the name than a corruption of Upton. In some ways, it is Professor Atwood, member of the 1930–31 Miskatonic expedition to Antarctica (*At the Mountains of Madness, CF* 3), who most resembles Winslow Upton, although the resemblance is superficial. Atwood was a physicist, not an astronomer. However, he was also a meteorologist, navigator, and surveyor, skills possessed by Upton, and, like Upton, he was willing to sally forth on scientific expeditions.

Lovecraft wrote in self-deprecating fashion that his "incessant questioning" of the Ladd staff made him a nuisance. Exactly what that questioning was about we do not know, although one supposes most questions were related to astronomy and, perhaps, to Lovecraft's wish eventually to become a professional astronomer. Lovecraft might have shown the Ladd Observatory staff at least some of his hectographed scientific magazines, such as the *Rhode Island Journal of Astronomy*, but, if he did so, we do not know what they thought of them. We have speculated (Smith, "Eratosthenes" 167 and chapter 4) that Upton, or perhaps Frederick Slocum, cautioned against Lovecraft's initially rosy view of

William Pickering's belief in life on the moon, as expressed in those magazines. That remains a reasonable but an unverified conjecture.

In fact, Upton and other members of the Ladd Observatory staff generally remain behind the scenes in the juvenile scientific publications Lovecraft wrote in the years he frequented the observatory. Lovecraft included sketches of Ladd Observatory in his *Rhode Island Journal of Astronomy* and in the *Science Library*. He also described visits to the observatory in the *Rhode Island Journal of Astronomy*, although with a charmingly journalistic tone. For example, when reporting on his visit to the observatory in the 1 November 1903 issue of the *Journal*, Lovecraft's headline proclaimed: "The Ladd Observatory Visited by a Correspondent Last Night." However, there are no guest articles by the Ladd staff, nor are there interviews with them or descriptions of them. Instead, Lovecraft is reticent in discussing the Ladd astronomers. If he was getting the benefit of questioning Upton and the other staff members, why do they not appear in a more direct way in his juvenile writing? Did he think that would be beneath them, at least as regards professors Upton and Slocum? Lovecraft did include a column in the August 1906 *Journal* informing the reader that Upton had been awarded an honorary Sc.D. degree by Brown University. Lovecraft commented that the "honour was well merited, for Mr. Upton has taught at Brown for 22 years in the best possible manner, being one of the clearest demonstrators in the university." Lovecraft does not address Upton's research prowess, possibly because Upton had published little research recently. His words suggest that Lovecraft had seen Upton teach, perhaps instructing students at the observatory, but they include nothing beyond what might have been written by a reporter who did not know Upton personally. We are left in the dark regarding Upton's personal relationship to his young admirer.

Frederick Slocum

This brings us to Frederick Slocum, second on the academic ladder at the Ladd Observatory and another of those whom Lovecraft claimed to have pestered. Slocum was connected with the sea as well as the stars. Born in Fairhaven, Massachusetts, in 1873, he came from a seafaring family. His father was a whaling captain and Frederick grew up acquainted with boats and fishing, but it was in academia that he found his métier. In 1895 he obtained a bachelors degree from Brown University, going on to receive a masters degree and then, in 1898, a Ph.D. from the same institution. He was appointed instructor in mathematics at Brown in 1895 and was promoted to assistant professor of astronomy in 1900.

For a time he lived in the home of Winslow Upton, a circumstance that may have encouraged his interest in an astronomical career. In 1899 he married Carrie E. Tripp of New Bedford, Massachusetts.

Slocum left Providence to spend the summer of 1907 as a volunteer assistant at the Yerkes Observatory, which boasted a 40-inch telescope, then the largest working telescope in the world.[14] Although by 1907 founder George Ellery Hale had already departed to establish the Mount Wilson Observatory in California, Yerkes Observatory was a much more vibrant center of research than the much smaller Ladd Observatory. That visit may have whetted Slocum's desire to be more engaged in research, for he returned only briefly to Providence, leaving again for the 1908–09 academic year. This time he headed abroad, visiting the Royal Astrophysical Observatory in Potsdam, Germany, which, like Yerkes, was an active center of astrophysical research. Upon his return to the United States, Slocum joined the staff of the Yerkes Observatory, where he would stay five years.

In 1914 Slocum returned to New England, not to Providence but to Middletown, Connecticut, where plans were under way to build a new astronomical observatory at Wesleyan University. He was appointed professor of astronomy and his first task was to design what would become Wesleyan's Van Vleck Observatory. He would briefly return to Providence to teach navigation during the First World War, but was back at Wesleyan after the war concluded. Slocum made the determination of stellar distances the main research program of the new observatory.

If we know little of Upton's relationship with Lovecraft, we know even less about Slocum's association with him. One need not call upon Slocum's experience with the sea to explain coastal locations such as Innsmouth in Lovecraft's stories. Lovecraft's upbringing in Providence and his travels along the New England coast suffice. A minor character named Charles Slocum appears in *The Case of Charles Dexter Ward,* but the name need not have been inspired by the astronomer. Lovecraft may very well have read of Joshua Slocum, who completed the first solo round-the-world voyage between 1895 and 1898 (on a ship he coincidentally built in Frederick's hometown of Fairhaven), and who wrote of it in his 1900 book, *Sailing Alone Around the World.*

---

14. The Yerkes telescope remains the largest operating telescope of the refracting type. In 1908, the Yerkes telescope would be surpassed in size by Mount Wilson's 60-inch reflecting telescope.

Frederick Slocum tweaks a spectroscope attached to the Ladd Observatory's 12-inch telescope in March 1905. Courtesy of the Brown University Library.

Slocum was the last of the Ladd Observatory three to die, outliving Lovecraft by seven years and passing on 4 December 1944, two months before his seventy-second birthday. He had been set to teach as Wesleyan University's fall 1944 semester began, kept in the saddle by the need for astronomy and navigation teachers during World War II. Obituaries are seldom overly critical of their subjects, but in his obituary of Slocum, Oliver Justin Lee declared that "I never heard him say an unkind thing to or about any person." That kindness presumably extended to Lovecraft, but we do not know how it was expressed.

Slocum, like Upton, had stories of adventure that he might have told to the young frequenter of the observatory. Lovecraft does not, however, mention such tales. Perhaps that is not surprising, for Lee in his obituary remarks: "Slocum was not much of a talker. Only rarely was it possible to get him to speak of the drama and adventure of the sea, such as, for example, shipwrecks around Cuttyhunk, when the colony of islanders were thrown into immediate action to recover what they could . . ." We cannot tie any of the shipwrecks or seafaring episodes in Lovecraft's fiction to Slocum, although it is just possible that he heard some of Slocum's stories of the sea.

2. Ladd Observatory and Three Whom Lovecraft Pestered 69

This postcard, mailed in 1925, shows the Van Vleck Observatory which Slocum directed. Its main instrument was a 20-inch refracting telescope. Like Ladd Observatory, it is still in existence. Astronomers gathered there in 1925 to observe the total solar eclipse. H. Smith collection.

Frederick Slocum returned to Brown University to teach navigation during World War I. Slocum is at the desk in Rogers Hall. Courtesy of the Brown University Library.

As far as we have been able to learn, Slocum left no reminiscences of Lovecraft. Nor, apparently, did Lovecraft ever visit the Van Vleck Observatory or write to Slocum. Perhaps Lovecraft's embarrassment over his lack of academic qualifications kept him away, or perhaps his acquaintance with Slocum was always slight.

John Edwards

Last, but not least as far as Lovecraft was concerned, we come to John Edwards, he of the misplaced h's. John Edwards was not a professor, as were Upton and Slocum. He was an assistant at the observatory who carried out mechanical and routine tasks needed to keep the observatory running. It is only in the case of Edwards that Lovecraft mentions specific ways in which the Ladd staff member aided him. In the letter to Jonquil Leiber quoted above, Lovecraft recalled several items of practical help that Edwards provided.

Edwards was an immigrant to the United States. Lovecraft did not look kindly on all immigrants, but Edwards came from England, which was perfectly fine for the Anglophile Lovecraft. In different letters, Lovecraft called Edwards a Cornishman and a cockney, contradictory designations as the former refers to someone from Cornwall while the latter applies to a working-class Londoner. That led one of us to dig into Edwards's life story, as detailed in a guest post included in David Haden's *Tentaclii* website (Smith, "Guest Post"). As spelled out in that post, there is evidence that Edwards was neither Cornish nor cockney by birth, but that instead he was born in 1858 in Lancashire, in northwestern England. Together with his wife, Mary, and their son Joseph, Edwards appears to have arrived in Boston in 1887. John and Mary would have two more offspring after their arrival in the United States, but by 1903, when Lovecraft began to visit Ladd Observatory, two of their three children had died, leaving only a son, Alban.

We do not know when John Edwards was hired to assist at Ladd Observatory, but it was within several years of the observatory going into operation. Professor Upton took a sabbatical from Brown University for the 1896–97 academic year, going to the Harvard College Observatory southern station in Arequipa, Peru. His temporary replacement, Frank W. Very, commended Edwards for "conscientious care" in meteorological and time service observations in his report to the university president. Edwards was apparently already employed by the observatory before Very arrived in July 1896. He assisted with observations of the Leonid me-

2. Ladd Observatory and Three Whom Lovecraft Pestered 71

teors in 1898 and in 1900 was a member of the Ladd Observatory expedition to observe the total eclipse of the sun from Centreville, Virginia.

We do not know whether Upton encouraged Edwards to help Lovecraft. Perhaps Edwards needed no encouragement and enjoyed talking, and passing along his expertise, to the enthusiastic young amateur astronomer. There would have been no academic barrier to instill formality between the teenage Lovecraft and Edwards, as there might have been with professors Upton and Slocum. Edwards lacked both a college degree and upper-class credentials. Moreover, Lovecraft was only two years younger than Edwards's surviving son. Lovecraft and Edwards surely discussed many issues regarding astronomical observing and equipment and Lovecraft's account of Edwards, brief though it is, indicates a fond appreciation of the assistant's skills, patience, and kindness.

Ladd observers prepare to photograph the Leonid meteors in November 1898. John Edwards is on the left. Frederick Slocum is on the right. Cropped from a photograph in the Brown University Library.

Edwards assisted at the observatory for two decades. When Upton died in 1914, Professor of Pure Mathematics Roland Richardson assumed directorship of the observatory. As he worked to get the new Van Vleck Observatory up and running, Slocum remembered his former Ladd Observatory associate. The Providence *Evening Tribune* for 29 September 1915 stated that "John Edwards, for 20 years assistant at the Ladd Observatory, Brown University, will soon leave to take charge of the field and routine work at the Van Vleck Observatory of Wesleyan University."

Sadly, Edwards's position at Middletown would not last long. *Wesleyan University Bulletin* 64 (May 1918) reported:

> John William Edwards, Assistant in the Van Vleck Observatory since 1915, died suddenly of heart trouble on April 24. Mr. Edwards came to Wesleyan after over twenty years of service in the Ladd Observatory of Brown University, and had already earned recognition here for faithful and efficient performance of duty.

Edwards and his wife, who had died the year before, are buried in Attleboro, Massachusetts, where his son Alban lived at the time of their passing. Thus ended the life of the member of the pestered trio who was least in academic rank but greatest in practical aid to the teenage Lovecraft's astronomical endeavors.

Students

There are two other people associated with the Ladd Observatory who deserve mention here. They were not staff members, but were students at the time that Lovecraft visited the observatory. The first of these, Leah Brown Allen (1884–1973), was a 1903 graduate of Providence's Hope Street High School (*Blue and White,* June 1903), the same high school that Lovecraft attended. She studied astronomy with Professor Upton, graduating from Brown University's Women's College (Pembroke College) with an A.B. in 1907. Upon graduation, and with Upton's recommendation, she was appointed a Carnegie assistant at the Lick Observatory in California (*Fall River Daily News,* 21 August 1907; *San Francisco Call,* 23 August 1908). Allen's article "A Brown Graduate at Lick Observatory" appeared in the April 1910 issue of the *Brown Alumni Monthly*. In 1912, she obtained an M.A. from Wellesley College, became instructor of astronomy there, and eventually was appointed professor of astronomy at Hood College in Maryland. She thus succeeded in following a career path similar to the one that Lovecraft once traced for himself. Lovecraft and Allen may very well have crossed paths in the Ladd Observatory hallway, but we have no direct evidence that the two met.

The second student we consider here, Harlan True Stetson (1885–1964), was not a native of Providence. However, he took astronomy courses at Brown University and received a Bachelor of Philosophy degree in 1908.[15] After getting a Ph.D. from the University of Chicago,

---

15. Some sources give 1912 as the date of Stetson's undergraduate degree;

he would go on to faculty appointments at Harvard and at Ohio Wesleyan University. We find the names of both Lovecraft and Stetson among the borrowers of books from the Ladd Observatory library in 1906. We might imagine the teenage Lovecraft sitting across from Stetson at a library table, but we have no definite evidence that the two met.

Leah Allen (on the left) at the Harvard College Observatory for a meeting of the American Association of Variable Star Observers in 1917. To her right are two well-known Harvard College Observatory astronomers: Annie Jump Cannon and Henrietta Leavitt. Cropped from the meeting photograph.

The cases of Leah Allen and Harlan Stetson demonstrate that, at the very time Lovecraft roamed the hallways of Ladd Observatory, Brown University and its associated women's college were graduating students who did go on to careers in astronomy. The career successes of Allen and Stetson were still mostly in the future when Lovecraft's hopes of

---

however, the *Brown University Historical Catalogue* (1914) lists him with the 1908 graduates.

attending Brown University ended. Any acquaintance with Allen or Stetson in the years leading up to 1908 might have encouraged Lovecraft in his dreams of an astronomical career. After his failure to graduate from high school, those students might have seemed a rebuke. All, however, must remain conjecture unless evidence of the relationships, if any, between Lovecraft and the Brown University astronomy students can be discovered.

Non-University Barbarian

Lovecraft's relationship with the Ladd Observatory changed once he realized that he himself would never become a professional astronomer. This occurred about 1908, when he experienced the breakdown that prevented him from graduating high school, dooming any thought of college. As discussed in chapter 1, S. T. Joshi has suggested that Lovecraft's realization that his mathematical skills were not adequate for a professional astronomer, and that therefore he could not himself become one, played a part in this breakdown (*IAP* 127–28). In 1918, Lovecraft wrote:

> I no more visit the Ladd Observatory or various other attractions of Brown University. Once I expected to utilise them as a regularly entered student, and some day perhaps control some of them as a faculty member. But having known them with this "inside" attitude, I am today unwilling to visit them as a casual outsider and non-university barbarian and alien. (Letter to Rheinhart Kleiner, 4 December 1918; *RK 126*)

As we have seen, Slocum departed Ladd Observatory after 1908. Upton died in 1914. Edwards left soon after Upton's death and died a few years later. By the end of 1915, none of the three remained at the observatory. Even were he not too ashamed to return, these changes may have meant that, after 1914, Lovecraft no longer retained privileged access there. However, his avoidance of the observatory apparently started earlier, with the collapse of 1908, for he wrote in 1927 that he had visited the observatory for the first time in twenty years (letter to James Morton, 26 February 1927; *JFM* 128). When he visited the observatory in 1936 to see Peltier's comet (see chapter 12), it was as a member of the public, a "casual outsider," rather than someone who held rights or privileges there.

Lovecraft used astronomical imagery to help set the mood of several stories. As T. R. Livesey noted (*DPO* 31–36), when specific descriptions are given for celestial phenomena, Lovecraft took pains to make

2. Ladd Observatory and Three Whom Lovecraft Pestered 75

those descriptions accurate. However, nowhere in Lovecraft's fiction do we find anything that explicitly resembles Ladd Observatory or its staff. That is somewhat surprising, since places Lovecraft visited and buildings he saw were, if sufficiently striking and appropriate, often recast as backdrops for his tales. In Providence, one need only recall the house at 135 Benefit Street that was the model for "The Shunned House," or the Fleur-de-Lys building in "The Call of Cthulhu."

Why was that other Providence location, the Ladd Observatory so familiar in his youth, without counterpart in Lovecraft's fiction? Fictional Miskatonic University is surely based at least in part upon the university Lovecraft knew best, Brown University. Miskatonic University had professors of physics, chemistry, history, geology, zoology, anthropology, archaeology, medicine, political economy, psychology, linguistics, English, engineering, and mathematics, but Lovecraft names no astronomer. Perhaps the reason for this lacuna is simple: the right story never came along. However, another possibility comes to mind. Was it a lingering regret at his own banishment from the "dark-domed enchanted castle" that banished the Ladd Observatory from his fiction?

Chapter 3
A Rooftop of Lovecraft's Astronomy

H. P. Lovecraft spent much of his life in penury. That was not, however, true of his childhood and teenage years. At that time, with the indulgence of his mother, and perhaps unwisely, Lovecraft acquired books and scientific instruments with an abandon impossible during most of his adult life.[1] As he accumulated these items, those that were related to astronomy often found mention in his handwritten and hectographed *Rhode Island Journal of Astronomy,* which he began in August 1903 (chapter 1). By the end of 1906, the *Journal* was on its last legs. Although there would be a failed attempt to restart the *Journal* as late as 1909, the year 1906 was its last full year of publication. However, the *Journal* ended that year with a splash.

The cover of the December 1906 issue offers a striking illustration, presumably by Lovecraft's hand, of astronomical paraphernalia arrayed across a flat rooftop or platform, bordered by a railing. Does it depict Lovecraft's own astronomical apparatus? He does not state that such is the case, but a careful consideration of the items suggests that that is indeed true, or at least mostly true. In this chapter, we consider that cover illustration and reflect on what the items depicted meant to the sixteen-year-old Lovecraft.

Atop the flooring we see, from left to right, an orrery, a shelf of books, an astronomical telescope on a tripod, a globe, a transit telescope, and, resting on the base of the transit instrument, a sextant. Are these consistent with items that we know Lovecraft possessed at the end of 1906?

---

1. HPL would later exclaim, "Ah, them golden days, when I didn't have to worry about what I spent!" (letter to the Gallomo, 19 September 1919; *Misc* 72).

3. A Rooftop of Lovecraft's Astronomy

Is this a depiction of Lovecraft's astronomical equipment? Courtesy of the Brown University Digital Repository. Howard P. Lovecraft Collection, Ms. Lovecraft, Brown University Library.

Let us begin with the central object in the drawing, the astronomical telescope. The *Rhode Island Journal of Astronomy* for October 1906 reveals that on 14 September Lovecraft purchased a new telescope with two eyepieces (a 50-power terrestrial eyepiece[2] and a 125-power astronomical eyepiece), a telescope that he would retain until his death. It was a refracting telescope manufactured by the French firm of Bardou & Son, but sold in the United States for $50 through Montgomery Ward (*IAP* 81; letter to Richard F. Searight, 16 April 1935; *EHP* 370–71).[3] It was not Lovecraft's first telescope, but its 3-inch achromatic lens was larger than the 2¼-inch objective lens of the telescope that had previously been his main instrument, letting him see fainter objects and resolve finer detail.[4] Rather than use the claw and pillar table-mounting that came with it, Lovecraft set his new telescope in an altazimuth mounting atop the tripod that he had previously purchased for the 2¼-inch telescope. Tripod-mounted 3-inch refracting telescopes by top-rated U.S. firms, such as Brashear or Alvan Clark & Sons, cost about $150 ($4,800 in 2022), and were perhaps out of reach even for a free-spending Lovecraft.

Was the telescope illustrated in the *Rhode Island Journal of Astronomy* modeled on Lovecraft's 3-inch Bardou telescope? The tube looks a little long compared to its width, but is not too far out of line to be the Bardou instrument. The focus knob appears to be of the right type. The drawing shows a small finder telescope attached to the main telescope. A finder telescope is a low-power instrument that helps in pointing the main telescope at a desired target, but we don't know whether Lovecraft actually attached a finder telescope to his 3-inch Bardou. It is unlikely to have come with one, and no finder is shown in photographs of the telescope in recent years. Perhaps Lovecraft didn't need a finder to target the bright objects that he usually observed, as the field of view of his telescope may have been close to a degree (two moon diameters) with its 50-power eyepiece. Aside from the questionable finder telescope, we have a satisfactory match between the drawing and Lovecraft's Bardou telescope.

---

2. A terrestrial eyepiece has extra optics to produce a right-side-up instead of an inverted image.

3. Eyepiece powers are listed in HPL's *Astronomical Notebook*.

4. HPL's Excelsior telescope had a theoretical resolution of about 6 seconds of arc. The resolutions of his 2¼-inch and 3-inch telescopes would have been about 2.1 and 1.6 seconds of arc, respectively—a second of arc being 1/3600 of a degree.

3. A Rooftop of Lovecraft's Astronomy

A 3-inch Bardou telescope advertised in a 1912 Montgomery Ward catalog, six years after Lovecraft bought his.

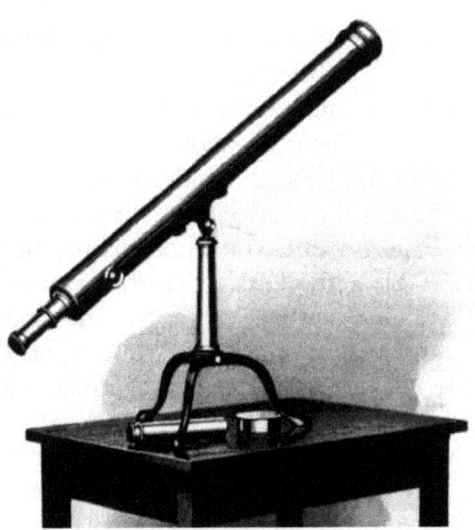

A 3-inch Bardou & Son telescope with claw and pillar table-mounting. From a 1911 catalogue.

Lovecraft's 3-inch Bardou telescope in its box, as it now appears. With permission of the telescope's present owner.

We next turn to the orrery. Orreries, mechanically illustrating the arrangement and motions of the solar system, were a widely used educational mechanism in the nineteenth and early twentieth centuries. Elaborate orreries had multiple gears allowing them to mimic the motions of the planets. Gearing is not obvious in Lovecraft's drawing but could be present in the actual device, if there were a physical model for the sketch. Around 1900, orreries for schools could be purchased for about $20 ($690 in 2022), although fancier orreries went for considerably more. In the nineteenth century, long before the modern projection planetarium, the term planetarium was sometimes applied to devices of this sort. Lovecraft would certainly have been familiar with the concept of an orrery, but did he ever own one?

Seeking an answer, we began by examining Lovecraft's juvenile scientific publications in the Brown Digital Repository, but without finding an indication that he owned an orrery. Nor have we found mention of his owning one in those of his letters that we have perused.[5] However, since all the other objects depicted appear to be, as we shall see, items

---

5. HPL does, however, mention an orrery in a letter of April 1920 (*Misc* 91).

that he owned, we can't help but think that the drawing of the orrery must at least be based upon something that Lovecraft actually saw, even if he did not own it. Schools used orreries as educational aids. Could his high school have owned one? Or did Brown University have one similar to the one depicted, perhaps at Ladd Observatory, which Lovecraft frequented?

Detail of the orrery and bookcase. To the far left Saturn and its ring are only partly shown. To Saturn's right, a belted Jupiter has four moons. Earth and its moon may be depicted to the right of Jupiter. The sun is perhaps spotted. On the far right we see a world with two moons, possibly Mars. Howard P. Lovecraft Collection, Ms. Lovecraft, Brown University Library.

Dr. Michael Umbricht, curator of Ladd Observatory, provided a possible answer. Ladd Observatory has an orrery that might very well have been on display in the early 1900s. In response to our query, Dr. Umbricht replied that, based on the number of moons for the outer planets, it was suspected that the Ladd Observatory orrery was made between 1789 and 1846, possibly by William Mason Stiles (1787—1871). The basic appearance of the Ladd orrery matches Lovecraft's drawing, but there are differences in detail. Perhaps the Ladd Observatory orrery inspired Lovecraft's sketch, but he may have felt free to invoke artistic license—drawing, for example, a few belts on the globe representing Jupiter and adding two moons to Mars that were unknown

A celestial globe as depicted in *Astronomy* by Russell, Dugan, and Stewart (1926).

in Stiles's lifetime.

Near the telescope's tripod, a globe rests on the floorboards. We cannot distinguish a terrestrial from a celestial globe in the drawing, but we know that Lovecraft owned globes of both types. Celestial globes depict stars and constellations, and, given the setting, a celestial globe seems more likely than a terrestrial one. In the September 1906 issue of the *Rhode Island Journal of Astronomy,* Lovecraft noted "the R. I. Journal has now acquired a 12 in Celestial Globe." It is quite plausible that the globe depicted is intended to represent that acquisition. Unfortunately, no other details about Lovecraft's celestial globe are given. In 1906, a brand new 12-inch celestial globe designed for school use could be had for about $25 ($800 in 2022), but Lovecraft may have found a better bargain.

3. A Rooftop of Lovecraft's Astronomy

Let us next consider what seems to be the small telescope in the right-hand side of the illustration. Its mounting indicates that it is a transit telescope. Transit telescopes of various types were used by astronomers, clockmakers, and surveyors. With a transit telescope an astronomer can measure when a particular star crosses (transits) the meridian, the north-south line in the sky. Such timings can be used to measure star positions in the sky. Alternatively, if the celestial coordinate of right ascension (the celestial version of longitude) is already known for the star in question, the calculation can be reversed to determine the local time. The altitude of a star when it crosses the meridian can be used to determine the declination of the star, the celestial version of latitude. Once again, the calculation can be reversed to determine the observer's latitude if the declination of the star is already known. Lovecraft would have been well acquainted with the transit telescopes at the Ladd Observatory, which allowed the observatory to provide accurate time to Providence subscribers.[6] The transit telescope shown in Lovecraft's cover illustration is not set up for proper use, but sits on the flooring. To be used, a transit telescope mounting must be leveled and, for many astronomical purposes, oriented so that the telescope swings in a north-south plane.

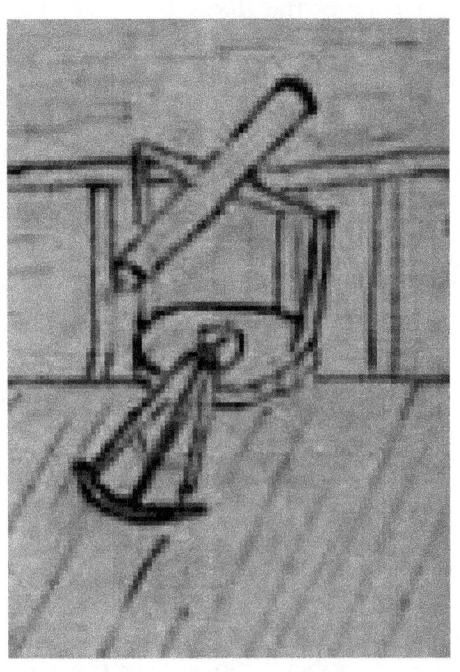

A transit telescope sits on the floor, with what appears to be a sextant resting on its base. Howard P. Lovecraft Collection, Ms. Lovecraft, Brown University Library.

---

6. We do not know whether he ever encountered it, but HPL might have been amused by the title of Latimer Clark's 1882 book, *A Treatise on the Transit Instrument as Applied to the Determination of Time for the Use of Country Gentlemen.*

Lovecraft owned a transit telescope but not, apparently, one in operating condition. In the very first issue of the *Rhode Island Journal of Astronomy*, Lovecraft offered for sale "a transit without vernier, or lenses, or wires." In the *Annals of the Providence Observatory*, written in 1904, Lovecraft reports owning a dismantled transit telescope with a 1-inch lens. Lovecraft does not state where he obtained his incomplete transit instrument. It was his before he turned thirteen, so it may have been a gift, perhaps from grandfather Whipple Phillips. Lovecraft never mentions observing with his transit telescope, so he may never have owned one in working order. In the October 1906 issue of the *Journal*, Lovecraft advertised "Wanted a cheap transit instrument," but reliable transit telescopes were not inexpensive devices. The second number of his *Science Library*, which came out in 1904, included an advertisement for Providence optician R. L. Allen's offering of a second-hand transit worth $300 for $50 ($9,750 and $1,600 in 2022), inviting readers to "come and see it." Fifty dollars was a good price for a working transit telescope, even a used one, but could not have been counted cheap by Lovecraft, and he did not take up Allen's offer. As noted, a transit telescope is accurate only when placed in a carefully adjusted and oriented mounting, an arrangement that would have been more difficult to establish once Lovecraft and his mother moved to rented quarters at 598 Angell Street in 1904.

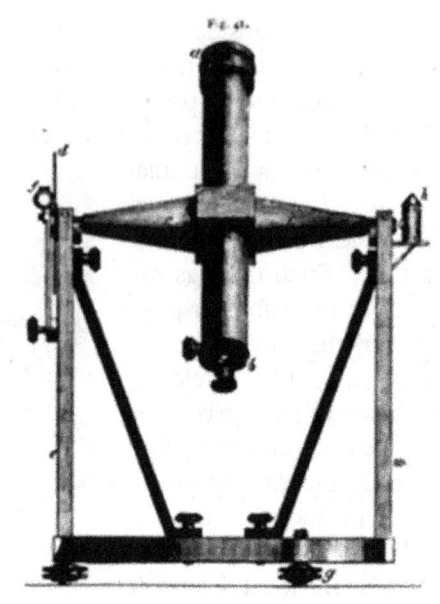

Drawing of a portable transit telescope from George Chambers's *A Handbook of Descriptive and Practical Astronomy* (1889).

That quintessential navigational device, a sextant, appears to lean upon the transit instrument in Lovecraft's illustration, although the drawing of the instrument is not detailed and it could possibly be an octant. However, the former is more likely, since Lovecraft owned a sextant.[7] The June 1906 issue of the *Rhode Island Journal of Astronomy* announced that "On May 7, 1906, the R.I. Journal procured a sextant for measuring celestial angles. It is by Blunt & Co., N.Y." If the Blunt & Co. name is correct, Lovecraft's sextant was not a new one, dating to about 1868–72, when that business name was in use. Lovecraft tested his sextant by measuring angles between stars and angles from the moon to various stars, apparently with satisfactory results. In the June 1906 issue of the *Rhode Island Journal of Astronomy*, Lovecraft reported that he had used the sextant to determine the latitude of his observing location to be 41°50′ north, and its longitude to be 71°23′ west, although he does not tell exactly how he made the calculation. Lovecraft's results correctly match the location of 598 Angell Street. Algebra may have disheartened Lovecraft (chapter 1), but he seems to have had no difficulty with the straightforward calculations of practical astronomy. Of course, besides carefully making his observations, he needed only to apply well-established prescriptions to determine his location.

We next turn to the array of shelved books, which of course fits quite well with the collection of astronomical volumes that Lovecraft had by then accumulated. A few of these books, including his edition of Elijah Burritt's *Geography of the Heavens*, were inherited from his grandmother, as noted in chapter 1, but many were his own purchases. Lovecraft wrote that he bought his first new astronomy book, Charles Augustus Young's *Lessons in Astronomy*, on 12 February 1903. As he rode home on a streetcar, Lovecraft "looked over the pictures & chapter headings with perhaps the most delightful sense of breathless anticipation I have ever known." Mentions of subsequent book acquisitions regularly appeared in the *Rhode Island Journal of Astronomy*, although they may never have provided Lovecraft quite the joy of that initial purchase.

Leaning against the bookshelf is an oversized volume, with writing that can be only partially read. The writing may be the beginning of the words Star Atlas. In the September 1906 *Journal*, Lovecraft wrote that he had purchased a copy of Winslow Upton's *Star Atlas*, "conceded to be the best in the United States." That large book, written by the director of Ladd Observatory who had allowed young Lovecraft access to the observatory, perhaps inspired the book in the drawing. Another book sits open before the telescope. It might be one of several guides to amateur astronomy that Lovecraft owned. Possibilities include Garrett Serviss's

---

7. HPL also owned a quadrant, but the drawing does not match such an instrument.

Pleasures of the Telescope, R. A. Proctor's *Half Hours with the Telescope,* or one of the volumes of T. W. Webb's *Celestial Objects for Common Telescopes.*

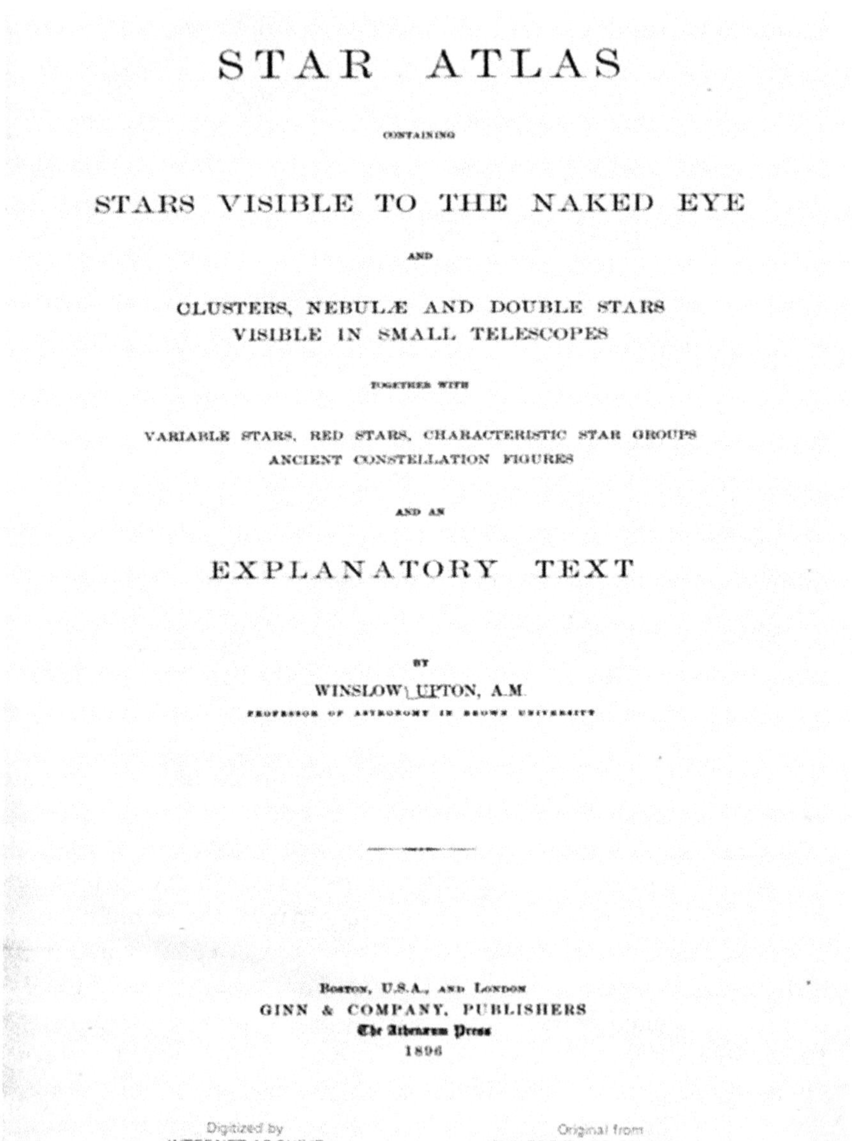

STAR ATLAS

CONTAINING

STARS VISIBLE TO THE NAKED EYE

AND

CLUSTERS, NEBULÆ AND DOUBLE STARS VISIBLE IN SMALL TELESCOPES

TOGETHER WITH

VARIABLE STARS, RED STARS, CHARACTERISTIC STAR GROUPS
ANCIENT CONSTELLATION FIGURES

AND AN

EXPLANATORY TEXT

BY

WINSLOW UPTON, A.M.
PROFESSOR OF ASTRONOMY IN BROWN UNIVERSITY

BOSTON, U.S.A., AND LONDON
GINN & COMPANY, PUBLISHERS
The Athenæum Press
1896

Digitized by
INTERNET ARCHIVE

Original from
UNIVERSITY OF CALIFORNIA

Title page of Winslow Upton's 1896 *Star Atlas*. Internet Archive.

What about the setting for this array of astronomical devices—a flat surface floored with boards and bounded by a railing? We are not certain whether Lovecraft's drawing was intended to show a real location. However, in a letter to the Gallomo,[8] he wrote:

> the roof of 598 Engelstrasse is approximately flat, and in the days of my youth I had a set of meteorological instruments there. Hither I would sometimes hoist my telescope, and observe the sky from that point of relative proximity to it. The horizon is fair, but not ideal. One can see the glint of the Seekonk through the foliage of Blackstone Park, and the opposite bank is quite clearly defined. With a terrestrial eyepiece of fifty diameters on my telescope, I can see some of the farms in the heart of East Providence, and even Seekonk, Mass., across the river. One in particular delights me—a typical bit of ancient agrestick New England with eighteenth century farmhouse, old-fashion'd garden, and even archaic well and well-sweep—all this bit of primitive antiquity visible from a roof in the prosaic modern town!! (30 September 1919; *Misc* 72)

The landscape shown in the drawing includes what might be a far-off church and farmhouse (and perhaps a hilltop observatory, although that is uncertain because of the obscuration caused by the banner carrying the title of the *Journal*). Perhaps, then, the instruments and books are imagined arrayed atop Lovecraft's 598 Angell Street home.

However, was there a railed-in area atop the house at 598 Angell Street? No railing is evident in older photographs of the house that we have seen, although the roof is not clearly shown in them. If the roof of his Angell Street home was not depicted, then an alternative inspiration for the setting might have been Ladd Observatory, where a portion of the roof was (and remains) both flat and fenced in. Lovecraft wrote that its "railed roof forms an excellent place for constellation study." He plausibly may have imagined and drawn his astronomical paraphernalia on the familiar Ladd Observatory rooftop, a location he still freely visited as 1906 drew to a close.

We thus can plausibly account for all the items shown in Lovecraft's cover illustration, either as things he is known to have owned or, in the case of the orrery, as something he might have seen close at hand. We are now free to imagine Lovecraft, having turned sixteen years old in 1906, peering through the illustrated telescope, entranced by the craters

---

8. A correspondence circle of Alfred Galpin, HPL, and Maurice W. Moe.

of the moon or the belts of Jupiter. Or we can imagine him using the sextant to measure the angular distance of the moon from a star of the first magnitude. It takes little imagination to picture the bibliophile Lovecraft lost within the pages of one of the volumes in the bookcase, although daylight or a well-lit room is more plausible for a good read than a spot under a starry sky.

Lovecraft drew this view of the Ladd Observatory for the 22 November 1903 issue of the *Rhode Island Journal of Astronomy*. See also the illustrations of the observatory in chapter 2. Howard P. Lovecraft Collection, Ms. Lovecraft, Brown University Library.

To conclude, we ask whether there was some particular reason why Lovecraft decorated the December 1906 cover with this array of his own astronomical instruments and books. The appearance of a January 1907 issue of the *Journal* indicates that Lovecraft did not intend the December issue to end the run of that publication. Of course, one might say, "What hobbyist doesn't want to show off?" Plenty of telescopes, books, and planispheres are proudly displayed on Facebook. The cover of the January

3. A Rooftop of Lovecraft's Astronomy

1906 issue of the *Journal* shows books, a star chart, and a different small telescope, perhaps Lovecraft's 2¼-inch instrument. The December cover may have been intended as a counterpoise to the January cover, the two of them bookending the year. Perhaps there is no more to it than that.

However, the year 1906 marked a change in the focus of Lovecraft's astronomical endeavors. That summer he began to write astronomical articles for the Providence *Tribune* and the *Pawtuxet Valley Gleaner*, while his self-published magazines would soon fade. The heyday of Lovecraft's own observing was also passing, although he would never give up all astronomical observations. The cover illustration perhaps signifies an awareness of these changes. By the end of 1906 Lovecraft had become a skilled and experienced amateur astronomer, but he had met algebra in high school and found it daunting (*IAP* 100–101; see also chapter 1). That weakness in mathematics would soon contribute to the end of Lovecraft's dreams of an astronomical career. Perhaps he thought it fitting pictorially to summarize his achievements as an amateur at a time when his professional future in the field was beginning to look doubtful. We might then take the obscuration of the hilltop observatory (if that is indeed what it is) by the banner carrying the word ASTRONOMY to be a foreshadowing of Lovecraft's looming separation from Ladd Observatory and from the gentlemanly world of academic astronomy that it had come to represent for him.

Chapter 4
Lovecraft Seeks the Garden of Eratosthenes

Sixteen-year-old H. P. Lovecraft chose a title for his article in the 14 September 1906 issue of the *Pawtuxet Valley Gleaner* that was likely to attract notice: "Is There Life on the Moon?" Its conclusion makes strange reading for the modern student of astronomy, aware of the desolate and apparently lifeless nature of the lunar surface: "Now all the evidence is very convincing, and in all probability is correct, so we must consider our satellite to be a body which, although not containing any high or animal life, is yet not wholly dead" (*CE* 3.26–27). The evidence to which Lovecraft alluded was that obtained by one whom Lovecraft called the "greatest living selenographer," Harvard professor William Henry Pickering (1858–1938). There is, however, more behind this article than is at first apparent. Not mentioned in the account are the young Lovecraft's own efforts to don the mantle of observational astronomer and verify for himself Pickering's startling discoveries.

William Pickering and Life on the Moon

William Pickering joined the staff of the Harvard College Observatory in 1887, an institution that his older brother Edward Charles Pickering had already directed for a decade. The elder brother is remembered as a pioneer of modern astrophysics, whose work in stellar spectroscopy, photometry, and photography during his long directorship paved the way for twentieth-century developments in the field. William (whom we shall just call Pickering, unless there is a chance of confusion with Edward) is regarded as one of astronomy's eccentrics. He deserves credit for his early work in photography; for his photographic discovery of Phoebe, the ninth

---

This chapter is a revised version of an article that appeared in the *Lovecraft Annual* No. 13 (2019): 153–74.

moon of Saturn, in 1899; and for a number of innovative ideas. Despite these laudable contributions, his career had a too-imaginative side that damaged his reputation. His extensive studies of our own moon drew him to conclusions that were dismissed as nonsense by most professional astronomers of his day. William Sheehan and Thomas Dobbins in *Epic Moon: A History of Lunar Exploration in the Age of the Telescope* somewhat uncharitably title the chapter on Pickering's work "the Madman of Mandeville"—Mandeville, Jamaica, being the location of Pickering's final observatory.

William Henry Pickering in 1909. Library of Congress.

Astronomers scrutinized the moon through telescopes of increasing capability as the nineteenth century progressed, attempting to settle what were still open questions as that century dawned: Was the moon a changing and living world, or a changeless and dead one? Early in the century, life on the moon seemed a real possibility. However, as the century progressed, that seemed less likely. In 1874, James Nasmyth and James Carpenter in their influential book, *The Moon: Considered as a Planet, a World, and a Satellite,* argued against lunar life.[1] A consensus emerged that the moon was an airless, lifeless, and largely immutable place. It should be recalled, however, that it had not at this time been accepted that the craters of the moon were created by impacting objects. Nasmyth and Carpenter, for example, regarded the lunar craters as volcanic, although they believed that volcanic activity was mainly if not entirely a thing of the past on the moon (see Haden, "Volcanoes on the Moon").

Taking up the study of the moon in earnest during the 1890s, Pickering soon rejected that consensus. Alterations in the appearance of certain lunar features, he announced, were not mere plays of light and

---

1. By 1904, HPL owned an edition of Nasmyth and Carpenter (*LL* 120).

shadow. The moon, he believed, had a tenuous atmosphere, permitting the deposition and evaporation of hoarfrost. More astonishing was Pickering's contention that the moon harbored plants, or even, as he suggested later in his life, hordes of small animals, perhaps insects, that could be seen migrating en masse across the floors of particular craters. Life on the moon had adapted to its strange conditions, Pickering proposed, so that cycles of lunar life were ruled not by the annual motion around the sun but by the monthly sequence of lunar phases. In reaching these unorthodox conclusions, Pickering relied mainly upon visual observations, believing with some justice that the eye at the eyepiece could detect finer details than could the photographic emulsions of the time. He made his views known early enough for his vision of lunar life to have influenced H. G. Wells when he wrote *The First Men in the Moon*, published in 1901 (Dobbins and Baum 105–9; Sheehan and Dobbins 255). Among the craters Pickering believed held life was Eratosthenes. In the 1920s, when he published a map of Eratosthenes, Pickering was inspired to name areas after flowers—Azalea, Aster, Dahlia, and Violet, among others—turning the crater in name into the garden of the moon that he believed it actually was (Pickering, "Eratosthenes No. 4" 69).

The reception of Pickering's ideas was not to his liking. While other astronomers agreed that craters seem to change during the course of the monthly lunar cycle, few interpreted what they saw along Pickering's lines. Most professional astronomers placed Pickering's lunar vegetation in the same disreputable category as his contemporary Percival Lowell's artificial Martian canals (a subject in which Pickering was also very interested). Even his brother Edward was reluctant to accept William's interpretations of what he saw. He advised caution in private letters to his younger sibling, but in vain, and these and other differences led to strained relations (Plotkin 103; Sheehan 172–73). In a letter to Edward dated 12 September 1912, William wrote: "Whatever reputation as an astronomer I lost when I published my former observations, will be nothing to the destruction produced when these [new results] get into print, & especially the drawings. I have seen everything practically except the selenites themselves running round with spades to turn off the water into other channels!" (Jones and Boyd 373). William was being facetious, since even he did not advocate the existence of shovel-toting inhabitants of the moon, but he clearly knew what most astronomers thought of his ideas.

4. Lovecraft Seeks the Garden of Eratosthenes 93

An illustration by Claude Allin Shepperson for the first edition of *The First Men in the Moon* (1901).

In February 1903, Lovecraft was delighted to purchase his first new book on astronomy, Princeton professor Charles Augustus Young's *Lessons in Astronomy* (see chapter 1). When Lovecraft turned to its section on the moon, he would have found that Young described a moon devoid of air and water, without "satisfactory evidence" of ongoing volcanic activity, and without "conspicuous changes." In other words, *Lessons in Astronomy* presented Lovecraft with the consensus picture of a dead and immutable moon. Young only briefly mentioned Pickering's belief in perceptible lunar changes, and he made no mention of Pickering's belief in life on the moon (Young 105–28).

Lovecraft Discovers Pickering

Nonetheless, it was the contentious question of life and change on the moon that quickly attracted Lovecraft's attention when, barely a teenager, he trained his own telescope on our nearest celestial neighbor. It is not certain how Lovecraft first learned of Pickering's ideas, but there are likely places. He must have encountered Young's mention of Pickering when he read his prized *Lessons in Astronomy,* but that mention is brief and not too enlightening by itself. Pickering had published results of his lunar studies in 1895 in the *Annals of the Harvard College Observatory,* a publication aimed at professional astronomers. However, as Livesey has noted, Pickering's displeasure at the reception of his ideas by the professional astronomical community led him, as the twentieth century began, to publish in magazines where his work would be seen by amateur astronomers and the general public. Among these was *Popular Astronomy* magazine, a publication little mentioned by Lovecraft but which Livesey (DPO 12) has persuasively argued was read by him. Nonetheless, it is perhaps likely, as Livesey (DPO 11) suggests, that Lovecraft first became aware of the details of Pickering's ideas through a pair of articles that Pickering wrote for the widely circulated *Century Magazine.*

The first of Pickering's *Century* articles, "Is the Moon a Dead Planet?" appeared in the May 1902 issue. The sequel, titled "The Canals in the Moon," appeared in June. The focus of the second article was Eratosthenes. Pickering presented drawings and photographs of the crater, calling attention to the way it changed in appearance through the course of the lunar day. As the crater warmed in the sun after the long and cold lunar night, vegetation darkened areas on its floor, or so Pickering informed his readers. Vegetation on the moon! Life on the moon! What young amateur astronomer's enthusiasm would not be whetted by such a hypothesis? Lovecraft's certainly was. Could he, too, see the markings that revealed that life existed a quarter of a million miles away?

After more than a century, what resources remain for tracing Lovecraft's interest in Pickering's ideas? There are such of his letters as address the subject of astronomy, but they seldom are detailed and look back on his early observing days from a remove of years or decades. Better are the weekly and monthly articles on astronomical topics which Lovecraft contributed to newspapers between the years 1906 and 1918 (available in *CE* 3). Those, however, are meant for a general audience, and, while they disclose his interests and are likely to have been shaped by Lovecraft's own observations, they rarely describe them. Most important are the juvenile scientific periodicals that Lovecraft published between 1903 and 1909, at the very time when his enthusiasm was taking him to the telescope.

Recall that the term "publication" is generous in connection with Lovecraft's juvenile scientific periodicals (see chapter 1). They consist of hand-drawn and, later, hectographed magazines, each just a few pages in size. His readers surely included family and friends, but we do not have any lists of subscribers. Several of these publications have astronomical content, with titles such as the *Scientific Gazette, Astronomy, Annals of the Providence Observatory,* and the *Rhode Island Journal of Astronomy*. It is the last which is most important to this discussion, for within its pages Lovecraft recounted his astronomical observations.

The survival of Lovecraft's juvenile periodicals is essential to investigating his early attempts at astronomical research, but this investigation is impeded by the loss of other documents. Some issues of his magazines, including some of the *Journal*, appear to be lost (*CE* 3.351). Moreover, surviving issues of the *Journal* frequently include drawings of astronomical objects as Lovecraft saw them. Those drawings must have been copied from originals made at the telescope. However, any original records Lovecraft made at the eyepiece now appear to be lost, although Lovecraft must have kept them for a time, since the *Journal* occasionally incorporated observations made well before the issue date.

Lovecraft at the Telescope

As we get our first glimpses of Lovecraft the observational astronomer in the pages of the *Journal,* we find him exploring the moon and planets with what is, by the standards of today's amateur astronomy, a rather modest telescope, purchased in July 1903, from the mail order firm of Kirtland Brothers & Company for $16.50 (*IAP* 81). This refracting telescope had an objective lens 2¼-inches in diameter and was set upon an altazimuth tripod mounting, purchased from Reuben L. Allen, a local supplier of optical instruments, for $8. It came with a terrestrial eyepiece magnifying 45 times, and an astronomical eyepiece providing a power of 100. In 1905, issues of the *Journal* mention a power of 135, that being about as high a power as a telescope with a 2¼-inch aperture can usefully employ, implying that a third eyepiece or perhaps a Barlow lens had been acquired at some point.

The *Journal* debuted on 2 August 1903, and in the first issues the reader sees Lovecraft immediately jumping into a research project. It does not, however, involve the moon. Instead, it is the determination of the then-unknown rotation period of cloud-shrouded Venus. Young's *Lessons in Astronomy* may have helped direct Lovecraft to that problem. The 1903 edition noted that the Venusian day might be 23 hours 21 minutes long, but that it might instead be equal to Venus's year, 225 Earth days. Rather a big difference! Could Lovecraft, with his small telescope, determine the right answer? For a time he seemed to think he might, but it was a hopeless project, as Lovecraft would eventually realize, and as will be discussed in chapter 7. Nonetheless, the fact that he attempted it demonstrates that, even as a novice observer, he strove to be not only a sightseer but also an investigator.

Lovecraft recalled his early nights as an amateur astronomer in a letter to Alfred Galpin:

> My observations (for I purchased a telescope early in 1903) were confined mostly to the moon and the planet Venus. You will ask, why the latter, since its markings are doubtful even in the largest instruments? I answer—this very MYSTERY was what attracted me. In boyish egotism I fancied I might light upon something with my poor little 2¼-inch telescope which had eluded the users of the 40-inch Yerkes telescope!! And to tell the truth, I think the moon interested me more than anything else—the very nearest object. I used to sit night after night absorbing the minutest details of the lunar surface, till today I can tell you of every peak and crater as though they were the topographical features of my own neighbourhood. I was highly angry at Nature for withholding from my gaze the other side of our satellite! (21 August 1918; *AG* 199)

The first weeks of the *Journal* show Lovecraft becoming familiar with observing and with the appearance of common celestial objects in his small telescope. Lovecraft's targets encompassed more than the moon and Venus, and are just such objects as we would expect a new observer, guided by amateur astronomy manuals of the day, to study. Drawings of modest fidelity appear in the *Journal* depicting ringed Saturn, Borrelli's comet, a crescent Venus, Jupiter with its Red Spot, sunspots, and the moon. A healthy dose of basic astronomical information is also served to

4. Lovecraft Seeks the Garden of Eratosthenes

Lovecraft's readers, whoever they might have been. At this time he seems to have rarely let a clear night pass without attempting some observing, though his observations were made chiefly in the evening rather than the predawn hours. As he noted, "even astronomers are loath to arise early" (*Journal*, 11 October 1903). The light pollution that brightens the skies and dampens the spirits of today's urban amateurs would have been much less evident in the Providence of 1903, but in any case Lovecraft focused his attention on bright objects that could be easily found and seen to advantage with his modest telescope. The modern amateur's annoyance with cloudy weather soon finds its counterpart in the *Journal*'s pages. As Lovecraft's letter to Galpin indicated, the moon saw particular attention. We find Lovecraft gradually acquainting himself with the moon's major craters, following its mountain ranges and making his own maps of the lunar seas.

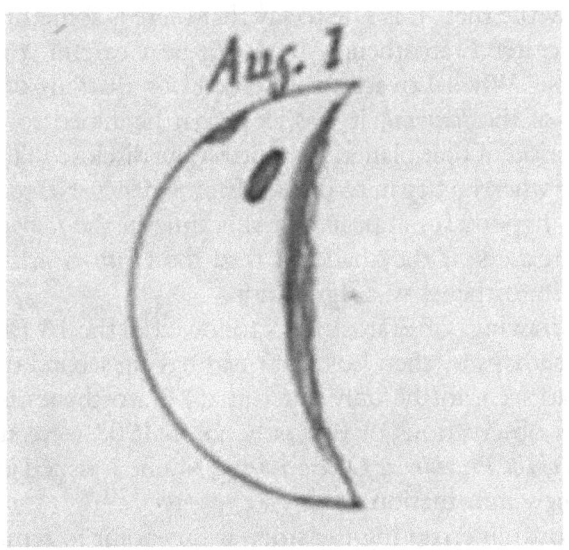

When Lovecraft first turned his small telescope to the planet Venus, he thought he saw markings that might be used to discover its rotation period. This drawing appeared in the first issue of the *Rhode Island Journal of Astronomy*, dated 2 August 1903. Howard P. Lovecraft Collection, Ms. Lovecraft, Brown University Library.

It is after Lovecraft had gained some experience as an observer, in the *Journal* for 6 December 1903, that drawings of Eratosthenes first appear.

On the 1st some strange markings were visible in the crater Eratosthenes at the end of the [lunar] Apennines they resembled the canals of Mars. Also a shading on the SE. side extending opposite to the shadows, proving it's [sic] independence. It was seen again on the 4th. On the 5th one of the canals reached *over* the E. wall and other markings were visible. Their nature is unknown.

Lovecraft used the term canal for dark narrow features on the moon, as had Pickering, and he explicitly referenced Pickering's second *Century* article.

These observations provide the first evidence that Lovecraft had undertaken a special observational study of Eratosthenes. Undeterred by the small size of his telescope, Lovecraft sought to see the markings that Pickering had ascribed to life. In the same *Journal* issue, he compared his own drawings of Eratosthenes to the much more detailed drawings published by Pickering, who of course used much larger telescopes. Lovecraft wrote that "it is safe to say that there is something changeable about the crater Eratosthenes. It would bear careful study with large instruments." When Lovecraft presented observations of Venus in the first issues of the *Journal*, it was clear that he aimed to determine the rotation period of that planet. In contrast, he disclosed far less about his motivation when he began to discuss Eratosthenes. No recapitulation of Pickering's hypotheses appeared at this time in the *Journal*, and it was left to his readers, if they had not read the *Century* articles, to puzzle over why Eratosthenes was significant.

Small drawings of Eratosthenes followed in the 13 December 1903 issue, but perhaps by then Lovecraft was having second thoughts about what he had seen, for he only noted that "Eratosthenes is very complicated." His observations of Eratosthenes in 1903 were summarized in the *Annals of the Providence Observatory,* Volume I, issued in 1904, which added no new information.

It is worth interrupting the story at this point to remind the reader why seeing genuine features within Eratosthenes was a daunting task for Lovecraft. Eratosthenes is a relatively large crater, about 59 kilometers in diameter. Its walls and central mountains cast long and easily seen shadows soon after sunrise and again two weeks later as sunset approaches. However, as the sun climbs above Eratosthenes, the crater walls become less conspicuous in the telescope and various lighter and darker spots, lines, and patches gradually appear and grow more pronounced in and around the crater floor. As the sun once more sinks toward the horizon, the spots and patches become less visible until they are lost in shadow.

4. Lovecraft Seeks the Garden of Eratosthenes

To Pickering, the evolution of these features during the course of a single lunar day could only be explained by the presence of something like vegetation. Any changes in spot development from one lunar cycle to another would only enhance that probability, for shadows and fixed rocky terrain would look much the same at the same phase, month after month, but perhaps not so frost or vegetation. In seeking to confirm Pickering's observations, Lovecraft had to study the crater carefully, looking for changes in Eratosthenes from one night to the next and also from month to month.

Pickering observed the moon with the 13-inch Boyden telescope at Harvard's southern observing station in Arequipa, Peru. This photograph of the Arequipa station, with El Misti volcano in the distance, was taken subsequently to Pickering's earliest observations. Ladd Observatory director Winslow Upton spent a sabbatical at Arequipa in 1896–97. From *Popular Science Monthly*, April 1904.

Lovecraft quickly discovered that many of the features drawn by Pickering were beyond the reach of his small instrument. While Pickering sketched a complex web of spots and lines, Lovecraft could see only a few dark, linear features. Of course, he was limited to a magnification of 100 or 135, whereas Pickering used powers of several hundred, reaching as high as 795 when he observed with the Harvard 13-inch telescope at Arequipa, Peru. Moreover, even were his telescope optics excellent, and the air through which he gazed perfectly steady, a telescope of only 2¼-inch aperture would have trouble seeing features smaller than about 2 or 3 seconds of arc in angular size, little better than a tenth of the apparent angular diameter of Eratosthenes.

Thus, in his search for changes, a direct comparison of his own drawings of Eratosthenes with those of Pickering was out of the question. Instead, Lovecraft had to intercompare his own drawings of the crater, taking into account differences in lunar phase and observing circumstances. Those features that he did detect tested the limits of his telescope. It was no simple task for him to see markings in Eratosthenes, to sketch those markings on multiple nights, and then confidently to establish the reality of any differences among his drawings. Experience and practiced judgment would be necessary to separate the real from the imagined, and the ordinary from the extraordinary, as Lovecraft again and again turned his telescope toward the moon.

Lovecraft's initial study of Eratosthenes continued into the winter of 1904, with observations reported in January. Either Lovecraft's aversion to cold weather was not as pronounced in his youth, or his desire to observe overcame any discomfort (a point also raised by Livesey *DPO* 78–79). At this time, he dithered as to the reality of the features he saw. In the *Journal* for 31 January 1904, he noted that he had observed Eratosthenes twice but that "the reality of the markings will be answered to-morrow night if clear." Alas, there ensued a long break in the publication of the *Journal*. In an undated note, Lovecraft later wrote that "After Jan. 31, 1904 a long skip in the publication of the R. I. Journal occurs, marked by temporary attempts (not preserved) to recommence it. The resumption was really begun Ap 16 '05 after which it was hectographed every week. In September it was made fortnightly but it was issued irregularly."

The cause of the interruption is not stated. 1904 was, however, not an easy year for Lovecraft. His grandfather, Whipple Phillips, died that March, leading to the traumatic removal of Lovecraft and his mother from the house he regarded as an ancestral home. Still, one wonders what happened that next night, which would have been well before his grandfather's passing. Perhaps it was cloudy.

4. Lovecraft Seeks the Garden of Eratosthenes 101

When at last the *Journal* resumes, it is quickly apparent that Eratosthenes had not been forgotten. A day after the publication of the first issue of the resumed *Journal*, on 17 April 1905, Lovecraft rushed out an "Extra" edition. The headline exclaimed

MORE CHANGES ON ERATOSTHENES
Crater Proven Variable Tonight at 8^h30^m
Has not changed before since May 28, 1904.

The extra edition bears the time 9:00, indicating that this discovery was proclaimed only half an hour after it was made. Lovecraft noted that "On Decr. 1, 1903, the work of observing the crater was taken up here, with successful results until May 28, 1904, after which no change could be found." The conclusion that Eratosthenes was invariable after 28 May was, according to Lovecraft, reported in the *Journal*, but that issue must have been one of the aborted restarts that is now missing.

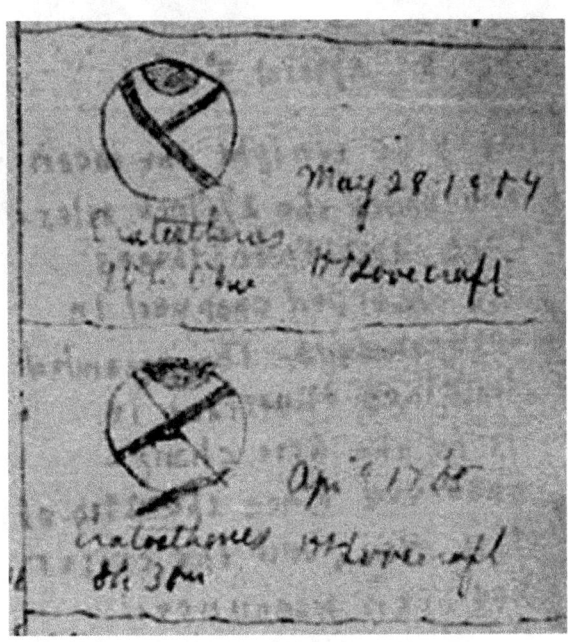

Two of Lovecraft's drawings of Eratosthenes from the extra edition of the *Journal*. Howard P. Lovecraft Collection, Ms. Lovecraft, Brown University Library.

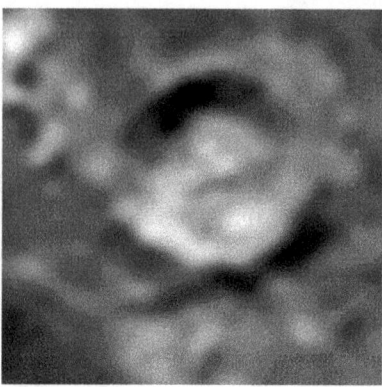

Lovecraft's drawings can be compared with this low-resolution photograph of Eratosthenes, taken before full Moon in 2018.

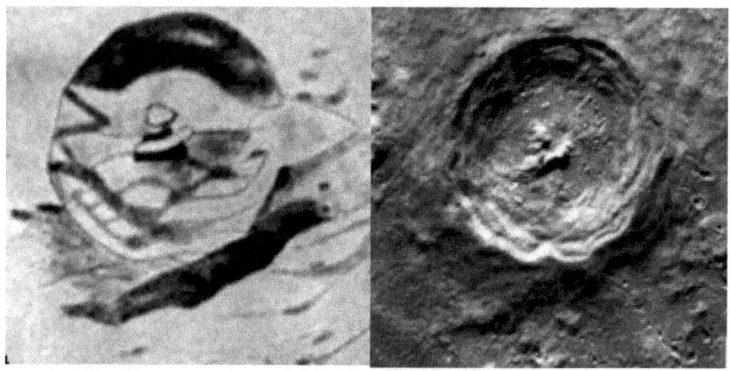

The crater Eratosthenes, as sketched by Pickering in 1901, rotated to be more easily compared with Lovecraft's drawings (Pickering, "Canals in the Moon" 190). A 1967 image taken by *Lunar Orbiter 4* is shown for comparison (Lunar Orbiter Photo Gallery, LPL Institute). Lovecraft's resolution of detail in Eratosthenes is obviously very poor compared to either of these images. Pickering's drawing is not bad, but his interpretation was wildly imaginative.

Whatever his earlier doubts, Lovecraft was now sure that he had observed genuine features in Eratosthenes and that those features had changed in a manner that could not be attributed to shifting shadows, and he was excited about that. The extra included a box containing the exhortation: "NOTICE / Would the local owners of telescopes over 2 in. aperture please notify us what Eratosthenes appears to be in their instruments / SYSTEMATIC OBSERVERS." Following "Systematic Observers," the last line in the John Hay Library copy ends with what appears to be "PAI," which runs off the page before the word is finished. Could Lovecraft have been so enthused as to have meant to pay such observers? Below that box is another: "WANTED Amateur drawings of Eratosthenes." The discussion of Eratosthenes continues on the next page, noting that "Eratosthenes was first brought to general notice by an article in the 'Century' written by Prof. W. Pickering of Harvard." One may infer from this extra that Lovecraft believed that some copies of the *Journal* would fall under the eyes of those who not only had astronomical interests but who possessed telescopes as large or larger than his own. Lovecraft vowed to resume regular observations of Eratosthenes, which had apparently lapsed. Subscribers who wished to decorate with a Lovecraft original could take advantage of the offer: "FOR SALE Drawings of the variable crater ERATOSTHENES Reasonable rates Apply Office."

Surprisingly, no observations of Eratosthenes appear in following issues, though in several Lovecraft complained of poor observing conditions. Nor do we discover whether anyone answered his call for observations. The *Journal* for 23 April 1905 mentioned Pickering's 1903 book on the moon, which expanded upon his *Century* articles and provided a photographic atlas of the moon. However, Lovecraft only discussed Pickering's depictions of the "faces in the Moon" visible to the naked eye, not his controversial findings. Not until the 3 September 1905 *Journal* does Lovecraft return to the question of lunar life. When he does it is with a serial titled "Is There Life on the Moon?," which runs over three issues of the *Journal*. That series is not based upon Lovecraft's own observations, but instead describes Pickering's results. The verdict of the series is nonetheless a strong one:

> Now all the evidence is very positive and convincing, the only way to 'get around' it being to tell the observers that they either lie or are mistaken, but neither of these is possible with a man of Prof. Pickering's skill, experience, and integrity, so, except for chronic skeptics there remains little more to be said than that there is life on the moon.

At the time, Lovecraft apparently did not place himself in the category of chronic skeptic, but he may have counted himself among the unnamed other observers. It was the first time that Lovecraft presented the gist of Pickering's hypotheses to his *Journal* readers.

Lovecraft Has Doubts

Why is there no further mention of his own result, touted in headlines in the 17 April extra? Had he lost confidence in his observations? Had someone he respected passed him a word of caution? The question of the Ladd Observatory and its astronomers comes to mind at this point. In writing to Rheinhart Kleiner in a letter dated 16 November 1916, Lovecraft stated:

> The late Prof. Upton of Brown, a friend of the family, gave me the freedom of the college observatory, & I came & went there at will on my bicycle. Ladd Observatory tops a considerable eminence about a mile from the house. I used to walk up Doyle Avenue hill with my wheel, but when returning would have a glorious coast down it. So constant were my observations, that my neck became much affected by the strain of peering at a difficult angle. It gave me much pain, & resulted in a permanent curvature perceptible today to a close observer. (*RK* 71; see chapter 2)

Did Lovecraft disclose his study of Eratosthenes to his acquaintances at Ladd Observatory? Did he attempt to use their much larger telescope to study the crater? Neither the director of the observatory, Winslow Upton, nor the second astronomer on the staff, Frederick Slocum, specialized in lunar and planetary observations. However, they were professional astronomers with much more knowledge and experience than Lovecraft. Did they see his *Journal* issues and did he rush to them with his 17 April extra?

We can only hazard doubtful answers to these questions. The letter to Kleiner at first glance implies that Lovecraft was free to use Ladd Observatory's 12-inch telescope, but more thought renders that unlikely. It would be one thing to give the teenage Lovecraft free access to the observatory library and quite another to allow him to use its major instrument at will. In the *Journal* Lovecraft makes only two, possibly three, mentions of observing through the Ladd Observatory telescope. The 27 September 1903 *Journal* reported that the transit of a Jovian moon was seen at the Ladd Observatory on the 21st, but it is not specified that it was Lovecraft who saw it. He might not have been the observer on that occasion, but little more than a month later the *Journal* for 1 November 1903 recounted Lovecraft's visit to Ladd Observatory on 31 October. He certainly looked through its telescope on that occasion, observing the moon, Jupiter, and Saturn, and even criticizing the telescope's chromatic aberration. Two and a half years later, he observed the sun, Mercury, and Venus through the Ladd Observatory telescope on 21 March 1906,

4. Lovecraft Seeks the Garden of Eratosthenes 105

according to the April issue of the *Journal*. However, other than these few instances, whenever Lovecraft reported telescopic observations in the *Journal*, they appear to be those made with his own telescope.

In a letter to Duane W. Rimel, Lovecraft reminisced: "I suppose I pestered the people at the observatory half to death, but they were very kind about it" (29 March 1934; *FLB* 157). In that letter Lovecraft recalled seeing the observatory equipment in action, reading endlessly in the observatory library, and being supplied with lecture slides made there, but he made no claim to extensive use of the 12-inch telescope. A letter to Jonquil Leiber, dated 29 November 1936, also indicates only intermittent use of the telescope: "As a boy I used to haunt the Ladd Observatory of Brown University—looking through the 12" refractor now & then, reading the books in the library, & probably making an unmitigated nuisance of myself through my incessant questioning of everybody present" (*CLM* 290).

Surely, if Lovecraft had been able to direct a telescope much larger than his own, he would have turned it toward Eratosthenes, whatever he thought of the telescope's chromatic aberration. Nowhere in the *Journal* does he mention such observations, and it would thus seem that none took place. It would appear that any astronomy-induced curvature to his neck was more likely the result of his many nights with his own telescope, rather than the Ladd Observatory instrument.

Lovecraft does not reveal whether he ever told the Ladd Observatory staff of his Eratosthenes project, though it would seem a likely subject for his "incessant questioning." Had he done so, he might have been disappointed in their response. At the least, they might have directed Lovecraft to the eminent observer Edward Emerson Barnard's very critical review of Pickering's book on the moon, recently published in the *Astrophysical Journal*, but Upton may have gone further.

We know something about Professor Upton's opinion regarding life on the moon. On 18 October 1907, Upton lectured on "The Question of Life on Other Worlds" to the Rhode Island Institute of Instruction. The manuscript of Upton's talk is held by Brown University's John Hay Library. In it, Upton states:

> I need hardly say that the evidence regarding life on the Moon is emphatically in the negative. . . . Some recent observations have however shown that in its long day, 14 × ours, some areas seem to regularly grow darker, and that there may be a minute gaseous envelope lingering in

some of the depressions. Plant life of a low order such as lichens, may possibly exist then in limited degree. But that is all.

Upton is clearly referring to Pickering's observations in this comment. He appears skeptical but not entirely dismissive of Pickering's lunar life. Had he held the same views in 1905, we could imagine him providing a word of caution to an overly enthusiastic Lovecraft. In 1905, Lovecraft still harbored ambitions for a career in astronomy, and any word of caution from Professor Upton, however gently phrased, might have seemed a significant rebuke. That, however, is speculation, for no such criticism is mentioned in the *Journal*.

With or without advice from the Ladd astronomers, by the spring of 1906 the more experienced Lovecraft was becoming a critic of his early astronomical observations. In the April 1906 *Journal,* he dismissed his 1903 and 1905 observations of markings on Venus as probably imaginary. Caution recurs in the August 1906 *Journal,* in which he noted that, although the cusps of the moon appeared prolonged in his telescope on 28 June (possibly indicative of a lunar atmosphere), this "was probably imagination."

On 14 September 1906, Lovecraft acquired the 3-inch Bardou & Son telescope that he would keep for the rest of his life. In the October issue of the *Journal* that announced the acquisition, Lovecraft showed himself dissatisfied with his older telescope, noting that "2¼ inches is much too small an aperture for our work" and that views of the moon in the 3-inch telescope were "superb."[2] He went on to state that the shadings of Venus that he had seen with his 2¼-inch instrument could not be verified with the 3-inch Bardou telescope, something that may have further shaken his confidence in his observations of changes in Eratosthenes. No observations of Eratosthenes with the Bardou telescope would ever be reported, although Pickering himself would later declare that a 3-inch telescope was sufficient to see the major features within that crater (Pickering, "Eratosthenes I" 579).

At this point we must pause to consider two Lovecraft documents whose places in our story are not completely clear. The first is a somewhat puzzling short essay by Lovecraft titled "My Opinion as to the Lunar Canals" (*CE* 3.15). As we have already noted, these lunar canals are not the water-filled bodies that the word usually brings to mind.

---

2. HPL would later be more critical of the Bardou telescope, writing to August Derleth that it "was never very good." See chapter 12.

Lovecraft proposed that the canals are dark natural features of the moon analogous to the bright lunar rays that surround some craters. Surprisingly, he went on to write: "As to Prof. Pickering's theory—i.e.—That they are streaks of vegetation, I have but to say that any intelligent astronomer would consider it unworthy of notice, as our satellite is wanting in both water and atmosphere, the two essentials for life either animal or vegetable." Joshi (*IAP* 82) states that this note is dated 1903, but that the date is not in Lovecraft's handwriting.

If the 1903 date is correct, it would make the essay one of Lovecraft's first astronomical writings, and it would confirm a very early awareness of Pickering's work. A 1903 date for the note is actually supported by its strong rejection of Pickering's ideas. Lovecraft's writings during the years following 1903 would in contrast be either supportive of Pickering or, at worst, neutral. Accepting a date of 1903 does require, however, that Lovecraft quickly raised his opinion of Pickering. Clearly, Lovecraft had heard of Pickering by the time he wrote the note, but perhaps he had not yet fully digested Pickering's *Century* articles, in which Pickering argued that, even if the moon had no liquid surface water, it did have a thin atmosphere. As late as the 27 September 1903 *Journal*, Lovecraft stated flatly that "the Moon has no atmosphere," contrary to Pickering's contention. By the time of his observations in December 1903, Lovecraft appears to be more open to Pickering's views. Thus, a date between the winter and the autumn of 1903 is plausible.

The second item's place in this story is uncertain not because it has no date but because it bears two dates. It is an essay optimistically titled "The Moon: A Brief account of all that is known concerning our satellite, 7th edition." The essay carries two dates, first stating that it was written 26 November 1903, but then noting that it was revised on 24 July 1906 (*CE* 3.17–20). Parts of this essay are incorporated into Lovecraft's article in the *Pawtuxet Valley Gleaner* for 19 October 1906 (*CE* 3.32–35) and in an unfinished serialization begun in the August 1906 *Journal*. The essay includes a brief account of Pickering's conception of a moon with atmosphere, hoarfrost, volcanism, and simple vegetation, noting that "this question will be more fully described in another volume." It concludes with the statement: "The writer confidently believes that there is no pursuit more interesting than the study of the moon, and all are urged to devote themselves to this branch of knowledge for in the history of the world some of the most recondite facts have been brought to light by the efforts of an amateur."

If the conclusion was written on 26 November 1903, it shows a Lovecraft already primed to begin his observational study of Eratosthenes the following month. On the other hand, if the wording has been changed at a later date, perhaps as late as July 1906, then there may be hindsight embedded in the words. Considering that Lovecraft was at work on Eratosthenes at the start of December 1903, it seems likely that the 1903 first edition of the document already included both a mention of Pickering and the encouragement for amateurs to pursue selenography.

Lovecraft experienced a partial breakdown in late 1905 continuing into 1906 that may have contributed to the abrupt cessation of his research efforts (*IAP* 100–101). His collapse in 1908 has been attributed at least in part to his realization that his weakness in mathematics meant that he would never become a professional astronomer (*IAP* 127–28; chapter 1). Lovecraft's observational study of Eratosthenes of course required no mathematics.

There is no denying that at the time of his 1905 *Journal* extra, Lovecraft was convinced that, like Pickering, he had seen genuine changes in Eratosthenes—changes that could not be attributed to the varying reflections of sunlight from a fixed and rocky terrain. However, the changes he reported pushed to the limit his ability to see details on the moon. Through experience Lovecraft gradually became more aware of the problems that bedevil all lunar observers—nights of poor definition, tricks of changing light, and the limitations of telescopes. By 1906, with or without advice from the Ladd Observatory astronomers, he had become a more severe judge of his own observations. Lovecraft never repudiated his observations of changes in Eratosthenes, as he did his detections of markings on Venus, but he stopped mentioning them. After 1905, questions regarding lunar life would hang on Pickering's observations, not his own.

A serial titled "Will Man Ever Reach the Moon?" in the April–July 1906 issues of the *Journal* (and the similar article in the *Pawtuxet Valley Gleaner* for 12 October of that year) noted only that, were such a trip possible, Professor Pickering's discoveries might be verified. Nevertheless, the article in the *Pawtuxet Valley Gleaner* for 14 September 1906 quoted at the start of this paper, "Is There Life on the Moon?," tells us that his flirtation with Pickering's theories was not entirely over. By the time he wrote these articles, Lovecraft is likely to have read Waldemar Kaempffert's article "Life on the Moon" in the August 1905 *Munsey's Magazine*, which described Pickering's ideas. *Munsey's Magazine* was read by Lovecraft as early as 1903 (*IAP* 139–40). Livesey (DPO 19) has also plausibly suggested that Lovecraft is the unidentified writer whose identically titled article came to the attention of the editor of *Popular Astronomy* magazine early in 1906.

Pickering and lunar vegetation do not often figure in Lovecraft's writings after 1906. We are not aware that Pickering is mentioned in his letters. It seems likely that Lovecraft, so skeptical about the supernatural, likewise developed a greater skepticism regarding Pickering's lunar vegetation. Exactly when that happened is unclear. The last mention of Pickering's hypotheses by Lovecraft of which we are aware does, however, adopt a neutral tone. In an article published on 6 March 1915 in the *Asheville Gazette-News* (*CE* 3.287–290) titled "The Earth and Its Moon,"[3] he wrote: The moon is generally considered to be a dead world; a body without air, water, life, or volcanic activity. Prof. W. H. Pickering, however, has lately concluded from his observations that slight traces of atmosphere, hoar-frost, and vegetation of a low type, as well as feeble remnants of volcanic force, are to be found upon our satellite." The article continued: "The conjectures of the earlier astronomers concerning 'the inhabitants of the moon' seem now quite amusing." Lovecraft's amusement was not explicitly directed at Pickering but toward earlier and more extreme adherents of lunar life, such as Franz von Paula Gruithuisen (1774–1852), who thought that he had detected signs of lunar inhabitants and their cities (Sheehan and Dobson, 75–94; chapter 5). Still, Lovecraft's tone had become arguably more reserved and no clear support was given to Pickering's conclusions.

Pickering himself remained true to his ideas. He continued to contemplate the moon and Mars from his Jamaican home until the end of his life in 1938, fine-tuning his ideas concerning life on both worlds and encouraging amateurs to examine for themselves the garden of Eratosthenes. A crater on the moon is named Pickering after both William and his brother Edward.

In a letter to Rheinhart Kleiner in 1920, Lovecraft stated that "I should describe mine own nature as tripartite, my interests consisting of three parallel and dissociated groups—(a) Love of the strange and fantastic. (b) Love of the abstract truth and of scientific logick. (c) Love of

---

3. Livesey (DPO 13) has suggested that Pickering's article, "Meteorology of the Moon" (*Popular Astronomy* 23, March 1915) may have been published early enough to have inspired HPL's return to the subject.

the ancient and the permanent" (*RK* 158). Lovecraft's astronomical investigations are clearly linked to the second of these, and raise the question of whether some kind of scientific career might have been possible for him. In this connection, Livesey (DPO 76–78) questions whether Lovecraft had the perspective to be a good scientist. He suggests that Lovecraft placed too much weight on his sometimes outdated science books, to the point that they became a part of his identity. New discoveries that overthrew the ideas in his books therefore threatened that identity and might be resisted—obviously not the frame of mind wanted in a scientific researcher. Livesey calls attention to Lovecraft's early failure to embrace relativity as an example of this resistance.

In the astronomical observations discussed here, the young Lovecraft was not dealing with anything as transformative as the replacement of Newtonian physics by relativity. A new value for the rotation period of Venus would not change Lovecraft's developing worldview, no matter what number was found. Life on the moon is a weightier subject, and Lovecraft probably hoped to confirm Pickering's results. In the end, however, he appears to have restrained his enthusiasm and backed off from claiming that his own observations proved Pickering right. Lovecraft's observational projects can be criticized as naïve, but they show a basic appreciation of evidence-based science. Although we do not see any flashes of fledgling genius (he was just in his teens, after all), there is nothing in these first investigations to suggest that Lovecraft, under different circumstances, could not have become a solid scientist. Whether the science could have been astronomy is a different question. Livesey (DPO 76–78) points out that, even if he could have mastered his mathematical shortcomings, Lovecraft's sensitivity to cold as an adult, as well as the increasing dependence of astronomy upon the tedious analysis of photographic plates, might have steered him toward other fields.

Pickering's hypotheses also touch on the strange and the fantastic, so we might ask whether Lovecraft's youthful search for life on the moon influenced his fiction. We would say that there is nothing as specifically influenced as was H. G. Wells's account of lunar conditions in *The First Men in the Moon*. Livesey (DPO) has already noted that Lovecraft's knowledge of astronomy colors his fiction in many places, but these cannot be directly tied to his interest in Eratosthenes or Pickering. Lovecraft's juvenile stories, written around the time of his observations, do not appear to draw upon Pickering's ideas, though there was apparently a now-lost tale based upon astronomer Peter Andreas Hansen's proposal that there could be an atmosphere and life on the far side of an ellipsoidal Moon (*IAP* 87). There are frequent references to the moon in Lovecraft's later stories (Livesey DPO 82–83; Hite 34–36), but nothing that closely resembles Pickering's vision of lunar life. A loose connection can perhaps be made with the creatures and plants that dwell on the moon in *The Dream-Quest of Unknown Kadath,* but that fictional moon bears little resemblance to the one posited by Pickering. Nor do the ill-fated inhabitants of Ib, who are said to have descended from the moon in "The Doom That Came to Sarnath," appear to have arrived from Pickering's moon. Some of Lovecraft's alien creatures do have an element of the vegetable about them. The fungi from Yuggoth, the vegetable entities of Mercury in "The Shadow out of Time," and the Elder Things in *At the Mountains of Madness* come to mind, but it would be a stretch to connect them with Pickering's lunar plant life. The narrator in *At the Mountains of Madness* in fact goes so far as to refer to "the sterile disc of the moon," though the context allows an ironic reading. Nor does it appear that any of Lovecraft's fictional scientists is modeled upon Pickering, although some of them do make discoveries that set them apart from their more conventional peers.

We venture a few final comments about Lovecraft as a young astronomer. Aside from any unspecified help he may have received from the Ladd Observatory staff, Lovecraft seems to have learned observational astronomy on his own, through reading and doing. In his studies of Eratosthenes and Venus, he attempted to see details that, to be generous, challenged the capabilities of his small telescope. He would eventually learn to doubt observations made at the limits of visibility, but it took him three years to develop his acumen in that regard. Not until 1932 would the Providence amateur astronomy association, The Skyscrapers, be organized. Lovecraft attended a meeting in 1936, shortly before his death, and left impressed (letter to James Morton, unfinished at Lovecraft's death; *JFM* 392). Had such an organization existed thirty years earlier, it might have provided valuable advice for the beginning observer, and for better or worse have directed Lovecraft along different paths.

In the next chapter, we move beyond Eratosthenes to examine Lovecraft's relationship to Moon voyages, literary and prospective.

Chapter 5
Lovecraft's Lunar Cycle

Introduction

Seven years after H. P. Lovecraft's death, his onetime co-author Kenneth J. Sterling reflected on a discussion the two had had on what would become the Hale Telescope of Palomar Observatory: "On one occasion when the 200-inch telescope was being discussed, the question arose as to how great an area of the moon's surface could be seen with it. Lovecraft knew the moon's diameter and the distance between earth and moon, and was able to compute in a few moments the area which could be viewed by the telescope" (Sterling 423). Lovecraft was very interested in the 200-inch telescope project, but one wonders whether Sterling recalled this incident entirely correctly. It would have required an adept Lovecraft indeed to proceed instantly with such a calculation. Not that the formulae are really difficult, even for someone such as Lovecraft who shied from the mathematical side of astronomy, but several optical and practical details would also need to be at instant recall. However, Lovecraft could have used a shortcut to arrive at a quick solution. Had he read of the expected angular field of view of the 200-inch telescope, he could have immediately used that number and his knowledge of the moon's real and apparent diameters to answer the question. Nonetheless, even if time and a youthful admiration for his mentor colored Sterling's reflections, that Lovecraft would have the knowledge required for such a calculation was plausible for someone who knew him as Sterling did. Astronomy was, after all, Lovecraft's beloved science, and he had spent many nights in his youth scrutinizing the moon in his small telescopes. Kenneth Hite noted that the more mature Lovecraft discussed the moon in fifty-four of his works of fiction and poetry (Hite 25–36), while S. T. Joshi noted that the first science fiction story that Lovecraft probably wrote, now lost, was set on the far side of the moon.[1]

---

1. It centered around the theory (largely rejected since 1868, as HPL knew)

5. Lovecraft's Lunar Cycle

However, Lovecraft was not merely interested in remote observation of the moon; he was also interested in its exploration—as it might hypothetically happen in the future, as well as how it had already happened in the realm of fiction. Fred S. Lubnow offered a potential explanation for these interests in his essay "The Lovecraftian Solar System." In it, he noted that the moon and Venus were of particular interest to Lovecraft because of his belief that they were the likeliest places in the solar system to contain life (Lubnow, LSS 3). T. R. Livesey, in his essay "Dispatches from the Providence Observatory," comprehensively noted how Lovecraft incorporated astronomical knowledge and motifs into his fiction (DPO 30–50). In this chapter, we take up a corollary of Livesey's observations—Lovecraft's incorporation of themes and motifs of astronautical fiction into his writing, with emphasis on his treatment of the moon.

A logical starting point to explore his interest in both spheres of lunar exploration is the sixteen-year-old Lovecraft's article "Can the Moon Be Reached by Man?" Originally appearing under the title "Will Man Ever Reach the Moon?" in the *Rhode Island Journal of Astronomy* for April to July 1906, it was published under its new title in slightly revised form in the 12 October 1906 issue of the *Pawtuxet Valley Gleaner* (*CE* 3.31–32). At the start of the article, Lovecraft gives an overview of several works of lunar fiction, which will be reviewed below, but the majority of the article focuses on how an actual lunar voyage might be mounted. Lovecraft identifies "the greatest problem of all" to be the "motive power," to which he provided three methods that are "worthy of notice":

(a) To fire an inhabited projectile from an immense cannon.
(b) To interpose between the earth and the selected vehicle a screen, consisting of some material impervious to gravity.
(c) To send off a projectile by electrical repulsion.

Of them, Lovecraft dismisses the giant cannon as impossible both due to the extreme acceleration it would impose, as well as the fact that no known explosive existed to sufficiently accelerate a capsule. Lovecraft rejects the second option, as no such antigravity material is known to

---

of Danish mathematician Peter Andreas Hansen (1795–1874) that, due to the moon's supposedly irregular shape, a lunar atmosphere might condense on the far side (*RK* 49–50; *IAP* 87; Faig, *Lovecraftian Voyages* 112; Brunner 157, 211–13; Crowe 390–91).

exist and, moreover, it would also make a return to Earth impossible without continuing out to Mars first (unintentionally presaging the 2010s NASA debate over whether or not to return to the moon before mounting a Mars mission). As a result, there "remains but one hope, electrical repulsion, and of all the three plans this seems, at present, the most rational." Lovecraft believes that within a century a device would be invented that could generate sufficient electrical or magnetic repulsion to accelerate a vessel into space. Notably, in "The Shadow out of Time" the Great Race travels "over wild regions in closed, projectile-like airships lifted and moved by electrical repulsion" (*CF* 3.401), which suggests that Lovecraft had a continued interest over the span of his life in the electromagnetic propulsion he first described here.[2]

What might have been the inspiration for "Can the Moon Be Reached by Man?" A hint may be found in the 27 September 1903 issue (its sole issue) of the *Rhode Island Journal of Science & Astronomy*, which opens with:

CAN MEN VISIT THE MOON?
This is the title of an article in the October "Munsey" which has attracted considerable attention. The author, E. G. Dodge, A.M. seems to believe that it will some day be attempted. He considers the repulsion plan as the best. He predicts that *summer hotels* will soon dot the face of our satellite, and also that trains will be run regularly. But what will the "summer boarders" do if there is no air to breathe? he [*sic*] finds a feasible (?) explanation. The tourists will be equipped with a diving suit, supplied by a chemical generator. The north & south polar regions of the earth might be mapped with ease if the observer were only on the moon, for the earth could be examined with a telescope. But, however, it is not likely that anyone now living, will ever step off his native PLANET.

In a way, Lovecraft was correct in his closing sentence, for no one alive in 1903 would travel into space. The earliest space voyager by birth was the Soviet cosmonaut Georgi Beregovoi, born in 1921, who flew into space on *Soyuz 3* in 1968. However, on the same day Lovecraft offered a shorter, pithier take on the front page of his main publication, the *Rhode*

---

2. One of the few other pieces of "future technology" in HPL's writings is also from an early work: a "a swift and pond'rous ark" capable of crossing the Atlantic in a single day, from his first published poem, printed in the 4 March 1912 Providence *Evening Bulletin*, "Providence in 2000 A. D." (*AT* 201).

Island Journal of Astronomy: "The October 'Munsey' published an interesting article about reaching the moon by the repulsion. The author E. G. Dodge, A.M. had better attempt what he considers so feasible."

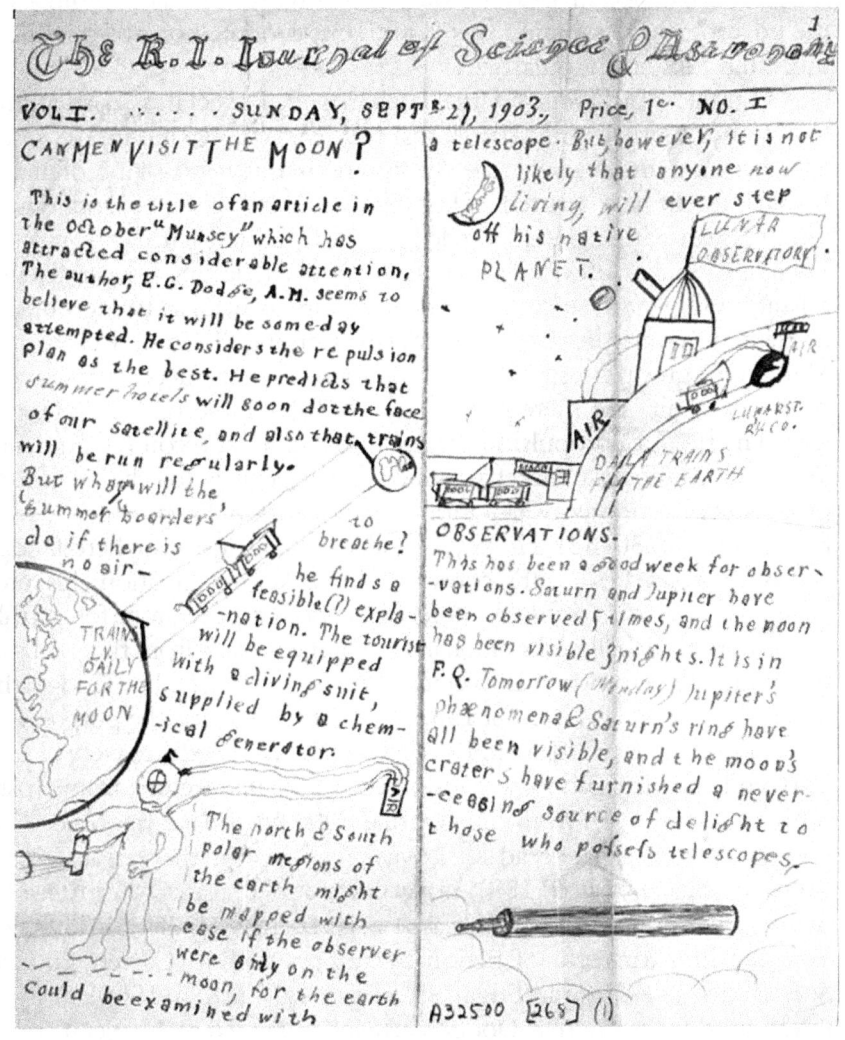

The cover of the *Rhode Island Journal of Science & Astronomy*, featuring Lovecraft's illustrations of a cosmic train, lunar observatory, and space suit.

Exactly who Dodge was, or what his master's degree was in, is not clear. Based on information from Ancestry.com, there was an Ernest Green Dodge, born in 1870, who received an A.M. from the University of Chicago in 1895, and was acting professor of Greek and instructor of mathematics at Berea College in 1898–99. He wrote a book of poems and was a professor at Urbana College (Urbana, Ohio) in 1903. He seems to have died in 1954 in Maryland, a retired special examiner for the government. Assuming this is the same Dodge, none of this sheds much light on his moon article.

Regardless of Dodge's actual background, Lovecraft's scorn at him in his latter journal seems hardly justified. Indeed, writing in 1983, science fiction grand master Isaac Asimov praised it as "the kind of article I myself might have written eighty years ago" and spoke of Dodge as "a rational man with a good knowledge of science and with a strong, but disciplined imagination" (Asimov 120).[3] Indeed, despite Lovecraft's dismissal, Dodge's article clearly stuck with him as well, as two groups of its elements clearly inspired segments in "Can the Moon Be Reached by Man?" One group consists of the difficulties of space travel: zero gravity, cold, lack of air, and meteors (Dodge 29–30). The second includes potential methods of propulsion: firing from a cannon, recoil (i.e., the motive force of modern rocketry, which Dodge rejects for the weight of propellants), anti-gravity levitation, and electric repulsion, which Dodge favors (Dodge, 30–32). However, it is in his conclusions where Dodge clearly outpaces Lovecraft's conservative Yankee imagination: his proposals of lunar observatories, hotels, and power generators for earthly consumption, all hallmarks of lunar development plans from the 1950s to today, are not set down in Lovecraft's article (Dodge 32). For Dodge, the moon was the destination; for Lovecraft, the voyage was the purpose.

A number of the ideas in Lovecraft's article, therefore, were clearly inspired by Dodge. But where did the other elements come from? Joshi offers an explanation from the fact that "Can Men Visit the Moon?" is the first known article read by Lovecraft in one of the various Frank Munsey magazines (*IAP* 139). Lovecraft would become a steady reader of the Munsey magazines, such as *Argosy All-Story* (Callaghan 69–82), exposing him to works of fiction by authors such as Garrett Putnam Serviss (1851–1929) and Edgar Rice Burroughs (1875–1950). It is interesting to speculate that Dodge's article is what led to Lovecraft reading the Munsey magazines to begin with, and the science fiction

---

3. Given Asimov's dislike of HPL (*IAP* 1049; Joshi, *Recognition* 187n6), it is perhaps not surprising that they would have different opinions of Dodge. Despite this, Kenneth Hite has compared Arkham to Asimov's city-planet Trantor, as both are "a permanent part of the atlas of the imagination" (Hite 13).

within—as it is science fiction that is the other source of inspiration for "Can the Moon Be Reached by Man?"

Outside of "In the Walls of Eryx," set on Venus, which he co-wrote in almost the final year of his life, human exploration of other worlds through semi-realistic means is not prominent in Lovecraft's fiction. However, the thought clearly did remain in his mind for most of his life. In particular, he considered interplanetary exploration in a letter to Natalie H. Wooley (27 November 1933; *RB* 194–95). In the letter, Lovecraft discusses the difficulty of building "space ships" as being "perhaps a little beyond probability (the obstacles to their operation being really much greater than popular science indicates) but I certainly think that some sort of rocket voyage to the *moon* (whose extreme nearness puts it in a separate category) will be attempted—first with an untenanted projectile, & later perhaps with a human cargo." On the other hand, Lovecraft was less sanguine about the possibilities of rockets reaching other planets in the solar system. But even his use of rockets as a method of reaching the moon shows a change in thought, one he expanded on in a letter to Sterling:

> About rockets—certainly I realise that the major experiments involve really serious research. They can probably get higher up in the stratosphere than anything else ever can, & it is surely fitting that all their possibilities be investigated. But I trust that repeated accidents will cause experimenters to take additional precautions—excluding spectators when anything problematical or of unusual magnitude is attempted. The *newness* of all this business is quite bewildering to an old man—when I was young the rocket principle was never heard of in connexion with locomotion, so that in writing my ponderous essay "Can the Moon Be Reached by Man?" in 1906 I enumerated only three possible motive powers—shooting from a cannon, screen to cut off gravity (if such be ever discovered), & some future manipulation of electrical propulsion. How times do change! (20 November 1935; *RB* 254)

As stated in chapter 1, Lovecraft's first astronomy book was an 1853 edition of Elijah Burritt's *Geography of the Heavens*, whose passage on the hypothetical faster-than-light flight across the cosmos by a seraph was perhaps the basis for Lovecraft's association of interplanetary fight with winged creatures. As Joshi has noted, space travel is ubiquitous among Lovecraft's intelligent extraterrestrials, but all perform it by using wings to fly through the luminiferous aether, a supposed medium existing in space which would allow light waves to flow. Its existence was disproven in 1887 by the Michelson-Morley experiment, which helped lead to Einstein's theory of relativity (Joshi, "LOP" 8; Joshi, "Civilizations" 9). Lovecraft's continuing use of luminiferous ether into the twentieth century has been criticized by Joshi, Livesey, and Richard L. Tierney as a case of Lovecraft ignoring the science of his day (Joshi, "LOP" 7; Livesey, DPO 52–55). However, it may not be a case of Lovecraft *ignoring* science, but rather *explicitly rejecting* the established physics of his time in favor of pseudoscience.[4] And indeed, a year after the Michelson-Morley experiment, the astronomy popularizer and science fiction author Garrett Serviss, whom Lovecraft admired, noted in one of the nonfiction astronomy books owned by Lovecraft, "Without the all-pervading luminiferous ether, narrow indeed would be our acquaintance with the physical creation. This is a sympathetic bond by which we may conceive that intelligent creatures throughout the universe are united" (Serviss, *Opera* 147).

In his letter to Sterling of 25 May 1936, Lovecraft mentions that on 4 May he attended a lecture by Dayton Miller (1866–1941), a physicist at what is now Case Western Reserve University and the leading critic of the Michelson-Morley experiment. Lovecraft wrote that, in his defense of the ether theory, Miller "produced some impressive data, & showed that many widely-accepted accounts of the Michelson-Morley experiment . . . are definitely erroneous [and] he surely sounded like one not easily disposed of. Is our view of the universe due for another jolt? We shall see!" (*RB* 277). In his seminal 1966[5] essay "Through Hyperspace with Brown Jenkin," Fritz Leiber offered the suggestion that the wings of Lovecraft's creatures were solar sails working off photon pressure, a retcon that has remained popular (Leiber, "Hyperspace" 168–69; Barlowe, Summers, and Meacham 68–69; Clarke, *Astounding* 98). However, it is clear that spaceflight using wings in ether was something that Lovecraft truly believed had at least some grounding in science as he understood it.

Despite his clinging to some disproven nineteenth-century ideas, Lovecraft's 1933 and 1935 letters show two changes in thinking from his 1906 article, reflecting evolutions that had happened in the wider

---

4. For a more extensive analysis of HPL's use of science and pseudoscience, see Joshi, "Time."

5. An early version of the essay was published in 1963, but the 1966 version is revised and is the version that has been subsequently reprinted.

culture: the use of rockets as propulsion and the use of uncrewed rockets as predecessors to crewed expeditions. These ideas, and their applications toward lunar voyages, had been promoted by several scientists by this point in the early twentieth century, most notably the Austro-German Hermann Oberth (1894–1989), the Russian Konstantin Tsiolkovsky (1857–1935),[6] and the American Robert H. Goddard (1882–1945). Indeed, Asimov noted that Tsiolkovsky began seriously writing about rocket travel into space the year that Dodge rejected the notion of reaction-based space propulsion (Asimov 128; Dodge 31).

But it is Goddard who is of particular relevance, as his *A Method of Reaching Extreme Altitudes* was published in 1919 by the Smithsonian Institution.[7] Goddard's work was mentioned on the front page of the *New York Times* on 13 January 1920, and then severely mocked in an editorial in the paper the next day, the basis of which was a severe lack of knowledge of physics leading to an assumption that thrust was impossible in a vacuum—exactly the sort of common misunderstanding of science that Lovecraft criticized in both his own early astronomy articles and his personal letters. Goddard was a New England local, having been born in Worcester, Massachusetts (about halfway between where Lovecraft placed Arkham and Dunwich), and gaining both education and employment from that city's Clark University.[8] On 16 March 1926, Goddard launched the world's first liquid-fueled rocket from the Asa Ward Farm in nearby Auburn, Massachusetts. The rocket flew a total distance of 184 feet, landing in a cabbage patch. In November 1929,

---

6. Tsiolkovsky was later adopted by the Soviet space program as its spiritual founder. Sergei Khrushchev, an engineer for the Soviet space program and son of Soviet premier Nikita Khrushchev who initiated the Soviet space effort, later emigrated to Rhode Island, became a faculty member of Brown University, and donated his papers to the John Hay Library.

7. On 19 January 1920, the Ladd Observatory library acquired a copy of Goddard's text (*The Library of Ladd Observatory of Brown University List of Books and Pamphlets, in Order of Their Receipt* 121; contained in the John Hay Library, MS-1ZAS-1 Department of Astronomy Papers Box 4). However, HPL ceased his youthful visits to the observatory, so it is extremely unlikely he would have read it there.

8. Clark University was founded by Jonas Gilman Clark, while its president at Goddard's time was Wallace Walter Atwood—two auspiciously Lovecraftian names.

aviation pioneer Charles Lindbergh (1902–1974) contacted Goddard, became a firm supporter, and began using his celebrity status to try and secure funding. In the spring of 1930, Lindbergh succeeded in convincing the Guggenheim business family to fund Goddard's research. With this backing, Goddard relocated to a remote area more suitable for rocket testing—the sleepy town of Roswell, New Mexico. However, Goddard would die in August 1945, just under two years before that town's more substantive July 1947 brush with cosmic notoriety.

Perhaps not surprisingly, Lovecraft was aware of Goddard's research. In an April 1920 letter to the Gallomo Lovecraft wrote, "Speaking of astronomical things—is either of youse guys interested in (a) the supposed new trans-Neptunian planet,[9] (b) the talk of telegraphic communication with Venus or Mars, and (c) the Goddard plan for sending a rocket to the moon? If so, just speak up! Grandpa has heaps to say about all these things!" (*Misc* 93). Those "heaps to say" about Goddard would remain in Lovecraft's mind until the final years of his life, as evidenced by his comments in his letter of 4 December 1935 to Sterling: "Glad you heard a good rocket lecture. I don't doubt but that this form of propulsion is getting to be more & more a thing of exact & dependable study. Yes—I saw an item about the Lindbergh-Guggenheim backing of the Goddard experiments. I always realised that Goddard was a serious investigator" (*RB* 257). It is perhaps notable that the only reference to rockets in Lovecraft's fiction[10] is at the end of "The Colour out of Space," when the departing colour "shot vertically up toward the sky like a rocket or meteor, leaving behind no trail and disappearing through a round and curiously regular hole in the clouds" (*CF* 2.396). The colour being compared to a rocket launching from a farm in central Massachusetts was perhaps inspired by the news accounts of Goddard's historic flight, exactly a year before Lovecraft wrote his story.[11] Unfor-

---

9. Early in 1920, newspapers carried reports of searches for a new planet, based upon perturbations in the motion of Neptune.

10. HPL's 1929 revision story "The Electric Executioner" mentions "Stephenson's 'Rocket'" (*CF* 4.188). However, this *Rocket* was an early locomotive, built in 1829 by the British engineer Robert Stephenson (1803–1859). HPL had an early interest in trains, writing one (extant) issue of the *Railroad Review* in December 1901 (Joshi and Schultz 134).

11. Of potential interest to future pastiche authors is that Goddard was born in October 1882, only a few months after the colour out of space landed on

tunately, there is no evidence that Lovecraft ever interacted with Goddard. However, Goddard did correspond with occultist and Jet Propulsion Lab scientist Jack Parsons (1914–1952), who had some circumstantial links to Lovecraft (Goddard 2.931; Harms and Gonce 124–26; Carter 6–7, 12, 60, 102).

Goddard was rare among early rocketry advocates in that his inspiration came from the Martian speculations of Percival Lowell and the works of H. G. Wells and his imitators, including Serviss (Goddard 1.7; Callaghan 72–73; Sagan, *Cosmos* 116–17). Most space advocates of the time, however, drew their inspiration from Wells's predecessor, the more scientifically grounded Jules Verne (1828–1905), and his 1865 *From the Earth to the Moon*. It is Verne's influence that looms largest in Lovecraft's essay. This is not surprising given that Verne was particularly beloved by young Lovecraft (*IAP* 87). Indeed, Lovecraft owned both French and English versions of *From the Earth to the Moon;* the former was given to him by Richard Ely Morse in 1935, but the translated version was presumably owned by Lovecraft from a young age (*LL* 160). Indeed, as Dodge's article specifically rejects as impossible Verne's method of space travel in *From the Earth to the Moon* (Dodge 30), one can speculate that perhaps this helped contribute to young Lovecraft's dismissive take on "Can Men Visit the Moon?"

However, Lovecraft's references to the books of Verne and Wells were not merely through inference; both are specifically cited within the text. And while those novels are the most influential of the works of fiction mentioned in "Can the Moon Be Reached by Man?," they are not the only ones. It is to a discussion of the lunar fiction Lovecraft mentions in that article—as early works of interplanetary fiction read during his youth, and therefore presumably formative on his views of both other planets and the beings that might inhabit them—that we now turn.

Lovecraft's Literary Lunar Canon

At the start of his article, the young Lovecraft cites *A Trip from the Earth to the Moon, Performed by Domingo Gonzales, a Spanish Adventurer* by the French translator Jean Baudoin (1590–1650), and states that "from that time on, hundreds of similar works have appeared, some

---

Nahum Gardner's farm—and that Goddard's own father was named Nahum. Perhaps Goddard's desire to explore space was a subconscious lure to return to the colour's cosmic home?

good, some bad; the most prominent having been written by Locke, Poe, Verne, and Wells." Verne's and Wells's tales have already been identified above; the first two are "The Unparalleled Adventure of One Hans Pfaall" (1835) by Edgar Allan Poe (1809–1849) and the Great Moon Hoax, a newspaper account in 1835 by Richard Adams Locke (1800–1871). Whether Lovecraft realized it or not, these five works exist in conversation with one another, to a degree that they can be considered part of a loose "lunar cycle" with some interesting parallels to Lovecraft's own later works. In addition, while these five works of fiction mentioned in "Can the Moon be Reached by Man?" are the bulk of the lunar fiction we know Lovecraft read, there are several other works he either certainly or probably read, which will be discussed at the end of this section.

Baudoin wrote *A Trip from the Earth to the Moon* in 1649, and Lovecraft described him as one of the first of "many authors who wished to make a startling piece of fiction [and therefore] have recounted imaginary journeys to the moon." But as Joshi noted when compiling the article for Hippocampus Press, Lovecraft seemingly did not recognize (at least at the time) that Baudoin's work was simply a French translation of *The Man in the Moone* by the English bishop Francis Godwin's (1562–1633), published posthumously in 1638 (Brunner 96–99; Crowe 13–14). Lovecraft was not alone in this misunderstanding, probably getting it from both Poe's and Verne's references to the French translation as the original in their own stories, with Verne himself probably drawing it from Poe. The lunar ship in the work being a spherical vessel of gravity-repellant metal would probably also influence Wells's lunar novel, but in all likelihood Lovecraft never read Baudoin's work, only knowing it from it being mentioned by Verne and Poe.

Poe's mention of Baudoin occurred in his short story "The Unparalleled Adventure of One Hans Pfaall," initially published as "Hans Phaall—A Tale" in the June 1835 issue of the *Southern Literary Messenger* (Brunner 107–9; Crowe 213). The majority of the story is framed as a journal kept by the eponymous resident of Rotterdam in the Netherlands, an account of the five years he spent on the moon, having reached it by means of a nineteen-day voyage on a unique balloon.[12] The

---

12. During his ascent to the moon, Hans passes over the North Pole, observing that it contains a giant hole leading into the Hollow Earth (Poe, "Phaall" 98–99), a popular theory at the time to which Poe also alluded in "MS. Found in a Bottle" (1833) and *The Narrative of Arthur Gordon Pym of Nantucket*

balloon then returned to Earth with a lunarian envoy seeking to determine if Hans could himself return, given that he had fled Rotterdam in the first place due to having murdered several creditors (Poe, "Phaall" 107–9). Poe apparently intended this initial story to be the first part of a series, but was upstaged by a report in the 25 August 1835 issue of the *New York Sun* concerning amazing discoveries on the moon's surface made by the British astronomer Sir John Herschel (1792–1871), who at the time had set up an observatory near Cape Town in modern-day South Africa.

The reports in the *Sun* continued for a total of six issues, appearing under the headline "Great Astronomical Discoveries Lately Made by Sir John Herschel at the Cape of Good Hope." The fantastic discoveries—which included enormous quartz obelisks near forests inhabited by giant single-horned goats (Locke 563–65) and intelligent bat-winged orangutans (Locke 568–69)—became too incredible to maintain, and the story was eventually revealed to be a hoax written by the reporter Richard Adams Locke (Brunner 109–10; Crowe 210–16). One of the early skeptics who declared it a hoax was Poe, who thought it to be similar to his own "Hans Phaall" tale—although he noted in 1848 that "Having stated the case, however, in this form, I am bound to do Mr. Locke the justice to say that he denies having seen my article before the publication of his own; I am bound also to add, also, that I believe him" (Poe, "Locke" 120; Tresch 85–87). Throughout the 1840s, Poe had been revising his "Hans Phaall" tale, although the end result was only published posthumously in 1850, under its full and revised title of "The Unparalleled Adventure of One Hans Pfaall." For our purposes, the most notable changes are the additions of notes at the end, which begin with a draw from his 1848 comments on Locke:

> Strictly speaking, there is but little similarity between the above sketchy trifle, and the celebrated "Moon-Story" of Mr. Locke; but as both have the character of *hoaxes,* (although the one is in a tone of banter, the other of downright earnest,) and as both hoaxes are on the same subject, the moon—moreover, as both attempt to give plausibility by scientific detail—the author of "Hans Pfaall" thinks it necessary to say, *in self-defence,*

(1838) (Tresch 95–96, 102–03). HPL would later write a letter to the editor of the *Providence Sunday Journal* (12 August 1906) denouncing Hollow Earth claims (*CE* 3.21–22). Ironically, *At the Mountains of Madness* would later contribute toward the late twentieth-century conspiracy theories associating the Hollow Earth entrances with the polar regions (Navroth 190).

that his own *jeu d'esprit* was published, in the "Southern Literary Messenger," about three weeks before the commencement of Mr. L's in the "New York Sun." Fancying a likeness which, perhaps, does not exist, some of the New York papers copied "Hans Pfaall," and collated it with the "Moon-Hoax," by way of detecting the writer of the one in the writer of the other. (Poe, "Note" 110–11)

It may be this passage in question was where the young Lovecraft drew most of his knowledge of the Moon Hoax. Verne mentions it in *From the Earth to the Moon* but does not state the author (Verne 14–15). In his book *Astronomy with an Opera-Glass* (1888), Garrett Serviss refers to the "crystallized mountains described in the celebrated 'Moon Hoax' of Richard Adams Locke" (125), and notes, in reference to a mysterious white streak in the lunar Sea of Serenity, that

the author of the "Moon Hoax" was fairly entitled to take advantage of the romancer's license, and declare that "its edge throughout its whole length of three hundred and forty miles is an acute angle of solid quartz-crystal, brilliant as a piece of Derbyshire spar just brought from the mine, and containing scarcely a fracture or a chasm from end to end!" (128)

However, these are the limit of the references to the hoax and its contents in the book.

The story was reprinted as "The Moon Hoax" under Locke's authorship in the September 1926 issue of *Amazing Stories,* which Lovecraft owned (*LL* 24). The opening lines of "The Moon Hoax" contain the passage:

It seems almost a presumptuous usurpation of powers denied us by the divine will, when man, in the pride and confidence of his skill, steps forth, far beyond the apparently natural boundary of his privileges, and demands the secrets and familiar fellowship of other worlds. We are assured that when the immortal philosopher to whom mankind is indebted for the thrilling wonders now first made known, had at length adjusted his new and stupendous apparatus with a certainty of success, he solemnly paused several hours before he commenced his observations, that he might prepare his own mind for discoveries which he knew would fill the minds of myriads of his fellow-men with astonishment, and secure his name a bright, if not transcendent conjunction with that of his venerable father to all posterity. And well might he pause! (Locke 558)

There are clear similarities to the opening lines of "The Call of Cthulhu," with its famous evocation of cosmic dread. Lovecraft wrote his most famous story in the fall of 1926, having probably completed it by the end of September (*IAP* 636). Given that magazines shipped before their publication dates, the *Amazing Stories* issue with "The Moon Hoax" would probably have arrived during Lovecraft's writing of "The Call of Cthulhu." Did Locke inspire Lovecraft, just as Lovecraft's idol Poe inspired Locke? Speculative, as mentioned above—but intriguing speculation.

The incredible details of the moon revealed via the telescope of "Herschel," including creatures on the left with a passing resemblance to the Elder Things. (Public domain; Project Gutenberg)

Poe himself, several paragraphs below the passage given above, continues:

> There have been other "voyages to the moon," but none of higher merit than the one just mentioned. That of Bergerac is utterly meaningless. In the third volume of the "American Quarterly Review" will be found quite an elaborate criticism upon a certain "Journey" of the kind in question:—a criticism in which it is difficult to say whether the critic most exposes the stupidity of the book, or his own absurd ignorance of astronomy. I forget the title of the work; but the *means* of the voyage are more deplorably ill conceived than are even the *ganzas* of our friend the Signor Gonzales. The adventurer, in digging the earth, happens to discover a peculiar metal for which the moon has a strong attraction, and

straightway constructs of it a box, which, when cast loose from its terrestrial fastenings, flies with him, forthwith, to the satellite. The "Flight of Thomas O'Rourke," is a *jeu d' esprit* not altogether contemptible, and has been translated into German. Thomas, the hero, was, in fact, the game-keeper of an Irish peer, whose eccentricities gave rise to the tale. The "flight" is made on an eagle's back, from Hungry Hill, a lofty mountain at the end of Bantry Bay. (Poe, "Note" 117)

Here we see Lovecraft exposed not only to the references of Baudoin's *A Trip from the Earth to the Moon*, but also to *A Voyage to the Moon* (1827) by the Virginia politician George Tucker (1775–1861), one of the first American science fiction novels, as well as its substantial review in 1828 by Robley Dunglison (1798–1869), an English-born physician at the University of Virginia (Dunglison 61–88). Tucker had instructed Poe during the author's brief stint at the University of Virginia (Brunner 104–7). Poe also references the *Comical History of the States and Empires of the Moon* (1657) by the French playwright Cyrano de Bergerac (1619–1655), itself influenced by Baudoin. The "Flight of Thomas O'Rourke" is an error on Poe's part, referring to the 1828 tale *Daniel O'Rourke* by the Irish folklorist Thomas Crofton Croker (1798–1854), depicting the titular character's flight to the moon on the back of an eagle in a tale influenced by Irish fairy legends (Croker 18–20). There is no evidence that Lovecraft read any of these works cited by Poe, however. Poe's condemnation of Cyrano's work as "utterly meaningless," is ironic given that it is the first story to depict the use of (solid fuel) rockets to reach the moon, albeit in an unrealistic way—and it would no doubt interest Lovecraft that Bergerac's voyager launches in his rocket machine from colonial Quebec City (Bergerac 33–34; Brunner 99–100; Crowe 379).

It is generally accepted that Poe wrote "The Balloon-Hoax" (1844) as a parody of the Great Moon Hoax, particularly as it was published in the *New York Sun* as a hoax article. It has even been argued that Poe's novel *The Narrative of Arthur Gordon Pym of Nantucket* (1838) was structured as a direct parallel of the Great Moon Hoax (Koenigs 176–78), which would make *At the Mountains of Madness* a distant descendent of the Moon Hoax. "The Balloon-Hoax" would itself go on to inspire several of Verne's works, including his debut novel *Five Weeks in a Balloon* (1863) and his *Around the World in Eighty Days* (1872), bringing it full circle. One other Poe story is worth mentioning, one of the final published in his lifetime—"Mellonta Tauta" (1849). The story is the form of a letter written by a female balloonist, Pundita, to a friend in the year

5. Lovecraft's Lunar Cycle

2848, transmitted back in time by a psychic (suggestive of "The Shadow out of Time"). In her letter, Pundita mentions that by using the "captain's spy-glass" she

> watched with much interest the putting up of a huge impost on a couple of lintels in the new temple at Daphnis in the moon. It was amusing to think that creatures so diminutive as the lunarians, and bearing so little resemblance to humanity, yet evinced a mechanical ingenuity so much superior to our own. One finds it difficult, too, to conceive the vast masses which these people handle so easily, to be as light as our own reason tells us they actually are. (Tresch 324; Poe, "MT" 1126–27)

Lovecraft owned the five-volume 1903 Raven edition of *The Works of Edgar Allan Poe* (*LL* 129). The first volume includes both "The Unparalleled Adventure of One Hans Pfaall" and "The Balloon-Hoax," the latter of which was also reprinted in the April 1927 issue of *Amazing Stories*, which Lovecraft owned as well (*LL* 24); the fourth volume contains "Mellonta Tauta."

But the Verne novel with the largest debt to "Hans Pfall" is, of course, *From the Earth to the Moon*. Given his childhood admiration of Verne, it is not surprising that the influence of Verne's lunar novel can be found in young Lovecraft's essay on lunar travel. As quoted above, the first method Lovecraft described of reaching the moon was "To fire an inhabited projectile from an immense cannon"—the exact method used in *From the Earth to the Moon*, with the projectile, the cannon, and its fuel being described in great detail (Verne 32–46). But this subsequent passage of Lovecraft's essay is also worth interrogating:

> The greatest impediment to extra-terrestrial travel is lack of air, but in an air-tight compartment one could easily store enough to last the journey, carrying oxygen to revivify and lime to purify it. Another obstacle is the lack of gravity, which would render everything unsteady; but all essentials could be fastened to the sides of the chosen vehicle, while the passenger might support himself by convenient rests. A third difficulty is the extreme cold, but of course, artificial heat could be had. Lastly, there is always a danger of colliding with meteoric bodies, but this is so slight, that I doubt if it would deter any enthusiast.

This makes it clear that Lovecraft was not only influenced by *From the Earth to the Moon* but by Verne's sequel, *Around the Moon* (1870), which depicts the actual space flight itself. Verne's three astronauts not only carry a supply of oxygen, but also use potash to remove carbon dioxide from the air they breathe (Verne 53). To Verne, true lack of gravity occurs only at the "neutral line" between the Earth and the moon (the L1 point), and the crew use just such handles to navigate the capsule as their gravity reduces as they approach the gravitational midway (Verne 63–65). The occupants of the projectile use a gas burner for heat to protect against the intense cold of space (Verne 96–99). And finally, en route to the moon, they narrowly avoid collision with a passing meteor (Verne 105–6). All the potential difficulties Lovecraft illustrates about a voyage to the moon are therefore present in *Around the Moon*.

The commander of Verne's lunar expedition is Barbicane, president of the Baltimore Gun Club, the group of enthusiasts who build the capsule and its launch cannon in the first place—choosing as their location "Tampa Town." Tampa is twenty-four miles east of Henry S. Whitehead's home in Dunedin, and less than 130 miles southwest of R. H. Barlow's home in DeLand, and Lovecraft would visit it on a vacation to Florida in 1931, the first of three trips over the next four years (Jordan 32–45; *OFF* 107). Barbicane and his companions make their way to Tampa via New Orleans, which Lovecraft visited in 1932, meeting future collaborator E. Hoffmann Price. Verne's Gun Club would later get its own minor incorporation into Lovecraftian pastiche in the anthology *The Starry Wisdom Library* (2014), intended to be an 1877 auction catalogue for the library of the Church of Starry Wisdom from "The Haunter of the Dark" (*CF* 3.460). The entry for each book in the collection was written by a different author, and the fake biography for Peter Rawlik (who contributed the entry on the *Qanoon-e-Islam* from *The Case of Charles Dexter Ward*) identifies him as having been treasurer of the Baltimore Gun Club from 1865 to 1869 (Pedersen vii).

In the initial planning of the proposed lunar expedition, President Barbicane gives a speech to the membership of the Gun Club, outlining prior ideas of voyages to the moon and the inhabitants that might be found there:

> In the seventeenth century a certain David Fabricius boasted of having seen with his own eyes the inhabitants of the moon. In 1649 a Frenchman, one Jean Baudoin, published a 'Journey performed from the Earth to the Moon by Domingo Gonzalez,' a Spanish adventurer. At the same period Cyrano de Bergerac published that celebrated 'Journeys in the Moon' which met with such success in France. Somewhat later another Frenchman, named Fontenelle, wrote 'The Plurality of Worlds,' a *chef-d'oeuvre* of its time. About 1835 a small treatise, translated from the New

York *American,* related how Sir John Herschel, having been despatched to the Cape of Good Hope for the purpose of making there some astronomical calculations, had, by means of a telescope brought to perfection by means of internal lighting, reduced the apparent distance of the moon to eighty yards! He then distinctly perceived caverns frequented by hippopotami, green mountains bordered by golden lace-work, sheep with horns of ivory, a white species of deer and inhabitants with membranous wings, like bats. This *brochure,* the work of an American named Locke, had a great sale. But, to bring this rapid sketch to a close, I will only add that a certain Hans Pfaal [*sic*], of Rotterdam, launching himself in a balloon filled with a gas extracted from nitrogen, thirty-seven times lighter than hydrogen, reached the moon after a passage of nineteen hours. This journey, like all previous ones, was purely imaginary; still, it was the work of a popular American author—I mean Edgar Poe! (Verne 14–15)

In this passage alone we see a familiar litany of names: Baudoin, Bergerac, Locke, and Poe, but also two new names. David Fabricius (1564–1617) was a German Lutheran pastor and astronomer, as was his son Johannes, an early observer of sunspots. However, Fabricius claiming to see inhabitants on the moon seems to be an invention of Verne's (Lucibella 2). Given that most of Fabricius's astronomy was before the telescope was used, and that he is mainly remembered for discovering the variability of the star Mira and for being murdered by someone he had denounced as a goose thief, he was a strange choice indeed for Verne. Lovecraft would go on to mention Fabricius's observation in 1596 of the star Mira in a 30 September 1914 article in the Providence *Evening News* (*CE* 3.126). Bernard Le Bovier de Fontenelle (1657–1757) was an early science popularizer of the French Enlightenment, and his *Conversations on the Plurality of Worlds* (1686) was a promotion of Copernican heliocentrism as well as a speculation of life on said other worlds (Brunner 94; Crowe 18–21).

Barbicane's recitation of fictional stories of the moon's inhabitants is quickly followed by a description of real attempts to contact them:

Thus, a few days ago, a German geometrician proposed to send a scientific expedition to the steppes of Siberia. There, on those vast plains, they were to describe enormous geometric figures, drawn in characters of reflecting luminosity, among which was the proposition regarding the 'square of the hypothenuse,' commonly called the 'Ass's Bridge' by the French. 'Every intelligent being,' said the geometrician, 'must understand the scientific meaning of that figure. The Selenites, do they exist, will respond by a similar figure; and, a communication being thus once established, it will be easy to form an alphabet which shall enable us to converse with the inhabitants of the moon.' So spoke the German geometrician; but his project was never put into practice, and up to the present day there is no bond in existence between the Earth and her satellite. (Verne 15)

The proposal is typically attributed to the German mathematician Carl Friedrich Gauss (1777–1855) in 1820, although study of his papers revealed no evidence of him having proposed it. But by the time Verne wrote his novel (and still by the time Lovecraft read Verne's novel) the proposal continued to be widely accepted as having been made by Gauss. Of additional relevance for Lovecraft aficionados is that in 1813 Gauss pioneered the development of non-Euclidian geometry (Crowe 205–7). The combination of non-Euclidian geometry and the use of mathematical symbols to communicate with extraterrestrials also has an obvious connection to "The Dreams in the Witch House."

However, the pseudo-Gauss is not the only astronomer whose theories are discussed by Verne; ones with much closer connections to Lovecraft are also mentioned. As discussed in chapter 4, Lovecraft's 1903 essay "My Opinion as to the Lunar Canals" and its 1906 follow-up "Is There Life on the Moon?" contained speculation on the supposed canals on the moon, and the related claims of the Bavarian astronomer Franz von Paula Gruithuisen (1774–1852) to have observed cities of intelligent lunarians (Brunner 18–20). The young Lovecraft scoffed at Gruithuisen, an opinion he maintained throughout his life. Lovecraft ended his speculation on space travel in 1933 to Natalie Wooley by stating his belief that intelligent life was exceedingly rare elsewhere in the universe (*RB* 194–95). Indeed, one of Lovecraft's final works, his 1936 collaboration with R. H. Barlow, "The Night Ocean," also indicates that the moon is dead now but was perhaps inhabited in the past (*CF* 4.655). This may reflect the continuing influence of Serviss, who in *Astronomy with an Opera-Glass* wrote that

> To declare that no possible form of life can exist under the conditions prevailing upon the lunar surface would be saying too much, for human intelligence can not set bounds to creative power. Yet, within the limits of life, such as we know them, it is probably safe to assert that the moon is a dead and deserted world. In other words, if a race of beings resembling ourselves, or resembling any of our contemporaries in terrestrial life, ever existed upon the moon, they must long since have perished. (137)

But while Lovecraft may not have taken the speculation of Gruithuisen seriously, Verne's astronauts do, and attempt to observe both the canals and the cities as they fly by:

> Thus they remarked that, during full moon, the disc appeared scored in certain parts with white lines; and, during the phases, with black. On prosecuting the study of these with still greater precision, they succeeded in obtaining an exact account of the nature of these lines. They were long and narrow furrows sunk between parallel ridges, bordering generally upon the edges of the craters. Their length varied between ten and 100 miles, and their width was about 1,600 yards. Astronomers called them chasms, but they could not get any further. Whether these chasms were the dried-up beds of ancient rivers or not they were unable thoroughly to ascertain. The Americans, among others, hoped one day or other to determine this geological question. They also undertook to examine the true nature of that system of parallel ramparts discovered on the moon's surface by Gruithuysen [sic], a learned professor of Munich, who considered them to be "a system of fortifications thrown up by the Selenitic engineers." (Verne 28)

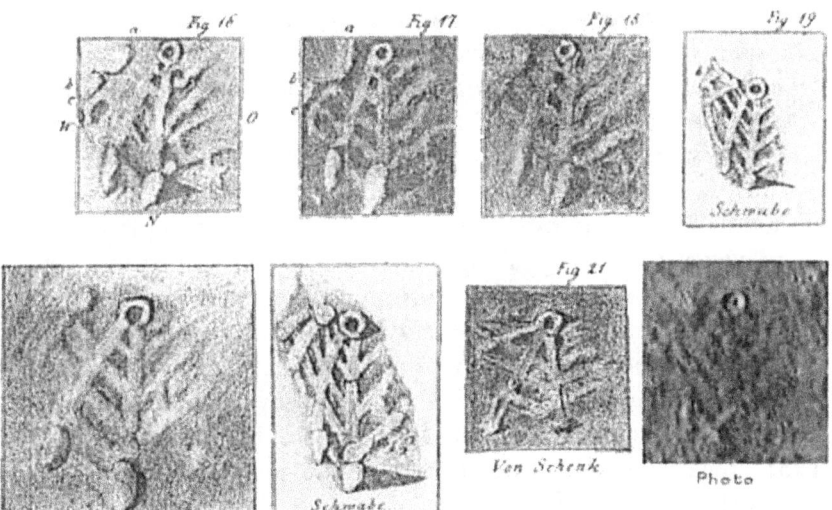

Gruithuisen's illustration of the supposed lunar city. (Public domain)

Later on, Barbicane observes the "rifts" and "long parallel ramparts" observed by "Pastorff, Gruithuysen, Boeer, and Moedler," with crewman Michel Ardan proposing the same idea as Julius Schmidt: "might it not be possible that the dark lines forming that bastion were rows of trees regularly placed?" (Verne 87). Aside from Gruithuisen, the cited astronomers, all German, were Johann Friedrich Julius Schmidt (1825–84), who became director of the National Observatory of Athens; Johann Wilhelm Pastorff (1767–1838), who, like Gruithuisen, claimed to have observed the hypothesized innermost planet Vulcan (to be described in chapter 7); and the friends Wilhelm Beer (1797–1850) and Johann Heinrich von Mädler (1794–1874), who created the first accurate map of the moon (Brunner 57–60). The astronauts also observe a lunar volcano during their flyby, contributing to their discovery of "real clouds formed in the midst of a very confined atmosphere" around the moon (Verne 104–6); as also described in chapter four, lunar volcanism and atmosphere were also of interest to the young Lovecraft in his two essays.

It is far too simple, as well as completely wrong, to claim that young Lovecraft received all his notions on the speculative lunar surface from Verne's fiction, but at the very least Verne and the nonfiction astronomy works Lovecraft read both built up similar speculation and drew from the same sources. Outside of Verne's two lunar stories, however, it is worth mentioning the novel *A Journey in Other Worlds* (1894), which Lovecraft owned (*LL* 28). The novel was written by John Jacob Astor IV (1864–1912), a businessman who would later become the namesake of the Waldorf-Astoria Hotel in New York, fight in the Spanish-American War, and die in the sinking of the *Titanic*. *A Journey* was his sole work of fiction (Fallon 102). The hotel Astor built would later be frequented by Hugo Gernsback, who would try to impress prospective authors he was wooing by taking them there to eat (Ashley and Lowndes 131). Set in the year 2000, it is more concerned with terrestrial technology development and the exploration of the outer solar system, and as such will be more of a focus in chapter 10. Although the novel's spaceship, the *Callisto*, does not go to the moon—save for a brief flyby where its complete deadness, and absence of all air and water, is noted (Astor 125)—the cosmic voyage described by Astor has some relevant elements in it, including a cylindrical design of light metal and insulation from the cold with observational portholes (Astor 101–2); the motive force being "apergy," which allows for the *Callisto* to fly into space via electrically repelling the magnetic field of local matter (Astor 86–89); the ship's atmosphere being maintained from liquid oxygen reserves and carbon dioxide scrubbing (Astor 132); and a voyage with near-misses of both a comet and Mars' moon Phobos (Astor 139, 144–45). All these elements show up in Lovecraft's article a dozen years later, although it is worth pointing out that Astor probably drew his own inspiration from Verne, especially given that a key early element of *A Journey in Other Worlds* is to use geoengineering to reduce the axial tilt of the Earth to eliminate extreme weather (Astor 24–31). This had earlier been the plot of Verne's novel *The Purchase of the North Pole* (1889), a sequel to *From the Earth to the Moon* and *Around the Moon*.

Astor's novel has not left a major impact on science fiction, nor did Lovecraft seem to mention it explicitly. This is in contrast to Verne, whose technically oriented and well-researched writings have an obvious appeal to the young, astronomically minded Lovecraft. Verne's successor in the realm of science fiction, however, draws somewhat less from the tradition of hard science fiction—but even so, its influence can be found in Lovecraft's essay and later work, even outside its explicit mention. H. G. Wells, the British author of science fiction and socialist political speculation, published *The First Men in the Moon* in 1901. The novel is the story of two Englishmen—the businessman Bedford, who serves as the first-person narrator, and the scientist Cavor—who design a spherical space capsule powered by an antigravity material termed Cavorite, after its inventor (Wells, *FM* 37–46). The pair use it to fly to the moon, where they are captured by a civilization of insectoid aliens, the Selenites, ruled over by the Grand Lunar. Bedford escapes in the Cavorite capsule and returns to Earth, while Cavor remains behind. However, despite being stranded, Cavor manages to use a radio to transmit back reports of the Selenite civilization, culminating in apparent plans to invade the Earth.

The First Men in the Moon was the last of Wells's initial, and greatest, forays into science fiction writing, which had begun in earnest in 1895. All Wells's best-known works were published in that six-year period (Bergonzi 164). But despite *First Men* being part of Wells's initial output of fiction, its appearance at the end demonstrates that the author was seemingly reaching the limits of his creativity. Verne himself criticized *First Men*'s lack of scientific accuracy in comparison to *From the Earth to the Moon* (Bergonzi 157–58). Wells appears to have anticipated this criticism; Bedford mentions Verne's "*A Trip to the Moon*" [*sic*] but Cavor, "not a reader of fiction," does not get the reference, although he does note that the launching of the Cavorite ship would cause "no more disturbance than firing a big gun" (Wells, *FM* 28–29). Indeed, in crafting a novel around a lunar voyage, Wells lacked the originality of his earlier novels, as the trope had been used many times before, in contrast to topics like invisible men, time machines, and Martian invasions (Bergonzi 157). Indeed, this connection goes back to the start of the genre, the *True History* of second-century C.E. Roman satirist Lucian of Samosata, perhaps the first piece of fiction about a voyage to the moon (Brunner 94–95; Crowe 5). Several critics have noted that *First Men* appears to draw heavily from Lucian's work, not only in tone but with direct quotations and parallels (Bergonzi 157; Keen 105–20). Another reader of Lucian was Lovecraft, who by August 1922 had purchased a copy of the *True History* (*LL* 107). Steven J. Mariconda has proposed that a magic mirror owned by the king of the Moon in Lucian's tale was an influence on the Shining Trapezohedron from Lovecraft's "The Haunter of the Dark" (Mariconda 16). The Cavorite itself, and its use in a spherical vessel, is perhaps an indication of the influence of Bergerac, Godwin, and Baudoin on Wells (Lake 3–9).

A final, intriguing nod by Wells to both his predecessors and contemporaries in the lunar voyage genre comes from the late chapter where Bedford receives a communique that

> informed me that Mr. Julius Wendigee, a Dutch electrician, who has been experimenting with certain apparatus akin to the apparatus used by Mr. Tesla in America, in the hope of discovering some method of communication with Mars, was receiving day by day a curiously fragmentary message in English, which was indisputably emanating from Mr. Cavor in the moon. . . . The reader will no doubt recall the little excitement that began the century, arising out of an announcement by Mr. Nikola Tesla, the American electrical celebrity, that he had received a message from Mars. . . . Ever since 1898 [Wendigee] had devoted himself almost entirely to this subject. (Wells, *FM* 129–30)

In 1899, Nikola Tesla asserted that he had received radio messages from intelligent Martians, a claim Lovecraft knew of, and which will be discussed in further depth in chapter 9. In this passage, the dating of 1898 as the start of Wendigee's interest is perhaps an attempt by Wells to link it to the publication of *The War of the Worlds*. Similarly, the reception of messages from space by a Dutchman is perhaps a nod to the titular Dutchman of Poe's "Hans Pfaall." The transcribed messages received by Wendigee form the final part of the novel, Cavor's description of Selenite society. This segment presaged Wells's twentieth-century turn toward utopian and dystopian political speculation, far more than his meager description of Martian society in *The War of the Worlds* from three years earlier (Bergonzi 161–63; Lake 9–11; Rieder 74–75).

Lovecraft himself claimed in his essay "Some Notes on Interplanetary Fiction" (1934) that when it came to the titular genre, "Social and political satire are always undesirable, since such intellectual and ulterior objects detract from the story's power as a crystallisation of a mood" (*CE* 2.181). However, this seemingly did not stop him from reading Wells's novel as a youth; Lovecraft owned an original 1901 printing of the novel, the only complete version of a Wells novel he owned, rather than his nonfiction works or magazine reprints (*LL* 164–65). Lovecraft also owned reprints of *First Men,* from when it had been serialized in the December 1926–February 1927 issues of *Amazing Stories* (*LL* 24). But the novel's influence on young Lovecraft can be seen not only from his inclusion of Wells's name among the authors of speculative lunar voyages in "Can the Moon Be Reached by Man?" but from his inclusion of "some material impervious to gravity" as a potential method of reaching the moon, seemingly a reference to Wells's Cavorite. Similarly, two of Lovecraft's stories from 1921, "The Moon-Bog" and "The Other Gods," feature characters falling into the sky toward the moon as gravity is reversed (*CF* 1.264, 278; Hite 31).[13]

Perhaps the plot trope in those stories is a memory of Cavorite.[14] Indeed, that Lovecraft continued to hold Wells's work in high esteem can be seen from the fact that at the start of his 1934 essay, he even allows "that not more than a half-dozen of these things [space travel

---

13. Both of these stories show influence from the fantasy of Lord Dunsany. A fantastical role for the moon is also evident in two of HPL's commonplace book entries. Entry 51 proposes an "Enchanted garden where moon casts shadow of object or ghost invisible to the human eye" (*CE* 5.222) while entry 138 suggests "Someone or something cries in fright at sight of the rising moon, as if it were something strange" (*CE* 5.227).

14. In the conclusion to volume one of Alan Moore and Kevin O'Neill's comic *The League of Extraordinary Gentlemen,* Professor Moriarty dies when he grabs a Cavorite sphere and is whisked upwards into space, ultimately impacting the moon. Given Moore's reading of HPL, it is possible that this fate originated from the two HPL stories, with the explicit Cavorite connection coming full circle (Moore and O'Neill 143–44). It should also be noted that "The Other Gods" also includes the titular characters flying on "cloud-ships," perhaps influenced by Cyrano de Bergerac's attempts to reach the moon by harnessing the levitating qualities of clouds (*CF* 1.274; Bergerac 30–31).

fiction], including the novels of H. G. Wells, have even the slightest shadow of a claim to artistic seriousness or literary rank" (*CE* 2.178).[15]

Other Moon Voyages

Out of the young Lovecraft's short essay on potential travel to the moon, we have analyzed the works of the five authors he mentioned—Jean Baudoin, Edgar Allan Poe, Richard Adams Locke, Jules Verne, and H. G. Wells—as well as the mutual references they drew from, their connections to one another, how Lovecraft may have learned of them, and what he drew from them. But beyond the works of those authors and their own individual references, what other examples of lunar fiction might Lovecraft have been exposed to?

One speculative potential work, about a moon, is the serialized novel *The Brick Moon* (1869–70) by Edward Everett Hale (1822–1909), a Unitarian minister from Boston and grandnephew of Revolutionary War hero Nathan Hale, who served as Chaplain of the US Senate from 1903 until his death. The story involves the construction of the titular space station, accidentally launched into orbit with a crew onboard using a waterwheel, its designers rejecting the concept of a cannon launch to space (Scharmen 22–29). Science fiction author (and vice president of the H. G. Wells Society) Stephen Baxter has called *The Brick Moon* "probably the first fictional depiction of a manned space station" and the longest work about a satellite of any sort until Arthur C. Clarke's 1952 novel *Islands in the Sky* ("From" 297). While there is no direct evidence that Lovecraft read *The Brick Moon*, he certainly knew of Hale, not only due to his pedigree but from owning his 1903 book *New England History in Ballads* (*LL* 78). Baxter himself would also write a piece of Lovecraftian lunar fiction, his novelette "The Shadow over the Moon" (2018), which blends Lovecraftian horror with the *Apollo* moon landing hoax trope,[16] linking transient flashes of color observed in the lunar Aristarchus crater since the 1880s with the colour out of space taking over an underground settlement of the Great Race (Baxter, "Shadow" 199–200). The horror film *Apollo 18* (2011), directed by Gonzalo López-

---

15. However, HPL was unimpressed by R. H. Barlow's correspondence with Wells, arguing that it would only be of interest to write *like* Wells, not *to* Wells (*WBT* 411).

16. It is interesting that in the 1983 film *The Right Stuff*, *Apollo* astronaut Gus Grissom was played by actor Fred Ward, who would go on to play (an) H. P. Lovecraft in the 1991 film *Cast a Deadly Spell*.

Gallego, also connects both *Apollo* hoaxes and the equivalent "lost cosmonaut" Soviet urban legend with lunar Lovecraftian beings. Also in this vein is James S. Dorr's short story "Dark of the Moon" (2002), in which a Russian cosmonaut on an international moon mission experiences a colour out of space—alongside other objects, like Hans Pfaall's balloon and the Gun Club's projectile—during a landing that may or may not be a figment of her emotional turmoil (Dorr 200–205).

Another potential influence of lunar fiction on Lovecraft was *The Moon Maid* by Edgar Rice Burroughs. *The Moon Maid* depicts a decades-long war in which a US–UK alliance destroy the Soviet Union, before launching an expedition to the moon in 1967. There, the Anglo-American alliance wages a war against the similarly villainous Kalkar regime, which in turn invades and occupies the Earth. Compiled into book form in 1926, it had originally been published in three serialized segments in the *Argosy All-Story* magazine in 1923 and 1925. The young Lovecraft was an enthusiastic reader of Burroughs's earlier stories in the magazine (Callaghan 70–72), and his specific influences from Burroughs will be discussed in chapter 9.

A less hypothetical connection is the essay "The Last Judgment" (1927) by British biologist J. B. S. Haldane (1892–1964), which Lovecraft also owned (*LL* 414). Haldane's speculative essay is on the future evolution of humanity and ultimate destruction of the Earth, caused by the collision of the moon as its orbit decays and as narrated to schoolchildren on Venus (Haldane, "Judgment" 292–93). Critics have identified numerous sources of Haldane's inspiration, including six works of Wells, among them *First Men,* with the Selenites serving as a basis for Haldane's future humans (Adams 471). Of note as well in this regard is that Wells's development of the Selenites, as with the Martians, Eloi, and Morlocks, derived from his knowledge of Darwinian evolution as mediated through Thomas Henry Huxley, "Darwin's bulldog" under whom Wells studied biology from 1884 to 1887 at the Normal School of Science (Williamson 189–98). It was also through the works of Huxley that Lovecraft largely derived his knowledge of Darwinian evolution (*IAP* 322).

Another work of Wells that influenced the essay was *The War of the Worlds* (Adams 471). While that story will be explored in greater depth in chapter 9, for now it suffices to say that in it, the Martian invasion is carried out via ten massive cylindrical spacecraft, launched from Mars via immense cannons (Wells, *WW* 8–10, 13–14). In "The Last Judgment," the colonization of other planets is done via cylindrical spacecraft ten meters wide and fifty meters long, launched from kilometers-long cannons embedded into mountains, to help eliminate air resistance. These spacecraft are one-way vehicles only, with many that survive the launch being destroyed by meteors or on impact. After leaving the atmosphere, solar sails of one square kilometer in size are deployed to help navigate through space. Using these projectile craft, the first successful landings on the moon are not made until the year 8 million, when two vessels land intact. Their crews manage to map the far side and radio back their findings before expiring as their oxygen runs out. In the year 9.7 million, two expeditions reach Mars, only to be exterminated by the canal builders, who are blind to visible light but able to perceive their surroundings through some unknown sense. In the year 10.3 million, the first crews land on Venus, but die from the low oxygen content in its atmosphere (Haldane, "Judgment" 296–98). Only after a prolonged program of artificial selection is a population of several hundred thousand humans prepared to colonize Venus. In the year 25 million, a fleet of 1734 ships are launched to Venus; of those, eight land successfully, and from their crews come the Venusian survivors of humanity (Haldane, "Judgment" 301–5). In Haldane's future history of space exploration we not only see the influence of *The War of the Worlds* far more than *The First Men in the Moon,* but also Verne and his space cannon. We also see a possible reinforcement of the notion of winged navigation of space that originated from Lovecraft's reading of Burritt.

While Haldane's essay was inspired by the fiction of Wells, it served in turn as an inspiration for another piece of fiction, *Last and First Men* (1930) by British author Olaf Stapledon (1886–1950), himself also an aficionado of Wells (Adams 468–69). A sprawling history of the far future, the humans of *Last and First Men* are forced to emigrate to Venus due to a strange development in the moon's celestial mechanics, causing its orbit to start to decay and spiral toward the Earth (Stapledon 243–49). In reality, tidal forces are causing the moon to move slowly *away* from the Earth. It will reach a maximum distance in about 50 billion years, with a lunar orbit then taking 47 current days. At that time the moon and Earth would be tidally locked, with one Earth rotation also taking 47 days. From there, solar tides will cause the moon to move closer to Earth. However, before all that happens, the sun will have become first a red giant—engulfing Mercury and Venus, and potentially Earth and moon as well—and then a white dwarf.

Because its primary celestial concern is Venus, *Last and First Men* will be discussed in greater depth in chapter 7, but for now we can note that Lovecraft held both the novel and Stapledon in high regard (*CE* 2.182). Indeed, there is a sort of inverse influence from both Haldane and Stapledon evident in *At the Mountains of Madness*. The two British authors depict a collision of the moon into the Earth as a catalyst for the evolution of human into posthuman. In *At the Mountains of Madness*, the Elder Things arrive on Earth and eventually direct human evolution "not long after the matter forming the moon was wrenched from the neighbouring South Pacific" (*CF* 3.100). This reflected the contemporary theory—proposed in 1878 by Charles Darwin's astronomer son George, modified several years later by the geologist Osmond Fisher, and not conclusively disproven until the 1960s—that the depression of the Pacific Ocean was the 'scar' left by the early Earth's rapid rotation flinging its molten contents into space, where they coalesced into the moon (Haldane, "Judgment" 294; Brunner 126–29; Hite 28).

The last major author of lunar fiction who influenced Lovecraft was the aforementioned Garrett P. Serviss. Serviss was not a professional astronomer. Like Lowell, Serviss never earned a degree in the subject; unlike Lowell, he never worked in the field either. After graduating from Columbia Law School, Serviss instead worked as a journalist for sixteen years, writing for the same *New York Sun* newspaper that had published the Great Moon Hoax forty years earlier. But while not a professional astronomer, he was certainly an amateur astronomer, a writer on the subject (as well as occasional forays into science fiction), and one of the most prominent American popularizers of astronomy in the late nineteenth and early twentieth centuries. Lovecraft was a great admirer of Serviss; David Haden has written an overview of the author and his influence on Lovecraft (Haden, *LH4* 141–51). Lovecraft owned three of Serviss's nonfiction books, *Astronomy with an Opera-Glass* (1888), *Pleasures of the Telescope* (1901), and *Astronomy with the Naked Eye* (1908), and quotes from the last at the end of his 1919 story "Beyond the Wall of Sleep" (*LL* 139–40; *CF* 1.85; Lubnow, *LSS* 4–5). Even at the end of his life, Lovecraft still recommended those three books as good introductions to astronomy in his 1936 suggestions for reading (*CE* 2.194). In a 1914 letter, Lovecraft further claimed by that point to have read *every* published work of Serviss (Callaghan 72–73; Moskowitz 374)—which would presumably include Serviss's *Edison's Conquest of Mars* (1898), an unauthorized sequel to *The War of the Worlds*.

This work and whether Lovecraft read it will be further discussed in chapter 9, but for now it will be noted that in the novel, Thomas Edison is chosen to build a space fleet to launch a counterattack on Mars because he had already built a small vessel in which he had secretly launched an expedition to the moon (Serviss, *ECM* 7–9). Further, the description of the motive power of Edison's lunar spacecraft is notable:

> Now, what Mr. Edison had done was, in effect, to create an electrified particle which might be compared to one of the atoms composing the tail of a comet, although in reality it was a kind of car, of metal, weighing some hundreds of pounds and capable of bearing some thousands of pounds with it in its flight. By producing, with the aid of the electrical generator contained in this car, an enormous charge of electricity, Mr. Edison was able to counterbalance, and a trifle more than counterbalance, the attraction of the earth, and thus cause the car to fly off from the earth as an electrified pithball flies from the prime conductor. (Serviss, *ECM* 8)

This could potentially contribute to the use of electrical propulsion mentioned by Lovecraft in "Can the Moon Be Reached by Man?" and still kept in mind in "The Shadow out of Time," although it should be noted that Dodge's article also proposed it (Dodge 31–32). Livesey has also speculated on the Serviss connection for electrical propulsion, particularly given the similar phrasing to Serviss that Lovecraft used to describe the electric field's operation (Livesey, "Green" 93). Further, Edison's electric lunar ship consists of a "brilliantly lighted chamber that formed the interior of the car, and where stores of compressed air had been provided together with chemical apparatus, by means of which fresh supplies of oxygen and nitrogen might be obtained for our consumption during the flight through space" (Serviss, *ECM* 8), while after the invasion fleet's launch one of its ships is damaged by a meteor impact (Serviss, *ECM* 42–43)—both of these passages reflecting elements of the hypothetical lunar voyage described by Lovecraft in "Can the Moon Be Reached by Man?"

When Edison's invasion fleet passes by the moon on its way to Mars, the crew observes the

> ruins of what appeared to be an ancient watch tower. It was evidently composed of Cyclopean blocks larger than any that I had ever seen even among the ruins of Greece, Egypt and Asia Minor. Here, then, was visible proof that the moon had been inhabited, although probably it was not inhabited now. I cannot describe the exultant feeling which took

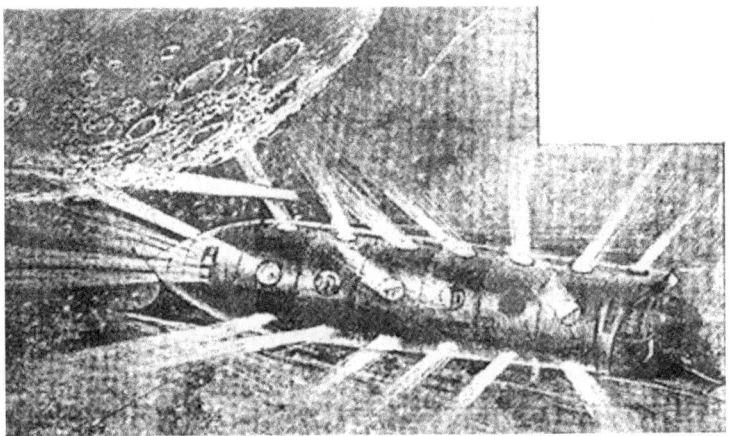

Edison's "Ship of Space" on its voyage to the Moon. (Public domain; Project Gutenberg)

possession of me at this discovery. It settled so much that learned men had been disputing about for centuries. (Serviss, *ECM* 45–48)

The passage is notable, not only for its reflection of the debates over intelligent inhabitants of the moon that interested both young Lovecraft and the astronomers and authors he drew from, but also for its use of the term "Cyclopean" in connection with the buildings of vanished ancient aliens—a key trope of the future Cthulhu Mythos, drawing to mind both R'lyeh and the Antarctic city of the Elder Things.

Whether Lovecraft did in fact read *Edison's Conquest of Mars* is not known for certain, though the above (as well as other details to be discussed in chapter 9) provide strong circumstantial evidence. Further, if Lovecraft had truly read the whole of Serviss's fiction by 1914, that would not necessarily have been the case in 1906. At the very least, Lovecraft did eventually know about *Edison's Conquest of Mars*, including it in a list of works that his friend H. Warner Munn was seeking to acquire (*CE* 5.262; *ES* 1.194). However, as Lovecraft compiled the list in 1929, it again is not necessarily evidence that Lovecraft knew of the story before this date.[17] That being said, one piece of Serviss's fiction that Lovecraft certainly did read was his novella *The Moon Metal* (1900), reprinted in the *All-Story* in May 1905. In his 1914 letter, Lovecraft

---

17. Thanks to Martin Andersson and Bobby Derie for information on the Munn list.

claimed to have read every issue of *All-Story* from its January 1905 debut, so he certainly would have read *The Moon Metal* (Callaghan 70). As it was reprinted in the July 1926 issue of *Amazing Stories,* Lovecraft may have read it again as an adult (*LL* 24).

The novella begins with an expedition to Antarctica discovering a vein of gold with enough worth to collapse the world economy. Into this crisis steps the mysterious Dr. Max Syx, who provides an alternative basis of currency in the form of a new metal, artemisium. David Haden has suggested that Syx, particularly a passage where he is compared to a devilfish keeping the world under his tentacles, may have influenced Cthulhu (Haden, *LH4* 149; Serviss, *TMM* 334). Over the course of the story it is revealed that Dr. Syx actually mines artemisium directly from the moon, through the use of a particle beam that can teleport the metal down to Earth. Gavin Callaghan has claimed that *The Moon Metal*'s apocalyptic imagery was an inspiration for Lovecraft's 1920 stories "Nyarlathotep" and "The Crawling Chaos" (Callaghan 73). Its opening with an expedition to Antarctica making a world-changing discovery is also a plot device with a clear echo in Lovecraft's later work. But there is also a hint of another Lovecraft story in the description of the effects of artemisium on Mr. Boon, president of the world financial congress:

> As he held the card up to get a better light upon it a stray sunbeam from the window fell across the metal and instantly it bloomed with exquisite colors! The president's chair being in the darker end of the room, the radiant card suffused the atmosphere about him with a faint rose tint, playing with surprising liveliness into alternate canary color and violet. The effect upon the company of clear-headed financiers was extremely remarkable. The unknown metal appeared to exercise a kind of mesmeric influence, its soft hues blending together in a chromatic harmony which captivated the sense of vision as the ears are charmed by a perfectly rendered song. (Serviss, *TMM* 324)

A mysterious cosmic element that produces undefinable colors and cognitive impacts—perhaps if President Boon had wanted to break Dr. Syx's monopoly on artemisium, he would not need to commission an electric lunar lander from Edison, but merely sponsor an expedition to the blasted heath nestled in the hills west of Arkham? As mentioned, if *The Moon Metal* was an inspiration for "The Colour out of Space," it would not be the first time that Lovecraft drew from Serviss in his fiction.

There is one final indirect connection between Serviss and Lovecraft. Serviss lived in New York City until his death in 1929, residing at

8 Middagh Street in Brooklyn Heights. In 1932, Lovecraft's friend Samuel Loveman moved into 17 Middagh Street, only a few hundred feet from the late author's home. In his letter to Barlow of 10 April 1934, an apparently oblivious Lovecraft stated his belief that Loveman and Serviss may have possibly been aware of each other "at the nodding stage" from passing by on the street (*OFF* 130). Needless to say, an encounter with Serviss on the streets of Brooklyn three years after his death would be extremely unlikely, but could make for an interesting sequel to "Cool Air" or "Herbert West—Reanimator."

While the works of Serviss complete the survey of printed lunar fiction, there remains one more type of fiction that may have influenced Lovecraft: the movies. Perhaps the earliest science fiction film was the French director Georges Méliès's *A Trip to the Moon* (1902), loosely based on an amalgam of the Verne and Wells novels (Brunner 208–9; Colavito, *Cult* 111). In 1919, a proper adaptation of Wells's *The First Men in the Moon* was released in Britain, but details about it are scant as copies of it no longer exist. More intriguing is the German film *Woman in the Moon* (1929), directed by Fritz Lang of *Metropolis* fame. *Woman in the Moon* is a depiction of an extremely realistic rocket voyage, courtesy of its technical advisor, Willy Ley, who worked with Wernher von Braun both before and after World War II. Among other things, the film pioneered the concept of a countdown before a rocket launch. The film does depict a habitable far side of the moon, but even this had an element of support from the same theory by Peter Andreas Hansen that inspired young Lovecraft (*IAP* 87). Finally, in 1936, the movie *Things to Come* was released, which featured a screenplay by H. G. Wells partially adapted from his 1933 novel *The Shape of Things to Come* (Adams 472). Both stories are post-apocalyptic, depicting the development of a utopia after a then-hypothetical World War II. However, in the film version the climax of the march to utopia is the first crewed mission to the moon—notably launched not by Cavorite, but by a Verne-type space cannon.

There is, sadly, no direct evidence that Lovecraft saw any of those films, but there are some tantalizing connections nonetheless. The most direct is Fritz Lang, who like Ley fled the rise of Hitler and resided in the United States from 1935 to 1957. Lang was an avid reader of science fiction and collected complete runs of, among other magazines, *Astounding* from 1933 to 1957 and *Weird Tales* from 1935 to 1957 (Gold 6–7). This meant that Lang would have read a sizeable portion of Lovecraft's fiction output,[18] including *At the Mountains of Madness* and "The Shadow out of Time" (*Astounding Stories*, 1936); "Out of the Aeons" (with Hazel Heald) and "Arthur Jermyn" (*Weird Tales*, 1935); "Dagon," "The Temple," "Pickman's Model," and "The Haunter of the Dark" (*Weird Tales*, 1936, with "Dagon" also reprinted in 1952); "The Thing on the Doorstep," "The Disinterment" (with Duane W. Rimel), "The Picture in the House," "The Horror in the Burying-Ground" (with Hazel Heald), "The Statement of Randolph Carter," "The Shunned House," "Hypnos," and "Polaris" (*Weird Tales*, 1937); "From Beyond," "The Diary of Alonzo Typer" (with William Lumley), "Beyond the Wall of Sleep," "The Doom That Came to Sarnath," "The Tree," "The Other Gods," and "The Nameless City" (*Weird Tales*, 1938); "Medusa's Coil" (with Zealia Bishop), "The Quest of Iranon," "The Evil Clergyman," "The Curse of Yig" (with Zealia Bishop), "Celephaïs," "Imprisoned with the Pharaohs" (with Harry Houdini), "Cool Air," and "In the Walls of Eryx" (with Kenneth Sterling) (*Weird Tales*, 1939); "The Mound" (with Zealia Bishop) (*Weird Tales*, 1940); *The Case of Charles Dexter Ward* (*Weird Tales*, 1941); "The Shadow over Innsmouth" (*Weird Tales*, 1942); and "Herbert West—Reanimator" (*Weird Tales*, 1942–43).[19] Of the core Lovecraft canon, all that Lang would have missed is "The Call of Cthulhu," "The Whisperer in Darkness," and *The Dream-Quest of Unknown Kadath*. For his part, Lovecraft saw Lang's film *Siegfried* (1924) in its 1925 New York City debut, writing that "it was an ecstasy & a delight to be remembered forever!" (*LFF* 388; McInnis 313–14; Haden, "Siegfried").

Of the moon movies, Lovecraft actually mentioned two. In a letter to Barlow, apparently in response to comments by Barlow on upcoming Wells adaptations, Lovecraft stated that he had not seen the 1919 *The First Men in the Moon* (10 December 1932; *OFF* 45). Mentioned several more times is *Things to Come*. In a letter to Lovecraft dated 24 June 1936, Catherine L. Moore mentioned seeing the film; she "was tremen-

---

18. In addition to the prose works listed here, the same range of *Weird Tales* contained twenty of HPL's poems, a number of works by others in the Lovecraft Circle, and several memorials to HPL in the 1937–38 range.

19. As far as can be discerned, the reading of HPL by Lang is an unexplored aspect of either the director's interest or the author's legacy, and could serve as a fruitful project for a future cinematic historian, particularly in regard to Lang's later films, *Ministry of Fear* (1944) and *The Thousand Eyes of Dr. Mabuse* (1960).

dously impressed" with its depiction of futuristic aircraft, warfare, architecture, and clothing (*CLM* 135–36). Lovecraft wrote to Robert Bloch in late June 1936 that he was hoping to see it and had heard good things about it (*RB* 172). But in a letter to Duane W. Rimel dated 30 December 1936, Lovecraft mentioned that he had missed the film when it was shown in Providence in June, that he was envious of Rimel having seen it, and that his hopes that it would soon return to Providence for a second run had not yet materialized (*FLB* 340). In a letter to Willis Conover, Lovecraft stated that he still had not seen it, making it unlikely that he would do so before his death two months later (10 January 1937; *RB* 410). *Things to Come*'s director was William Cameron Menzies, who would go on to direct the *Invaders from Mars* (1953). Skeptic Jason Colavito argued that scenes from that film combined with the legacy of Lovecraft's fiction to create a foundation for the modern myth of UFOs and alien abductions (Colavito, *Cult* 123). A more concrete admirer of *Things to Come* was Arthur C. Clarke, who used it as one of the inspirations for *2001: A Space Odyssey* (Clarke, *Lost* 35)—a work that has some clear Lovecraft influences of its own, particularly *At the Mountains of Madness*, as will be discussed in chapter 10. Indeed, Chuck Hoffman has suggested that rather than Antarctica, an *At the Mountains of Madness* film adaptation would best be set on the moon (Price, "Episode 20").

Meanwhile, as of 2020, there was a remake of Méliès's *A Trip to the Moon* in pre-production, although as of 2022 it appears to be abandoned. Intriguingly, both Méliès and Lovecraft were listed as co-writers ("Trip to the Moon"). This seems to indicate that the planned adaptation would have incorporated some element of Lovecraft into the original's use of Verne and Wells. As late as his letter to Richard F. Searight of 10 September 1933, Lovecraft argued that when it came to science fiction, "Verne & Wells really worked the vein out, leaving little save colourless imitation for others" (*EHP* 289). Given those sentiments, Lovecraft would have to be pleased to be associated with their company in the prospective *A Trip to the Moon* remake.

Conclusion

In a letter to Rimel dated 22 December 1934, Lovecraft declared that "No one can appreciate interplanetary fiction without a smattering of astronomical knowledge. I missed a good deal through reading Verne *before* I studied astronomy in 1902 & thereafter" (*FLB* 246). Through this statement, we can see something of the dialectical view Lovecraft had toward astronomy and science fiction, that the former not only aided in the appreciation of the latter, but the best examples of the latter (as Lovecraft considered Verne to be) should also be built upon the former. It is this fiction/nonfiction feedback loop that this chapter has sought to illuminate.

In his 1975 memoir of Lovecraft, Frank Belknap Long speculated that if Lovecraft had lived into the 1970s, two of the world developments that would have "seemed unbelievable" to him would have been "the launching of the first earth satellite [and] the moon landing" (Long 86–87). As we have seen, neither was particularly unbelievable to Lovecraft in theory, but the timing would have been. Lovecraft ended his article "Can the Moon Be Reached by Man?" by stating that "it is not probable that, within the lifetime of anyone who now reads these pages, a journey to the moon, or any more distant orb, will be either thought of or attempted" (*CE* 3.32). This was obviously a severely pessimistic view, given that many of Lovecraft's own associates lived beyond not just *Apollo 11* but the conclusion of the *Apollo* program itself. His widow Sonia died at age eighty-nine in 1972, exactly one week after the return of the final lunar mission, *Apollo 17*. Indeed, Lovecraft himself would have been only seventy-eight at the time Neil Armstrong and Buzz Aldrin walked on the Sea of Tranquility, not an impossible age by any means. Perhaps appropriately, Peter Cannon ended his alternate history novel *The Lovecraft Chronicles* (2004) with a seventy-year-old Lovecraft happy at the election of John F. Kennedy in 1960, the president who would go on to initiate the *Apollo* program (162). It is apt that, given the fictional inspirations in Lovecraft's 1906 article on travel to the moon, it was a fictional Lovecraft who would live to see the dawn of the lunar era in 1960.

Chapter 6
Stop the Presses—Venus in the West!

Okay, there won't really be any "stop the presses" moments in this chapter. In fact, some of the columns on astronomy that Lovecraft wrote for newspapers may strike readers—at least those who are not dyed-in-the-wool astronomy enthusiasts—as being a little on the dull side. They nonetheless have their interesting points and illuminate Lovecraft's beginnings as a writer for the public. Through these columns we also get a glimpse of an alternative Lovecraft, one whose writing centered on science journalism rather than weird fiction.

Before radio and television, and long before the Internet, came the heyday of the newspaper. Several dailies battled for sales in Providence as the twentieth century dawned. In 1906, when Lovecraft's newspaper columns began, the *Providence Journal* was, as it still is, the largest newspaper in the Rhode Island capital, then a growing city of some 200,000 inhabitants, holding almost half the population of the state.

Lovecraft's start in newsprint was hardly impressive, consisting of slightly embarrassing excerpts from a letter he wrote in connection with his entry for a 1905 weather forecasting contest (Bleiler; Whyte). Not until the following year did items he clearly intended for publication see print. Lovecraft's letter critical of an astrologer was published in the 3 June 1906 issue of the *Providence Sunday Journal* (*CE* 3.16; see "Lovecraft against Charlatanry" below). Soon thereafter, his letter of 16 July 1906 to the *Scientific American* was published in its 25 August issue, encouraging observatories to cooperate in the photographic search for a trans-Neptunian planet (*CE* 3.16).[1] Two weeks after this letter was written, astronomy columns carrying Lovecraft's byline began to appear in two Rhode Island newspapers.

---

1. Both the 1893 and 1903 editions of Young's *Lessons in Astronomy*, the book that introduced HPL to modern astronomy, noted that photographic surveys might soon discover a planet beyond Neptune, if one existed.

The Providence *Tribune* and *Pawtuxet Valley Gleaner*

Lovecraft's astronomy articles would not appear in the *Providence Journal*, the city's largest circulation newspaper. The *Journal*[2] already published a monthly astronomy column written by Winslow Upton, director of Brown University's Ladd Observatory and key to Lovecraft's access to that facility (see chapter 2). Lovecraft's articles appeared instead in newspapers of lesser circulation. The first of these initially monthly, but soon-to-be-weekly, articles appeared in the *Pawtuxet Valley Gleaner* for 27 July 1906. Almost simultaneously, he began a monthly astronomy column in the Providence *Tribune*, commencing with the 1 August 1906 issue.

Lovecraft's astronomy articles saw print as he recovered from a near-breakdown that had forced him to withdraw from high school in November 1905. He did not return to school until September 1906, when the next school year began (*IAP* 100–101), just weeks after his astronomy columns began to appear. As his birthday was not until 20 August, Lovecraft became the astronomy writer for two newspapers when he was a precocious fifteen years old. It was an impressive start. It is understandable that a newspaper might want astronomy columns by someone of Professor Upton's stature, someone who had clear credentials as an astronomer. It is also understandable that a teenage Lovecraft might seek to emulate the Ladd Observatory director. But why would a newspaper editor want an astronomy column written by a fifteen-year-old high school student?

The *Pawtuxet Valley Gleaner* was a weekly paper, published in Phenix, Rhode Island. Subtitled "And the New England Summer and Winter Resort Register and Hotel Guide," the *Gleaner* was obviously not intended to compete directly with metropolitan Providence dailies. Politically, the *Gleaner* promoted the Lincoln Party, a short-lived political party that claimed to fight corruption. Although grandfather Whipple Phillips had died in 1904, Lovecraft attributed his own appearance in the *Gleaner* to the lingering esteem accorded the Phillips name in the area of Rhode Island from which the *Gleaner* originated: "the Gleaner was more than willing to print & feature anything from Whipple V. Phillips' grandson" (*IAP* 121). Nonetheless, exactly how the connection was made between young Lovecraft and then editor J. Davis Hall is apparently unknown. Hall may have welcomed the new contributor as,

---

2. At this time officially named the *Providence Daily Journal*, except on Sundays.

6. Stop the Presses—Venus in the West! 149

aside from advertisements, much of the *Gleaner* was taken up by items such as a list of new laws, accounts of sermons, and a discussion of hickory nuts. Lovecraft's articles on voyages to the moon and life on Mars were certainly not dull compared to such material, and his column would continue to appear in the *Gleaner* for two years, until the newspaper folded.

By contrast, the second newspaper to which Lovecraft contributed, the Providence *Evening Tribune,* was a daily paper competing in the Providence market. From 1906 to 1908, the *Evening Tribune* was joined by morning and Sunday editions, and Lovecraft's columns would sometimes appear in the morning as well as the evening. How Lovecraft became the *Tribune*'s monthly astronomy columnist is a bit of a mystery, but there are a few clues. The *Evening Tribune* was in a sense a new newspaper, having begun publication in March 1906 as the *Tribune and Telegram* when those two newspapers merged. Faig (*Lovecraftian Voyages* 98) suspected that Professor Upton might have had something to do with Lovecraft becoming the *Tribune*'s astronomy columnist. That remains conjecture, but the idea gains support from the circumstance that the new editor of the *Tribune,* Frederick H. Howland, had previously been manager of the *Providence Journal,* the newspaper that ran Upton's

Lovecraft announced his new astronomy column in the July 1906 issue of the *Rhode Island Journal of Astronomy*. The *Evening Tribune* soon dropped the *Telegram* part of its name.

astronomy column. In that position, Howland may have met Upton, leading him to seek his advice regarding an astronomy columnist for the new newspaper. Were Upton aware of Lovecraft's hectographed astronomy publications, his young acquaintance might have come to mind. Upton may even have encouraged Lovecraft to accept the *Tribune* position. Lovecraft makes no mention of being paid for his newspaper columns, and the opportunity to obtain an astronomy column for free, or for a slight payment, may have been a lure for the *Tribune*'s editor. In whatever way the editors of the *Gleaner* and *Tribune* learned of Providence's teenage astronomy enthusiast, Lovecraft willingly stepped into the role of newspaper writer—at a time when he had not given up hope of a professional career in astronomy.

Lovecraft's articles in the *Pawtuxet Valley Gleaner* (available in *CE* 3.22–44, and in Google newspapers) started off with straightforward introductions to the sky for August and September 1906. After that, however, Lovecraft's articles became weekly and ranged more widely in subject. For example, the topic of his column in the 7 September 1906 issue was "Is Mars an Inhabited World?" Subsequent issues took up the question of life on the moon, the occultation of a star by the moon, and whether man can reach the moon, among other subjects (see also chapters 4 and 5). Clearly, in his *Gleaner* articles Lovecraft was not content just to describe what was visible in the night sky; he wanted to educate the public on what he considered to be interesting aspects of astronomy. When Lovecraft's *Gleaner* articles began, he was still producing the hectographed *Rhode Island Journal of Astronomy* (chapter 1), and it is not surprising that there is overlap between the contents of the two, with Lovecraft sometimes drawing upon issues of the *Journal* for material to use in the *Gleaner*.

Years later, Lovecraft disparaged his *Gleaner* articles. In a 1933 letter to the young Robert Bloch (*RB* 88), he remarked that he dumped reams of "callow scientific prose" on the rural weekly. Lovecraft the mature writer undoubtedly could have improved upon the output of his teenage self. Nonetheless, he was being hard on himself. Young Lovecraft's articles stand comparison to many similar products turned out in the heyday of newspapers.

It is not clear when Lovecraft's final article in the *Pawtuxet Valley Gleaner* appeared. Issues of the newspaper after 1906 are not known to exist, but apparently the *Gleaner* continued publication after that year. Lovecraft wrote that his articles continued until 1908 (*RK* 73) when the

6. Stop the Presses–Venus in the West!   151

Gleaner ceased publication. Faig (*Lovecraftian Voyages* 96) wondered whether Lovecraft's memory failed him on that point. However, Joshi (*IAP* 121) has found evidence that the *Gleaner* did continue after 1906 and is inclined to accept Lovecraft's statement.

Lovecraft's articles in the *Tribune* were more restrained than those in the *Gleaner*, consisting of straightforward descriptions of monthly sky phenomena (*CE* 3.44–84). In this, he followed Upton's approach to his own monthly astronomy articles, and we do not see the imaginative subjects that livened Lovecraft's articles in the *Pawtuxet Valley Gleaner*. If a reader wished to be apprised of the date of the full moon or wondered what that bright star was before dawn, then Lovecraft's column in the *Tribune* was just the thing to satisfy the reader's curiosity. While his *Tribune* columns provided pertinent information to stargazers of the time, today's reader is unlikely to be thrilled to learn that Mars could be seen mornings in March 1907. Today's reader might, however, take passing interest in the column's star charts in Lovecraft's hand. His *Tribune* column ceased to appear following his description of the sky for June 1908. Frederick H. Howland, editor of the *Tribune* when Lovecraft began his column, had left that post in the summer of 1907, to be succeeded by associate editor Frederic Luther. Whether that change had anything to do with the termination of Lovecraft's series in the following year is unknown. In any case, as the summer of 1908 arrived, Lovecraft suffered the most serious breakdown of his life (see chapter 1).

With both his *Journal* and *Gleaner* columns concluded or concluding, Lovecraft withdrew from most social interactions. There would be a lapse of almost six years before Lovecraft's byline appeared again over a newspaper column. In *I Am Providence,* Joshi wrote that it is only for

> **THE HEAVENS FOR AUGUST**
>
> **Celestial Phenomena to Happen Next Month.**
>
> WRITTEN FOR THE GLEANER.
>
> Venus is, without doubt, the chief planet for August, shining each night in the west with unrivalled brilliancy. In the telescope it appears gubbous, like the moon a few days from full. Next in order of interest comes Saturn, which rises about 7.30. Its rings, which make it so attractive, are becoming less and less visible, so that in a small telescope, they appear simply as a band of light. Saturn will be nearest the earth September four.

The opening paragraph of Lovecraft's first article in the *Pawtuxet Valley Gleaner* for 27 July 1906.

the 1908–13 interval that we find ourselves ignorant of Lovecraft's day-to-day activities.

The Providence *Evening News* and the *Asheville Gazette-News*

By 1913, Lovecraft was beginning to re-engage with the world around him. He was now in his twenties. The days of high school and precocity were behind him, as were dreams of attending Brown University to pursue a career in astronomy. The issue of 1 January 1914 saw the return of Lovecraft's byline as his first astronomy article appeared in the Providence *Evening News*, inaugurating a monthly series that would continue until May 1918 (*CE* 3.100–260). It would be his longest-lasting column. As Joshi noted (*CE* 3.10), these newspaper articles also represent a milestone in Lovecraft's emergence from the isolation that marked so much of his life after 1908.

Lovecraft was once again contributing to what he called one of the "lesser Providence newspapers." Exactly how he secured his position with the *Evening News* is unclear. He did, however, have one advantage that he did not have in 1906. In 1914, Lovecraft could present an editor with columns from the *Tribune* and the *Pawtuxet Valley Gleaner* as evidence of competence in astronomy and in writing. Joshi believes that Lovecraft was paid for these articles, although any pay was likely to have been small, perhaps

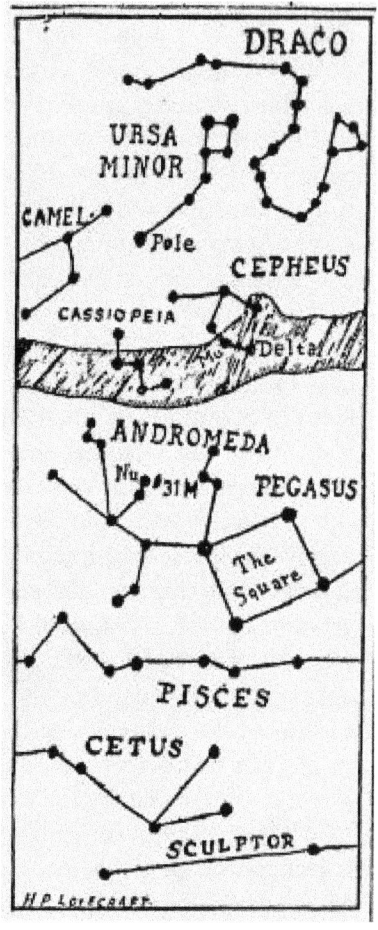

Lovecraft's illustration for his article in the Providence *Evening Tribune* of 1 November 1907. The shaded area represents part of the Milky Way. 31M stands for Messier 31, a catalogue designation of the Andromeda Nebula, now but not then known to be a galaxy separate from our own.

insignificant (*IAP* 182–83). Given the already serious decline in family wherewithal, and despite Lovecraft's principle of not writing for money alone, the prospect of adding even a few dollars to the family coffers may have provided at least a small impetus to resume astronomy writing.

As with his *Tribune* columns, the articles in the *Evening News* focused on the appearance of the heavens each month. However, they soon grew to be more far-reaching in scope, though they lacked the *Tribune*'s occasional star chart. Elements of astronomical history and mythology appeared after the first few articles. Lovecraft sometimes drew upon personal experience or recent events to increase the appeal of his columns. In the column "March Skies" (published 27 February 1915), he noted a lecture recently given at the Providence YMCA by astronomer William Brooks, which it seems likely that Lovecraft attended. "One of the rarest treats yet afforded local lovers of astronomy was the able and beautifully illustrated lecture on the heavens given by Prof. Brooks" (*CE* 3.142). Brooks, a famous discoverer of comets, had advanced the (now long-disproved) idea that the fifth moon of Jupiter was a portion of a comet captured by the giant planet in 1886. Lovecraft was rightly skeptical of the idea, but the "startling" theory did enliven the column. His 31 October 1916 column noted an exhibition of Lowell Observatory photographs at the Roger Williams Park Museum. Following Percival Lowell's death on 12 November 1916, Lovecraft devoted a substantial part of his 1 December column to Lowell's commemoration.[3] The column would occasionally reflect Lovecraft's growing involvement in amateur journalism. He twice calls the attention of his readers to Leo Fritter's essay "The Spiritual Significance of the Stars." Fritter was an amateur journalist from Ohio, known to Lovecraft (*CE* 3.139–40). Excerpts from poems (including some of Lovecraft's own, but without attribution) also made their way into the *Evening News* articles.

At the conclusion of his *Evening News* article for 2 October 1917, Lovecraft paints a vivid picture of the distant future. Contemplating a remote time when stars and nebulae have ceased to produce significant light, he imagines a "vast sepulchral universe of unbroken midnight gloom and perpetual arctic frigidity, through which will roll dark, cold suns with their hordes of dead, frozen planets, on which will lie the dust

---

3. HPL's 1917 poetical elegy to Percival Lowell (*AT* 122) is not, however, regarded as one of his better efforts. See, for example, *Tentaclii*, 26 March 2021.

of those unhappy mortals who will have perished as their dominant stars faded from the skies" (*CE* 3.238). One is reminded of Lovecraft's poem "Nemesis," in which "black planets roll without aim," written soon after this newspaper article (in the "sinister small hours of the black morning after Hallowe'en") and first published in the June 1918 issue of the *Vagrant* (*AT* 46–48). Although our ideas of stellar evolution are very different from those of 1917, science still pictures a cold and gloomy far future.

The immensity of time and space had come to impress Lovecraft deeply by the time he wrote for the *Evening News*. In his column for May 1917 (*CE* 3.222), Lovecraft wrote that "the consideration of boundless time and space is indeed the most thought-provoking feature of astronomical science. Humanity with its pompous pretentions sinks to complete nothingness when viewed in relation to the unfathomed abysses of infinity and eternity which yawn about it." The notion of a universe beyond human comprehension, and in comparison to which humanity is insignificant, would become a theme of Lovecraft's weird fiction (see also Livesey DPO 24).

Lovecraft wrote that his *Evening News* column came to an end when the editor asked him to simplify its language (*CE* 3.11). He had already attempted to explain some common astronomical terms in his March 1917 column, perhaps in response to complaints by his readers or the editor. However, little changed thereafter in the level of Lovecraft's articles. Among the topics that appeared in the final entries of the series was the determination of distances to stars using stellar parallax, not a trivial notion to readers unversed in the idea. Things seem to have come to a head when the *Evening News* was sold. Its new owners took charge on 27 April 1918, and the name of the newspaper would be changed to the *Providence News*. Lovecraft apparently objected to anything that might have seemed to be a dumbing-down of his column. He wrote that the "late *Evening News* was not a newspaper—it was a joke. And I am not much interested in its successor, since the request of its editor for me to make my articles 'so simple that a child might understand them' caused me to withdraw from the field" (letter to Alfred Galpin, 27 May 1918; *AG* 187). Lovecraft's last article appeared in the edition for 2 May. Perhaps by this time, he was also growing bored with the necessarily repetitive nature of much of that series.[4]

---

4. HPL thought well enough of the *Evening News* in late 1917 to write the poem "Lines on the 25th. Anniversary of the *Providence Evening News*,

6. Stop the Presses—Venus in the West!

Lovecraft's fourth series of astronomy articles differs from the others in that it was published in a newspaper located far from Providence. The *Asheville Gazette-News* was a North Carolina paper published daily except Sundays. Boyhood friend Chester Pierce Munroe had moved to Asheville and forms a probable link between Lovecraft and that city (*CE* 3.11). His columns appeared there, usually twice a week, from 16 February 1915 until 17 May 1915 (*CE* 3.273–317), and the series was intended to have fourteen parts. However, the column ended abruptly with what appears to be a second section of the thirteenth part. The "to be continued" promise at the end of the column for 17 May does not appear to have been made good, so that all fourteen parts did not appear.[5] Lovecraft may have received some payment for his series in the *Gazette-News*, which would certainly have been welcome, but any recompense was surely modest.

Mysteries of the Heavens Revealed By Astronomy In XIV Parts. By H. P. Lovecraft.

The heading to Lovecraft's article in the 16 February 1915 issue of the *Asheville Gazette-News*.

Lovecraft's articles in the *Asheville Gazette-News* did not concentrate on the current appearance of the heavens, but attempted to provide readers with a non-mathematical introduction to astronomy. Among their topics are such fundamental subjects as constellations, the nebular hypothesis, and the rings of Saturn. Publishing under the general heading, "Mysteries of the Heavens Revealed by Astronomy," Lovecraft hoped not only

---

1892–1917" (*AT* 124–25), although Joshi regards its sentiments as hypocritical (*IAP* 196).

5. Joshi (*CE* 3.11) speculates that the conclusion of HPL's series might have been printed in missing issues of the *Gazette-News*. However, issues apparently missing when Joshi did his search but now available contain no columns by HPL.

to educate readers about astronomy but also to destroy belief in the "pernicious and contemptible superstition" of astrology (*CE* 3.273). He may have been displeased when he discovered that the *Gazette-News* also ran a horoscope column ("the stars incline but do not compel"), which proved longer-lasting than his own edifying series.

Lovecraft's *Gazette-News* columns reflect the prevailing scientific views of the day. The column for 13 April 1915 devoted but a single paragraph to the "structure of the universe." When writing of that structure, Lovecraft regarded our own Milky Way galaxy as the entire universe. The Milky Way he described was the flattened star system outlined by William Herschel a century before. By the time he wrote this article, Harlow Shapley had begun his studies of globular star clusters. Within a few years he would overthrow the picture of the galaxy presented by Herschel and his successors, although another decade would pass before the existence of galaxies other than our own was established (see, for example, *The Expanding Universe* by Robert Smith). Nonetheless, the universe described by Lovecraft was already immense. In the 23 March 1915 column, he suggests that the vast distances of the stars might help humanity realize its own insignificance. "To what mean and ridiculous proportions is thus reduced our tiny globe, with its vain, pompous inhabitants and arrogant, quarrelsome nations!" Quarrelsome indeed, as World War I was then raging, although the United States was not yet a combatant.

Lovecraft had by this time become more skeptical of the claims of life on other worlds by astronomers William Pickering (chapter 4) and Percival Lowell. When he discussed Mars in the *Gazette-News* for 9 March 1915 (*CE* 3.291–94), Lovecraft outlined Percival Lowell's hypothesis that canals built by intelligent beings stretched across the deserts of Mars. Lovecraft went on to call Lowell's ideas baseless speculation. It was not the first time that he had used those words in connection with Mars. He had used them before in the *Pawtuxet Valley Gleaner* for 7 September 1906. However, in 1906, Lovecraft had also thought Lowell's ideas "not only possible, but even probable." In 1915, Lovecraft stated that, while some form of life might exist upon Mars, he left it to his readers or the "ingenious novelist" to imagine the nature of that life (see chapter 9).

A Newspaper Series That Never Was

There might have been yet one more series of astronomy articles, a series that never was because of Lovecraft's untimely death in March

1937. In his correspondence, Lovecraft noted[6] that Charles B. Johnston had asked him to write a series of elementary astronomy articles for a local newspaper, presumably in DeLand, Florida, where Johnston was connected in some fashion with Stetson University and its astronomy club. Lovecraft had visited DeLand on his trips south to see R. H. Barlow, and had met Johnston when he was a hired hand for the Barlows (*IAP* 883).

Lovecraft began preparations for the new series, which sounds as though it might have been an updated version of the *Gazette-News* columns. However, when he reread his old articles, he found that "their obsoleteness bowled me over." He realized how much astronomy had advanced during the past few decades and concluded that "I'd have to do a helluva lot of brushing up" before he could write the new series. To that end, he began a reading program, using astronomy books from the public library (see chapter 12).

Astronomy had indeed progressed since Lovecraft concluded his columns in 1918. As his *Evening News* series ended, Harlow Shapley was revolutionizing the conception of our own galaxy. A few years later, Edwin Hubble used Henrietta Leavitt's Cepheid period-luminosity relation to demonstrate that our galaxy was only one of many great star systems. As the 1920s drew to a close, Hubble and George Lemaître discovered the expansion of the universe. Meanwhile, Cecilia Payne, Henry Norris Russell, and others began to decipher the relative abundances of the chemical elements in the stars. Pluto, initially designated a ninth planet of the solar system, was photographically discovered by the Lowell Observatory's Clyde Tombaugh in 1930 (chapter 10). None of these discoveries would matter if the proposed column content were merely to describe the appearance of the night sky, but they would be essential to anything more ambitious. There can be no doubt that, had Lovecraft been willing and able to write a new introduction to astronomy in 1937, he would have had to do much more than recycle earlier articles from the *Gazette-News*. Unless he was expecting to be paid for this labor—and toward the end of his life even a small recompense might have been warmly received—he would have found researching the new columns a time-consuming chore. The task would, however, have been lightened by Lovecraft's enduring personal interest in astronomy.

Thomas Schwaiger (*Lovecraftian Proceedings No. 4* 128–29) proposed

---

6. Unfinished letter to James F. Morton, found after HPL's death (*JFM* 392–93), and letter to August Derleth (17 February 1937; *ES* 768).

that an undated, typed letter to Lovecraft attributed to R. H. Barlow (online through the Brown Digital Repository) may actually have come from Charles Johnston. Schwaiger's arguments on this point seem strong, and the letter appears to be in reply to one from Lovecraft that must have told of his illness and his inability to complete the requested series. Johnston (if he is indeed the author of the letter) had lined up Charles Greeley Abbott, a well-known astrophysicist and secretary of the Smithsonian Institution, as well as teachers at Stetson University to replace Lovecraft as author. Johnston noted that he had picked a "worthy successor," but, if the letter was mailed near the time of his death, Lovecraft may never have seen the implied compliment.

Lovecraft against Charlatanry

Before concluding, we need to examine one more aspect of Lovecraft's newspaper writing—his letters to the editor (also included in *CE* 3). Those letters are particularly revealing of his opinion of pseudoscience, and of his willingness to combat it. We have already mentioned his letter in the 3 June 1906 issue of the Providence *Sunday Journal*. In it, Lovecraft calls attention to a letter promoting astrology in the 27 May issue. The astrologer noted a coming transit of the sun by Mars. After scoffing at the pseudoscientific nature of astrology, Lovecraft explains that, as it is farther from the sun than Earth, Mars can never be seen in transit between the Earth and the sun—although Mars would be in conjunction on the far side of the sun in July. The point is well taken, although astrologers do not always use the term transit in the same way as astronomers, and the alignment of Mars and the sun in apparent position can suffice for an astrological transit. Fifteen-year-old Lovecraft had already taken a stance against astrology, and the opposition to pseudoscience and fallacy expressed in this first letter would be a continuing theme.

As Christmas 1909 approached, news of a (hoax) airship swept across New England (see Whalen and Bartholomew; Smith *Willimantic Skies* 79–103). By that time, Lovecraft's first newspaper columns had ended, and he had suffered the breakdown of 1908. His subsequent withdrawal into isolation, though severe, was not total. One window into his life as 1909 drew to a close is provided by a letter published in the *Providence Sunday Journal* for 26 December (*CE* 3.99–100). Lovecraft recounted how, on Christmas Eve, he came upon excited groups of people who stood amazed by what they believed to be the searchlight of a mysterious airship. Lovecraft pointed out to one such group that

6. Stop the Presses—Venus in the West! 159

what they were seeing was not an airship, but the planet Venus, brilliant in the southwest after sunset. He comments in dismay that "The general ignorance of the public as regards the science of astronomy has often been noted and deplored." He believes that those who followed Professor Winslow's monthly astronomy column in the *Journal* would not be likely to fall into such an obvious mistake. Lovecraft would later recall this event in one of his regular *Evening News* articles (1 September 1914) and in one of his articles for the *Asheville Gazette-News* (27 February 1915). We will touch upon the airship hoax again in chapter 7.

Perhaps the most entertaining of Lovecraft's letters to the editor are the exchange in 1914 in the *Evening News* between Lovecraft and astrologer Joachim F. Hartmann (*CE* 3.334–48), which has been extensively discussed by Joshi (*IAP* 183–88). Lovecraft was not pleased when he discovered the astrologer's 4 September 1914 article, in which Hartmann discussed astrological predictions relating to the new war in Europe. Nor was he amused by Hartmann's opening sentence: "The vulgar prejudice against the noble science of astrology by otherwise learned men is greatly to be deplored." Lovecraft's reply appeared in the *Evening News* for 9 September (*CE* 3.262–64). The resultant back and forth contin-

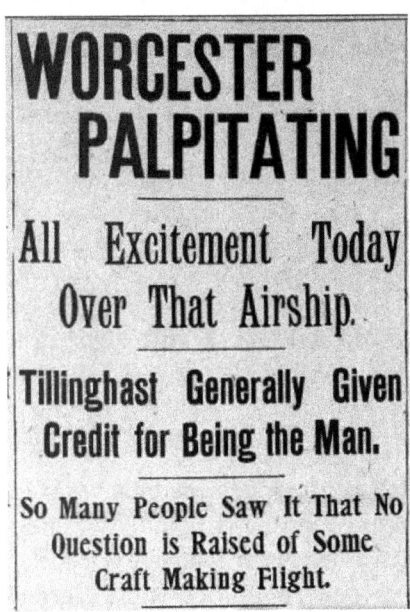

As Christmas approached in 1909, New Englanders scanned the skies for Wallace E. Tillinghast's airship. These headlines from the evening edition of the *Boston Globe* for 23 December illustrate the excitement. The next evening, Lovecraft was dismayed as residents of Providence mistook Venus for the mysterious airship.

ued in that newspaper until December. Lovecraft gave his version in a letter to Maurice Moe, penned before the final letters between the two appeared in the *Evening News*:

Recently a quack named Hartmann, a devotee of the pseudo-science of Astrology, commenced to disseminate the usual pernicious fallacies of that occult art through the columns of *The News,* so that in the interest of true Astronomy I was forced into a campaign of invective and satire. I began seriously, with "Science versus Charlatanry", which I followed up with "The Falsity of Astrology", but eventually the stupid persistence of the modern Nostradamus forced me to adopt ridicule as my weapon. I thereupon went back to my beloved age of Queen Anne for a precedent, and decided to emulate Dean Swift's famous attacks on the astrologer Partridge, conducted under the nom de plume of Isaac Bickerstaffe (or Bickerstaff—I have seen it spelled both ways). Accordingly I published a satirical article wherein I gave with an air of solemn gravity the most nonsensical collection of wild prophecies that my brain could conceive; the whole entitled "Astrology and the Future", and signed "Isaac Bickerstaffe, Jr." I there "predicted" the end of the world by an explosion of internal gases in the year 4954. Hartmann scarce knew whether or not to take me seriously, and kept up his mountebank performances, so I prepared another Bickerstaffe paper whose ridicule should become more open toward the end. In this final effort, "Delavan's Comet and Astrology", I explained how the human race shall be preserved after the destruction of the earth, by transportation to the planet Venus! Even the obtuse intellect of the charlatan must have discovered the sarcastic nature of this ponderous prophecy, for he has now quietly ceased to inflict his false notions on a gullible public. (8 December 1914; *MWM* 38)

Lovecraft had the final word in the exchange. His penultimate contribution on 17 December was published under his own name and took a reasoned approach to the debate. However, he returned to satire in his final letter, published on 21 December 1914 under the Isaac Bickerstaff, Jr. pseudonym. Faux astrologer Bickerstaffe began his letter with a parody of the opening of Hartmann's first letter: "Seasoned though I am to the heartless attacks of the vulgar scientific public, I was cut to the quick by the recent insinuations concerning me, made by my fellow-astrologer, Prof. J. F. Hartmann." Lovecraft's letter contains a series of ridiculously obvious predictions, supposedly derived through astrology. That "several men will die either in Belgium, France, or Prussia" was a pretty good bet during World War I, as were "ill-feelings between Austrians and Serbians."

The closing of the exchange with Hartmann was not the last time that Lovecraft's contempt for astrology would be on display. As noted above, opposing astrology was one of the expressed goals of his astronomy series in the *Asheville Gazette-News,* although nothing as combative as the exchange with Hartmann actually appeared in the series.

Astrology was also intended to be a topic in *The Cancer of Superstition*, to be written by C. M. Eddy and Lovecraft at the behest of Harry Houdini. Work on that book was scarcely begun before Houdini's death in 1926, and it was never completed (*CE* 3.320–22). It is true that stars sometimes have a baleful influence on humanity in Lovecraft's stories (e.g., "Beyond the Wall of Sleep" and "Polaris"), but not in the manner of traditional astrology (Hite 148; chapter 10). Astrology briefly surfaces in *The Case of Charles Dexter Ward,* in which necromancer Joseph Curwen's library "was a treasure-house of lore in the doubtful realms of alchemy and astrology." However, Curwen's delving into astrology could hardly have been seen as an endorsement.

An Alternative Lovecraft?

What insights into Lovecraft's life are provided by his writing for newspapers? They provide information on the breadth of his reading in astronomy, a subject explored by Livesey (DPO). In fashioning his columns, Lovecraft drew upon a mixture of popular astronomy books, such as Burritt's *Geography of the Heavens* and Simon Newcomb's *Astronomy for Everybody*. He also drew upon astronomy news in the popular press, and in the less technical astronomy journals, especially *Popular Astronomy*. At the time, *Popular Astronomy,* published from Carleton College's Goodsell Observatory, was read by both amateur and professional astronomers, and was the chief magazine of its type in the United States.

Lovecraft's newspaper articles reinforce our view of him as an erudite amateur astronomer. Livesey (DPO 22–23) does take Lovecraft to task on a few points, and his knowledge of astronomy was not perfect.[7] His astronomy columns also give us a glimpse of a Lovecraft who never was—not a writer of stories for *Weird Tales,* nor a professor of astronomy at Brown University, but a science journalist appearing in the popular press. His articles are competent and informative, and would have been useful to stargazers of his day. Some of them have a matter-of-fact dullness, but the best of them play on imaginative themes. Had he continued along these lines, Lovecraft might today be remembered as an adept writer of science articles for newspapers and magazines, possibly

---

7. Although we think HPL can be exonerated on one of Livesey's criticisms, as discussed in Appendix II.

even as an author of popular science books. The best astronomy popularizers of his day, such as Garrett P. Serviss—who honed his literary skills as a newspaper writer—have their admirers today. However, few readers would trade the invention and thrill of "The Colour out of Space" for the measured speculation of "Can Man Reach the Moon?" Only Lovecraft could have crafted the former; many science enthusiasts could have written the latter. Lovecraft would not pursue a career as a science journalist, nor is there evidence that he contemplated such a career. Commercial science writing, while congruent with his desire to educate others, was less suited to Lovecraft's aesthetic of writing, not for money, but for self-expression. Aside from the series of newspaper articles aborted by his death, and the similarly uncompleted *Cancer of Superstition*, we are unaware of any attempt by Lovecraft to resume science writing after 1918. His interest in science remained, but his science writing, at least for the public, ended as his writing of weird fiction was just beginning to flourish.

Goodsell Observatory, home of astronomy at Carleton College, Minnesota, as depicted on a postcard mailed in 1911. Carleton College was the home institution of *Popular Astronomy* magazine, a source of information for Lovecraft. H. Smith collection.

Chapter 7
Lovecraft Ventures to Venus

Introduction

On 24 June 1947, pilot Kenneth Arnold claimed to have seen nine objects flying past Mount Rainier, Washington, moving like saucers skipping across water. Two weeks later, the US Army Air Force announced that it had captured one such "flying disc" from where it had crashed near Roswell, New Mexico (Colavito, *Cult* 107–9).[1] From those two incidents came the birth of the modern UFO era—though not the start of strange objects being reported flying through the sky by even stranger pilots. Take, for example, a wave of "mystery airship" sightings across the American West and Southwest that spanned from November 1896 to May 1897 (Colavito, *Cult* 110–11; Clark 122–23; Jacobs 3–46). Near the end of the wave, on 17 April, the supposed culprit's airship crashed in the sleepy town of Aurora, Texas. The local newspaper claimed that the residents identified the pilot as a Martian and buried it in the town cemetery (Colavito, *Cult* 110; Jacobs 17–19). As Aurora is only 34 miles from Robert E. Howard's birthplace of Peaster, it is

---

Thanks to Justin Mullis for several suggestions on themes of Venusian fiction to incorporate here, and to Russell J. Hawley for permission to use his artwork.

1. One of the features of the "Roswell Myth" as it emerged in the 1980s was that the flying saucer wreckage was initially discovered by a team of archaeologists from an "eastern university" led by a Dr. Buskirk, before the military arrived to swear them to silence (Ziegler 16–17). Were Dr. Buskirk and his students perhaps from Miskatonic University, possibly following the route taken by the explorer Pánfilo de Zamacona y Nuñez prior to his arrival at K'nyan? If so, this raises the question: were the aliens who crashed at Roswell somehow summoned either by the members of the Miskatonic expedition, or something they discovered? Until the records of Majestic-12 are disclosed, we may never know.

tempting—though entirely speculative, particularly given how peripatetic his family was during his youth—to imagine him hearing about it as a child, and later relaying the information of a buried Martian pilot to Lovecraft.

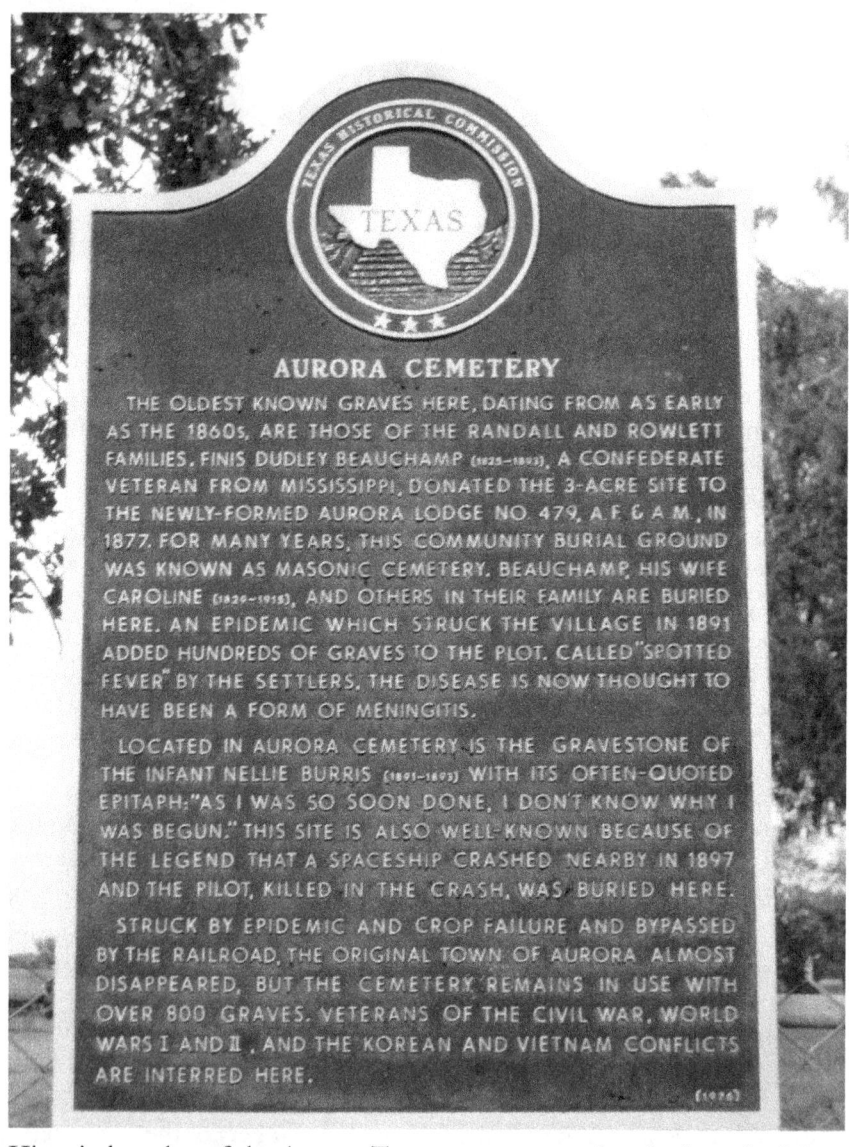

Historical marker of the Aurora, Texas, cemetery, noting the legend of the 1897 alien burial there. Photograph by Edward Guimont.

There were waves of "airship" sightings across the world in the fifty years between Aurora and Roswell, but those tended not to stick to historical memory (Clark 123). Additionally, despite the claims of Aurora's residents, the pilots of the airships were not typically identified as aliens, but rather as brilliant American inventors—with Thomas Edison often a culprit (Clark 125, 132; Jacobs 26–30). Take, for example, Garrett Putnam Serviss (1851–1929), mentioned in chapter 5 as perhaps the most prominent American popularizer of astronomy in the decades on either side of the century. Serviss also ventured into science fiction writing, such as his serialized novel *Edison's Conquest of Mars* (1898). The language around the public reveal of Edison's secret spacefaring airship in the novel clearly draws from the "mystery airship" wave of the previous year:

> Nevertheless, inklings of the truth leaked out. The flying machine had been seen by many persons hovering by night high above the Orange[, New Jersey] hills and disappearing in the faint starlight as if it had gone away into the depths of space, out of which it would re-emerge before the morning light had streaked the east, and be seen settling down again within the walls that surrounded the laboratory of the great inventor. (Serviss, *ECM* 6)

While not on the scale of the 1896–97 wave, another such series of mystery airship sightings emerged in December 1909–January 1910; and just as the earlier wave have been centered in the West and Southwest, this one was centered in New England. And just as the earlier wave was blamed on the eccentric inventor Thomas Edison, this one was blamed on another supposed inventor, the businessman Wallace E. Tillinghast of Worcester, Massachusetts (Whalen and Bartholomew 466–76). In his book *New Lands* (1923) Charles Fort describes the involvement of the businessman:

> Upon the night of September 8, 1909, a luminous object had been seen sailing over New England, and sounds from it, like sounds from a motor, had been heard. Then Mr. Wallace Tillinghast, of Worcester, Mass., announced that this light had been a lamp in his "secret aëroplane," and that upon this night he had travelled, in said "secret aëroplane," from Boston to New York, and back to Boston. At this time the longest recorded flight, in an aëroplane, was [Henri] Farman's, of 111 miles, from Rheims, August, 1909; and, in the United States, according to records, it was not until May 29, 1910, that [Glenn] Curtiss flew from Albany to

New York City, making one stop in the 150 miles, however. So this unrecorded flight made some stir in the newspapers. Mr. Tillinghast meant his story humorously of course. I mention it because, if anybody should look the matter up, he will find the yarn involved in the newspaper accounts. If nothing else had been seen, Mr. Tillinghast might still tell his story, and explain why he never did anything with his astonishing "secret aëroplane;" but something else was seen, and upon one of the nights in which it appeared, Tillinghast was known to be in his home. (Fort, *NL* 217–18)

While showing a skepticism of the association of the New England airship with Tillinghast, Fort instead offers a literally more outlandish connection:

An association between the planet Venus and "mysterious visitors" either illumines or haunts our data. In the *New York Tribune*, Jan. 29, 1910, it is said that a luminous object, thought to be Winnecke's comet, had been seen, Jan. 28, near Venus; reported from the Manila Observatory. . . . Certainly enough it was no "secret airship" of this earth, unless its navigator went to extremes with the notion that the best way to keep a secret is to announce it with red lights and a searchlight. (Fort, *NL* 219)[2]

By September 1927, Lovecraft had read *New Lands,* though he thought it somewhat inferior to Fort's *The Book of the Damned* (*DS* 1.145). However, he did not need Fort to tell him either of Tillinghast's "airship" or of its potential connection to Venus—for Lovecraft was a firsthand witness to both. As noted in chapter 6, on Christmas Eve of 1909, Lovecraft found himself in downtown Providence, in the middle of a crowd of people excitedly observing what they believed to be the searchlight of Tillinghast's airship. Lovecraft, however, identified it as simply the planet Venus, shining with its usual evening brilliance. Nor was this the first time Venus had been misidentified as a terrestrial aircraft; Lovecraft noted an incident that occurred in 1887, described by Serviss in

---

2. It should be noted that either Fort or the *Tribune* is probably wrong. Comet Winnecke, now usually called Pons-Winnecke, was a faint comet, already receding from Earth at this time; its orbit was well known. Instead, Fort and the *Tribune* are possibly referring in a very confused fashion to the Great January Comet of 1910, which had been a surprise appearance and at its brightest was visible in daylight. The Great January Comet was occasionally confused in the media with Halley's Comet, which returned a few months later.

the introduction to *Astronomy with an Opera-Glass* (1888), in which large numbers of New York City residents mistook the planet for an electrically lit balloon launched by Edison (Serviss, *Opera* 2). It was one of the three Serviss books that Lovecraft actually owned (*LL* 139–40).

The 1909 Tillinghast sighting clearly stuck with Lovecraft. He mentioned it again in an article on the September sky for the *Providence Evening News* on 1 September 1914 (*CE* 3.122) and an article on the inner planets for the *Asheville Gazette-News* (27 February 1915; *CE* 3.283), and several times in World War I he would wonder whether Venus might be misidentified as a German airplane or Zeppelin (*CE* 3.183, 241).[3] But more concretely, Lovecraft would recycle the surname Tillinghast into his fiction, using it in his story "From Beyond" (1920), appropriately as the name of the mad scientist Crawford Tillinghast (*CF* 1.192); his 1924 short story "The Shunned House" (*CF* 1.465), albeit in the form of a reference to the historical Providence resident Pardon Tillinghast (1625–1718); and his 1927 novel *The Case of Charles Dexter Ward* (*CF* 2.225), in which a number of Tillinghasts appear in connection with Joseph Curwen. The mass sighting of the "Tillinghast airship" in 1909 that Lovecraft witnessed would also be dramatized in the eighth issue (2016) of Alan Moore and Jacen Burrows's comic book *Providence* (Moore and Burrows 129; Derie and Linton); the comic establishes that Wallace is the cousin of Henry Annesley, *Providence*'s analogue for Crawford Tillinghast. In his short story "In the Hall of the Yellow King" (2011), Peter Rawlik would take the airship connection one step further, turning the Tillinghasts into a future family of starship navigators, piloting between Earth and the planet Carcosa (Rawlik 13–14).

It can safely be said, therefore, that Lovecraft was not a firsthand witness to a spaceship visiting from Venus—although depending on one's definition, it can perhaps be stated that he was present at a mass UFO sighting. But the notion that Venus might harbor life, even intelligent life, was perhaps not so outlandish to the nineteen-year-old skeptical amateur astronomer. Fred S. Lubnow has noted that Lovecraft always thought that

---

3. Nor was Venus the only such culprit in HPL's experience. In his astronomy column for 1 October 1915, he writes of Mars that "The writer recollects that at the opposition of 1907 a number of persons inquired whether it was a signal or artificial light of some sort sent up from a point southeast of Providence" (*CE* 3.161).

Venus was a better candidate for life than the more popular candidate of Mars (Lubnow, LSS 6–7). Take for example Lovecraft's comments from a 1916 article in the Providence *Evening News:*

> Speculation concerning the inhabitants of other worlds is always fruitless, but in view of popular and extended discussions about possible intelligent life on Mars, it seems excusable to indulge in similar discussion regarding Venus, whose conditions are certainly better adapted to the maintenance of life than are those of the small and frigid Mars. (*CE* 3.180)

Lovecraft perhaps was perhaps inspired to think this from Serviss's *Astronomy with an Opera-Glass,* which states that "there is rather more reason to regard Venus as possibly an inhabited world than any other of the Earth's sister planets, not excepting Mars" (139–40). The thirteenth chapter of Serviss's *Curiosities of the Sky* (1909), a credulous take on the American astronomer Percival Lowell's claims of Martian canal builders, nevertheless included the caveat that Venus

> is almost the exact twin of the earth in size, and many arguments may be urged in favor of its habitability, although it is suspected of possessing the same peculiarity as Mercury, in always keeping the same side sunward. Unfortunately its atmosphere appears to be so dense that no permanent markings on its surface are certainly visible, and the question of its actual condition must, for the present, be left in abeyance. (Serviss, *Curiosities* 240)

This interest in Venus would span Lovecraft's entire life. The issue of the *Rhode Island Journal of Astronomy* for 20 September 1903 advertises a ten-page-long manuscript titled "On Venus," which would be available to read in full for interested visitors to 454 Angell Street, as well as a twenty-seven-page-long "Solar System" and an impressive sixty-page-long "Astronomy." Unfortunately, none of these essays remain extant (*IAP* 84–85).[4] At the other end of his lifespan, Lovecraft set one of his final stories on Venus. This was his sole completed entry into the space opera genre, "In the Walls of Eryx" (1936), co-authored with the teenage Kenneth Sterling (1920–1995). "Eryx" was set on Venus, not the Mars that so many others, including his acquaintances Clark Ashton Smith and C. L. Moore, had chosen for their own interplanetary

---

4. *CE* 5 erroneously refers to these unpublished essays as having been printed in the late 1920s or early 1930s (*CE* 5.316). With thanks to S. T. Joshi for the clarification.

fiction. Chapter 9 will discuss more about why Lovecraft may not have been interested in Mars—but what was the pull that drew him inwards to Venus? The immediate temptation is to credit Lovecraft's personal love of heat and association of high temperatures with vitality—though this of course is purely speculative. But with so much of his personality, a more substantive answer can be found in the eighteenth century.

The Solar Order

Scientific consideration of how the solar system was created and developed, and how it might evolve in the future emerged in early modern Europe, with René Descartes providing perhaps the first model, in which the sun and planets had condensed individually out of cosmic whirlpools (Williams and Cremin 40). However, in the eighteenth century an alternative view emerged, the "nebular hypothesis," independently proposed by the Prussian philosopher Immanuel Kant (1724–1804) and French polymath Pierre-Simon Laplace (1749–1827) (Williams and Cremin 50–51). In the original incarnation of the hypothesis, largely discredited since the late nineteenth century, the solar system was formed by an interstellar cloud cooling from the outside in, with planets progressively younger the closer they were to the sun (Crowe 77, 276–77, 373–74). As mentioned in chapter 1, the book that introduced Lovecraft to astronomy was Charles Augustus Young's *Lessons in Astronomy*, which includes a section conditionally endorsing the nebular hypothesis, although questioning the degree by which the outer worlds were older than the inner planets (Young 286–89).

In the United Kingdom, one of the great promoters of the nebular hypothesis was the Scottish astronomy popularizer John Pringle Nichol (1804–1859), who saw it as a scientific example of the laws of natural reform that political progress should be based on. So successful was Nichol in this popularization of his interpretation of the nebular hypothesis that one of his converts was across the Atlantic: Lovecraft's literary inspiration Edgar Allan Poe. Indeed, in his seminal 1841 detective story "The Murders in the Rue Morgue," Poe's character C. Auguste Dupin speaks both of "Dr. Nichols" [*sic*] and how "the vague guesses of that noble Greek [Epicurus] had met with confirmation in the late nebular cosmogony" (Schaffer 145; Tresch 6–7, 163; Poe, "Morgue" 661). S. T. Joshi has noted "Rue Morgue" as inspiration for Lovecraft's 1904 juvenile story "The Beast in the Cave" and that Lovecraft may conceivably have read Poe's work years before (*IAP* 52, 116).

Given that Lovecraft did not turn to astronomy until 1902 or 1903, as described in chapter 1, it is possible that Nichol, via Poe, was Lovecraft's introduction to the nebular hypothesis. Poe's linking of the theory to ancient Greek thought would undoubtedly have appealed to the classically interested Lovecraft. Another possibility for Lovecraft's discovery of the theory was when the astronomer Winslow Upton gave a public talk at Brown University's Sayles Hall on 11 February 1907, titled "The Failure of the Nebular Hypothesis."[5] Given this was a free public lecture, and Lovecraft knew Upton as described in chapter 2, it is entirely possible that Lovecraft attended—particularly given that we know he attended a lecture in the series one month earlier, on 7 January, by Lowell (Faunce 73).

However he was introduced to it, Lovecraft wrote of his acceptance of the nebular hypothesis in several of his astronomical writings of the first two decades of the twentieth century (*CE* 3.25, 42, 237, 310–11). In the nebular theory, Venus was younger than Earth, and therefore its life would have emerged later and be more primitive, but also would last longer than Earth's life as it was closer to the sun and would receive its heat for longer. Mercury's life would, in turn, have the same increased youth and extended longevity in comparison to that of Venus. Or, as Serviss wrote in *Astronomy with an Opera-Glass*, with flourishes somewhat anticipating Lovecraft's cosmic view,

> the dead and barren moon shows us, as in a magician's glass, the approaching fate of the earth. Fortunately, human life is a mere span in comparison with the æons of cosmic existence, and so we need have no fear that either we or our descendants for thousands of generations shall have to play the tragic *rôle* of Campbell's "Last Man,"[6] and endeavor to keep up a stout heart amid the crash of time by meanly boasting to the perishing sun, whose rays have nurtured us, that, though his proud race is ended, we have confident anticipations of immortality. (Serviss, *Opera* 73)

---

5. The manuscript of this speech can be found in the Ladd Observatory records of the John Hay Library, MS-12AS-1, Box 72: 30897 Upton—notes on eclipses of 1878, 87, 83 Correspondence 1886–1913, Notebooks, offprints, graphs—unalphabetized Ladd Observatory, folder 7:14. Nichol's theories are part of the lecture (13–14).

6. Thomas Campbell (1777–1844) was a Scottish poet. His 1823 poem "The Last Man" features the eponymous character on an apocalyptic Earth as the sun dies.

For Lovecraft, the nebular hypothesis was more than a scientific model for the universe; it also underpinned his developing notion of cosmicism and the minute irrelevance of the Earth and its inhabitants, as outlined in his brief July 1918 essay "Time and Space" (*CE* 5.30). The role of the nebular hypothesis in cosmicism can be seen from the fact that according to the Laplacian theory, a cornerstone element is that in the future the Earth will become as cold and dead as Mars currently is.

Prior to the 1938 discovery of nuclear power, this cooling of the Earth was seen as only a few million years in the future, given the only known source for the sun's light and heat would be its fixed contraction left over from the solar nebula (Beer 159–80; Haldane, "Judgment" 290). Just such a cold, dark, dead Earth is featured at the end of H. G. Wells's *The Time Machine* (1895), when the Time Traveller visits the darkened Earth of the year 30 million. Lovecraft read *The Time Machine* in 1924 during his honeymoon, stating that it was that it was "thoroughly entertaining in every detail" (Wells, *TM* 193–202; *IAP* 532). Another work based on the assumption that the future of the Earth would be cold darkness is William Hope Hodgson's *The Night Land* (1912). In "Supernatural Horror in Literature," Lovecraft praised this "tale of the earth's infinitely remote future—billions of billions of years ahead, after the death of the sun" as its "picture of a night-black, dead planet, with the remains of the human race concentrated in a stupendously vast metal pyramid and besieged by monstrous, hybrid, and altogether unknown forces of the darkness, is something that no reader can ever forget" (*CE* 2.115). But Lovecraft did not read Hodgson until 1934. In articles from both 1915 and 1918, Lovecraft cites the work of the astronomer Simon Newcomb (1835–1909) in stating that as the sun's heat and light were a byproduct of its contraction, its ultimate death (and that of the Earth) would be only ten million years in the future. However, even then Lovecraft notes an escape route for the future Earth: the 1898 discovery of radium provided a possible mechanism by which the lifespan of the sun could be extended (*CE* 3.247, 281–82). The temporal aspects of solar energy would also form the basis for Lovecraft's entry 94 in his commonplace book: "Change comes over the sun—shews objects in strange form, perhaps restoring landscape of the past" (*CE* 5.225).

At the end of his writing career, Lovecraft would again reference the nebular hypothesis and its progressive cooling of the solar system's planets in his ghostwritten tale "Out of the Aeons" (1933; see chapter 10) and, more substantively, in "The Shadow out of Time" (1934–35). From the viewpoint of Peaslee on modern-day Earth, the inhabitants of Jupiter's outer moon lived "six million years in the past" (*CF* 3.398), the inhabitants of Venus "would live incalculable epochs to come" (*CF* 3.398), and "as the earth's span closed" (*CF* 3.399) the Great Race would migrate to Mercury, as Earth will be a "cold planet," its survivors "burrowing to its horror-filled core" for heat (*CF* 3.400). Peaslee's recollection of the sun from his time as a guest of the Great Race also reveals a potential related astronomical theory that contributed to Lovecraft:

> Once in a while, though, there would be glimpses of the sun—which looked abnormally large—and of the moon, whose markings held a touch of difference from the normal that I could never quite fathom. When—very rarely—the night sky was clear to any extent, I beheld constellations which were nearly beyond recognition. Known outlines were sometimes approximated, but seldom duplicated; and from the position of the few groups I could recognise, I felt I must be in the earth's southern hemisphere, near the Tropic of Capricorn. (*CF* 3.381)

Peaslee is of course, recounting views of the night sky from the distant past. The abnormally large sun may reflect the now-obsolete theory of stellar evolution propounded by American astronomer Henry Norris Russell (1877–1957). In Russell's conception, somewhat following that of British astronomer Norman Lockyer (1836–1920), stars begin their lives as very-low density giant gaseous spheres, which shrink through gravitational contraction, the friction of which creates their heat and light. When it was realized that gravity could not provide enough energy to keep the sun shining as long as it has been, Russell kept to his contraction idea but revised it, postulating some unknown but temperature-sensitive process for transforming matter to energy that might halt the contraction—getting closer to the modern view. Peaslee viewing the large sun in the past would be in the same continuum of astronomical belief that would assume the sun would be dim and cool in the distant future.

Lovecraft's use of the nebular hypothesis is one of many aspects of "The Shadow out of Time" that August Derleth misinterpreted in his 1957 sequel, "The Shadow out of Space," which states that the Great Race "had fled outward into space, at first to the planet Jupiter, and then farther" (Derleth, *Watchers* 238). This is one of numerous examples of Derleth's misunderstanding of basic astronomical knowledge across his science fiction (Howard 55).[7] The ultimate death of the Earth is also alluded to several times in Lovecraft's 1936 collaboration with R. H. Barlow, "The Night Ocean" (*CF* 4.647, 649, 658).

It should be noted that during most of Lovecraft's adult life, the nebular hypothesis was eclipsed by an alternate proposal, the "planetesimal hypothesis," by which the sun developed first, and the planets emerged as a result of matter being pulled off of the sun by the nearby passing of another star. This idea emerged in the first years of the twentieth century—as stated above, by 1907 Lovecraft's acquaintance Upton was giving public talks on the problems of the nebular theory—but by the late 1930s the planetesimal hypothesis had become heavily challenged (Williams and Cremin 42–46). Throughout most of his life, and as expressed in most of his astronomical writings, Lovecraft did not give the planetesimal hypothesis any consideration. However, this changed by 1929, when he wrote in a letter to Woodburn Harris:

> I never allow my irritation to hamper my acceptance of the new theory as soon as positive evidence warrants it. Thus I have reluctantly exchanged the old nebular for the planetesimal hypothesis, and am beginning to accept the main points of relativity despite a profound intellectual distaste. (*WH* 88)

Lovecraft seemed to retain this late conversion to the planetesimal hypothesis until his death, as will be discussed in chapter 10. However, the lateness and reluctance—after all, as stated above, its influence is still evident in "The Shadow out of Time," written six years later—of his conversion to the planetesimal hypothesis shows a similar instinct for scientific accuracy to Lovecraft's use of the then-disputed theories of continental drift and the Bering land bridge in *At the Mountains of Madness* (*CF* 3.106; Guimont, "Arctic" 141). However, in his nonfiction Lovecraft does show one philosophical affinity to the planetesimal hypothesis, even before outright accepting it in 1929. The theory requires planetary formation to be the byproduct of the near-collision of stars,

---

7. But the possibility should be allowed for the opposite, that Derleth could be attempting to correct HPL's own error with the later knowledge that the sun will actually expand as it ages. It should also be noted that HPL's 1935 collaboration with R. H. Barlow, "'Till A' the Seas,'" features a distant future Earth killed by the more scientifically accurate overheating from an expanding sun (*CF* 4.537; Lubnow, *JLS3* 56–61).

and as a result planetary systems—and therefore life—would be exceedingly rare in the universe, something Lovecraft certainly agreed with in his letters (*FLB* 350). In the revised nebular hypothesis, which is now the dominant model for solar system formation, the planets all condensed from the solar nebula at the same time, removing the staggered age component of the original theory that colored Lovecraft's views of Venusian and Martian life.

It is therefore clear that Lovecraft believed in a model of solar system formation whereby the outer planets are progressively older than the inner planets, and Venus therefore is younger, and further from eventual extinction, than the outer worlds. But if that was his view of Venus, what of the world inside its own orbit—or, indeed, the potential for *worlds* to exist closer to the sun than Venus?

The Innermost Solar System

In his article "Are There Undiscovered Planets?" for the *Pawtuxet Valley Gleaner* (5 October 1906), Lovecraft concludes by saying that "It is not likely that the limits of our solar system are yet found, and sooner or later Mercury and Neptune must lose the distinction that they now bear" (*CE* 3.30). This is perhaps more understandable for Neptune, as there is plenty of open space beyond it for additional planets. But Mercury is only 36 million miles from the sun; what evidence was there that another world might be squeezed within its orbit?

For a time, as it turns out, there was at least enough evidence for such a claim to be considered by some—as Lovecraft describes in that article. In 1846, the French astronomer Urbain Le Verrier (1811–1877), solely by applying mathematics to unexpected discrepancies in the orbit of Uranus, accurately located the new planet Neptune. In 1848, as Lovecraft notes, Le Verrier turned to disturbances in Mercury's orbit and in 1859 predicted an interior world whose gravity was similarly impacting it just as Neptune's had Uranus, which he named Vulcan (Levenson 69–91; Young 264). That year, the French amateur astronomer Edmond Modeste Lescarbault (1814–1894) claimed to have observed Vulcan, as did the American astronomers James Craig Watson (1838–1880) and Lewis A. Swift (1820–1913) during an 1878 eclipse (Levenson 71–78, 101–8). But, as Lovecraft noted, none of those "discoveries" was substantiated by further viewing. Indeed, the observations of the 1883 total solar eclipse in which Upton took part, as described in chapter 2, helped further discredit the belief in Vulcan.

Around the same time that Lovecraft wrote "Are There Undiscovered Planets?" he wrote another essay, apparently unpublished, on the specific topic: "Does Vulcan Exist?" (*CE* 3.331). As Joshi observed, the material in "Does Vulcan Exist?" approximately covers the relevant section of "Are There Undiscovered Planets?," particularly the observational claims of Lescarbault, Warson, and Swift, and was probably written around the same time. As noted by Joshi, August Derleth's initial 1945 claim that this article was published in the *Providence Sunday Journal* does not seem to be true. Given its similarity to the published article, therefore, it is worth asking: just for what venue was "Does Vulcan Exist?" written?

As the essay stands, it would need to be expanded or supplemented to make a full article for the *Pawtuxet Valley Gleaner*. Nor is it long enough to be an article submitted to *Popular Astronomy* magazine, or hold enough new material to merit publication there as a letter. It was unlikely to have been prepared for the *Providence Tribune,* where Lovecraft's articles focused on what was happening in the sky in that month. It seems unlikely that he would have submitted it to the *Providence Journal* once he was being published in a competing newspaper, as noted by Kenneth Faig as early as 1973 (*Voyages* 97–99). Why, then, might it have been written? There are three possibilities. The first is that it was intended to be an article for the *Rhode Island Journal of Astronomy* (or possibly one of his other juvenile publications), but never published when the *Journal* ceased regular publication. The second is that it was the start of a draft for an article in the *Pawtuxet Valley Gleaner,* perhaps published (after expansion) in one of the lost issues. However, the style of the essay appears somewhat different from what Lovecraft typically used often used in his *Pawtuxet Valley Gleaner* articles. As an example, the essay's first sentence jumps immediately into a discussion of intra-Mercurial planets, with no explanation as to what that means. Moreover, too much of the material is covered in his published *Pawtuxet Valley Gleaner* article on undiscovered planets. Thus, it is unlikely that it was never actually published in a lost *Pawtuxet Valley Gleaner* issue. The third possibility, as speculated by Joshi, is therefore the most likely: that it is one of several of Lovecraft's unpublished juvenile science manuscripts which Derleth acquired after Lovecraft's death.

Vulcan's entirely speculative nature did not prevent it from being used in pseudoscience, of course. A notable example was American meteorologist John Hower Tice (1809–1883), who claimed to be able to predict the weather using the orbital position of Vulcan (Tice 389). This meteorological use of the by-then debunked Vulcan was denounced by Lovecraft in articles in the Providence *Evening News* on 1 April 1916 (*CE* 3.181–82) and 2 January 1917 (*CE* 3.211).

The gravitational perturbations in Mercury's orbit that led to Le Verrier predicting Vulcan's existence would eventually be resolved in 1915 by none other than Albert Einstein, with his theory of general relativity explaining the disturbances as being due to Mercury's proximity to the sun's immense gravitational field. This would eventually be confirmed by observations during the 29 May 1919 solar eclipse. Observations of stars around the eclipsed sun indicated the predicted gravitational bending of starlight passing near the sun (Levenson 142–73). Nevertheless, Vulcan would remain in Lovecraft's memory, and he would mention Lescarbault's 1859 claim to have observed the planet in his letter to Kenneth Sterling (20 November 1935; *RB* 255).

Ironically, Lovecraft perhaps wrote more of interest about the nonexistent Vulcan than the actual innermost world of the solar system, Mercury. In his various nonfiction astronomical works, there is not much of note about the planet named for the messenger of the gods. Most markedly, in articles for the Providence *Evening News* on 29 May 1914 (*CE* 3.113–14) and 1 February 1917 (*CE* 3.212–13) and for the *Asheville Gazette-News* on 27 February 1915 (*CE* 3.282), he notes controversies over whether Mercury has an atmosphere, whether it has mountains that can be observed from Earth (older astronomers believed so, while more recent ones did not), and what the period of its rotation is. For that last dispute, Lovecraft noted that older astronomers had believed Mercury's rotation to be 24 or 25 hours, while more modern astronomers, such as Percival Lowell and the Italian astronomer Giovanni Schiaparelli (1835–1910), believed that Mercury was tidally locked to the sun much as the moon is to the Earth, and always showing the same face toward it. Lovecraft sided with Schiaparelli and Lowell's position, not surprisingly given his views of their claims about Mars, as will be discussed in chapter 9. In reality, Mercury takes 88 Earth days to orbit the sun, but 59 Earth days to rotate around its axis, as it is locked into a resonance of three Mercurian days to every two Mercurian years.[8]

Mercury-set fiction was not (nor is) as common as fiction set on the

---

8. The combination of the two gives Mercury a synodic (solar) day equal to 176 Earth days.

moon, Venus, or Mars, but it did exist in Lovecraft's time. Ray Cummings (1887–1957) worked as the personal assistant to Thomas Edison from 1914 to 1919, before making a career writing for the pulp magazines. His novels *Tama of the Light Country* (1930) and *Tama, Princess of Mercury* (1931) are feminist allegories set on a Mercury whose inhabitants are winged humanoids, and the protagonist is an Earth man who accidentally crashes onto Mercury when his moon rocket goes astray (Valdron, "Tama"). However, there is no evidence that Lovecraft read those specific novels, although he had certainly read (and disliked) some of Cummings's space operas (*DS* 187). Despite his dislike, on learning that Cummings was in Florida in 1934, Lovecraft entertained trying to meet him during his visit to R. H. Barlow, as stated in his letter to Barlow of 10 April 1934 (*OFF* 127). For his part, Cummings was a fan of Lovecraft, praising both "The Outsider" and "The Tomb" in a letter to *Weird Tales* (Joshi, *Recognition* 43–44).

Lovecraft did, however, read *The Worm Ouroboros* (1922) by British author E. R. Eddison (1882–1945). Eddison's novel is a fantasy set on Mercury, though one in which the planet is merely a stand-in for a heroic fantasy setting, not unlike the role of the moon in Edmund Spenser's poem *The Faerie Queene* (1590). Indeed, characters in *The Worm Ouroboros* refer to Mercury as "Middle-earth"; perhaps not coincidentally, the novel's admirers included J. R. R. Tolkien and C. S. Lewis. But it was also highly popular within the Lovecraft circle, being enjoyed by Lovecraft, Clark Ashton Smith, Frank Belknap Long, and E. Hoffmann Price. Indeed, Lovecraft owned multiple copies of *The Worm Ouroboros,* as Price lost the copy Lovecraft sent him (*EHP* 52–53, 57; *LL* 63). It was in a letter to Price dated 2 March 1933 that Lovecraft elaborated on the novel and its relation to the actual Mercury:

> Glad you're succumbing to the unique & haunting charm of "Ouroboros". There is nothing else quite like it—even by the same author. It weaves its own atmosphere, & lays down its own laws of reality. At first one tends to rebel at the laying of the scene in [sic] *Mercury* without any attempt to depict conditions peculiar to that planet & alien to the earth (if we except the rather whimsical *horns* of the population), but gradually we come to accept or forget the gesture—taking the whole thing in the spirit of an enthralling fireside tale. (*EHP* 67)

In a letter to Henry Kuttner, Lovecraft further elaborated:

What a chronicle of dream! When it was first circulated around 1927 half our gang were swearing great oaths by Koshtra Pivrarcha [a Mercurian mountain in the novel]! . . . I do think the supposed setting on Mercury is a bit clumsy. . . . But never again has [Eddison] struck the heights of Ouroboros. Koshtra Pivrarcha, alas, can be scaled only once! (20 November 1935; *CLM* 277)

In terms of Lovecraft's own fiction, as mentioned above, "The Shadow out of Time" establishes that Mercury in the future will be home to a species of "bulbous vegetable entities" who will become hosts to the Great Race's minds after the Earth has cooled into frozen inhospitability (*CF* 3.400). Interestingly, in his above-cited 1915 article on Mercury, Lovecraft wrote that "The excessive amount of solar light and heat received by Mercury on account of its proximity to the sun precludes the possibility of the existence upon its surface of inhabitants in any way similar to those of earth" (*CE* 3.282). Presumably, either bulbous vegetables are different enough from Earth life to pass Lovecraft's qualifiers or, in light of the nebular hypothesis they only evolve on Mercury after the sun dims sufficiently (or are perhaps shielded by the shadow of Koshtra Pivrarcha).

"The Shadow out of Time" is the sole reference to Mercury in Lovecraft's fiction. However, reality has left an even stronger link between Lovecraft and the planet. In 2013, a crater near Mercury's southern pole was named Lovecraft by the International Astronomical Union. Appropriately enough, Lovecraft crater is located next to a crater named after the Russian artist Nicholas Roerich (1874–1947), whose work helped inspire *At the Mountains of Madness* (*CF* 3.18; Lubnow, LSS 10–11). One imagines that in the distant Lovecraftian future, those craters serve as the redoubt of the Great Race in their bulbous hosts.

Both the hypothetical and actual innermost planets in the Lovecraftian cosmos have therefore been surveyed. Continuing outward, in the manner of Derleth's Great Race, we come to the planet that is arguably most prominent in Lovecraft's fiction: Venus.[9]

"Old Venus"

Venus is in many respects the Earth's sibling. Its diameter is only several hundred miles less than Earth's; it is the closest planet to Earth;

---

9. Depending, of course, on whether one considers Yuggoth to be a true planet, a dwarf planet, or an extradimensional location.

it is the only other rocky planet with a significant atmosphere; and it is the brightest natural object in the night sky, after the moon. Due to its brightness, it has long attracted interest from terrestrial observers—the irony being that its brightness is partially due to the fact that its atmosphere is entirely shrouded in clouds that obscure the surface from visual observation. However, after centuries of observation the permanent clouds of Venus were not confirmed, leading to suspected glimpses of the surface. Due to the nebular hypothesis, Venus was believed to be younger than Earth, meaning that life on it would be similar to that of Earth millions of years ago. Along with its proximity to the sun, Venus was therefore often assumed to be a steamy, tropical jungle (Grinspoon, *Venus* 50–54). Indeed, a common trope depicted the planet as populated by dinosaurs (Hawley 46–47). In spite (or perhaps more accurately, because) of the obscuring atmosphere, there were still two features of Venus that astronomers noted over the years and fed into speculation of life on the planet: "ashen light" and the "spokes."

Ashen light is a phenomenon still not fully explained, by which observers have occasionally claimed to see a glowing light on the night side of the planet. Ashen light was first observed by the Italian Jesuit astronomer Giovanni Riccioli (1598–1671) in 1643, who gave the phenomenon its name. Over the centuries, various explanations have included auroras, lightning, sunlight refracted through the thick atmosphere, or optical illusions that do not actually exist (Beatty 27; Levine 1081–87; Grinspoon, *Venus* 42–44). The Bavarian astronomer Franz von Paula Gruithuisen (1774–1852), whose theories on intelligent moon-dwellers (and Lovecraft's reception thereof) were discussed in chapters 4 and 5, had a different explanation. He believed that the ashen light was the fires of giant festivals fueled by the abundant tree growth of the young Venus, celebrating either religious occurrences or the coronations of new rulers. Regarding the latter, Gruithuisen calculated that "if we take the ordinary life span of a Venusian to be 130 Venus years . . . then the reign of an absolute monarch may easily last 76 years" (Crowe 204).

In contrast to the disputed nature of the ashen light, the spokes of Venus were almost certainly an optical illusion. In 1894, Percival Lowell established Lowell Observatory in Arizona, built for the purpose of examining what he believed to be the canals of Mars. In 1896, after having installed a new telescope in the observatory, Lowell had several months before Mars entered optimal viewing conditions. Following inconclusive efforts of Schiaparelli to map permanent features on Venus, Lowell decided to use the observatory's period of free time to observe Venus. Over the course of several nights, Lowell sketched a series of linear spokes spanning the Venusian globe, converging on a central "node." These observations were never confirmed by the observatory's other staff, and for a brief period in the early 1900s Lowell himself retracted his claims, before recommitting to them in 1903. Explanations for the spokes have included Lowell's mental strain or a reflection of the capillaries in his eyes onto the telescopic view piece (Sheehan and Dobbins 53–63; Grinspoon, *Venus* 40–42).

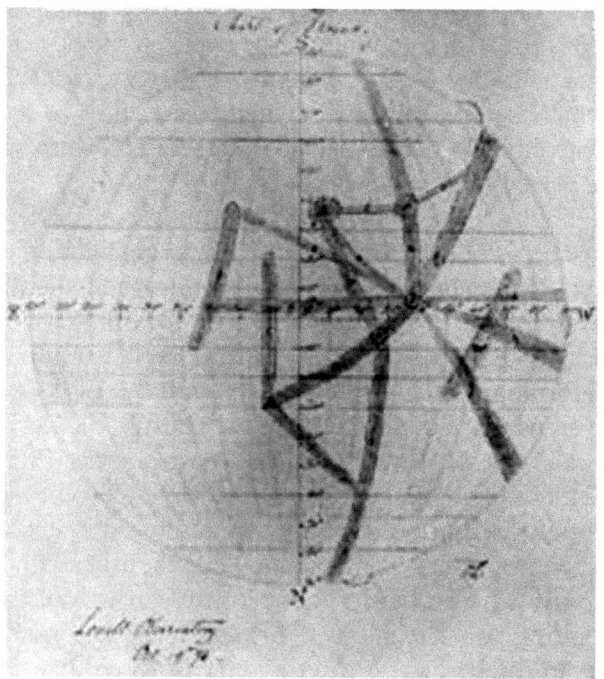

1896 map of the Venusian spokes by Lowell, as printed in a 1909 *Popular Science* article on Venus by him (courtesy Wikimedia).

These speculations around Venus are only lightly represented in Lovecraft's published work. In his column in the Providence *Evening News* for 29 May 1914, Lovecraft did briefly mention Lowell's spokes, but pointed out that the features observed by both him and Schiaparelli were not confirmed by other astronomers (*CE* 3.114). In his article "The Inferior Planets" (*Asheville Gazette-News*, 27 February 1915), there is no mention of ashen light, though the intense atmosphere and its funneling of the sun's light around it is mentioned (*CE* 3.283), as is the apparent fact that "Dark, indefinite shadings, with perhaps a few high mountains, are probably the principal features of the disc of Venus, though Lowell insists on the reality of certain spoke-like markings which he says radiate outward from the centre of the surface" (*CE* 3.284).

In *The Book of the Damned* (1919), Charles Fort devotes several paragraphs to another controversy: whether Venus had a moon or not. Fort notes that between 1645 and 1767 astronomers occasionally reported seeing a moon of the world. Fort goes on to describe that in 1884 the Belgian-American astronomer Jean-Charles Houzeau (1820–1888) not only gave the name Neith to this hypothetical object, but proposed that it was actually a planet of its own—or, in the words of Fort, a "world, planet, super-construction"—orbiting the sun in a resonance with Venus that would account for it only occasionally being visible from Earth (Fort, *Damned* 185–86). As mentioned above, Lovecraft read and enjoyed *The Book of the Damned,* but there is no indication he took the claims of Neith that Fort collected to be anything more serious than Fort's other bits of trivia. Lovecraft does not seem to have written about Neith, and ashen light and the spokes are only briefly mentioned by him. As an example linking such indirect reference to the spokes with his interest in Venusian life, Lovecraft mentioned in a letter to Alfred Galpin:

> I began to study astronomy late in 1902—age 12. . . . I think I really ignored the abysses of space in my interest in the habitability of the various planets of the solar system. My observations (for I purchased a telescope early in 1903) were confined mostly to the moon and the planet Venus. You will ask, why the latter, since its markings are doubtful even in the largest instruments? I answer—this very MYSTERY was what attracted me. In boyish egotism I fancied I might light upon something with my poor little 2¼-inch telescope which had eluded the users of the 40-inch Yerkes telescope!! (21 August 1918; *AG* 199)

However, Lovecraft did more extensively discuss a less sensational controversy of Venusian observation: its period of rotation.

In "The Inferior Planets," Lovecraft writes that since 1666 astronomers believed that Venus rotated once every 23 hours and 21 minutes, though he notes that in the past quarter-century this idea had come under dispute by astronomers such as Schiaparelli and Lowell, both of whom claimed that Venus was tidally locked to the sun. In actuality, it rotates once every 243 Earth days, making a Venusian day longer than the 224.7-day-long Venusian year (Grinspoon, *Venus* 44–46). Like Mercury, its day is longer than its year; and like Uranus, it rotates in reverse compared to the rest of the planets in the solar system. Young Lovecraft sided with the 23-hour rotation "favoured by those best informed on this subject" (*CE* 3.284). As briefly mentioned in chapter 4, Lovecraft had attempted to measure the rotation period of Venus with observations made through his 2¼-inch telescope. He thought that he had found a period of just under 24 hours, as reported in the debut issue of the *Rhode Island Journal of Astronomy*, but he later recanted his Venus observations.

However, this mundane controversy over the planet's period of rotation did not preclude Lovecraft from speculating on what potential Venusians might encounter when they looked to the stars:

> If the planet possesses inhabitants, as possibly it may, they must seldom see the heavens on account of the cloudy canopy which seems to envelop them. However, when their sky is clear, the earth must appear in their eyes as resplendent as is their abode in ours; in other words, our terraqueous globe must shine in the heavens of Venus as a brilliant planet, having motions like those of Mars as seen by us. The moon, of course, would also be conspicuous, resembling a small star beside its primary. (*CE* 3.284)

This imagery clearly stuck in Lovecraft's head, as more than twenty years later he would use it in "In the Walls of Eryx." The story's narrator, Stanfield, remarks that "A heavy mist obscured most of the stars and planets, but the earth was plainly visible as a glowing, bluish-green point in the southeast. It was just past opposition, and would have been a glorious sight in a telescope. I could even make out the moon beside it whenever the vapours momentarily thinned" (*CF* 4.613).

However, even by the time of "Eryx," a Venus where a visitor from Earth could walk comfortably in just a mask was outdated—an apparent contradiction to Lovecraft's repeated admonition of authors of science fiction who did not confirm to scientific realities (*CE* 2.180). Joshi has said that it would not have been preposterous, and indeed this swampy Venus was still dominant in popular culture (*IAP* 964). But in the scientific community it had already faded away into the realm of fiction. By the early 1920s, analysis of the atmosphere of Venus had turned away from the notion, indicating the planet was hot and waterless. Radio observations of Venus in the 1940s and 1950s confirmed the blistering heat of the world's surface under the runaway greenhouse effect, and this early study of the Venusian atmosphere actually helped early global warming modeling on Earth (St. John and Nicholson 208–9; Grinspoon, *Venus* 63).

The final death knell to the "Old Venus" would come on 14 December 1962, when the US *Mariner 2* became the first space probe to fly by not only Venus, but to fly by another planet (Hand 16). On 12 June 1967, the Soviet *Venera 4* became the first probe to enter the atmosphere of Venus; on 17 August 1970, *Venera 7* became the first probe to land on either Venus or another planet. For almost two decades, until 1985, the Soviet *Venera* program would become arguably the most successful series of interplanetary probes thus far, achieving a number of firsts in planetary exploration through its range of orbiters, landers, and atmospheric balloons (Grinspoon, *Venus* 72–76).

Much as with Mars, the Space Age was the final nail in the coffin for the romance of Old Venus, but spaceships had been making their way to the planet for decades before the arrival of *Mariner 2*. These were the spaceships of interplanetary fiction, for which Venus had a particular resonance. Several notable works were written in the years on either side of "In the Walls of Eryx," and it is these works to which we will turn next.

Old Venus in the Literary Imagination

In 1875, the Russian émigré Helena P. Blavatsky (1831–1891) founded the occult religion of Theosophy, by grafting Western ideas of occultism and supernaturalism onto (sometimes shaky) frameworks provided by Hinduism and Buddhism. Among the tenets of Theosophy established by Blavatsky and her followers are the *The Book of Dzyan,* an ancient tome containing the true history of humanity, as well as the fact that humans owe our civilization to the "Lords of Venus" who came to our world from theirs millions of years ago (Colavito, "Dzyan"; Stanley 27–29). Lovecraft mentioned Theosophy in "The Call of Cthulhu" (1926; *CF* 2.29) and in "Supernatural Horror in Literature" (1927; *CE* 2.95) but seems not to have known much about it until learning details from E. Hoffmann Price in 1933 (*DS* 404). The combination of extraterrestrial origins of humanity (in this case, from Venus) with a forbidden book of ancient lore was obviously going to be of interest to Lovecraft, and Kenneth Hite has argued that Theosophy played a major role in the development of the notion of geological deep time in Lovecraft's later works (Hite 198–203). As Lovecraft wrote in a letter to Price, "as I said before, I'm quite on edge about that Dzyan-Shamballah stuff. The cosmic scope of it—Lords of Venus, & all that—sounds so especially & emphatically in my line!" (15 February 1933; *EHP* 62).

Perhaps the first explicitly science fictional work to feature a voyage to Venus was the anonymously authored New Zealand novel *The Great Romance* (1881), whose final chapters depict the main characters building and piloting a spacecraft to Venus. As mentioned in chapter 5, the American businessman John Jacob Astor IV (1864–1912) published the novel *A Journey in Other Worlds: A Romance of the Future* in 1894, which Lovecraft owned (*LL* 28). One reason the novel's protagonists choose to explore the outer solar system rather than the inner is because

> Venus's axis is inclined to the plane of her orbit seventy-five degrees, so that the arctic circle comes within fifteen degrees of the equator, and the tropics also extend to latitude seventy-five degrees, or within fifteen degrees of the poles, producing great extremes of heat and cold. Venus is made still more difficult of habitation by the fact that she rotates on her axis in the same time that she revolves about the sun, in the same way that the moon does about the earth, so that one side must be perpetually frozen while the other is parched. (Astor 21)

The first novel to be primarily set on Venus would be *Journey to Venus* (1895), by the American author Gustavus W. Pope (1828–1902), a sequel to the prior year's *Journey to Mars,* which will be covered in chapter 9. The characters in Pope's novel make a point of specifically disproving "the theosophical theories of the occultists . . . Blavatsky and Co.," including the role of astral projection, reincarnation, and Venus (Pope, *Venus* 9–10). The novel is apparently also the first use in fiction of the trope of dinosaurs on Venus, Pope populating his world with "huge land reptiles, the Iguanodons, Megalosaurs, and Dinosaurs" (Pope, *Venus* 163; Hawley 46; Fallon 110–16).

Two years after Pope's Venusian novel, H. G. Wells would begin to write his serialized classic of alien invasion, *The War of the Worlds,* a work Lovecraft read and admired. While it will also be discussed in greater depth in chapter 9, it is worth noting that the novel ends with the Martians, having failed at their invasion of the Earth, launching an alternate invasion of Venus (Wells, *WW* 299–301). Given the Martian inability to handle the bacteria of Earth, one can only imagine how quickly they would succumb to the tropical biosphere of Old Venus—let alone the pressure-cooker atmosphere of the actual Venus. Given the differences between the three planets, the American science fiction writer Lawrence Watt-Evans playfully proposed that the crews of the invasion fleets sent to Earth and Venus were actually exiles deliberately sent to die by the leadership on Mars (Watt-Evans 169–70).

While Lovecraft did read *The War of the Worlds,* there is no indication he read either *The Great Romance* or *Journey to Venus*. The earliest confirmed Venusian novel that Lovecraft read was *A Columbus of Space,* by the aforementioned astronomy popularizer Garrett P. Serviss. Originally serialized in *All-Story* in 1909, it was published in book form in 1911. Serviss dedicated *A Columbus of Space* "To the readers of Jules Verne's romances. . . . Not because the author flatters himself that he can walk in the Footsteps of that Immortal Dreamer, but because, like Jules Verne, he believes that the World of Imagination is as legitimate a Domain of the Human Mind as the World of Fact" (Serviss, *ACS* x). As mentioned in chapter 5, young Lovecraft would certainly be included in that group of Verne fans. In a 7 March 1914 letter, Lovecraft stated that "I hardly need mention the author of *A Columbus of Space* further than to say that I have read every published work of Garrett P. Serviss, own most of them, and await his further writings with eagerness" (*Misc* 433). In a letter to Barlow dated 28 July 1932, Lovecraft mentions having read the work when it was originally published in the *All-Story* (*OFF* 34). He would get the chance to read it again when it was reprinted in the August–October 1926 issues of *Amazing Stories,* which he owned (*LL* 24).

The plot of *A Columbus of Space* follows the exploits of brilliant inventor Edmund Stonewall of New Jersey, who invents a spacecraft powered by his discovery of how to control the forces of radioactivity and which he decides to use to reach Venus. In testing his spacecraft, an onlooker mistakes it for a balloon (Serviss, *ACS* 14). Given the combination of Venus, New Jersey inventor, and balloon, this seems a callback to the Edison incident Serviss mentioned in *Astronomy with an Opera-Glass* and repeated by Lovecraft in his letter to the editor. The bulk of the narrative on Venus is described by one of Stonewall's friends, after Stonewall himself has disappeared, a technique obviously indebted to Wells's *The Time Machine* (Wells, *TM* 211–16). Notably, the narrator describes how his "dreams were disturbed by visions of the grinning nondescripts at the foot of the wall, which transformed themselves into winged dragons, and remorselessly pursued me through the measureless abysses of space" (Serviss, *ACM* 24–25), which David Haden suggests may have influenced the nightmare dreams experienced at the start of "The Call of Cthulhu" (*CF* 2.25–30; Haden, *LH4* 149–50). The actual voyage to Venus in the novel includes descriptions of both the vessel's atmosphere-scrubbing equipment and a near-miss with a meteor (Serviss, *ACS* 33–35), elements clearly taken from Verne's *Around the Moon* and echoed in Lovecraft's "Can the Moon Be Reached by Man?"

The actual adventures of Stonewall on the swampy Venus—the world containing neither spokes nor lizards, though ashen light is observed (Serviss, *ACS* 42–46)—are largely irrelevant here, but do contain some elements that suggest Lovecraft retained them in memory. First and foremost is the use of radiation in reaching Venus. "In the Walls of Eryx" is one of the only two stories of Lovecraft's where he uses the term "radiation" or any of its derivatives, albeit through the single reference to Stanfield's equipment including "D-radiation-cylinders" (*CF* 4.629).[10] Unlike in "Eryx," the *Columbus* Venus is tidally locked with Schiaparelli's observations cited, but that was not always the case, as deduced from the discovery of a seam of anthracite coal inside a cave on the side of eternal night:

> "A Carboniferous Age on Venus!" Edmund continued. "What do you think of that? But, of course, it was sure to be so; all the planets that are old enough have been through practically the same stages. Think of it! The plants that gave origin to this coal must have flourished here when Venus still rotated on her axis rapidly enough to have day and night succeeding one another on all sides of her, for now no vegetation except the insignificant plants that grow in these caverns can live on this hemisphere. And think, too, of the countless ages that must have been consumed in slowing down her rotation by the friction of her ocean tides." (Serviss, *ACS* 62–63)

The historical musings based on remnants of ancient life discovered bring to mind the discoveries of the Miskatonic expedition in *At the Mountains of Madness*. Similarly, Stonewall and his companions later come across an ancient Venusian city, including a great library with endless books dating back to prehistory (Serviss, *ACS* 203–08), bringing to mind Pnakotus.[11] The Venusians of Serviss have a largely non-verbal form

---

10. The other story is "The Shunned House" with its two references to "ether radiations" (*CF* 1.470, 475). "Through the Gates of the Silver Key" (*CF* 3.292) and "The Mound" (*CF* 4.202, 230) both use the term "radiation" in its more general sense of "expression" or "transmission."

11. "Pnakotus" is a fan term for the library city of the Great Race in "The Shadow out of Time." The name is used here for brevity, despite HPL never

of communication (Serviss, *ACS* 72) just as do the man-lizards of "Eryx." And, just like the Venus of "Eryx," the Venus of *A Columbus of Space* has enormous crystal deposits (Serviss, *ACS* 85–89).

The next works of Venusian fiction that Lovecraft read were both published in 1919. The first is *Station X* by British author George McLeod Winsor (1856–1939), in which Earthlings form an alliance with Venusians against their mutual Martian foes, a plot perhaps inspired by the aforementioned ending of *The War of the Worlds*. The context of *Station X* will be discussed in greater detail in chapter 9, but for now it suffices to say that in "Some Notes on Interplanetary Fiction" Lovecraft singles it out as one of the few good works of the genre (*CE* 2.182). The second 1919 work is the novel *The Three Eyes* by the French author Maurice Leblanc (1864–1941). Leblanc is best known for his character Arsène Lupin, a rough equivalent to Sherlock Holmes; young Lovecraft's interest in Holmes is perhaps what led him to read Leblanc. *The Three Eyes* focuses on a French scientist who makes remote contact with Venusians, who have the three eyes of the title; in its usage of an Earthling making remote contact with Venusians, it also has some similarities to *Station X*. However, Lovecraft did not view it in the same light as its British counterpart. The novel was translated into English in 1921 and read by Lovecraft in 1927. In a letter to Clark Ashton Smith dated 1 October of that year, Lovecraft simply opined that "In 'The Three Eyes' Maurice Leblanc ruins a splendid interplanetary theme by puerile popular treatment" (*DS* 1.145). Lovecraft wrote entry 157 in his commonplace book, "Vague lights, geometrical figures, etc., seen on retina when eyes are closed. Caus'd by rays from *other dimensions* acting on optick nerve? From *other planets?*" (*CE* 5.229) Perhaps this unused idea had its origins in the general plot of remote contact with Venusians from either *Station X* or *The Three Eyes*.

In the April 1925 *Weird Tales,* Nictzin Dyalhis published the story "When the Green Star Waned," which also features an expedition launched to Earth from Venus for the purpose of saving the humans from an invasion of third-party aliens. The story has been credited with inventing the venerable science fiction term "blaster" as an alternative to ray gun; it also has been speculated as being an inspiration for both the Superman comics and *Star Trek* (Hanley; Hite 150). Lovecraft certainly read "When the Green Star Waned," but did not appreciate it. In the

---

using it in the story.

story, the commander of the Venusian expedition is named Hul Jok; Lovecraft attacks the character by name as an unrealistic extraterrestrial in his letter to Natalie H. Wooley (27 November 1933; *RB* 195).

In contrast to "When the Green Star Waned," the Venus-set work that Lovecraft perhaps appreciated the most was the 1930 novel *Last and First Men* by British author Olaf Stapledon (1886–1950). A truly cosmic future history of humanity taking place across millennia and the entire solar system, it was first mentioned in chapter 5 and will be discussed again in chapters 9 and 10. *Last and First Men* was inspired by the 1927 speculative science essay "The Last Judgment" by British biologist J. B. S. Haldane (1892–1964), which Lovecraft also owned (*LL* 78). Haldane's essay is on the future evolution of humanity as narrated to schoolchildren on Venus, where humans have emigrated after a disaster befalls Earth. Stapledon took Haldane's framework and built an elaborate fictional setting around it. After a major interplanetary war with the Martians, the future "Fifth Men" are faced with the prospect of the moon slowly spiraling in toward a collision with Earth. The humans are forced to evacuate to Venus, which necessitates a million-year-long plan to terraform Venus and artificially evolve the human race so that both can meet in the middle. However, the terraforming process is interrupted by attacks by the Venerians, the world's intelligent natives who live in the oceans that envelop the majority of Venus. The Fifth Men of Earth commit to a policy of genocide against the Venerians, exterminating them so their world can be both adapted and cleared out for human habitation. Ultimately, Stapledon's future human race lasts longer on Venus than it did on Earth (Stapledon 243–72). In "Some Notes on Interplanetary Fiction," Lovecraft praised *Last and First Men* as one of the "few semi-classics" in "the serious exploitation of the astronomical tale" (*CE* 2.182) and included Stapledon in a 1936 list of recommended authors of "scientific fantasies" (*CE* 2.190). The genocidal policy against the sea-dwelling Venerians also brings to mind the government's efforts to defeat the Deep Ones in "The Shadow over Innsmouth."

A somewhat more prominent series of Venus fiction from contemporary standpoint—if by dint of their author more than anything in the text—was the Carson Napier of Venus series by Edgar Rice Burroughs (1875–1950). Despite their outward similarities, the Carson Napier series never received the attention of Burroughs's other planetary series, John Carter of Mars (let alone Tarzan). The John Carter books, as well as Lovecraft's early enthusiasm for Burroughs, will be discussed more extensively in chapter 9. Of the Carson Napier stories, only two were released in Lovecraft's lifetime: *Pirates of Venus*, serialized in six issues in *Argosy* in 1932 and then collected in book form in 1934; and *Lost on Venus*, serialized in *Argosy* in 1933 and collected in book form in 1935 (Lupoff, *ERB* 101–10). Although these stories came out shortly before Lovecraft and Sterling wrote "Eryx," there is only circumstantial evidence that Lovecraft read them. In a letter to Barlow dated 30 October 1932, in response to Barlow's description of an installment of Otis Adelbert Kline's serialized Venus novel *The Port of Peril*, Lovecraft replied that "it can't be much worse than the similar junk of Burroughs" (*OFF* 41). Of course, Lovecraft may have been referring to the general sword-and-planet concept of Burroughs's earlier John Carter stories, and there are certainly no specific inspirations in "Eryx" from the Carson Napier works. For Lovecraft especially, if not Sterling, these two novels came out long after his period of affection for Burroughs ended. However, there is one element of "Eryx" that may reflect a general influence from the second of those stories. While Gustavus Pope's *Journey to Venus* was the first novel to place dinosaur-like reptiles on Venus, it was Burroughs's *Lost on Venus* that resurrected and popularized the trope, with Napier encountering crocodile-like veres and dog-sized kazars, which Burroughs interestingly establishes as being feathered (Hawley 46). The man-lizards of "Eryx" seem to reflect a trope that, while started by Pope, owes more to its popularization by *Lost on Venus*.

Within Lovecraft's own circle, there were a number of authors who preceded the Old Gentleman and his teenage companion in penning interplanetary fantasies on Venus. Kline is perhaps the most prominent of the circle to voyage to Venus, with a trilogy of books: *Planet of Peril* (1929), *The Prince of Peril* (1930), and *The Port of Peril* (1932). The trilogy focuses on Earthman Robert Grandon, whose mind is telepathically exchanged with a Venusian slave—shades again of the Great Race. In 1936, Donald A. Wollheim published an article claiming a feud between Kline and Burroughs, alleging that Kline had deliberately written the Grandon novels as an infringement on John Carter, with Burroughs in turn writing his Carson Napier stories to trade on Kline's Grandon. This feud was accepted in the fandom community for almost thirty years, before Wollheim's article was revealed to be a hoax in 1965 by Richard A. Lupoff (Lupoff, *ERB* 108–10). In the aforementioned letter to Barlow, Lovecraft noted that the outline of *The Port of Peril* "is surely amusing. I probably shan't read it—for I never seem able to keep awake over one of Otis Adelbert's laboured, mechanical penny-thrillers" (*OFF* 41).

In the January 1934 edition of *Wonder Stories,* Richard F. Searight published a poem, "Impressions of the Planets—Venus." Searight's Venus is somewhat more modern than that his contemporaries; while it does contain oceans with rocky shores, they are shrouded in "acrid, sulphide fog," and the entire planet is a "mist-wrapped world where life is yet to rise . . . When heat shall wane" (*EHP* 452). C. L. Moore's first professional story, "Shambleau," published in the November 1933 *Weird Tales* and appreciated by Lovecraft, features "a sprinkling of Venusian swampmen" present on the human colony of Lakkdarol on Mars. The main character, Northwest Smith, also has a Venusian companion, Yarol, described as resembling a fallen angel as typical of his species, anticipating the religious connotations C. S. Lewis would give Venus (Moore 532, 544–45). The second Northwest Smith story, "Black Thirst," was published in the April 1934 *Weird Tales* and had Smith and Yarol going to the latter's Venusian home. The series would return to Venus in the fifth story, "Julhi," from the March 1935 *Weird Tales.* In Moore's cosmopolitan solar system, even when Smith and Yarol are on Mars or the moon, Venusians are often to be found in the various colonies and settlements.

Clark Ashton Smith also wrote several stories set on Venus, in a variety of settings. One of the more unique is "A Voyage to Sfanomoë" from the January 1931 *Weird Tales.* Set in the ancient past, it concerns an expedition to Venus by two Atlanteans, who hope to determine whether the arboreal planet could be a suitable refuge for those fleeing the upcoming sinking of Atlantis—something of the Theosophical model in reverse. The September 1931 *Weird Tales* featured "The Immeasurable Horror," Smith's story about the lone survivor of an expedition to Venus in 1979, where disaster is met at the hands (to so speak) of an enormous, miles-long monster of protoplasm that consumes all in its path—perhaps the natural endpoint of a terrestrial shoggoth, should it escape Antarctica? And in Smith's Martian-set "The Vaults of Yoh-Vombis" (*Weird Tales,* May 1932), the human narrator references exploring the ancient fortress of Uogam on the frozen nightside of the tidally locked Venus, which he compares to Machu Picchu.

As it would turn out, Lovecraft's own expedition to Venus would involve the discovery of an ancient building on Venus and a disastrous end for its narrator—though ironically, his death indeed arrives from an inability to measure.

"In the Walls of Eryx"

While "In the Walls of Eryx" is the most substantive work of Lovecraft's fiction to involve Venus, it is not the only one. In his 1927 novel *The Case of Charles Dexter Ward*, Lovecraft includes the minor character of Dr. Benjamin West, who had written a pamphlet on the 1769 transit of Venus across the sun (*CF* 2.248). West was a real figure who actually did observe the transit of Venus in Providence, and his pamphlet was titled *An Account of the Observation of Venus upon the Sun the Third Day of June 1769* (and one wonders whether his twentieth-century descendants included a certain Miskatonic medical student). Lovecraft would discuss the transit of Venus in letters (*JFM* 392), and the observation of the transit is the namesake for Planet Street and Transit Street in the East Side of Providence, the latter of which runs parallel to Angell Street, half a mile south. The telescope West used to observe Venus is displayed at Ladd Observatory.[12]

Venus is next referenced in Lovecraft's fiction in his novella "The Shadow out of Time" (1934–35). In it, among the other displaced visitors to Pnakotus, Peaslee encounters "a mind from the planet we know as Venus, which would live incalculable epochs to come" (*CF* 3.398). Later in 1935, Venus is mentioned in "The Diary of Alonzo Typer," which Lovecraft ghostwrote for William Lumley. In the story, the eponymous Typer's diary entry for 22 April 1908 notes that from reading the sixteenth-century occult manuscript of Claes van der Heyl, "I learned of the Book of Dzyan, whose first six chapters antedate the earth, and which was old when the lords of Venus came through space in their ships to civilise our planet" (*CF* 4.585). This clearly shows the influence of the information on Theosophy that Lovecraft learned from E. Hoffmann Price in 1933, as well as a fairly blatant early example of the ancient alien theory, particularly with Lovecraft's uncharacteristic use of "ships" as the means of navigating space for otherworldly beings (Hite 145; Colavito, *Cult* 89).

"In the Walls of Eryx," written the year after "Shadow" and "Typer," is the last of Lovecraft's fiction to incorporate Venus, as well as the most in-depth; it can well be said that he truly did save the best for last. In *The Tragic Thread in Science Fiction* (2019), Robert H. Waugh notes that "Eryx" is one of Lovecraft's least discussed works—perhaps a combination

---

12. However, the transit of Venus is not included in the 1769 section of Peter Cannon's *The Chronology out of Time* (15).

of the fact that it is one of his last works, one of his collaborations, one of his very few purely space-opera works, and one of his stories that is generally not seen as part of the "Cthulhu Mythos" for which Lovecraft is primarily known to the wider public (Waugh 208). "Eryx" does not, for instance, appear to have ever been the focus of any article in the premier Lovecraftian scholarly journals *Crypt of Cthulhu* or *Lovecraft Annual*. *Future Lovecraft* (2012) and *Ride the Star Wind* (2017) are both anthologies centered around Lovecraftian space opera, and neither contain stories inspired by "Eryx." Even Waugh's analysis of the story, one of those few interrogations of "Eryx," occupies a mere fifteen out of his book's 235 pages. Among Lovecraft's own surviving correspondence, he only mentions the story once—in a letter to August Derleth (11 February 1936)—and there not even by name (*RB* 13; *ES* 2.725).

Lovecraft co-wrote "Eryx" with Kenneth J. Sterling, his teenage protégé who lived in Providence in Lovecraft's final years of life. Sterling wrote an initial draft of 6000–8000 words, which Lovecraft very quickly rewrote and expanded into 12,000 words (*IAP* 963; Joshi and Schultz 126). The story is a first-person account by a certain "Operative A-49, Kenton J. Stanfield of 5317 Marshall Street, Richmond, Va.," an employee of the Venus Crystal Company, which operates on Venus out of the Terra Nova settlement. The Terra Nova outpost remains the only human settlement on the planet, despite the fact that the story is set seventy-two years after the first landing on Venus. Other than Stanfield's residence, the only details provided about conditions on Earth are that the Company's headquarters are in Chicago and terrestrial governments have the ability to project "a barrier of N-force . . . to mark a forbidden zone" (*CF* 4.603). Whatever N-force is, its barrier projectors are powered by the crystals mined by the company, as the Venusian crystals are used for generating energy back on Earth.

The removal of the crystals is hampered by the intelligent native race of "man-lizards" who worship them. The man-lizards tend to avoid the human employees of the Crystal Company, but even their tepid resistance to the theft of their religious ornaments spurs the prejudice of Stanfield:

> One can't call the damned things men for all their "cities" and towers. They haven't any skill except building—and using swords and poison darts—and I don't believe their so-called "cities" mean much more than ant-hills or beaver-dams. I doubt if they even have a real language—all the talk about psychological communication through those tentacles

down their chests strikes me as bunk. What misleads people is their upright posture; just an accidental physical resemblance to terrestrial man. I'd like to go through a Venus jungle for once without having to watch out for skulking groups of them or dodge their cursed darts. They may have been all right before we began to take the crystals, but they're certainly a bad enough nuisance now—with their dart-shooting and their cutting of our water pipes. More and more I come to believe that they have a special sense like our crystal-detectors. No one ever knew them to bother a man—apart from long-distance sniping—who didn't have crystals on him. (*CF* 4.598–99)

Beyond those details, Stanfield provides a few other descriptors of the natives throughout the story. The man-lizards have an average height of seven feet. They have flat heads with tapir-like snouts; "green, slimy, frog-like skin" (*CF* 4.618–19); and poor night vision. They communicate with four long, ropy tentacles down their chests, and possibly some sixth sense related to detecting the planet's crystals, which also have a religious significance.

Illustration of a man-lizard by Russell J. Hawley. Used with permission of the artist.

In addition to their swords and poison darts, they also carry glow-torches (*CF* 4.623). Russell J. Hawley identifies the man-lizards as part of the general trope of dinosaurs being featured on Venus in pulp space-opera stories; in line with this, Fred Lubnow notes that some of the Venusian flora in "Eryx" appear to be dinosaur-era lepidodendrons (Hawley 46; Lubnow, *Essays* 6).

The story takes the form of Stanfield's recordings as he prospects, using his crystal-detector to follow the signal indicating "the crystal I sought—a thing possibly no larger than a hen's egg, yet containing enough power to keep a city warm for a year . . . a crystal of the very finest quality" (*CF* 4.554). While approaching the location of the crystal, Stanfield literally stumbles into an invisible structure, determining it to be a maze. Nor is he the first to make this discovery: through the invisible wall is the corpse of Frederick N. Dwight, a veteran Crystal Company prospector, clearly having been drawn into the maze and trapped inside until his air supply ran out, and still grasping the crystal in his dead hands. Stanfield attempts to enter the maze to retrieve the crystal, marking his route, but ultimately becomes lost inside the invisible maze. As the days go by, his oxygen dwindles, and the man-lizards appear to watch, seemingly to taunt the human interloper for being caught in their trap. Dying, in one of his final journal entries Stanfield turns from hatred of the man-lizards and calling for their extermination to regret, hoping that his records will be found and that they

> may do more than merely warn men of this trap. I hope it may teach our race to let those shining crystals stay where they are. They belong to Venus alone. Our planet does not truly need them, and I believe we have violated some obscure and mysterious law—some law buried deep in the arcana of the cosmos—in our attempts to take them. Who can tell what dark, potent, and widespread forces spur on these reptilian things who guard their treasure so strangely? Dwight and I have paid, as others have paid and will pay. But it may be that these scattered deaths are only the prelude of greater horrors to come. Let us leave to Venus that which belongs only to Venus. (*CF* 4.627–28)

The final part of the story switches to a report from Wesley P. Miller, of the Venus Crystal Company's Support Group A, which arrived to rescue Stanfield only minutes after his death from asphyxiation. Ironically, both Stanfield and Dwight were only feet from the maze's exit—but facing the wrong direction—when they succumbed. The "later parts of this account shew mental decay" and are thus discounted. Dwight and Stanfield are buried in the company graveyard at Terra Nova, the crystal shipped back to Chicago, and the maze is given a perfunctory study before it is dynamited and completely destroyed. Then, "we shall adopt Stanfield's suggestion—the sound one in the saner, earlier part of his report—and bring across enough troops to wipe out the natives altogether. With a clear field, there can be scarcely any limit to the amount of crystal we can secure" (*CF* 4.630).

Outside of the threat of the man-lizards, Lovecraft and Sterling's Venus is semi-habitable. The world is covered with shallow mud and heavy vegetation; "these jungles are always half impassable after a rain. It must be the moisture that gives the tangled vines and creepers that leathery toughness; a toughness so great that a knife has to work ten minutes on some of them" (*CF* 4.597–98). As will be mentioned in chapter 11, it is also possible that Lovecraft incorporated some of his background development of the planet Yekub (*CE* 3.259) from the round-robin tale "The Challenge from Beyond" (1935) into the development of his Venus. The Venusian atmosphere contains enough cyanogen to render it deadly to a human after thirty seconds, necessitating the wearing of masks. Lubnow has proposed this aspect was inspired by the 1910 panic that life on Earth would be exterminated from the minor traces of cyanogen present in the tail of Halley's Comet (Lubnow, LSS 12; Sagan and Druyan 149–50). Stanfield wears a "Carter oxygen mask" whose weight is twice that of a "Dubois mask with sponge-reservoir instead of tubes" (*CF* 4.598). This technical description is from a part probably written by Sterling (Waugh 220); Lubnow suggests further that "many of the more scientifically based concepts and ideas in ["Eryx"] probably originated from Sterling" (Lubnow, *Essays* 13). It is tempting to assume that Sterling named the Carter mask after Burroughs's John Carter. The mechanism by which the mask creates breathable air from chlorate cubes was cutting-edge for the 1930s, based on masks developed by miners (Lubnow, LSS 12–13). The Venusian air also quickly rots paper, necessitating the use of a rotating metal-sheet "record scroll" (*CF* 4.612). However, the Venusian atmosphere is still clear enough to view stars from; indeed, Stanfield is able to observe the Earth and moon in the sky, reflecting Lovecraft's musings on Venusian astronomers from his 1915 article "The Inferior Planets" (*CF* 4.613; *CE* 3.284).

No specific period is given for Venus's length of day in the story, but Stanfield mentions at the start that its rotation is "slightly quicker" than Earth's. This seems to indicate that Lovecraft was using the 23-hour period he had sided with in "The Inferior Planets." This also perhaps aligns with the nebular hypothesis, given that Mars has a slightly slower rotation than Earth's, a reduction in speed being associated with a planet's aging in works such as Serviss's *A Columbus of Space* (although giant outer worlds such as Jupiter had still shorter rotation periods). Lubnow also notes that the story establishes that the sun sets in the west on Lovecraft's Venus, as opposed to the east on the actual planet (*CF* 4.610; Lubnow, *Essays* 5). In *The Chronology out of Time,* Peter Cannon notes that while the dating system Stanfield uses in "Eryx" is internally consistent, it is impossible to relate to a known dating system (7). The only comparison is at the very start of the story, where 18 March is equated to "VI, 9 of the planet's calendar" (*CF* 4.597).

In terms of geography, the Venus of "Eryx" contains two continents. Stanfield's crystal-hunting expedition takes him to the "plateau mapped by Matsugawa from the air fifty years ago, and called on our maps 'Eryx' or the 'Erycinian Highland'" (*CF* 4.601). This is in line with Lovecraft's thoughts in "The Inferior Planets" that the principal features of Venus were probably "a few high mountains" (*CE* 3.284). The name "Eryx" is a reference to the Sicilian mountain Eryx (modern Mount Erice), with its ancient temple of the goddess Venus at the peak, as mentioned by Virgil in the *Aeneid* (Waugh 221). Other geological features include the Dionaean Plateau, which contains "holes" that Stanfield muses might hide other higher life on the world (*CF* 4.599). In Greco-Roman mythology, Dione was a goddess who was sometimes identified with Aphrodite or Venus. The human colonists divide Venus into "mud regions" and "yellow clay regions," with water only potable in the latter. Terra Nova is in the former, but has long pipelines to the yellow clay regions, which the man-lizards often cut. The Venusian north pole contains "formations" of grayish clay, which also comprises the Venusian soil beneath the covering six inches of thin mud (*CF* 4.617).

Outside the man-lizards, the Venusian flora and fauna include farnoth-flies and efjeh-weeds, both of which feed on corpses; hallucinogenic mirage-plants; carnivorous skorahs; wriggling akmans; flying tukahs of the other continent; mud-dwelling sificlighs; ugrats; and bursting darohs. These were almost all references to various figures from Lovecraft's circle, including Farnsworth Wright, Forrest J Ackerman, Bob Tucker, the Science Fiction League, Hugo "the Rat" Gernsback, and Jack Darrow, respectively. The narrator Stanfield's name is an obvious play on Sterling's. These various names all probably came from Lovecraft, given their similarities to the ones used by him and Barlow in their parodies "The Battle That Ended the Century" (1934) and "Collapsing Cosmoses" (1935) (*IAP* 963–64; Joshi and Schultz 126; *RB* 13; Lubnow, *Essays* 15).

The most prominent feature of Venus in "Eryx" is the invisible maze. The concept was developed by Sterling, based on Edmond Hamilton's "The Monster God of Mamurth," published in the August 1926 *Weird Tales* and involving an invisible structure in the Sahara Desert (*IAP* 963; Joshi and Schultz 126; Lubnow, *Essays* 13); Hamilton will be discussed more extensively in subsequent chapters. However, the maze also has similarities with works closer to the Lovecraftian home. Foremost is entry 201 in Lovecraft's commonplace book: "Planets form'd of invisible matter" (*CE* 5.232). August Derleth's stories from 1933, "The Thing That Walked on the Wind" and "The Snow-Thing," feature the entity Ithaqua trapping its victims in walls of ice (Derleth, "Ithaqua" 76–77). There is also Lovecraft's letter to Price (24 March 1933) in which he mentions what Clark Ashton Smith had told him about Vedic astronomy: "The lore he has read says much of *invisible planets* whose substance is not exactly material in our sense" (*EHP* 72, 76). Stanfield muses about there being hidden cosmic forces behind the man-lizards (*CF* 4.627), including the invisible labyrinth being left on Venus by an ancient race of visiting aliens (*CF* 4.608). Perhaps the invisible maze is therefore indirectly Theosophical, possibly adding to the connection of the Lords of Venus?

This leads to another issue regarding "Eryx"—the assumption that the story is not part of the Cthulhu Mythos. This is made in most of the scarce criticism of "Eryx" (Emrys and Pillsworth), but there is really no evidence for this. Waugh argues that among Lovecraft's fiction, "Eryx" and *At the Mountains of Madness* are more quintessentially science fiction as Lovecraft understood the genre, especially going by "Some Notes on Interplanetary Fiction" (Waugh 219). *At the Mountains of Madness* is heavily discussed and incontrovertibly part of the Mythos (or Arkham continuity cycle, if one prefers); therefore, the SF aspect of "Eryx" cannot be the reason why it is either widely ignored or excluded from the Mythos. For example, the man-lizards, the Lords of Venus from "Alonzo Typer," and the future mind from Venus in "The Shadow out of Time" are not necessarily incompatible, given the different time periods. If anything, it is the Lords of Venus from "Typer" that are more incompatible with the Mythos as it stands.[13] But even so, it is possible that the future Venusian mind Peaslee encountered was a man-lizard, and the Lords of Venus one of the "cosmic forces" behind the man-lizards, or even their ancestors as suggested by Kenneth Hite (146). Or the cosmic forces of "Eryx" could be the man-lizard equivalent of the Cthulhu cult, or even the local Mi-Go agents. If connected with cosmic beings capable of travel between planets, it is also possible that the man-

---

13. Brian Lumley's Lovecraftian pastiche *The Transition of Titus Crow* (1975) establishes that intelligent mollusks would inhabit Venusian seas in the future, though eventually go extinct. They are also another candidate for the mind Peaslee encounters, and given their aquatic abode, not necessarily contradictory to the man-lizard dominance of the Venusian landmass.

lizards and the Serpent Men of Valusia—invented by Robert E. Howard, and referenced by Lovecraft in both "Typer" (*CF* 4.591) and "The Haunter of the Dark" (*CF* 3.467)—share some kind of distant common ancestry.

On a more thematic level, Waugh notes that Stanfield's call to commit genocide on the Venusians (*CF* 4.628–31) is a callback both to the government's deportation of the Deep Ones from Innsmouth in "The Shadow over Innsmouth" and the genocide of the Venerians by humans in Olaf Stapledon's *Last and First Men* (Waugh 221–22). In this case, a key plot point of "Eryx" reflects both a key plot point of an essential Mythos tale as well as a key plot point of an influential space-opera work. It should be noted that Stapledon's Venerians live in the planet's oceans—perhaps they actually *are* Deep Ones as well. And while Cannon in the *Chronology* did not include "Eryx" because of the inability to convert its dating system to a recognizable one, that only speaks to the lack of a framework, not an incompatibility.

It should be noted that its general lack of reception among critics does not mean that "In the Walls of Eryx" has been *completely* ignored. It has experienced something of a minor resurgence in the early twenty-first century, perhaps due to its perceived anti-imperial politics. Fred Lubnow briefly discusses the story in his 2019 article "The Lovecraftian Solar System," and far more extensively in a series of articles on his *Lovecraftian Science* website. In November 2021, Lubnow released the chapbook *Essays from Beyond the Walls of Eryx* (illustrated by Steve Maschuck) expounding on the ecology of what he terms "Sterling and Lovecraft's Venus" or "SLV." Notably, Lubnow acknowledges that "While Lovecraft loved to drop bits and pieces of the Cthulhu mythos into stories that he either revised or collaborated on, *In the Walls of Eryx* is one of the few that has no such references. This story is solely on its own; tucked away in its own little multiverse. A large part of this was more than likely due to the tale itself and the imaginative science Sterling brought on the planet Venus" (Lubnow, *Essays* 14). However, in another chapbook released at the same time, the *Journal of Lovecraftian Science, Volume 3,* Lubnow does ponder whether the Mi-Go, Elder Things, or star-spawn of Cthulhu were the ones who built the invisible maze, but ultimately settles on ancestors of the man-lizards (Lubnow, *JLS3* 70, 80–82).

In 2012, the H. P. Lovecraft Literary Podcast covered "Eryx" on episode 114, where the hosts noted the jungle setting and anti-colonial themes were similar to James Cameron's 2009 film *Avatar*; Lubnow also made that connection on his website and his chapbook (Lubnow, *Essays* 9–10). In their 2015 review of "Eryx" for the website of SF publisher Tor, Ruthanna Emrys and Anne M. Pillsworth argue that while the story is not one of Lovecraft's best, it still "starts out as a pure and perfect sci-fi pulp" before using that as a segue into more typical Lovecraftian themes. They also opine that "it's kind of sweet that Lovecraft took Kenneth Sterling's high school pulp and filled it in with tentacles and existential horror" and that, despite the name of Stanfield, the narrator is more of a stand-in for Lovecraft than Sterling. And they point out that the Venusian crystals of the story presage later SF objects like the dilithium crystals of *Star Trek*, the spice of *Dune*—and, of course, the unobtanium of *Avatar* (Emrys and Pillsworth).

Beyond the general similarities to *Avatar*, there is one other aspect of popular culture whose origins have been proposed to be traced back to "Eryx." Early in the story, Stanfield encounters one of "those curious mirage-plants [with] the shaggy stalk, the spiky leaves, and the mottled blossoms whose gaseous, dream-breeding exhalations penetrate every existing make of mask" (*CF* 4.600). The effects of the mirage-plant's gasses on Stanfield are rapid:

> I noticed a decided change in the landscape—the bright, poisonous-looking flowers shifting in colour and getting wraith-like. The outlines of everything shimmered rhythmically, and bright points of light appeared and danced in the same slow, steady tempo. After that the temperature seemed to fluctuate in unison with a peculiar rhythmic drumming. The whole universe seemed to be throbbing in deep, regular pulsations that filled every corner of space and flowed through my body and mind alike. I lost all sense of equilibrium and staggered dizzily, nor did it change things in the least when I shut my eyes and covered my ears with my hands . . . . Although everything was spinning perilously, I tried to start in the right direction and hack my way ahead. My route must have been far from straight, for it seemed hours before I was free of the mirage-plant's pervasive influence. Gradually the dancing lights began to disappear, and the shimmering spectral scenery began to assume the aspect of solidity. When I did get wholly clear I looked at my watch and was astonished to find that the time was only 4:20. Though eternities had seemed to pass, the whole experience could have consumed little more than a half-hour. (*CF* 4.600–01)

In other words, Stanfield encounters a plant whose leaves produce gases that, when inhaled, cause hallucinogenic effects; and the time at which he does so is 4:20. For decades, the number "420" has been associated with marijuana by the drug community. In 2002, counterculture author Victor Cypert proposed that the use of the number in conjunction with the drug came from the mirage-plant in "Eryx" (Bennett). This appears to be nothing more than a coincidence, as the origin of the 420 slang has been documented as originated among a group of San Rafael, California, high schoolers in 1971—albeit indeed relating to the use of 4:20 as a meeting time. Perhaps one of them had actually read the 1965 Arkham House volume *Dagon and Other Macabre Tales,* the first collection reprinting "Eryx" since the 1930s. Unless a member of the Great Race occupies their minds to observe the inspiration, the relation between marijuana and mirage-plants will remain elusive.[14]

In the Shadows of Eryx

"In the Walls of Eryx" remained unpublished in the short remainder of Lovecraft's lifetime after it was completed. After an initial rejection by *Weird Tales,* it was eventually published in its October 1939 issue, one of the final issues edited by Farnsworth Wright before his resignation in March 1940 and death three months later. As mentioned above, "Eryx" would not be reprinted in a publication until 1965, followed by *The Tomb and Other Tales* (1969) by British publisher Panther. In 1975, John Lawson McInnis III submitted his doctoral dissertation at Louisiana State University; titled "H. P. Lovecraft: The Maze and the Minotaur," the seventh chapter is based on "Eryx" (McInnis 331–401). However, as Joshi has noted, McInnis's analysis of the story's themes for Lovecraft—for example, proposing that the maze and the man-lizards represent the changing nature of Providence (McInnis 376)—is colored by the fact he was apparently unaware that the maze idea came from Sterling (Joshi, *Recognition* 185).

According to hplovecraft.com, as of 2022 there are only eight volumes of Lovecraftian fiction currently in print that include "Eryx," in contrast with the twenty-seven volumes currently in print that contain

---

14. The 420 theory also brings to mind Clark Ashton Smith's story "The Plutonian Drug" (1934), set in a twenty-first century where space travel is financed by the pharmacological products developed from the solar system's native flora. This includes mnophka, a narcotic from Venus. Interestingly, the titular drug from Pluto is a narcotic named plutonium, six years before the discovery of the identically named radioactive element.

"The Call of Cthulhu." But "Eryx" was obviously not the last story set on Venus. The planet remained a popular setting for science fiction into the twenty-first century, even after the discovery of its true atmospheric conditions. One notable standout is Lovecraft fan Stephen King's 1971 short story "I Am the Doorway," depicting an astronaut on a late twentieth-century expedition to Venus. On arriving in orbit, the astronauts send a probe on the planet's barren surface, revealing it to be shrouded by "equal parts methane, ammonia, dust, and flying shit . . . at about 600 mph." After returning to Earth and nearly dying in a crash, the astronaut realizes that he has become possessed by an alien intelligence, implied to have been summoned to their spacecraft from an experimental radio broadcast to potential extraterrestrials they transmit during the flight to Venus. The alien is soon manifested as a series of eyeballs that emerge on the astronaut's hand. The alien views humans as monsters and compels the astronaut to commit a series of murders on returning to Earth; despite burning his hands, the alien eyes start to appear elsewhere on his body, and the astronaut decides to kill himself to prevent the alien presence from continuing to exert its influence (King 63–75). Besides the visual similarity with shoggoths for the malevolent alien intelligence out of space, John Langan identifies the title of King's story as an allusion to "The Dunwich Horror" and its *Necronomicon* passage, "Yog-Sothoth is the gate" (Langan 158; *CF* 2.434). The Lovecraftian influence on King's story is also perhaps evident from commonplace book entry 191: "An odd wound appears on a man's hand suddenly and without apparent cause. Spreads. Consequences" (*CE* 5.231).

More recently there is the 2015 anthology *Old Venus*, featuring deliberately anachronistic stories by a variety of modern science fiction authors writing throwback stories set on Venus as imagined pre–Space Age. Two entries are of particular note. Lavie Tidhar's story "The Drowned Celestial" was compared by Russell Letson to the Venus of C. L. Moore's Northwest Smith stories in his review for *Locus* magazine (Letson; Tidhar 38–69). Michael Cassutt's "The Sunset of Time" was identified by reviewer Matt Ruff as a work that that in its approach to the

> old world presupposes an ocean populated by all kinds of wondrous dreams and structures; it implicates unimaginably ancient civilizations that unmake themselves, inexplicably disassembling their famed cities: "Where once was Twi-land," Michael Cassutt writes in a nicely eldritch yarn that would have done Lovecraft proud, "would now be Noon, or Nightside." (Ruff; Cassutt 358–95)

Of course, a full catalogue of post-1936 Venusian fiction would be impossible to limit to a single chapter and, more to the point, would be outside the remit of this book. However, beyond the above selections, there are two works on Venus, published only a few years after "Eryx," which are worth discussing in further depth: the 1941 short story "Logic of Empire" by Robert Heinlein, and the 1943 novel *Perelandra* by C. S. Lewis.

Robert Anson Heinlein (1907–1988) was considered one of the "Big Three" science fiction authors of the twentieth century, alongside Isaac Asimov and Arthur C. Clarke. Heinlein grew up in Kansas City, Missouri, leaving in 1925 for service in the Navy.[15] Given a medical discharge in 1934, he relocated to Los Angeles, joining with the burgeoning science fiction community there, which he coalesced into a group called the Mañana Literary Society. Among the Mañana crowd for whom Heinlein served as leader were a number of people Lovecraft corresponded with, and in some cases met, such as Henry Kuttner (whom Heinlein viewed as his obvious successor), C. L. Moore, Emil Petaja, Forrest J Ackerman, and L. Ron Hubbard (Nevala-Lee 181–82).[16] Heinlein was also at least aware of August Derleth; in his essay "Science Fiction: Its Nature, Faults and Virtues" (1959) he voiced his disagreement with Derleth's argument "that there is no clear distinction between fantasy and science fiction" (15). Notably, this essay was published in a volume that also included an essay by Robert Bloch.

Heinlein transitioned from fan to writer in 1939 with the publication of his first short story, "Life-Line." "Life-Line" was also the first entry in what became an interconnected continuity of his fiction, called the "Future History." The Future History will be explored more detailedly in chapter 11, but as the name implies, it followed the development of human civilization from the period roughly around when Heinlein became an author into a near-future of theocratic dictatorship on Earth, and ultimately as the human race became an interstellar civilization millennia in the future. From 1939 to 1941, Heinlein would publish thirteen Future History stories, until the American entry into World War II temporarily halted

---

15. Although this means that Heinlein left Kansas City eleven years before R. H. Barlow arrived in the city, one wonders whether he and Natalie H. Wooley ever unknowingly passed each other in the streets.

16. As mentioned in chapter 5, there are indirect links connecting HPL to Los Angeles fan, rocket scientist, and occultist Jack Parsons; the same for linking Parsons to Heinlein (Carter 65).

his writing career. The last of those initial Future History stories published was "Logic of Empire."

"Logic of Empire" is set on the Venus of Heinlein's universe, at a period early in the human expansion into the solar system. Heinlein's Venus is the typical swampy setting of Old Venus, complete with intelligent, amphibian natives. The only areas of the planet tolerable to humans are the polar regions, whose environments are equivalent to the Amazon rain forest, and where self-sustaining colonies have been established despite the presence of fungal diseases (Heinlein, "Logic" 316; McGiveron 248–49). The human colonies are company towns run by an unnamed corporation, which uses indentured labor imported from Earth, combined with a process by which the indentured workers

> wheedle and bully the little, mild amphibian people into harvesting the bulbous underwater growth of Hyacinthus veneris johnsoni—Venus swamproot—and to bribe the co-operation of their matriarchs with promises of bonuses in the form of "thigarek", a term which meant not only cigarette, but tobacco in any form, the staple medium in trade when dealing with the natives. (Heinlein, "Logic" 323)

The main character of the story is named Wingate, an employee of the nameless company who, on a drunken bet, signs himself up to become one of the company's Venusian workers (Heinlein, "Logic" 304). There, he learns that the conditions are more akin to slavery than he anticipated. He discovers the necessity of the local hallucinogen, rhira, to fall asleep; meets a religious worker named Hazel; and comes to despise the indigenous Venusians, especially as their presence causes the human workers to begin to develop a lisping speech in imitation of the native efforts to speak English (Heinlein, "Logic" 322–24). During his work, Wingate also befriends an elder worker, nicknamed Doc:

> [Wingate] had learned that the nickname title had derived from the man's former occupation on Earth; he had been a professor of economics and philosophy in one of the smaller universities. Doc had even offered a partial explanation of his presence on Venus. "A little matter involving one of my women students," he confided. "My wife took an unsympathetic view of the matter and so did the board of regents. The board had long considered my opinions a little too radical."
>
> "Were they?"
>
> "Heavens, no! I was a rockbound conservative. But I had an unfortunate tendency to express conservative principles in realistic rather than

allegorical language."

"I suppose you're a radical now."

Doc's eyebrows lifted slightly. "Not at all. Radical and conservative are terms for emotional attitudes, not sociological opinions." (Heinlein, "Logic" 355)

Doc explains to Wingate how the presence of slavery on Venus is not due to any moral failing or criminal banking system, but merely a logical outgrowth of colonialism, which he defends as a natural tendency of human civilization. Ultimately, Wingate manages to return to Earth and attempts to write an exposé. However, the ghostwriter resorts to lurid "cheap sensationalism," which Wingate rejects. When his friend advises him that sensationalist satire is perhaps the only thing that could get attention, as opposed to lobbying middle-class discussion clubs, Wingate plaintively asks,

"But- Oh, the devil! What can we do about it?"

"Nothing. Things are bound to get a whole lot worse before they can get any better. Let's have a drink." (Heinlein, "Logic" 340)

The relationship of the Big Three science fiction authors to Lovecraft varies. As briefly mentioned in chapter 5, Asimov had a low opinion of Lovecraft. In chapter 10, we will discuss Clarke's much more positive view of Lovecraft. Joshi has said that it is "highly questionable" whether Lovecraft had any "direct influence" on Heinlein (*IAP* 893). However, it seems that the Venus of "Logic of Empire" has a number of similarities to the Venus of "In the Walls of Eryx." Of course, some of these similarities are unavoidable as roughly mid-century works on Venus. After all, Joshi's point that the "already hackneyed use of Venus as a setting for ["Eryx"] is perhaps its one significant drawback" (*IAP* 964) is well taken. But even so, there are too many similarities to Lovecraft's oeuvre for pure coincidence.

The swampy Venus, amphibian natives as a metaphor for colonized peoples, hallucinogenic plants, and corporate exploitation are all elements of "Logic" that first appear in "Eryx." In particular, the company control and critical commentary on colonization are aspects of "Eryx" not particularly widespread in prior Venusian fiction. The fear over cultural decline of the human colonists when exposed to indigenous cultures reflects Lovecraft's xenophobia, not only of explicit colonial projects—"Arthur Jermyn" for example, or "Winged Death," which he wrote for Hazel Heald, who shares her name with Wingate's fellow worker—but also Lovecraft's fears over the end result of immigration. Wingate's rejection of sensationalist political satire could come straight from Lovecraft's invectives against the "hack writing" of Price or Long, as well as "Some Notes on Interplanetary Fiction."

So too could Doc's description of his politics, or Wingate's recognition of the limits of respectable reform, have come from Lovecraft's later letters on politics. In that realm of politics, Heinlein and Lovecraft have an almost inverse development. Young Heinlein was a liberal who evolved into a conservative whose views were most famously expressed in his novel *Starship Troopers* (1959). Lovecraft began as a conservative who by the end of his life considered himself to the left of Franklin D. Roosevelt, though still opposed to Marxism. After arriving in Los Angeles but before turning to fiction writing, Heinlein worked on the End Poverty in California (EPIC) campaign of the socialist Upton Sinclair, who was running for governor of California in 1934. In a letter to Clark Ashton Smith dated 30 September 1934, Lovecraft voiced his support for Sinclair's EPIC campaign (*DS* 568; *IAP* 915). EPIC symbolizes both the endpoint of Lovecraft's political transformation and the start of Heinlein's.[17]

According to a 1941 timeline of the Future History, "Logic of Empire" is set sometime between the years 2000 and 2012. It is therefore unlikely that the character of Doc was old enough to have also participated in the EPIC campaign, though one supposes that he may have studied it, given his former position of professor of economics and philosophy. One wonders if it was Miskatonic University's board of regents that shipped him off to Venus. But it is the Doc scene that gives perhaps the biggest clue about a Lovecraft connection. A character named Wingate, a professor of economics, and an alien setting: could these be references to "The Shadow out of Time"? Lovecraft's novella and "Logic of Empire" were both published in *Astounding*, after all, as was "Life-Line." That Heinlein was reading the magazine in 1936, only three years before he submitted "Life-Line" to it, is far from unreasonable.

---

17. Sinclair believed his wife possessed psychic powers, and he wrote the 1930 nonfiction book *Mental Radio* about their efforts to test her abilities. HPL began writing "The Shadow out of Time" the same month as Sinclair's failed gubernatorial election. It is tempting to speculate whether HPL's following of Sinclair's political career led to his interest in psychic powers, which in turn influenced the telepathy of the Great Race.

Ultimately, these connections between "Eryx" (and Lovecraft more broadly) and "Logic of Empire" are purely circumstantial. An even more tenuous potential link, between Lovecraft and Heinlein's Mars, will be discussed in chapter 9. But however circumstantial the evidence for a direct connection is, there is still some undeniable overlap in publishing between the two authors. Heinlein published a number of stories in *Weird Tales* beginning in 1949. Lovecraft's and Heinlein's works even appeared together, albeit as reprints, in the December 1951 issue of *Famous Fantastic Mysteries*. Lovecraft was represented by "Pickman's Model," while Heinlein's entry was his 1941 tale "—And He Built a Crooked House." While not part of the Future History, that story—about an architect who builds a four-dimensional house where the occupants, walking through its non-Euclidian geometry, are transported thousands of miles away—has obvious similarities to "The Dreams in the Witch House." Whether intentional or not of Heinlein, it was an appropriate choice to be reprinted alongside a Lovecraft story.

"Logic of Empire" shows, at the very least, clear parallels with Lovecraft's Venus. This is perhaps not surprising, given that both men were Americans who wrote science fiction in the 1930s, sharing a number of friends between them. The same similarities cannot be said to exist between Lovecraft and Clive Staples Lewis (1898–1963), a British novelist and literary scholar at both Oxford and Cambridge universities. Between 1938 and 1945, Lewis published his *Space Trilogy,* a mix of Christian allegory and interplanetary fiction, and perhaps his second most famous literary work after *The Chronicles of Narnia*. The first entry in the trilogy was *Out of the Silent Planet* (1938); as it is set on Mars, it will be discussed in chapter 9. The second entry, *Perelandra* (1943), is set on Venus.[18]

The basis of the *Space Trilogy* is that supernatural and incorporeal aliens of great power, the eldila, have evolved in the "Deep Heaven" of interstellar space. Certain more powerful members of the eldila, the Oyarsa, preside over individual planets, governing on behalf of the supreme entity, the Old One. The Oyarsa of Earth rebelled against the Old One and the other eldila, in an imitation of Satan's rebellion against God; this resulted in Earth being termed the "Silent Planet" (Thulcandra), with the distance of space being used as a cosmic quarantine. Mars,

---

18. Curiously, as of 2022 there was a health food store named Perelandra in Brooklyn Heights, several blocks away from the former homes of Garrett Serviss and Samuel Loveman.

or Malacandra, is a world where the Oyarsa and its species live in harmony with both one another and with the eldila. Venus, or Perelandra, is an oceanic world at present inhabited only by two green-skinned humans. They represent the world's Adam and Eve, and have not yet been tempted to rebel against the dictates of the Old One (Lewis, *Perelandra* 4–5, 174–75). In this way, Lewis perhaps deliberately maps a theological schema onto the nebular hypothesis: Venus is untouched by the temptation of sin, Earth has succumbed to it, and Mars has transcended it.

On an immediate level, Waugh comments that one major difference between *Perelandra* and "Eryx" is that Lovecraft and Sterling's story was far more explicitly science fiction than Lewis's religious parable (Waugh 221). However, beyond their respective approaches to genre conventions—which, based on "Some Notes on Interplanetary Fiction" and his appreciation of *The Worm Ouroboros,* Lovecraft may not have cared about—what connections are there between the two works? In a 1983 *Crypt of Cthulhu* article, Charles Garofalo noted that while he had found no evidence Lewis ever read Lovecraft, there was a decidedly Lovecraftian moment at the end of *Perelandra*. The hero Elwin Ransom chases the satanically possessed villain Weston (based on Haldane and Wells) beneath the surface of Venus, where Weston summons an insectoid "many-legged, quivering deformity" (Lewis, *Perelandra* 151–52). Garofalo points out the similarities to both the climactic scene of *At the Mountains of Madness* and the mutated flora and fauna of the Gardner farm in "The Colour out of Space." However, Garofalo notes that this is the sole "Lovecraftian" scene in Lewis's works, despite the use of the term "Old One" in *Out of the Silent Planet* (Garofalo 37; Lewis, *Silent* 56–57).

If Lewis did not read Lovecraft—as in all likelihood is the case—what could account for the similarities? For one, both drew from a common pool of inspiration. Lewis cited Wells's *The War of the Worlds* and *The First Men in the Moon;* the "The Last Judgment" by Haldane;[19] and Stapledon's *Last and First Men* (Lewis, *Silent* iii, 56–57; Lewis, *Perelandra* 3–4; Lewis, "OSF" 108–9; Adams 483). All these works had also been read and praised by Lovecraft, who also owned them save *Last and*

---

19. Haldane's essay was influenced by Wells's fiction and in turn served as an inspiration for Stapledon and Heinlein (see chapter 5). The framing device of Haldane's essay was a school lesson to the descendants of humans on Venus forty million years in the future, charting the evolution of humanity and ultimate decline of life on Earth (Adams 463–64, 483–85).

First Men. In his 1955 essay "On Science Fiction," Lewis lists some other works of speculative fiction for which his appreciation overlaps with Lovecraft: *The Worm Ouroboros, The Night Land, The Time Machine,* Jonathan Swift's 1729 satire *Gulliver's Travels,* William Beckford's 1786 Gothic novel *Vathek,* Edward Bulwer-Lytton's 1871 proto-conspiratorial novel *The Coming Race,* Robert Louis Stevenson's *Strange Case of Dr. Jekyll and Mr. Hyde* (1886), H. Rider Haggard's *She* (1887), Jules Verne's *Twenty Thousand Leagues under the Sea* (1870), and the *One Thousand and One Nights* (Lewis, "OSF" 93, 99, 108–12). Lewis also praises the work of several authors influenced by Lovecraft, including Clarke, Ray Bradbury—and Heinlein (Lewis, "OSF" 99, 109–10, 112).

Aside from the common authors they mutually admired, it can be argued that Lovecraft and Lewis had similar views about the role of humanity compared to the vastness of space. In his 1958 article "Will We Lose God in Outer Space?" Lewis expounds on one of the core tenets of the *Space Trilogy,* that the vastness of space serves as a cosmic quarantine of Earth and its theologically "fallen" population. He muses on the significance of humans discovering intelligent life elsewhere in the universe; on the one hand, he admits that there is absolutely no indication this will happen, and also that if life does exist elsewhere in the universe, it may take a form that makes it impossible to comprehend as life, let alone intelligence, to humans. However, if human astronauts do discover other intelligences, humanity may find itself to be the only fallen species in the universe. If so, it may be the humans who suffer the psychological blow of developing space travel only to discover sinless beings (literally) beyond us (Lewis, "God" 74–76). While applying a Christian sheen to the sentiment (in ways that August Derleth might approve of), there is certain overlap here with the fears over the investigation of humanity's place in the universe that Lovecraft expressed in the opening lines of "The Call of Cthulhu." In his alternate-history Mythos pastiche "A Colder War" (2000), Charles Stross similarly applies that sentiment to the Space Race: in the story's setting, Richard Nixon cancels the planned post-*Apollo* exploration program in favor of the extremely limited Space Shuttle precisely because, to quote Lovecraft, "it was not meant that we should voyage far" for risk of encountering the Old Ones (Stross 56).

Ultimately, *Perelandra* is included in this section for the opposite reason that "Logic of Empire" is. Heinlein's story seems to show that Lovecraft in general, and "In the Walls of Eryx" specifically, left an immediate impact on a classic work of Venusian fiction by a great of science fiction. Lewis's novel, however, shows how Lovecraft's "Eryx," despite being his sole major piece of interplanetary fiction, is a perfect fit for the genre, sharing both themes and sources of inspiration with a parallel but independent piece of great literature from a giant of genre fiction. While "Eryx" may therefore be one of Lovecraft's less-discussed works, and of a genre he is not typically associated with, its comparison with the equivalent works of Heinlein and Lewis demonstrates that Lovecraft's voyage to Venus is undeniably an important component of his oeuvre.

Conclusion

In 1950, self-educated and self-described classical historian Immanuel Velikovsky (1895–1979) published his most famous and influential book, *Worlds in Collision*. Among other controversial statements, it argued that the planet Venus did not exist until approximately 17,000 years ago, when it was ejected from the planet Jupiter as a comet, passing by Earth in its new orbit. The near-collisions of the Venus-comet with Earth before it stabilized into the current orbit of Venus caused multiple catastrophes on our planet, which were the foundation for various mythological events, such as those recounted in the Book of Exodus—and the destruction of Atlantis (Velikovsky 153–57). According to Velikovsky, evidence for his claims could be found in ancient folklore (299–302) and recordings in ancient temples and monuments (315–18)—none of which would be out of place for the protagonist of a Lovecraft story. In the years since its publication, *Worlds in Collision* and its sequels became increasingly popular among the fringe crowd and led to Velikovsky leading a movement alleging that the mainstream historians and scientists who rejected his ideas were part of a conspiracy to suppress the truth. From the late 1960s to the 1970s, Isaac Asimov and Ben Bova—the latter of whom took over as the editor of *Analog Science Fiction and Fact* after John W. Campbell's death in 1971—became main figures of the effort to push back against Velikovsky's claims, believing that the science fiction community needed to be at the forefront of defending true science against pseudoscience (Gordin 170–85; Kaveney 27–28).

What became known as the "Velikovsky Affair" is brought up here not only because of the centrality of Venus to its claims, but because there is a strange parallel between Velikovsky's catastrophism and Lovecraft's own science writings. As mentioned in chapter 6, in late 1914

Lovecraft became embroiled in a series of letters to the editor of the Providence *Evening News* debating the merits (or lack thereof) of astrology with astrologer Joachim F. Hartmann (*IAP* 183–88). This culminated in Lovecraft's letter to the editor (24 October 1914) in which he satirically took the persona of astrologer Isaac Bickerstaffe, Jr., who shared his incredible astrological divining on the future of human history. On 29 June 4898, the comet XY4 will pass by Earth. Its tail will swipe the human race into space, keeping it in suspended animation and depositing it safely on Venus. Venus would then become the new home for the human race—thankfully so, as the Earth will explode from an internal gas buildup in the year 4954. Several fragments of the exploded Earth will hit Venus; among these will be a segment of the Earth containing the Providence Public Library. The piece of the PPL will injure the leading astrologer, Señor Nostradamo Artmano, leaving him incapable of performing astrology any longer. This would lead the way for the introduction of the doctrine of "Logic" to the Venus-bound humans in the year 5012 by "an evil-minded individual named Serviss" (*CE* 3.267–68). Outside of predating the association of Venus and cometary destruction by Velikovsky, Bickerstaffe is to be commended for predicting the use of Venus as a replacement home for post-Earth humans in the writings of Haldane and Stapledon. There is also a certain poetic symmetry in starting this chapter with Lovecraft, Venus, and strange airship visitors, and ending it with Lovecraft, doomsday, and the human exodus to Venus.

It is also worth ending this chapter with commentary on the fact that, decades after the idea of life on Venus had been relegated to science fiction, it made a brief return to the scientific mainstream when, in 2020, it was claimed that traces of the organic compound phosphine were detected in the atmosphere of Venus in an amount too great to explain from abiotic processes and might indicate microbial life in the Venusian clouds. Upon re-examination, the anomalous findings were largely dismissed as measurement errors, but the idea of microbial Venusian life continues to be promoted by astrobiologists such as Jan Špaček and David Grinspoon (Špaček 1–19). If that minority view is indeed correct, perhaps—in an ironic inversion of H. G. Wells—it will be those microbes who are destined, in incalculable epochs to come, to evolve into the minds that will provide an emissary to the Great Race for Peaslee to converse with.

Chapter 8
In the Two-Corona Class

Lovecraft was in a celebratory mood. In a 1932 letter to his friend James F. Morton, he was able to crow that he "was in the two-corona class now." By that he meant that he had twice seen the gossamer glow of the solar corona encircling a totally eclipsed sun. Today, many members of the two-corona class have traveled thousands of miles and spent thousands of dollars to secure entry into that elite group. By contrast, Lovecraft's eclipse journeys were relatively short and inexpensive; fortunately so, since his wallet was always slim and an expedition to a distant land would have been out of the question. He saw his first total eclipse in 1925 from the northern environs of New York City. His second eclipse came seven years later, in 1932, when he saw the moon cross before the sun from Newburyport, Massachusetts.

Lovecraft was of course familiar with the geometry and phenomena of eclipses long before 1925. Before his thirteenth birthday he had read about eclipses in his astronomy books, and he later described solar eclipses in his newspaper columns. He was aware of the role that solar eclipses had recently played in testing Einstein's theory of general relativity (see the discussion in Livesey, DPO 61–64). However, the first solar eclipses Lovecraft himself saw were only partial. Partial eclipses of the sun are interesting but far less awesome than total eclipses, as the corona remains hidden by the light of the uneclipsed portion of the solar disk. When he left Providence for New York in 1924, Lovecraft was still stuck in the zero-corona class.

When a total eclipse occurs, only those within a narrow path swept across the globe see the moon completely hide the sun's disk. Those in a much wider area see the moon partly block the sun. This means that, although a total eclipse of the sun can be seen from some location on the earth about once every eighteen months, they occur very rarely at any particular location, much more rarely than partial eclipses. In the northern hemisphere, a given spot witnesses a total solar eclipse about once in 330 years. Thus, it is not surprising that Lovecraft had had no opportunity to see a total eclipse until he entered his thirty-fifth year. In fact, he was lucky to have even one total solar eclipse occur near his home. To have two such events occur in his vicinity only seven years apart was extraordinary.

Yonkers, 1925

Lovecraft's first total solar eclipse came during his unhappy sojourn in New York City, on 24 January 1925, a Saturday. The path of totality for this eclipse swept across the northeastern United States and parts of Canada before continuing out to sea. As the path of totality was to include densely populated areas, including part of New York City, the eclipse filled newspaper pages long before it actually arrived. Few in the affected region can have been ignorant of its coming, and astrophile Lovecraft certainly was not.

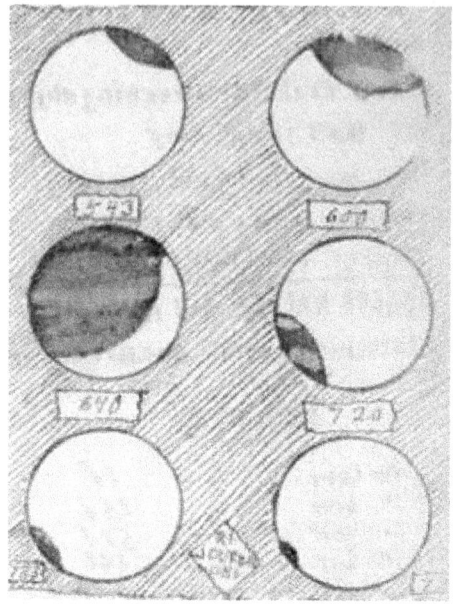

Lovecraft's drawing of the partial solar eclipse on 30 August 1905, as depicted in the 3 September 1905 issue of his self-published *Rhode Island Journal of Astronomy*. Howard P. Lovecraft Collection, Ms. Lovecraft, Brown University Library.

Lovecraft's enthusiasm for the coming eclipse is disclosed by a letter he wrote to his aunt Lillian Clark three days before the event. He reminded her that this was something she "must not under any circumstances miss" (*LFF* 237). He enclosed a dark film to dim the sun during the eclipse's partial phases and schooled her on the expected progression of eclipse phenomena. Clearly, Lovecraft was more than ready to join the one-corona class.

As the day of the eclipse dawned, thirty-four-year-old Lovecraft was newly installed at 169 Clinton Street in Brooklyn. His wife, Sonia, had moved to Cleveland to take new employment, leaving Lovecraft on his own in a city he increasingly disliked. The whole of that city would not see a total eclipse that January. Only those in the northern parts of New York City would see the sun's disk completely extinguished by the moon. Too far to the south and the eclipse would be almost but not quite total.

At Lovecraft's home in Brooklyn, the sun would diminish to a tiny sliver of light, but it would not totally vanish behind the moon. That remaining sliver, thin though it was, would be enough to hide the faint corona. Lovecraft would need to venture north if he wished to escape zero-corona ignominy. The deeper Lovecraft traveled north into the zone of the total eclipse, the longer would be the interval during which the glow of the sun was hidden. The line of longest eclipse duration would pass well north of New York City, around Newburgh, where the sun would be hidden for about two minutes. In the letter to his aunt dated 22 January, Lovecraft described his plans: "The Boys will view the sight from some good point in Yonkers—meeting at 6:00 a.m. in Van Cortlandt Park & faring northward by trolley or foot as the gods—or the schedule—may determine" (*LFF* 237).

The weather forecasts published by New York newspapers the day before the eclipse were in one sense hopeful, in another ominous. Skies might be clear, but temperatures would be exceptionally frigid. The chill of 24 January would be more than enough to tax the hardiness even of those not particularly sensitive to winter's freeze. Temperatures were forecast to be near zero Fahrenheit at sunrise (-18 Celsius), and would stay close to that frostbite-inducing number throughout the eclipse.

Venturing north on 24 January would, under those conditions, challenge Lovecraft. In his teenage years he had braved the cold to go outside in winter to view the skies. However, by 1925 his well-known sensitivity to cold had emerged, a sensitivity that could under the worst conditions lead to unconsciousness (Joshi, *IAP* 1006). Dare he venture into what might prove dangerous cold? Despite cold that Lovecraft would later call "marrow-congealing," he would not miss totality. North he would go. Lovecraft would not, however, go alone. He would be able to call upon assistance should the cold prove too much for him. The "Boys" accompanying Lovecraft on his eclipse expedition were James F. Morton, Arthur Leeds, George Kirk, and Ernest A. Dench. Kirk had earlier written to his fiancée, encouraging her to come to New York for the eclipse, when they might admire it from a Yonkers aqueduct.[1] Although his fiancée doesn't seem to have joined the eclipse party, the small group of hopeful eclipse watchers sallied forth early Saturday morning.

---

1. David Haden suggests that it may have been the Old Croton Aqueduct (*Tentaclii*, 1 January 2015).

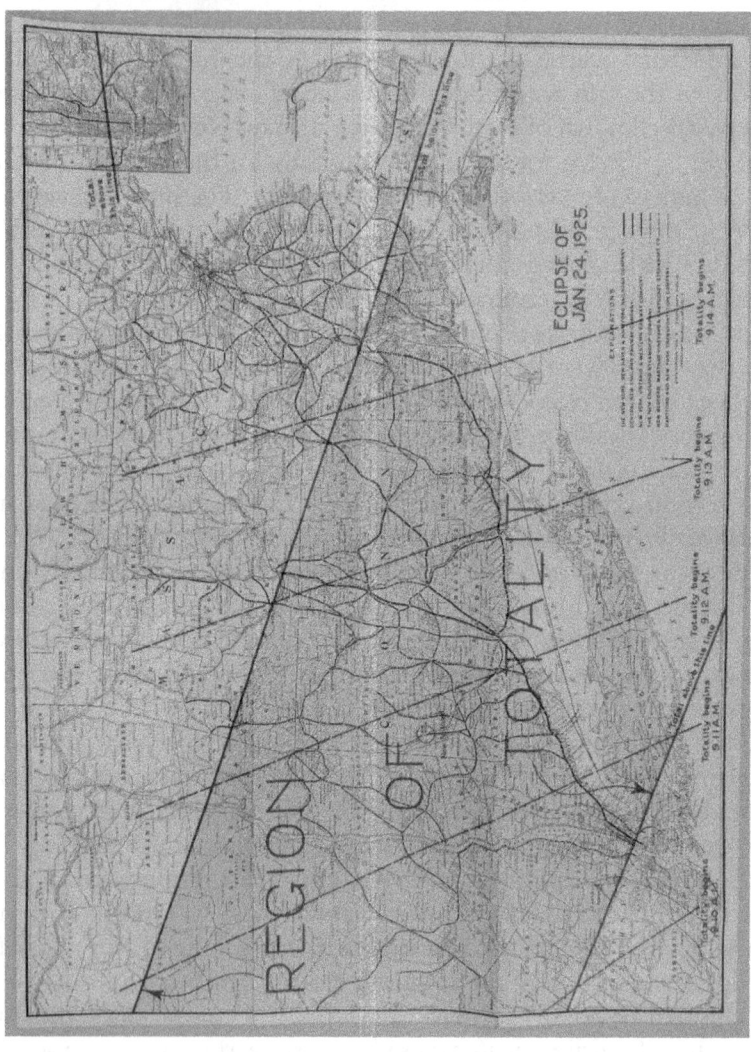

The path of the total solar eclipse of 24 January 1925 depicted in a brochure published by the New York, New Haven, and Hartford Railroad Company. Courtesy of David Haden.

8. In the Two-Corona Class

We do not know Lovecraft's exact viewing location for the eclipse, except that it was in snow-covered Yonkers. Lovecraft's diary for the day (online at the Brown Digital Repository) is rather telegraphic:

"Up 3:30 [a.m.]—to SL's & Van Ct. with GK—meet JFM, Dench, Leeds. M & D walk, rest ride Getty Sq. Yonkers. Walk up hills— ECLIPSE . . ." (CE 5.150)

The group appears to have met at Van Cortlandt Park as planned before heading further north to Getty Square in Yonkers. *SL* is Samuel Loveman, who apparently did not join the Boys. Lovecraft's party apparently watched the eclipse from a hill, but we don't know which one. A postcard Lovecraft wrote after the eclipse doesn't help in that regard. He merely noted that his party had watched the eclipse from the summit of a high hill. Park Hill, south of Getty Square, and Nodine Hill, east of Getty Square, were noted in newspapers as popular observing locations, and one of them might be the place from which Lovecraft saw his first corona.[2] The whole of Yonkers lay within the zone of totality, with a duration of total eclipse lasting more than a minute. From Park Hill, totality would have lasted about 1 minute 14 seconds.

The moon would begin to encroach upon the sun's disk at about 8 am, so the intrepid observers needed their early start. If Lovecraft and his companions wanted to look directly at the diminishing sun, they would have needed some sort of filter to dim the brilliance of its uneclipsed portion. Since Lovecraft had mailed such a filter to his aunt, he was apparently already well prepared in this regard. Various devices for viewing the eclipse were being hawked to the New York citizenry, often at a cost of only a dime (approximately $1.65 in 2022).

As the eclipse proceeded, more and more of the sun fell behind the disk of the moon—while undoubtedly Lovecraft became colder and colder. Perhaps he was able to shelter briefly in the warmth of a store or public building, but the progression of eclipse phenomena would not have let him linger long in welcome heat. Just before totality, the sun's disk was reduced to a single, glaring point of light, creating the so-called diamond ring effect. Suddenly, it was 9:10 A.M. and the sun's disk was totally eclipsed.

---

2. David Haden has suggested (*Tentaclii*, 11 February 2022) that the eclipse party may have returned south in the direction of High Bridge, which carried the Croton Aqueduct across the Harlem River. This would, however, have returned the group to the Bronx.

Filters could be dispensed with, and the sun became surrounded by the dim but beautiful corona. Lovecraft had escaped the zero-corona class!

A dime would purchase the SOL-A-CLIPSE, with a film through which one might see the partial stages of the eclipse. It included times for the eclipse at several locations, including Yonkers. H. Smith collection.

The Boys would have been able to see the planets Venus, Jupiter, and Mercury come into view as the sky dimmed, although even at totality the sky did not reach the full darkness of night. A postcard Lovecraft quickly dispatched to his aunt Lillian on the day of the eclipse reported: "... went up to Yonkers & had a magnificent view of the entire thing from the summit of a high hill. Corona was splendid & planets were brilliantly visible" (*LFF* 241).

Then totality was over. After little more than a minute, a blaze of sunlight came again and the corona quickly vanished. Newspapers reported that the temperature fell a couple of degrees during the eclipse, and one doubts whether Lovecraft lingered in the cold to savor every bit of eclipse as the sun recovered its luster, something not achieved until 10:30 A.M. Nonetheless, his postcard to his aunt joyfully exclaimed: "We suffered from the cold, but the experience was worth it!" Lovecraft's party had enough energy to visit the Philipse Manor House[3] on their return trip.

The diamond ring effect lingers as the corona comes into view. Public domain.

The Boys celebrated their success at Kirk's apartment the night of the eclipse. One wonders how much celebrating Lovecraft did, happy though he was to have seen the eclipse. Two years later he wrote to James F. Morton that the extra pounds he had put on thanks to Sonia's cooking had not spared him from the rigors of that day (*JFM* 138). When the 1932 eclipse approached, he wrote that the frigid morning of eclipse viewing left him nearly incapacitated: "God! Will I ever forget that eclipse expedition. . . . I was just about all in for the rest of the winter by the time I staggered back" (letter to Alfred Galpin, 29 September 1934, *AG* 89). Nonetheless, he had braved the cold, survived, and was now a bona fide member of the one-corona class.

---

3. A historic house in Yonkers. One of its occupants, Frederick Philipse III, was a notable Loyalist in the revolution. It opened as a museum in 1912.

The solar eclipse of 24 January 1925, as photographed by Frederick Slocum at the Van Vleck Observatory in Middletown, Connecticut. Two decades before the eclipse, Slocum had been one of Lovecraft's astronomical acquaintances at the Ladd Observatory. Published in the *Astrophysical Journal*.

Howard Russell Butler's painting of the 1925 eclipse is shown here in grayscale. Princeton University. Wikimedia Commons. Public domain.

8. In the Two-Corona Class 219

Headlines from page 1 of the *Yonkers Statesman* on the day of the 1925 eclipse.

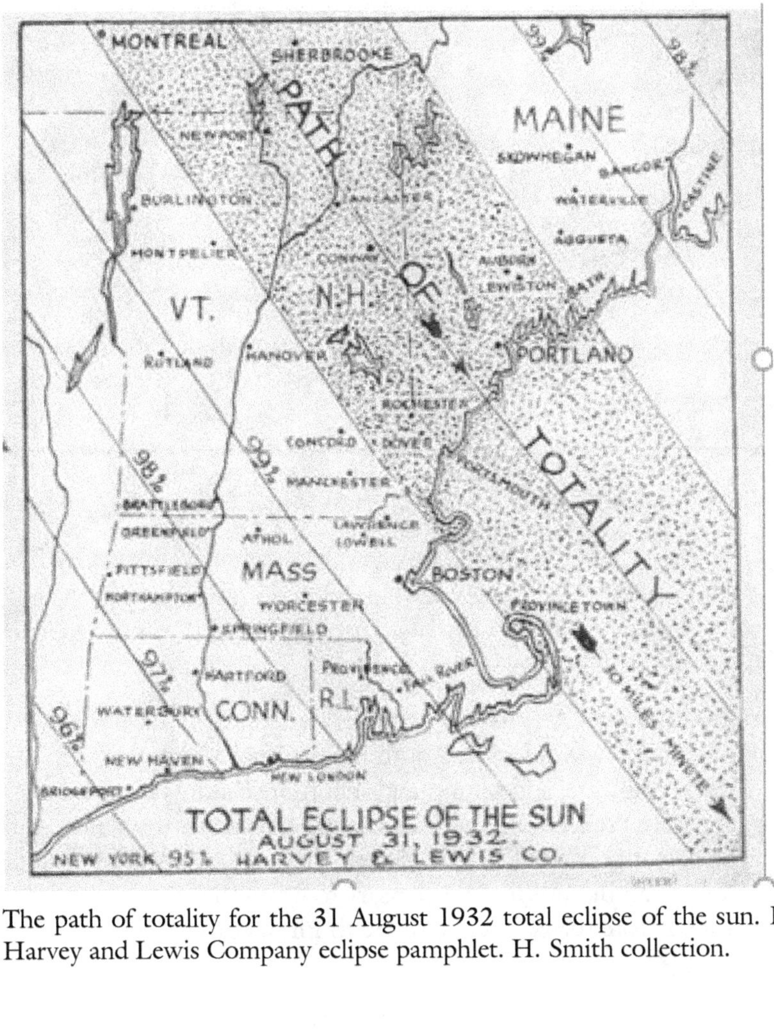

The path of totality for the 31 August 1932 total eclipse of the sun. From a Harvey and Lewis Company eclipse pamphlet. H. Smith collection.

Newburyport, 1932

Between his successful if dangerously frigid viewing of the 1925 eclipse and the arrival of his second total eclipse in 1932, Lovecraft's life underwent great changes. He left New York to return to his beloved Providence. His marriage to Sonia effectively ended. Some of his best-known stories were written and published, including "The Call of Cthulhu," "The Colour out of Space," "The Dunwich Horror," and "The Whisperer in Darkness."

A close-up of the eclipse path near Newburyport on a modern map. The line is the divide between a total and a partial eclipse. Courtesy of Eclipse Predictions by Fred Espenak, EclipseWise.com.

On the last day of August 1932, moon and sun would again conspire. The moon's shadow would race south from Canada, crossing into Vermont, New Hampshire, and Maine, and skimming coastal portions of Massachusetts before proceeding into the Atlantic Ocean. At the center of the eclipse path the moon would totally eclipse the sun for about 1 minute 38 seconds. Lovecraft did not find it necessary to travel to the centerline of the 1932 eclipse. Before the eclipse, he wrote to Elizabeth Toldridge:

I hope to get north of Boston—in the totality zone—during the eclipse of August 31, but am not sure whether I shall bother to go to Maine for the zone of maximum duration. It really matters relatively little whether an amateur sees the totality for half a minute, or for a minute & a half, so long as he does see it. Even a momentary flash gives the full benefit of the corona. In 1925 (when I was in New York) some of us tramped up to northern Yonkers to see the January eclipse, but Long (judging from his description) seems to have seen about as much from the roof of his apartment house in 100th St. (12 August 1932; *ET* 216)

One of Lovecraft's favorite cities, Newburyport, Massachusetts, would lie within the path of totality, and it was there that he decided to go. He had drawn upon his familiarity with Newburyport in writing "The Shadow over Innsmouth" late in 1931, and the narrator of that story passes through Newburyport on his way to Innsmouth.[4] The day before the eclipse Lovecraft traveled to Boston to meet his friend, W. Paul Cook, and the two set off to Newburyport the next day, with a brief stop along the way to visit Charles W. "Tryout" Smith[5] in Haverhill. The open area of Atkinson Common in the northern part of Newburyport provided a suitable observing spot.

On 31 August, a Wednesday, the moon would begin to eclipse the Sun at about 3:22 P.M. at Newburyport. At 4:31 P.M., the eclipse would be total, remaining so for just under a minute before the sun once more emerged. By 5:36 P.M., all would be over. It was summer and the cold of the 1925 eclipse was no longer a threat, for which we are sure Lovecraft was grateful. However, there was always the question of another aspect of the weather. Would the skies be clear during the brief period of totality? The headline in the *Boston Daily Globe* that morning was not encouraging: "Fair Weather Doubtful for Eclipse Today."

Lovecraft was by no means alone in selecting Newburyport as a location from which to view the eclipse. Factories and stores within the city announced plans to suspend operations temporarily so that their employees would be able to see the rare sight. In addition to the city's

---

4. The eclipse would have been total at Innsmouth, and one wonders whether Deep Ones who survived the raid of 1928 were drawn to the surface to see it. Would an eclipse have been featured in "The Shadow over Innsmouth" had the story been written several months later?

5. *Tryout* was the name of an amateur journal Smith published.

15,000 inhabitants, the *Boston Daily Globe* reported that 10,000 visitors swarmed the city hoping to see the eclipse. Eclipse eye protectors sold out on the morning of the crucial day. Might the would-be viewers be disappointed by the weather?

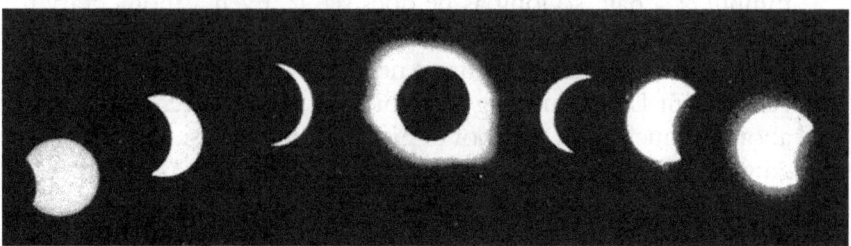

The eclipse of the sun as seen at Portland, Maine, 31 August 1932. From a John A. Marshall postcard. H. Smith collection.

Clouds obscured the Newburyport sky for most of the morning, and it appeared that the *Globe*'s pessimistic headline might prove true. The outlook became more promising in the afternoon as clouds began to thin and break. Lovecraft's good fortune was reported in a letter of 3 September to James F. Morton, a member of the 1925 eclipse party:

> Well—the card from me an' Culinarius [W. Paul Cook] no doubt appris'd you of our eclipse success.[6] Grandpa is in the two-corona class now—whereas you may get a rainy day in Peru in '37![7] In Prov. I am told it was rainy. Boston got a good view of its 99% obscuration—but as near as Medford it was half-ruin'd by clouds. I'm hoping that Smithy had as good luck at Haverhill (two sec. totality) as we did at Newburyport.

Lovecraft continued with a detailed account of the eclipse:

> As for harrowing details—we reached Bossy Gillis's[8] burg long before the eclipse started, and chose an hilltop meadow with a wide view—near

---

6. HPL and Cook evidently dispatched several postcards to friends with quick news of their success in seeing the eclipse.

7. The path of the total solar eclipse of 8 June 1937 would cross part of Peru near sunset. Evidently, Morton contemplated a Peruvian excursion. Professor Charles Smiley led a Brown University expedition to that eclipse.

8. Andrew "Bossy" Gillis was several times mayor of Newburyport and apparently a notorious character.

the northern end of High Street—as our observatory. The sky was mottled, and naturally we were damn anxious—but the sun came out every little while and gave us long glimpses of the waxing spectacle. The aspect of the landskip did not change in tone until the solar crescent was rather small, and then a kind of sunset vividness became apparent. When the crescent waned to extreme thinness, the scene grew strange and spectral— an almost deathlike quality inhering in the sickly yellowish light. Just about that time the sun went under a cloud, and our expedition commenced cursing in 33⅓ different languages including Ido.[9] At last, though, the thin thread of the pre-totality glitter emerged into a large patch of absolutely clear sky. The outspread valleys faded into unnatural night—Jupiter came out in the deep-violet heavens—ghoulish shadow-bands raced along the winding white clouds—the last beaded strip of glitter vanished—and the pale corona flicker'd into aureolar radiance around the black disc of the obscuring moon. We were seeing the real show! Though Newburyport was by no means close to the line of maximum duration, the totality lasted for a surprisingly long time—long enough for the impression to sink ineffaceably in. It would have been foolish if we had gone up to the crowded central line in Maine or New Hampshire. The earth was darken'd much more pronouncedly than in our marrow-congealing ordeal of '25, (the coldness of this damn train takes my memory back to that harrowing occasion!) tho' the corona was not so bright. There was a suggestion of a streamer extending above and to the left of the disc, with a shorter corresponding streamer below and to the right. We absorb'd the whole exhibition with open eyes and gaping mouths—I chalking down II whilst Khul-i-N'hari had to be content with I. Too bad about youse poor one-eclipse guys! Finally the beaded crescent reëmerged, the valleys glow'd again in faint, eerie light, and the various partial phases were repeated in reverse order. The marvel was over, and accustom'd things resum'd their wonted sway. (*JFM* 303)

Quite a nice description of the eclipse phenomena! A letter from Lovecraft to Wilfred Talman dated 24 September reiterated his pleasure with his second total eclipse, and his joy that it was a summer occasion: "The eclipse was magnificent, & I feel quite distinguished as being a veteran of *two* successful total eclipses. I nearly froze to death during the first one—Jany. 1925" (*WBT* 213).

Considering Lovecraft's ambition to join the two-corona class and his pleasure when he succeeded, is there evidence that witnessing these solar eclipses influenced his fiction? Somewhat strangely, the answer

---

9. Ido is an artificial language designed to be a second language for all.

seems to be no, or at least not directly. Lovecraft was obviously pleased and impressed by the changes in the appearances of land and sky associated with a total solar eclipse. After the 1932 eclipse, he even wrote to E. Hoffmann Price that the "spectacle was inexpressibly weird & suggestive of other-planetary phenomena" (letter dated 3 October 1932; *EHP* 21). However, we do not find the daytime darkness of a solar eclipse incorporated into his fiction. An eclipse does figure in his short story "The Other Gods," which was written in 1921 before Lovecraft entered even the one-corona class, but it is an eclipse of the moon, not the sun. An eclipse is mentioned in one line ("With moon-drugs in th' eclipse distill'd," from Thomas Moore's poem *Alciphron*) of the 1921 story "The Nameless City." David Haden (*LH* 152–53) has suggested that the sight of New York City in semi-darkness during the 1925 eclipse could have contributed to Lovecraft's depiction of R'lyeh, risen from the ocean in "The Call of Cthulhu." Had he lived longer, and had he once more turned his attention to fiction, perhaps Lovecraft would have eventually brought the diamond ring, the strange eclipse twilight, and the rays of the corona more directly to the Mythos.

Three-Corona Fantasies

After the Newburyport eclipse, Lovecraft was, as he proclaimed, a bona-fide member of the two-corona class. It would, however, be his final view of the solar corona. He died less than five years later, on 15 March 1937, and this chapter should properly come to a stop here. Suppose, however, that we venture into the realm of gentle fantasy. Had Lovecraft's life not been so abbreviated, had it extended to ripe old age, would he have had opportunities to better his two-corona standing without venturing to the far ends of the world?

Were Lovecraft gifted with long life, it seems plausible that his beloved Providence would have remained his home. The 1925 eclipse he witnessed in Yonkers was very briefly total as viewed from Providence. However, the next solar eclipse to be seen as total in that city will not come until the first of May 2079. A 188-year-old Lovecraft would seem unlikely without the assistance of Joseph Curwen, so Lovecraft would not have been promoted to the three-corona class unless he ventured from his home.

There would be close misses, however, in which the path of totality approached Lovecraft's city. A trip to coastal Massachusetts at dawn on 2 October 1959 might have caught the eclipsed sun right on the horizon, but the weather that morning was poor in most areas, and whether

8. In the Two-Corona Class

a sixty-nine-year-old Lovecraft could have obtained a good view on that occasion is doubtful. A trip to Maine or to Canada, south of Quebec City (Ville de Québec), would have brought the seventy-two-year-old Lovecraft into the path of the total eclipse of 20 July 1963, with better chances of success. Finally, as Lovecraft approached his eightieth birthday he might have crossed land and sea to reach Nantucket Island, which had entranced him in 1934. There, on 7 March 1970, the sun was totally eclipsed and he would have had another chance to join the three-corona class. As it happened, the weather on that occasion was good. Had the elderly Lovecraft decided instead to keep his old bones home in Providence, safe from any March chill, he could have stepped outside to see more than 97% of the sun's disk covered by the moon—only a thin sliver of sun remaining but still too much for the corona to be seen.

Lovecraft in May 1934, proud member of the two-corona class. Lucius B. Truesdell portrait. Wikimedia Commons. Public domain.

In the sadder reality, Lovecraft never had these opportunities to rejoice in the rarified fellowship of the three-corona class. Given his customary want of funds and his premature death, he was remarkably lucky to have seen the solar corona on two occasions. Many never see it once. He was entitled to be proud of his two-corona credentials: "I may never see another—but it is not everyone who has, like me, witnessed two total solar eclipses" (letter to Robert E. Howard, 3–7 October 1932; *MF* 426).

Chapter 9
At the Mountains of Mars

Introduction

In 2020, the *Atlantic* published an article that provocatively argued that Mars is "The Most Overhyped Planet in the Galaxy," based on the fact that it receives the overwhelming attention of the planetary exploration lobby—in large part due to the speculation driven by the science fiction of the prior century (Koren). However, this sentiment is neither original nor new. Consider these words of a sixteen-year-old H. P. Lovecraft: "No planet in the solar system has been the subject of more baseless speculation than Mars." Thus began "Is Mars an Inhabited World?," an article published in the *Pawtuxet Valley Gleaner* for September 1906 (*CE* 3.24–25). Although referring to contemporary scientific debates over the existence and meaning of the supposed Martian canals first observed in 1877 by the Italian astronomer Giovanni Schiaparelli (1835–1910),[1]

This chapter originated as the paper "At the Mountains of Mars: Lovecraft's Relationship with the Red Planet," presented at the Third Biennial Dr. Henry Armitage Memorial Symposium at NecronomiCon Providence on 18 August 2017. It was then revised and expanded for publication in *Lovecraftian Proceedings No. 3* in 2019, under the title "At the Mountains of Mars: Viewing the Red Planet through a Lovecraftian Lens" (Guimont, "Mountains" 52–69). This chapter is largely an edited and revised version of the 2019 published version. With thanks to David J. Halperin and Justin Mullis for their feedback and suggestions, and Bobby Derie for help with the Vrest Orton connection.

1. Young HPL only borrowed three books from Ladd Observatory's library (John Hay Library, MS-1ZAS-1 Department of Astronomy Papers Box 2: *Ladd Observatory Books Loaned* 12–13). The third, loaned from 11 June to 25 July 1907, was a work titled *The Planet Mars* by the astronomer William Henry Pickering, who was discussed in chapter 4. Pickering published a book titled *Mars* in 1921, but exactly what the book was that HPL took out

Lovecraft's comments were equally applicable to the science fiction of his time. His own first published work—a letter to the editor of the *Providence Sunday Journal* in June 1906 in response to basic errors in an astrology column—had been printed only three months earlier and itself focused on the astrologer's lack of understanding of Mars' orbit (*CE* 3.16).

The Boston-born astronomer Percival Lowell (1855–1916) took up the claims of Schiaparelli and from 1892 until his death in 1916 arguably did more than anyone to popularize the notion that the lines observed crisscrossing Mars were canals constructed by a dying civilization to irrigate their drying world with polar meltwater (Crowe 502–46). On 7 January 1907, Lowell gave a free public talk at Brown University's Sayles Hall, titled "Proofs of Life on Mars." Lovecraft not only attended, but was introduced to Lowell by Ladd Observatory astronomer Winslow Upton—who, as mentioned in chapter 7, would give his own talk at Sayles Hall criticizing the nebular hypothesis a month later (Faunce 73; *IAP* 122–23; *LFF* 1038).[2] As mentioned in chapter 4, on 18 October of the same year Upton would give a speech titled "The Question of Life on Other Worlds"[3] to the Rhode Island Institute of Instruction, an organization established in 1845 for the promotion of public education in the state. While it is unlikely that Lovecraft attended that talk, it is useful as a glimpse into Upton's views on Mars that he presumably would have shared with Lovecraft. Despite his criticism of the nebular

---

from Ladd is unclear. It was possibly a reprint of an article by Schiaparelli on Mars from 1894 that Pickering had translated into English. If so, then it presented a different concept of Mars, with the dark "seas" as actually being swampy in nature (much like the Venus HPL would later depict in "In the Walls of Eryx") and with the canals a completely natural phenomenon, albeit still channels carrying polar runoff water.

2. Upton's talk on the nebular hypothesis included a reference to "Schiaparelli, who was the first to draw attention to the canal-like markings on Mars," although the bulk of the discussion of Schiaparelli was to his theory connecting comets to the rings of Saturn (John Hay Library, MS-12AS-1, Box 72: 30897 Upton—notes on eclipses of 1878, 87, 83 Correspondence 1886–1913, Notebooks, offprints, graphs—unalphabetized Ladd Observatory, folder 7:14, p. 40).

3. John Hay Library, MS-12AS-1, Box 72: 30897 Upton—notes on eclipses of 1878, 87, 83 Correspondence 1886–1913, Notebooks, offprints, graphs—unalphabetized Ladd Observatory, folder 7:15.

hypothesis, Upton accepts that "Mars is older than the earth, or at least further along in its history" (18) and that, regarding Lowell's canal-building claims, "we may fairly conclude that Mars may support life not essentially different from what we know on the earth" (13).

In a letter to Rheinhart Kleiner, Lovecraft would claim:

> when I met [Lowell] I had just been attacking his theories in my astronomical articles with my characteristically merciless language. With the egotism of my 17 years, I feared that Lowell had read what I had written! I tried to be as noncommittal as possible in speaking, and fortunately discovered that the eminent observer was more disposed to ask me about my telescope, studies, etc., than to discuss Mars. (19 February 1916; *RK* 53)

Lowell's canals would indeed eventually be determined to be more fantasy than real, but they were widely debated at the time. Lovecraft's own fiction is filled with real astronomical objects and contemporary discoveries, most famously the 1901 GK Persei nova in his 1919 story "Beyond the Wall of Sleep" (*CF* 1.85) and the 1930 discovery of Pluto in his novella "The Whisperer in Darkness" (*CF* 2.538). The novella "The Shadow out of Time" alone features intelligent aliens from Mercury, Venus, a moon of Jupiter, and several extrasolar planets (*CF* 3.397–400). However, Mars and any potential inhabitants are curiously absent from Lovecraft's fiction, being only mentioned in a single sentence in his 1933 Dream Cycle story "Through the Gates of the Silver Key," technically co-written with E. Hoffmann Price, although it was almost entirely written

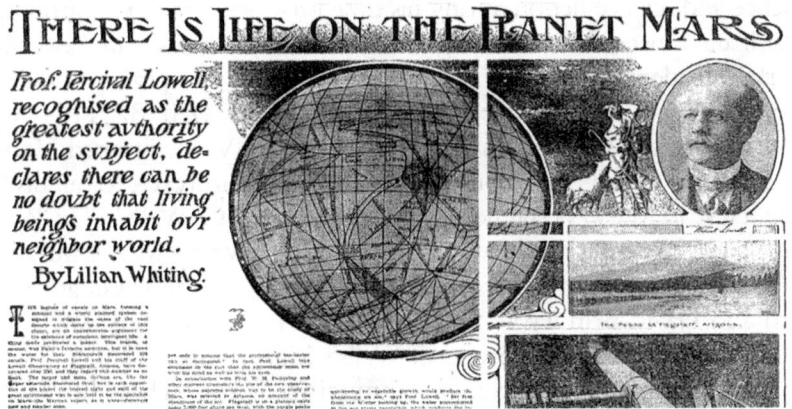

Percival Lowell and his claim of intelligent canal-building Martians gets an endorsement from *The New York Times* p. X1, 9 December 1906.

by Lovecraft (*ET* 274; Lubnow, *LSS* 14). Why might this be?

The reasons for the lack of Mars in Lovecraft's canon cannot be definitively stated, but given his political, scientific, and literary views, several reasons can be extrapolated. However, while the planet itself was almost completely absent, contemporary theories about Mars, especially those of Lowell, can be seen as influencing Lovecraft's later fiction—as can Mars-related works of fiction by such writers as Edgar Rice Burroughs, Garrett Putnam Serviss, and especially H. G. Wells in *The War of the Worlds*. But despite its terrestrial setting, it is *At the Mountains of Madness* that draws the most from the Martian themes of prior science fiction and fact alike. Indeed, with its depiction of a realistically planned expedition to an inhospitable environment, it serves as a sort of transition point between the more fantastic planetary romances of earlier authors and the more scientific bent of later authors—of both fiction and nonfiction—who speculated on what expeditions to Mars might be like. And even from Lovecraft's own lifetime up until the present, there have been no shortage of pastiche authors willing to bring the Cthulhu Mythos and its themes—and, sometimes, Lovecraft himself—to the Red Planet.

Searching for Mars

On the purely personal level of armchair psychology, we can perhaps wonder if, more than anything, Lovecraft avoided Mars due to his own dislike of cold and association of it with sluggishness and death—"[c]old and death to are to me synonymous," as he wrote in his final letter to Richard F. Searight (*EHP* 435). But scholarship on the role of Mars in science and science fiction during his time provides some more grounded, if still circumstantial, reasoning for the planet's absence in Lovecraft's works. He identified himself as a "Verne enthusiast [and] many of my tales showed the literary influence of the immortal Jules" (*IAP* 87, 114–15), as described in greater detail in chapter 5. But Jules Verne ignored Mars almost completely in his fiction (Harpold 29–35). However, for all his lack of interest in Mars, Verne nevertheless viewed H. G. Wells's *The War of the Worlds* as "a work for which I confess I have a great admiration" (Verne, "Commentary" 185). Further exploring this link, Gregory Benford and David Brin wrote the 1996 story "Paris Conquers All," which follows Verne during the events of Wells's Martian invasion.

Or perhaps Lovecraft's anti-communism (Joshi, "Thought" 20–24) was a reason, turning him off of Mars due to its adoption by socialist authors, who took its nickname of the Red Planet to heart (Lane 170–85;

Schroeder 13–14). Mars was particularly prominent in Soviet science fiction, most notably Aleksandr Bogdanov's *Red Star* (1908) and *Engineer Menni* (1913), both influenced by Wells, and Aleksei Tolstoi's *Aelita* (1923), influenced by Theosophy and including Atlanteans colonizing Mars to flee the destruction of their continent.[4] *Aelita* was popular enough that in 1924 it was adapted into the first Soviet blockbuster film (Crossley, *Imagining* 174–76; Yudina 51–55; Valdron, "Aelita"; Scharmen 56–69). Meddy Ligner used this combination to great effect in his 2011 short story "Trajectory of a Cursed Spirit," set in an alternate history where the Soviets relocated their gulags from Siberia to Mars. The story follows a purged Communist Party official who falls under the sway of the Great Old Ones once resident on Mars, and who were the cause of the once-lush world wasting away to the airless desert it now is. Lovecraft's typical Cyclopean monoliths are replaced by enormous sculptures of Karl Marx, Friedrich Engels, Vladimir Lenin, and Joseph Stalin, and the protagonist's ultimate physical obliteration in an underground tomb of a Great Old One mirrors his spiritual obliteration in the gulag (Ligner 209–20). Here, Ligner not only merges Lovecraft's supernatural themes and his anti-communism, but also Stalin's own use of Bogdanov's novels as inspiration for Soviet canal- and city-building projects in the 1920s (Graham 62). The association of Martian invaders and Soviet enemies would continue into the 1950s, becoming a staple of Cold War flying-saucer films (Colavito, *Cult* 118–19). Ligner was also presaged by filmmaker John Carpenter, director of such Lovecraftian films as *The Thing* (1982), *They Live* (1988), and *In the Mouth of Madness* (1994). Carpenter also directed the 2001 film *Ghosts of Mars*, which involved a team of colonists on Mars encountering ghosts of the planet's now-deceased civilization.

Aelita and *Ghosts of Mars* bring up another possible explanation for the lack of Mars in the filmgoing Lovecraft's output: its lack of appearance in film prior to the 1950s. As mentioned in chapter 5, meager as the offerings were, there were still a number of notable moon-themed films in the same era, including some with major impacts on science and culture alike. In the US, there were only two Mars films available during Lovecraft's lifetime. The first was *A Trip to Mars*, a four-minute Thomas Edison silent from 1910.[5] The second was the 1930 musical *Just Imagine*.

---

4. Similar to Clark Ashton Smith's "A Voyage to Sfanomoë," as mentioned in chapter 7.

5. It is worth noting that HPL's longtime correspondent Rheinhart Kleiner

Set in 1980, the final act features two future New Yorkers and one man revived from 1930 going to Mars, where they meet the king and queen, before returning home, where the honor of being a part of the first expedition to another planet lets the main character wed the woman of his dreams. Notably, the electrical props used to revive the 1930 man would be reused the next year in *Frankenstein*—which Lovecraft saw and disliked (*DS* 344)—and *Just Imagine* was the first science fiction film to be nominated for an Academy Award, in Best Art Direction (T. Miller 18–25). However, there was almost a third Mars film in Lovecraft's lifetime. In the early 1930s, MGM collaborated with Edgar Rice Burroughs to make an animated version of his *Barsoom* novels, but the studio shut down the effort in 1936 due to poor test audience responses to the footage. Had it gone forward, it probably would have beat Disney's December 1937 *Snow White and the Seven Dwarfs* and become the first American animated feature film (Hughes 311–22).

Beyond the political overtones of Martian fiction, another possible reason for the lack of the Red Planet in Lovecraft's work was that he was merely reflecting the science of his era. The 1930s were a time when astronomers were less attentive toward Mars and the planet's significance to science was at its nadir (Huntington 80–85; Crossley, *Imagining* 168–70). This was demonstrated in contemporary fiction by Martian tales increasingly focusing on the Red Planet as simply a setting for either "sword and planet" swashbuckling tales or satires of such earthly issues as sexuality, racism, war, and colonialism (Caidin, Barbree, and Wright 98–102; Lane 201–13). As noted in his 1934 essay "Some Notes on Interplanetary Fiction," Lovecraft believed that "Social and political satire are always undesirable" in speculative fiction (*CE* 2.181),[6] and in a letter to Wilson Shepherd of 29 May 1936, he lamented that the "average interplanetary tale is just a camouflaged 'western' with the pioneers & soldiers called 'space-explorers', & the Indians called 'Martians' or 'lunarians'" (*RB* 350).

Despite this, it should be remembered that *The War of the Worlds*, which Lovecraft admired, was a strong satire of British imperialism. In

---

worked for Edison Studios as both an actor and a scriptwriter (*RB* 274), but there is no indication that he was involved with *A Trip to Mars*.

6. This is a somewhat odd view for HPL to hold, given that Joshi has noted that "Satire had been a consistent strain in HPL's temperament and literary work from childhood" (Joshi, *Recognition* 22–23).

his seminal 1966 essay on Lovecraft's contribution to speculative fiction, Fritz Leiber argued that "clearly he seems to be thinking of the crude anti-religious element in Burroughs and perhaps of such books as Bellamy's *Looking Backward* and Jack London's *The Iron Heel*. He can hardly be referring to *Gulliver's Travels* or to such novels by H. G. Wells as *The First Men in the Moon,* or to Olaf Stapledon's *Last and First Men*" (Leiber, "Hyperspace" 165–66).[7] That being said, John Rieder has also argued that certain core elements of the Cthulhu Mythos—"invasion, human idolization and cultic worship of the invaders, and conspiratorial anticipation of the monster-god's return"—are distinctly evocative of imperialism and therefore implicit rejections of the satire in *The War of the Worlds* (Rieder 44–45).

As scientific interest in Mars revived after the 1930s doldrums, it became increasingly clear that there was no intelligent life, and perhaps no life at all, on the world. Martian fiction of this era tended to be set on a habitable, canal-ridden Mars based not on science but on nostalgia of the Lowell era. One major example of this from the end of the decade was C. S. Lewis's religious parable *Out of the Silent Planet* (1938), a work that was influenced by both *The War of the Worlds* and *The First Men in the Moon* by Wells (Lewis, *Silent* iii, 56–57; Lewis, *Perelandra* 3–4). It is the first entry in the *Space Trilogy,* of which the second installment, *Perelandra,* was discussed in chapter 7. In *Out of the Silent Planet,* the human protagonist discovers that the eldila, a species of entities that bridge the gap between extraterrestrials and deities, have placed the Earth under a sort of galactic embargo due to the fallen nature of its own eldila (Lewis, *Silent* 83–88). This was a reflection of Lewis's own pondering on whether "the vast astronomical distances may not be God's quarantine precautions [to] prevent the spiritual infection of a fallen world from spreading" (Hannay 11). In this cosmology, we find some very Lovecraftian (sprinkled with Derlethian) elements. Indeed, Leiber argued that the novel "reads as if it had been written to satisfy Lovecraft's criteria" (Leiber, "Hyperspace" 166). Despite this endorsement, Lewis

---

7. Edward Bellamy (1850–1898), Massachusetts author of the utopian *Looking Backward: 2000–1887* (1888); Jack London (1867–1916), Californian author of the dystopian *The Iron Heel* (1908); *Gulliver's Travels*, 1726 satire by Anglo-Irish clergyman Jonathan Swift (1667–1745). HPL owned London's 1915 *The Star Rover* (*LL* 103) as well as *Gulliver's Travels* and a volume of Swift's essays (*LL* 152).

does evade Lovecraft's strictures for scientific accuracy, writing years later that "When I myself put canals on Mars I believe I already knew that better telescopes had dissipated that old optical delusion. The point was that they were part of the Martian myth as it already existed in the common mind" (Lewis, "OSF" 109).

One of the most seminal works of post–World War II Martian fiction, Robert Heinlein's *Stranger in a Strange Land* (1961), features a group of incorporeal, esoterically religious Martians with the Lovecraftian name of the Old Ones (Heinlein, *Stranger* 92; McGiveron 249–51). But the archetypal example of this trope is Ray Bradbury's 1950 short story collection *The Martian Chronicles*. In the story "Night Meeting," the only story original to the collection, the main character encounters the spirit of a Martian from thousands of years in the past, projected into the future—reminiscent of "The Shadow out of Time" (Bradbury 78–86). Lovecraft is even mentioned in the story "Usher II," along with Edgar Allan Poe and Ambrose Bierce, as one of the authors whose works a character hopes to preserve on Mars from earthly censors (Bradbury 105). In another entry, "The Exiles," Lovecraft initially appeared, as the story depicted Mars as a sort of purgatory for authors whose works were being destroyed on Earth; Lovecraft eats ice cream and writes letters to L. Frank Baum, Samuel Johnson, and Charles Dickens. However, Bradbury removed Lovecraft's appearance from all subsequent reprints of the story for unknown reasons (Perridas). These Lovecraft references in early Bradbury works are not surprising, given that his earliest stories were published in *Weird Tales* and his first book, the short story collection *Dark Carnival*, was published by Arkham House only a decade after Lovecraft's death, in 1947 (Joshi, *Recognition* 131). Bradbury's early promotion by Arkham House was apt; another entry in *The Martian Chronicles*, "There Will Come Soft Rains" (Bradbury 166–72), was later parodied by August Derleth in his 1954 short story "The Mechanical House" (Howard 55).

While Lewis, Heinlein, and Bradbury were representative of one authorial tendency—that of simply ignoring the modern consensus on Mars—others dealt by transferring the trope of the dying desert world to different solar systems. The planet Anthea from Walter Tevis's novel *The Man Who Fell to Earth* (1963) and Arrakis from Frank Herbert's novel *Dune* (1965) are early examples of this Martian imposter syndrome (Crossley, "Cultural" 166–68; Caidin, Barbree, and Wright 110–36). Even in *Star Wars* (1977), in a scene on the desert world Tatooine, Greedo—the green-skinned, bug-eyed bounty hunter whom Han shoots first—was referred to by the production crew simply as "Martian" (Titelman 61). This trend was finalized by the arrival of the Space Age to Mars. On 15 July 1965—only two weeks prior to the publication of *Dune*—NASA's *Mariner 4* became the first spacecraft to return images from Mars. Showing a world that appeared completely desiccated and crater-blasted, it seemed to put the question of Martians to rest (Caidin, Barbree, and Wright 128–29).

The Lowell Influence

If other locations could symbolically step in for Mars after the start of the Space Age, why couldn't it have happened earlier, too? Lovecraft was, after all, a man ahead of his time in so many other genre innovations. Perhaps, therefore, an inhabited Mars is present in Lovecraft's fiction—if only in a mutated form.

Fred S. Lubnow has claimed that "Lovecraft never thought highly of the hypothesis of life on Mars" (Lubnow, LSS 6), but this is not entirely accurate. Indeed, up until the end of his life, he maintained that at least "primitive vegetation" almost certainly existed on Mars (*FLB* 351). Instead, it should be said that Lovecraft's view of Lowell's theory of intelligent canal-building Martians has a tumultuous history, as seen in a series of his early newspaper articles on astronomy. In 1903, he wrote that Lowell's claims were "perfectly ridiculous" (*CE* 3.15); in 1906, that they were "not only possible, but even probable" (*CE* 3.24–25); in 1915, 1917, and 1918, that the "true nature of the canals . . . is a matter of great dispute" but deserved consideration because Lowell was the "leading authority on all matters relating to the planet Mars" (*CE* 3.291–94, 319–20, 251–54); and in 1917, he wrote an elegiac poem dedicated to Lowell after the astronomer's death the year before (*AT* 107, 484–85). In the 11 June 1905 issue of the *Rhode Island Journal of Astronomy*, Lovecraft wrote on the Lowell Observatory's photography of the Martian canals, commenting that "from previous work at Mr. Lowell's observatory, we may well believe some seemingly improbable things," a tone that conveys some skepticism but also a degree of open-mindedness; Lovecraft's own telescopes were too small to show much on Mars, and his drawings do not show much detail that can be ascertained to be real. However, despite all these writings showing at least a measure of credulity, Lovecraft stated in his 1916 letter to Kleiner that "I never had, have not, and never will have the slightest belief in Lowell's speculations" (*RK* 53).

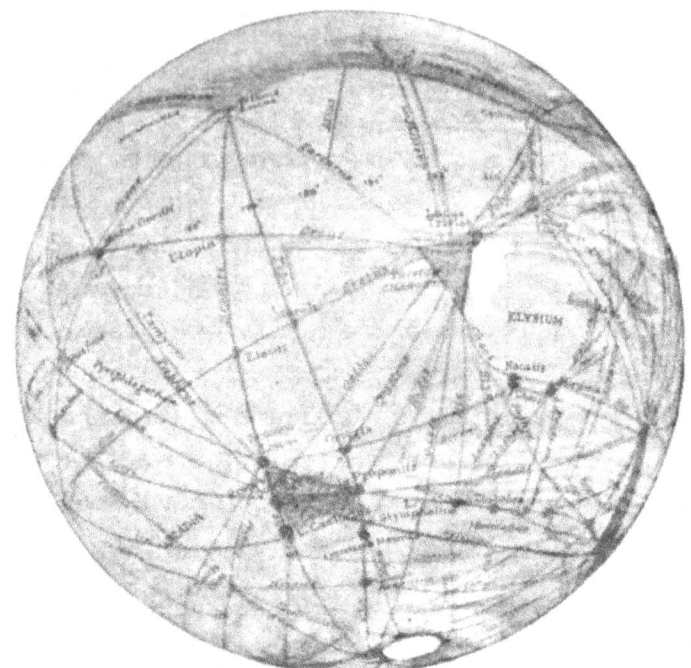

A SECTION OF THE CANAL EUMENIDES-ORCUS TERMINATING IN THE
JUNCTION TRIVIUM CHARONTIS

The length of this canal is 3500 miles. The remainder of the canal may be seen on the hemisphere shown on p. 156, where it starts from Phœnix Lake (Lucus Phœnicis).

One of Percival Lowell's maps of Mars and its canals (Lowell 150).

However, even if we acknowledge that Lovecraft fully dismissed Lowell's ideas, that would not preclude his use of said Martian speculation as the basis for fiction. After all, nearly the whole of Lovecraft's output contains material and topics that he himself, the atheist materialist skeptic, did not personally believe in. While Lovecraft did argue that interplanetary fiction needed to adhere strictly to the latest scientific knowledge (*CE* 2.180), as demonstrated in chapters 5 and 7, he did not always follow his own advice in his own (scant) planetary fiction. It would therefore not be inconsistent that Lovecraft could draw inspiration from Lowell's Martian theories, even if he disagreed with them as unscientific. From 30 July 1903 to 16 March 1923, the Ladd Observatory library received eighty-four issues of the *Lowell Observatory Bulletin*, the majority of which contained observational records of the Martian canals, polar ice caps, atmosphere, temperature, and moons, often written by Lowell himself before his 1916 death.[8] From these, young Lovecraft could easily have kept up with the latest speculation on Martian life and conditions from Lowell during his visits to the observatory library.

In particular, there are two aspects of Lowell's Martian canal theory that can be seen as influences on Lovecraft's work. The first is evident in Lovecraft's 1906 and 1915 articles on Mars, where he referenced the nebular hypothesis of solar system formation, as described in chapter 7. In line with this theory, in the words of Lovecraft, "as Mars is an old planet, compared to the earth, the population might be vastly more civilised and advanced than that of our globe" (*CE* 3.25). Indeed, in those words from his 1906 article, Lovecraft anticipates Lowell's thoughts in his 1908 book, *Mars as the Abode of Life*.[9] Lowell's telescopic observations demonstrated to him the "connecting link in the long chain of evolution from nebular hypotheses to the Darwinian theory" (Lowell 2) that results in the fact that on "Mars, we find what is but in its infancy on earth, there in full control" (Lowell 131).

Notably, the nebular hypothesis corollary that Mars was an older and dying world was evident in an early science fiction novel that Lovecraft owned, the 1894 *A Journey in Other Worlds* by American businessman John Jacob Astor IV (*LL* 28). As mentioned earlier, the novel concerns an expedition to the outer solar system in the year 2000, and so will be discussed more in the next chapter. However, one of the justifications for the novel's explorers deciding against landing on Mars is that "Mars is already past its prime" (Astor 262)—a clear nod to the nebular conception of solar system aging. Despite this, the expedition passes

---

8. *The Library of Ladd Observatory of Brown University List of Books and Pamphlets, in Order of their Receipt* 63–128; contained in the John Hay Library, MS-1ZAS-1 Department of Astronomy Papers Box 4.

9. Hugo Gernsback (1884–1967), the "father of science fiction" to many and "Hugo the Rat" to HPL, would later claim that reading a German translation of *Mars as the Abode of Life* at age ten in his native Luxembourg was what inspired him to become interested in science fiction. However, as a number of biographers have noted, the timeline of this does not add up, nor does it for any of Lowell's Mars-themed books. However, it is most likely that Gernsback had instead read newspaper accounts of Lowell's theories, and it was in this way that Lowell's Martian canal ideas led to both the field of science fiction and ultimately the *Amazing Stories* magazine in which "The Colour out of Space" would be published (Ashley and Lowndes 469).

Mars on its way to Jupiter, observing a snowstorm and southern glaciers, and determining that one quarter of the "Marsian" surface is covered in oceans; the moons Phobos and Deimos similarly show signs of former water and volcanos on their surfaces (Astor 134–40). No reference is given to intelligent life—or their canals.

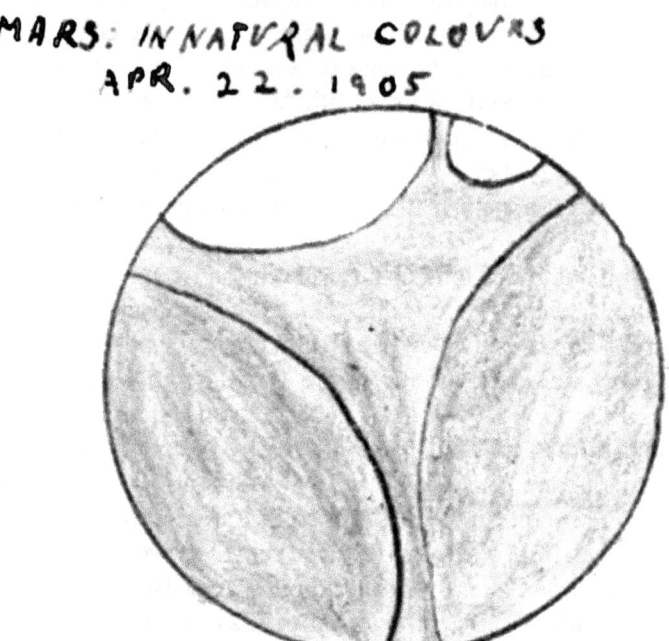

Lovecraft's map of Mars from the *Rhode Island Journal of Astronomy* III, No. II (23 April 1905)—a rare (and possibly unique) color illustration from the publication—ahead of the world's May 8 opposition. The center feature was drawn in green, the side regions in red. In the accompanying text, Lovecraft notes that on 18 April, "the 'oceans and continents' were plain, but no polar cap could be distinguished," but on the 22nd, the south pole could be seen. He ends by noting, "In all telescopes of over 12″ the principal canals are visible." Howard P. Lovecraft Collection, Ms. Lovecraft, Brown University Library.

The second possible influence from the canal theory can be discerned from Lovecraft's 1906, 1915, and 1917 Mars articles. In them, he noted that, to be seen from Earth, the Martian canals would have to be of an "immense scale, out of all proportion to the known works of mankind" (*CE* 3.292–93, 319) and that as "a thoughtful person will be apt to doubt the ability of humans to construct such great work" the canals would have to be made by beings "able to accomplish much more than our race in a mechanical way" (*CE* 3.25). A civilization far older than human history with the ability to engage in feats of Cyclopean construction, and yet for all their technology unable to prevent the slow death of their world: these are all hallmarks of Lovecraft—with R'lyeh, Pnakotus, and the Antarctic city of the Elder Things as the primary examples—which Lowell (and others) had prior claimed about Mars (Scharmen 58–59). Indeed, in his sole fictional reference to Mars in "Through the Gates of the Silver Key," the character Randolph Carter, his disembodied spirit traveling across space and time, "gazed at the Cyclopean ruins that sprawl over Mars' ruddy disc" (*CF* 3.315). Lubnow has speculated that the "ruins" sighted by Carter may have been inspired by Olympus Mons, the largest mountain on Mars, or any planet in the solar system. Olympus Mons is often the only part of the planet visible to terrestrial astronomers when dust storms engulf the rest of Mars (Lubnow, *LSS* 14–15). However, one wonders whether Carter was actually viewing the Face on Mars that would only be revealed to the wider public with its photography by *Viking 1* in 1976 (Colavito, *Cult* 251; Grinspoon, *Lonely* 358–62).[10]

Nor was Lowell the only popular scientific figure who made claims about intelligent Martians. In 1899, the inventor Nikola Tesla (1856–1943) claimed to have received radio messages from Mars, an event Lovecraft briefly mentioned in a letter to Maurice W. Moe (September 1906; *MWM* 333). Tesla was only one of several notable fin de siècle inventors to make such early SETI claims. British physicist Lord Kelvin (1824–1907) and Italian radio pioneer Guglielmo Marconi (1874–1937) were also reported to have made such early SETI claims around the time, although it is less clear whether they actually did make such claims, with Kelvin denying it in 1902. However, even in his denial Kelvin believed that some form of communication across worlds was possible (Crowe 398–99; Grinspoon, *Lonely* 291–92).[11] The British biologist J. B. S. Haldane alluded to these efforts in a 1923 speech on future human evolution

---

10. The Face on Mars had an even more direct science fiction predecessor, the 1958 comic book *The Face on Mars* by Jack Kirby and Joe Simon, where a human expedition to Mars finds an immense, ancient stone carving of a man's face (Kirby and Simon 1–5).

11. "There is one thing I wish to emphatically deny, and that is the absurd report which quoted me as saying that the planet Mars was signalling to

at Cambridge University titled *Daedalus, or, Science and the Future:* "I should have like had time allowed to have added my quota to the speculations which have been made with regard to inter-planetary communication. Whether this is possible I can form no conjecture; that it will be attempted I have no doubt whatever." Lovecraft owned the 1924 printed version of Haldane's speech (*LL* 78). This early mania for radio contact with Martians reached its peak in August 1924. As Earth and Mars reached their closest points in their respective orbits, US Secretary of the Navy Curtis D. Wilbur (1867–1954) ordered all naval radio stations to report any potential signals from the Red Planet. This included the use of a balloon-mounted radio developed by astronomer David Peck Todd at Amherst College in Massachusetts (Sconce 95–103; Schroeder 25; Hester). Not only is Amherst only twenty miles from where Lovecraft placed Dunwich, Winslow Upton had previously corresponded with Todd on observations of the total solar eclipse of 1 January 1889.[12]

These events were unsurprisingly reflected in contemporary science fiction, most notably the novel *Station X* (1919) by British author George McLeod Winsor (1856–1939) (Sconce 94). *Station X* features a Scottish radio operator working on a new Marconi wireless station located on a British outpost on a newly formed volcanic island in the Pacific. The narrator begins to pick up Martian signals on his receiver at the station he works at, presaging a psychic invasion of the Earth by Martian forces seeking to take over human bodies. The Martians are actually originally the inhabitants of the moon who had "emigrated" to Mars, taking over the Martian race as the moon died (Winsor 16, 39, 72, 101). *Station X* was reprinted in the July–September 1926 issues of *Amazing Stories,* which Lovecraft owned (*LL* 24), and in "Some Notes on Interplanetary Fiction" he singles it out as one of the few good works of the genre (*CE* 2.182). It is clear that Lovecraft read *Station X* in 1926, and David Haden has suggested that it not only influenced the Great Race in "The Shadow out of Time" but also—supposing that he read it

---

New York. What I really said was that the inhabitants of Mars, if there are any, were doubtless able to see New York, particularly the glare of the electricity" (*New York Times* [11 May 1902]: 29).

12. This can be found in the Ladd Observatory records of the John Hay Library, MS-12AS-1, Box 68: 30901 F. Seagrave—notes; A. Caswell—notebook—astro. observations; t. Andrews—diaries Ladd Observatory, folder 2:12.

prior to its *Amazing Stories* reprinting—"Beyond the Wall of Sleep" as well (Haden, "Angling" 13–17).[13]

Despite this signal boosting by radio enthusiasts, by the end of the nineteenth century Lowell's Martian canal theory was under increasing derision in the astronomical community. In 1906, Lowell attempted to rehabilitate his scientific reputation by initiating a search for what he called "Planet X," a world whose gravity could explain apparent discrepancies in the orbits of Uranus and Neptune. A young Lovecraft wrote of Lowell's search for Planet X in his article "Are There Undiscovered Planets?" (5 October 1906; *CE* 3.30). Lowell died in 1916, but his project continued, resulting in the discovery of Pluto at his observatory in 1930. Lovecraft would incorporate this into the end of "The Whisperer in Darkness," where Pluto is actually the Mi-Go planet Yuggoth, and its discovery due to the Mi-Go ending their psychic shrouding of the planet (*CF* 2.538; *ET* 137–38; Lubnow, LSS 23–26). Lovecraft had earlier developed Yuggoth in his 1929–30 poem cycle *Fungi from Yuggoth*. It is therefore ironic that, prior to equating Yuggoth with the planet found as a result of Lowell's attempt to escape from his own canal legacy, Lovecraft would devote sonnet XXIV of his poem to describing an abandoned, lifeless canal in Yuggoth:

> A deep, black, narrow channel, reeking strong
> Of frightful things whence oily currents race.
> Lanes with old walls half meeting overhead
> Wind off to streets one may or may not know,
> And feeble moonlight sheds a spectral glow
> Over long rows of windows, dark and dead. (*AT* 74)

The discovery of Yuggoth by astronomer Clyde Tombaugh, and its role in the post-Lovecraft Mythos, will be discussed in greater depth in chapter 10. But Pluto is not the only icy realm covered by Lovecraft with ties to Mars; another, more terrestrial locale also serves as a Martian stand-in.

The Martian Connection to *At the Mountains of Madness*

It is the 1931 novella *At the Mountains of Madness* where the most parallels to Lowell and the Martian fiction he inspired can be found in

---

13. Given the setting on a newly risen Pacific island, had HPL read *Station X* in 1919, it is possible it also contributed to the DNA of "The Call of Cthulhu."

Lovecraft's corpus. A small team of scientists use custom-built flying machines to establish a base in a distant, inhospitable frozen desert filled with mountains, valleys, and plateaus. There, the scientists find the ruins of an ancient alien civilization that, despite its advanced technology, was unable to halt the decline in its environment and the concomitant rise in attacks by barbarous lesser beings. Lovecraft himself seemingly originally intended what became *At the Mountains of Madness* to be a work of interplanetary fiction. In a letter to Clark Ashton Smith, he stated how

> I shall sooner or later get around to the interplanetary field myself—& you may depend upon it that I shall not choose Edmond Hamilton, Ray Cummings, or Edgar Rice Burroughs as my model! I doubt if I shall have any *living* race upon the orb whereto I shall—either spiritually or corporeally—precipitate my hero. But there will be Cyclopean *ruins*—god! what ruins!—& certain *presences* that haunt the nether vaults. (3 December 1929; *DS* 187)

As Lovecraft never wrote such an interplanetary story but did begin writing *At the Mountains of Madness* approximately a year later, it seems clear that the basic outlines of his Antarctic story originated in those ideas shared with Smith for a story set on another planet. Lovecraft even mentions Smith in *At the Mountains of Madness* itself; the professors recognize the Elder Things' remains because they are familiar with Smith's sculptures of them based on the *Necronomicon* (*CF* 3.40).[14] This sudden transposition of setting from one world to another is not as odd as it may seem when it is realized that in doing so Lovecraft was simply doing the inverse of connections between polar and interplanetary—specifically Martian—exploration that prior authors had been making for decades (Deischer).

From 1887 to 1893, a series of articles titled "Letters from the Planets" were published in the British *Cassell's Magazine,* portrayed as correspondence sent by the Venusian traveler Aleriel to the author via the power of Druid stone circles. In the first letter, Aleriel relays the discovery of the ruins of an ancient civilization on the moon; in the second, a visit to the south pole of Mars, where he chides his human correspondent on how "you actually know less of [your Antarctic regions] than of

---

14. It is likely that HPL was persuaded to change his story's location from another world to the terrestrial poles by the discovery in August 1930 of the remains of Swedish explorer Salomon August Andrée's failed 1897 Arctic balloon expedition (Guimont, "Arctic" 148–51).

the Antarctic realms of Mars, for these you can see in your most powerful telescopes—you can at least discern the outlines of land and sea. But of the Antarctic realms of the earth no man can tell whether they are land or sea, whether the Antarctic continent is a fable or a fact . . ." (Schroeder 103). The 1889 novel *Mr. Stranger's Sealed Packet* by Scottish mathematician Hugh MacColl (1831–1909) has an entire chapter centering around an aerial expedition over the "Marsian" south pole by the novel's titular Earthman and his native wife, Ree. At one point, Ree views an enormous dark storm cloud that she fears is an immense monster living in hiding at the south pole (MacColl 229). At the actual south pole, they encounter what appears to be an almost urban collection of glacial spires, along with evidence that some ancient heavenly body had impacted the south pole in the distant past (MacColl 232–34).

In the early 1910s, inspired by esoteric musings on the Hollow Earth by conspiracist Americus Symmes (1811–1896) and on the Egyptian pyramids by astronomer Charles Piazzi Smyth (1819–1900), infamous factoid compiler Charles Fort (1874–1932) wrote two novel manuscripts of his own, with the provisional titles *X* and *Y*. *X* was about humans on Earth being controlled by a civilization on Mars; *Y* was about a sinister civilization living in secret in Antarctica. Kaspar Hauser was a character in *Y*, revealed to have emerged from the Antarctic "Y-land" and been murdered to prevent him from leaking the secret. Fort wrote about the books to his friend Theodore Dreiser (1871–1945), the author who founded the Fortean Society in New York City in 1931. Dreiser was very enthusiastic about the drafts, but Fort nevertheless abandoned the stories and burned the manuscripts (Knight 55–56). Interestingly, Dreiser and Lovecraft shared acquaintances in the personages of Kalem Club member Wilfred B. Talman (1904–86) and Vermont author Vrest Orton (1897–1986). Orton offered to introduce the two during the time he was researching his 1929 biography of Dreiser, but Lovecraft declined (Long 159; Orton 344). One wonders if Fort's works might have come up had Lovecraft accepted Orton's offer to meet with Dreiser, and what impact that would have had on the soon-to-be-commenced writing of *At the Mountains of Madness*.

While the missives from Aleriel, the novel by MacColl, and Fort's manuscripts were and remain extremely niche, other novels by American authors Gustavus W. Pope (1828–1902) and Edwin Lester Arnold (1857–1935) were more influential. In Pope's 1894 novel *Journey to*

Mars, the survivor of a doomed US Navy expedition to Antarctica encounters a Martian expedition on the southern continent. After going with them to Mars, the sailor is eventually returned to the Antarctic sea (Pope, *Mars* 21–56, 515–31). As mentioned in chapter 7, Pope would publish a sequel the following year, *Journey to Venus.* Arnold's 1905 novel *Lieutenant Gullivar Jones: His Vacation* sees the titular US Navy officer transported to Mars by an "Oriental" magic carpet inscribed in suitably Lovecraftian form with a mix of symbols representing the solar system and "characters half-way in appearance between Runes and Cryptic-Sanskrit" (Arnold 6–7). On Mars, Jones has a prolonged adventure encountering unfriendly natives as he treks across the Martian Arctic (Arnold 157–82) and explores the "the ruins of a Hither [Arabesque Martian civilization] city, a haunted fairy town to which some travellers have been, but whence none ever returned alive" (Arnold 201). Pope's and Arnold's novels are widely seen as influences of Edgar Rice Burroughs, whose own works had an impact on Lovecraft's writing, including *At the Mountains of Madness* (Fulwiler 60–65; Price, "Warlord" 66–68; Callaghan 77–78; Ashley and Lowndes 41). Notably, the influence of Pope and Arnold on Burroughs was first argued by Richard A. Lupoff, who in addition to being a scholar of Burroughs was deeply interested in Lovecraft and wrote the first Lovecraftian space opera, as will be discussed in chapter 10 (Lupoff, *ERB* 19–23, 224–25).

In terms of real expeditions to terrestrial ice sheets, Lovecraft based his Miskatonic Antarctic Expedition on the US Navy's 1928–30 Byrd Antarctic Expedition, led by Admiral Richard Byrd (Eckhardt 31–38; Callaghan 78). In 1948, German rocket scientist Wernher von Braun developed the first technical outline of a Mars mission using available technology of the day; one of his influences for the structure of the Mars voyage was the US Navy's 1946–47 Operation Highjump expedition to Antarctica, also led by Byrd. Notably, von Braun's outlined expedition landed at the Martian south pole, the ice cap providing an easy surface for his airplane-like "landing boats." Just as with the Miskatonic Expedition and its transport ships, only some of von Braun's crew would make the final descent to Mars, the remainder staying on board the larger orbiting transfer spaceships (von Braun 65–66; Portree 1–2).

Although Lowell had long been discredited by the 1950s, his canals continued to have some influence into the 1960s, mostly upon drawings of Mars but also on some interpretations of photographs, for example in the 1962 book *The Photographic Story of Mars* published by Lowell

Observatory astronomer Earl C. Slipher. Even after *Mariner 4* in 1965, a few dissenters, including Carl Sagan (1934–1996)—who had been inspired by Burroughs's Martian stories as a youth (Sagan, *Cosmos* 115–16)—claimed the photographs returned by the probe were too few and too low-resolution to fully dismiss the existence of canals (Caidin, Barbree, and Wright 128–29). For his part, von Braun remained inspired enough by Lowell's theories to discuss the potential of finding canals on Mars. His 1956 book *The Exploration of Mars*, co-written with Willy Ley—a prominent cryptozoologist, Atlantis advocate, advisor to science fiction films, and friend of Arthur C. Clarke—included an illustration of an ancient Martian temple ruin (Ley and von Braun 66, 72, 158, 163; Scharmen 85). This was only one of many space advocacy projects on which von Braun and Ley collaborated in the 1950s (Scharmen 75–76). As mentioned in chapter 5, Ley was a friend of German film director Fritz Lang, who read a number of Lovecraft stories. After Lang returned to Germany in 1957, Ley handled the sale of Lang's voluminous collection of *Astounding* and *Weird Tales* volumes (Gold 6–7). Ley may also have known of Lovecraft through his correspondence with Jack Parsons (Carter 6, 65). In 1952, Ley co-wrote the nonfiction book *Lands Beyond* with future Lovecraft biographer L. Sprague de Camp; de Camp and Ley, along with Lin Carter, were also members of the Trap Door Spiders, a social club of New York City–based science fiction authors whose membership also included Isaac Asimov.[15]

It is tempting, but entirely speculative, to consider whether Ley experienced Lovecraft through either his Lang or Parsons connections, and whether Lovecraft influenced the ideas Ley brought to his collaborations with von Braun. For his part, von Braun had been such an avid reader of *Astounding* before World War II that, after the war broke out, he continued to receive a subscription under a false name and at great personal expense via the German embassy in neutral Sweden (Nevala-Lee 193–94). Depending on how long before the war von Braun had been a subscriber, it is very likely he could have read *At the Mountains of Madness* when it was serialized in *Astounding* in 1936 (as had Clarke, just a few hundred miles away in Britain). While we can say it might be likely that von Braun read *At the Mountains of Madness*, ultimately there is no clear evidence that von Braun was inspired, even indirectly, by

---

15. With thanks to Richard Jordan for bringing notice to the Trap Door Spiders.

Lovecraft, especially as both authors had other mutual inspirations, such as Jules Verne (Scharmen 87). But it does demonstrate that whatever the lineage, Lovecraft's Antarctic expedition and von Braun's Martian expedition—the prototype for all subsequent scientific plans for journeys to Mars—shared a common ancestor in Byrd's Antarctic journeys. More recent studies of Mars expeditions by NASA have emphasized the usefulness of Antarctic bases as models for Mars bases, but also the importance of exploring the poles of Mars for their potential preservation of ancient geological records—including life (Cockell 355–64). Even John M. Navroth opens his study of Lovecraft and the "Polar Myth" by noting the similarities to Antarctic and Martian exploration (190). And of course, the city of the Elder Things is located on the inspiration for "evilly fabled plateau of Leng" (*CF* 3.18); in his 2017 story "The Children of Leng," Remy Nakamura turns the plateau into a colony on the "fourth moon of Kepler 4557c" (7).

In its similarity to the later, more scientific postwar conceptions of expeditions to Mars, *At the Mountains of Madness* stands as a forerunner—despite its terrestrial setting—of the type of Martian tale to come, in contrast to those of Lovecraft's time. One Martian story that almost immediately reflected the shift embodied by *At the Mountains of Madness* is "The Vaults of Yoh-Vombis," by Lovecraft's friend Clark Ashton Smith, to whom Lovecraft had written the initial idea of *At the Mountains of Madness* in 1929, when he still considered that it would be part of the "interplanetary field" (*DS* 187). Smith published his story in 1932, the year after Lovecraft finished his draft of *At the Mountains of Madness* but before the story's 1936 publication. "The Vaults of Yoh-Vombis" also features the hospitalized last survivor of a scientific expedition to an abandoned city built by ancient aliens who cautions his peers not to return there, as apocalyptic creatures still exist in the ruins. The general plot parallels *At the Mountains of Madness,* with the location switched from the Antarctic to Mars (Gelatt, Ruth, and Mucci). Perhaps because of this similarity, Derleth was critical of Smith having set his story on Mars instead of Earth (Murray, "Mars" 12).

Smith would publish two subsequent Martian stories. The first was "The Dweller in the Gulf" (1933), which is most notable for drawing the condemnation of future leading fandom figure Forrest J Ackerman (1916–2008). Ackerman's attack on the story in the letter column of the *Fantasy Fan* led to a longstanding feud between the teenager and the Lovecraft circle (*IAP* 857–58). It was this conflict that led to Ackerman becoming the namesake of the wriggling, slimy Venusian akmans of "In the Walls of Eryx." Smith's third Martian story was "Vulthoom" (1935). The title character is the Martian equivalent of Satan, sleeping in the underground city of Ravermos, with parallels to Cthulhu and predating Lewis's Martian cosmology. Lovecraft thought that the story "had its moments but falls a bit beneath [Smith]'s best level," and Smith himself had varying opinions of its quality (*RB* 315; Murray, "Mars" 14).

Burroughs and Wells

If even the scientific von Braun could reflect the lingering influence of Lowell into the 1950s, the canal theorist cast an even larger shadow among science fiction authors in the first half of the century. Perhaps the most notable example is Edgar Rice Burroughs (1875–1950) in his *Barsoom* tales of John Carter of Mars, of which Lovecraft had been a youthful fan. Carter was a Virginian gentleman and Confederate cavalry officer in the Civil War before being transported to Mars while prospecting in Arizona (the location of Lowell Observatory). There, he marries Princess Dejah Thoris, a member of the humanoid Red Martian nobility who fight to sustain their idealized slaveholder society against hordes of degenerate inhuman savages. The first book, *A Princess of Mars,* was serialized in 1912 in the *All-Story* as *Under the Moons of Mars,* and published in novel form under its current title in 1917. The second entry in the series, *The Gods of Mars,* was serialized in *All-Story* in 1913 and published in book form in 1918. Lovecraft was an avid reader of *All-Story,* including the Burroughs tales (Callaghan 71–72; Fulwiler 60; Lupoff, *ERB* xxii). In a letter to Kleiner, Lovecraft noted that Burroughs

> is a clever writer of imaginative fiction, but is of course subject to the usual limitations of his kind. In his stories of the planet Mars he made a gross astronomical error (he spoke of the year as having 687 Martian days. This is not so. The Martian year is 687 days long by *our* reckoning, but the Martian day is over half an hour longer than ours, giving 668⅔ to one Martian year.), which I detected & exposed in the Log Book (or whatever corresponds to that column) of the *All-Story*. (27 December 1916; *RK* 80)

Lovecraft's letter to the editor correcting Burroughs's knowledge of Martian time was published in the 7 March 1914 issue of the *All-Story Weekly* (*RK* 81n5; *IAP* 142–43). Lovecraft's correction of Burroughs did not endear him to the other readers, one of whom in turn wrote in to call Lovecraft "an egotist of the worst type" (Joshi, *Recognition* 17–18). The error in question appeared near the end of *The Gods of Mars*. Unfortunately, Burroughs either did not read or take action on Lovecraft's letter, as the incorrect dating of a Martian year to 687 Martian days is retained in the book version of the novel—even with Burroughs acknowledging the factor of a (slightly inaccurate) 41-minute longer rotational period for the planet (Burroughs, *Gods* 318).

Perhaps because of this lack of attention to detail or the lack of correction when pointed out, Lovecraft's attitude toward Burroughs soured later in life. As mentioned above, in his 1929 letter to Smith Lovecraft grouped Burroughs together with Hamilton and Cummings as interplanetary authors he intended *not* to emulate. This attitude reflects opinions of Burroughs's later output, which was considerable. Burroughs ultimately published eleven volumes in the *Barsoom* series, the last coming out in 1943. The eighth in the series, *Swords of Mars,* was serialized in the magazine *Blue Book* in 1934–35 before being published in book form in February 1936. It was presumably the publication of *Swords of Mars* that occasioned a letter to Lovecraft from Kleiner, to which Lovecraft replied on 6 February 1936, stating "No—I don't think Burroughs worth counting as a serious interplanetary author. His stuff is really almost juvenile—with all the cheap & unconvincing stock devices of commercial quantity-production" (*RK* 205). But much like his later claims about never believing in Lowell's canal theories, the younger Lovecraft had quite clearly enjoyed reading the early work of Burroughs, including the initial *Barsoom* stories (*IAP* 142).

In the *Barsoom* series' first entry, *A Princess of Mars,* John Carter voyages to the atmosphere plant that sustains Mars' dying atmosphere; the factory is "a huge building which covered perhaps four square miles and towered two hundred feet in the air" (Burroughs, *Princess* 221). Carter also observes Martian cities surrounded by immense walls and containing mile-high towers (Burroughs, *Princess* 280). Perhaps these descriptions remained in young Lovecraft's mind and inspired the "Cyclopean ruins" observed on Mars by Randolph Carter in "Through the Gates of the Silver Key." Further, the climax of the third book, *The Warlord of Mars*—serialized in 1913–14 in *All-Story* and published in book form in 1919—includes (John) Carter leading an extended expedition to a lost city at the Martian north pole, with clear shades of *At the Mountains of Madness* (Burroughs, *Warlord* 163–66).

9. At the Mountains of Mars

The Southern gentleman Carter and his adoptive Red Martian society clearly parallel Lovecraft's own social and political views (*IAP* 113–14; Joshi, "Thought" 20–24). William Fulwiler and Robert M. Price have argued that Burroughs's *Barsoom* series was an inspiration for Lovecraft's Dream Cycle (Fulwiler 64–65; Price, "Warlord" 66–68). Alan Moore and Kevin O'Neill made the link explicit in their *League of Extraordinary Gentlemen* comic, establishing John Carter as Randolph Carter's granduncle (Moore and O'Neill 160).[16] Ironically, Lovecraft claimed that the name of Randolph Carter came from a real-life John Carter, a member of the Carter family of Virginia who relocated to Providence prior to the American Revolution, as the "transposition of a Virginia line to New England always affected my fancy strongly" (*ET* 75). This historical John Carter briefly appears as a character in the 1770 segment of *The Case of Charles Dexter Ward*, alongside Lovecraft's own distant relative Abraham Whipple (*CF* 2.248). Meanwhile, Joshi has argued that the fictional John Carter, via his transportation to Mars via astral projection, was perhaps an inspiration for the Great Race in "The Shadow out of Time" (Joshi, "Civilizations" 9).

Lovecraft criticized Burroughs for anthropomorphizing his Martians, and many of the tropes he attacked in "Some Notes in Interplanetary Fiction" are bedrocks of the *Barsoom* series (*CE* 2.180–81). The influence of Burroughs can be seen in C. L. Moore's "Shambleau," published in the November 1933 *Weird Tales* and featuring a swashbuckling Earthman adventurer, Northwest Smith, encountering the title character, a humanoid Martian enchantress with tentacles emerging from her head. Intriguingly, Smith's Venusian companion Yarol wonders whether the legend of the Medusa was inspired either by an earlier Earth civilization reaching Mars, or ancient Martians coming to Greece, particularly Lovecraftian tropes (Moore 549). Despite Moore's reliance on humanoid aliens, Lovecraft praised the story, while selectively criticizing parts of it to Derleth (Derie, "Shambleau"). But just as Lovecraft was able to praise Moore's Mars despite its embodiment of tropes he disliked, it is the Martians of Burroughs, far more than of Wells or Serviss, who reflect what Joshi identifies as the three values of Lovecraft's own aliens: "pure intelligence, sound political organization, and aesthetic sensibility" (*IAP* 142–43, 643; Joshi, "Civilizations" 22; Leiber, "Hyperspace" 177–78).

In contrast to Burroughs, another author whose Martians were

---

16. One wonders where Lin Carter fits into this extended Carter family tree.

widely praised for being truly alien were those of Stanley G. Weinbaum (1902–1935), in his two debut stories, both from 1934, "A Martian Odyssey" and "Valley of Dreams" (Weinbaum 7–51).[17] The first in particular remains highly influential, and includes additional Lovecraftian elements in the form of an expedition to the Martian south; pyramids built hundreds of thousands of years prior by unknown creatures lurking within; a tentacled, telepathic predator named the "dream-beast"; a city with an underground labyrinth full of automata; and a character from New York named F. Long (Weinbaum 8, 17–25). "Valley of Dreams" features a return mission to the Martian south, explicitly referred to as an analogue to the Antarctic, where the two human explorers find a city older than human civilization composed of "Gargantuan" structures "like a range of mountains" and containing both a library of strange lore and wall murals depicting the progress of Martian society, the discovery of the fact that the Martians visited Egypt in the distant past and were the inspiration for the god Thoth, and the contemplation of the fact that humans might never truly comprehend an alien intelligence (Weinbaum 35–37, 41–42). In a letter to Willis Conover dated 23 September 1936, Lovecraft stated that he had been introduced to Weinbaum's work by his "Eryx" co-author Kenneth Sterling, and praised Weinbaum as one of the few good modern "scientifiction" writers (*RB* 396). This was strong praise indeed from Lovecraft, given Weinbaum's Jewish heritage—which is expressed in the stories themselves by use of Yiddish, not least of which is one of the main characters being named Putz (Weinbaum 7). Weinbaum and Lovecraft even shared an acquaintance in the person of Robert Bloch, who met Weinbaum only a few months before the latter's December 1935 death by cancer (*RB* 147).

Outside of Burroughs, the author most closely associated with Mars in Lovecraft's lifetime was H. G. Wells, who published a trifecta of Mars fiction in 1897. In his short story "The Crystal Egg," a London shop owner discovers that an antique crystal egg is actually a device that projects images of Mars and its inhabitants, while in "The Star," Martian astronomers observe the apocalyptic effects of a rogue star passing by

---

17. Weinbaum's praises were sung not only by HPL, but also by space opera authors like Asimov and Clarke. Of interest also is that in the early 1920s, Weinbaum was a classmate at the University of Wisconsin–Madison with Robert Goddard's future rocket research patron, Charles Lindbergh (Clarke, *Astounding* 122).

9. At the Mountains of Mars

the Earth. The stories were respectively reprinted in the May and June 1926 issues of *Amazing Stories*, both of which Lovecraft owned (*LL* 24). Steven J. Mariconda has proposed that "The Crystal Egg" was an influence on the Shining Trapezohedron in "The Haunter of the Dark" (Mariconda 16–17). But the most significant Martian work for Wells in 1897 is, of course, *The War of the Worlds*, the pioneering work of the alien invasion genre, which began to be serialized in magazine form in 1897 before being printed as a book in 1898. Lovecraft's admiration for the novel as a cornerstone work of "scientifiction" remained strong throughout his life; he wrote in a letter to Searight that "I think Wells's 'War of the Worlds' remains the best of all 'outside invasion' stories to date" (25 August 1933; *EHP* 286).

Lovecraft would later claim to have first read *The War of the Worlds* when it was reprinted in *Amazing Stories* in 1927 (*DW* 147). If true, that would complicate some of the associations proposed in this chapter. However, was that claim true? He also claimed to have read *The Time Machine* for the first time in 1924 (*IAP* 532), but elsewhere recalled that he had read it in his youth (*DW* 29). As a youthful fan of both Verne and Serviss, it is hard to imagine Lovecraft did not search out Wells's space travel works; as noted in chapter five, he had likely read *The First Men in the Moon* by 1906. E. Walter Maunder's book, *Are the Planets Inhabited?* (1913), describes Wells's Martians; Lovecraft had read some of Maunder's earlier books, and may have come across this one. Lovecraft's 1920 dream (discussed below), with imagery that appears to be derived from *The War of the Worlds*, adds to the evidence that he was acquainted with the novel before 1927. If Lovecraft had not read the full novel early in his life, perhaps he at least skimmed it or read sections. In any case, he would have undoubtedly come across enough references to *The War of the Worlds* that he would have known the gist of the story, even if he did not read the complete novel until 1927.

Wells's Martian invasion can be interpreted as Lovecraft's quintessential "strange aeons" (*CF* 2.40): cosmic entities come to Earth to rule, reshaping the world and its ecology, with small bands of humans serving as collaborators. Even the Martian arrival in their cylindrical ships is originally viewed as simply a spectacular meteorite impact—the chapter of the initial Martian landing is even titled "The Falling Star" (Wells, *WW* 12). In other words, the Martian arrival is quite literally when "the stars are right." Lovecraft even directly connected the novel to his interest in astronomy. In a letter to E. Hoffmann Price dated 20 January

1936, he described his visit to New York City over the new year, which included two visits to the Hayden Planetarium at the American Museum of Natural History. To Lovecraft, the projector of the planetarium "looks like an Hamiltonian 'space ship' or like one of the armoured Martians in 'The War of the Worlds'" (*EHP* 219). The "Hamiltonian" here is a reference to Edmond Hamilton (1904–1977), who published a number of space-opera stories in *Weird Tales* and *Amazing Stories*, and will be discussed more in chapter 11.

During his flight from the Martians, Wells's unnamed narrator takes refuge in a farmhouse and witnesses the countryside overrun by alien "red weed," a precursor to the cosmically mutated farm plants in Lovecraft's "The Colour out of Space" (Wells, *WW* 212). There is an even more direct connection between Lovecraft's short story and Wells's novel: "The Colour out of Space" debuted in the September 1927 issue of *Amazing Stories*, alongside the second half of the magazine's reprint of *The War of the Worlds*. On a deeper level, the narrator pontificates on how the Martian invasion "has robbed us of that serene confidence in the future which is the most fruitful source of decadence" (Wells, *WW* 300), which he characterized at the novel's start as the "infinite complacency [by which] men went to and fro over this globe about their little affairs, serene in their assurance of their empire over matter" (Wells, *WW* 1). These ruminations on the Martian shattering of human importance and confidence are reminiscent of the cosmicism expressed by Lovecraft in the famous opening lines to "The Call of Cthulhu" (*CF* 2.21–22). Richard L. Tierney has suggested that *The War of the Worlds*, along with "The Star" and Wells's 1895 novel *The Time Machine*, may have indeed fueled Lovecraft's "cosmic outlook" (Tierney, "Cosmic" 194).

And with their octopus-like appearance and their "vast and cool and unsympathetic" intellects (Wells, *WW* 2), Wells's Martians have obvious parallels with Lovecraft's cosmic entities. Lovecraft himself may even have drawn visual inspiration for Cthulhu from the original *The War of the Worlds* illustrations of the Martians by Warwick Goble during its serialization (Wells, *WW* 27–29; Price, "Episode 9"). The narrator's comments on the Martians at the end of the novel also evoke the Great Race's temporal abilities: "To them, and not to us, perhaps, is the future ordained" (Wells, *WW* 301). Conversely, the narrator opens the novel by reminding the reader that "before we judge of them too harshly," the similarity of the Martians to human behavior should be remembered (Wells, *WW* 4). This conflates with Dyer's comments on the Elder

Things in *At the Mountains of Madness:* "whatever they had been, they were men!" (*CF* 3.143).

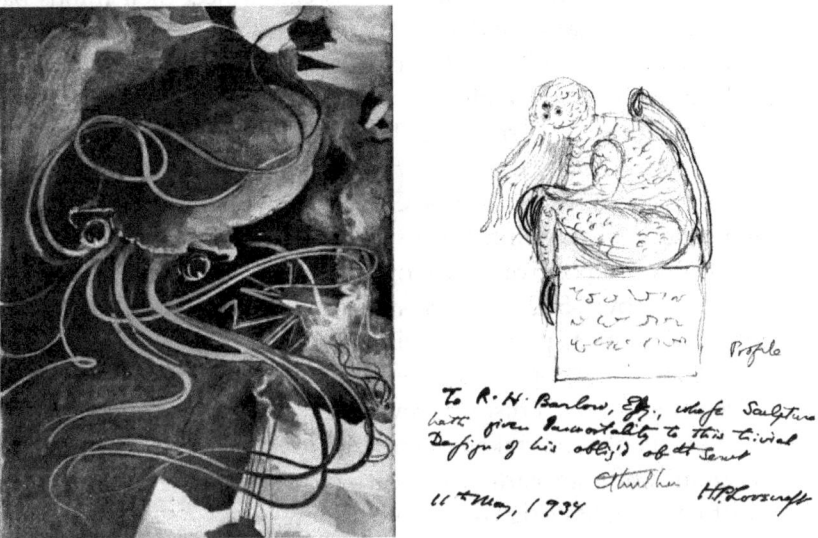

Left: Goble's 1897 Martian illustration, inverted (public domain; Wikimedia) Right: Lovecraft's 1934 illustration of Cthulhu for R. H. Barlow. Howard P. Lovecraft Collection, Ms. Lovecraft, Brown University Library.

The events of Wells's novel also provide for mirroring of other Lovecraftian elements. The ironclad ship *Thunder Child* ramming a Martian tripod to destroy it parallels the yacht *Alert* ramming Cthulhu to defeat it in "The Call of Cthulhu" (Wells, *WW* 183–87; *CF* 2.54). Just as Cthulhu re-forms itself after the attack, the Martians themselves are impervious to human attempts to defeat them, succumbing instead to bacteria, "slain, after all man's devices had failed, by the humblest things that God" had created (Wells, *WW* 282)—in other words, by a fellow divinity. Even so, the Martians are not truly defeated, as the narrator fears they may yet attempt a second invasion of the Earth, in addition to the subsequent invasion of Venus they undertake at the end of the novel (Wells, *WW* 299–301). This idea was taken up by Olaf Stapledon in *Last and First Men,* admired by both Wells and Lovecraft. Stapledon's "Second Race" of humans are tormented by repeated Martian invasions, halted only when a bacterial plague escapes and destroys the Martians on both worlds, and nearly wiping out terrestrial humans as well. The Third Race of humans incorporate remnants of Martian biology, granting them the

Martian powers of telepathy (Stapledon 151–88). One of the by-products of this is that by the time of the Fifth Race, a project of time travel is developed, by which certain individuals can project their minds back through time to "possess" individuals in the past for purposes of historical research (Stapledon 238–43)—clearly evocative of the Great Race.

Both Lovecraft's and Wells's cosmic entities are therefore shown to be beyond creation or destruction. This is not the case in the unauthorized 1898 sequel *Edison's Conquest of Mars* by American astronomy popularizer and science fiction author Garrett Putnam Serviss, serialized in the *Boston Post*. By this point, Serviss had already endorsed the canal theories of Lowell in a positive review of Lowell's 1895 book *Mars* for *Harper's Weekly* (Crowe 512). Serviss's novel recounts a US-led counter-invasion of Mars by a space fleet built by Thomas Edison, which inverts the anti-colonial satire of Wells (Rieder 136–38). Landing at the south pole of the Red Planet, Edison's crew encounters human slaves who are the descendants of those taken from Earth by a previous Martian invasion thousands of years earlier. In hearing one of the slaves recount the history of her people's origins, a professor exclaims,

> Gentlemen, gentlemen [. . .] is it that you do not understand? This Land of Sand and of a wonderful fertilizing river—what can it be? Gentlemen, it is Egypt! These mountains of rock that the Martians have erected, what are they? Gentlemen, they are the great mystery of the land of the Nile, the Pyramids; The gigantic statue of their leader that they at the foot of their artificial-mountains have set up—gentlemen, what is that? It is the Sphinx! (Serviss, *ECM* 143–48)

In other words, Serviss developed the concept of aliens being responsible for the creation of ancient religions and megalithic statuary on Earth. This is a clear predecessor to both the 'ancient alien theory' and the Cthulhu Mythos, especially as Lovecraft was a fan of Serviss, as mentioned in chapter 5. Among the more notably Lovecraftian passages is the statement that the Great Pyramid of Cheops "was not the work of puny man, as many an engineer had declared that it could not be, but the work of these giants of Mars" (Serviss, *ECM* 146)—language strikingly similar to that used by Lovecraft to describe the Martian canals in his 1915 and 1917 articles (*CE* 3.292–93, 319). Notably, while Lowell's canals are not mentioned by Wells, they are prominent features of the Mars of Serviss, as well as Burroughs, Smith, and Bradbury.

There is only circumstantial evidence that Lovecraft read *Edison's Conquest of Mars,* as described both in chapter 5 and by T. R. Livesey

("Green" 92–94); David Haden likewise argues that it is "highly likely" that Lovecraft read it ("Man-Gods"). If Lovecraft did read *Edison's Conquest of Mars,* he would have had to have read it in magazine form, as it was not republished as a book in his lifetime. That Lovecraft might have done so is not out of the question; his fellow New Englander, the rocket scientist Robert Goddard, kept the copies of the *Boston Post* with the novel in it, and noted reading it in his diary as late as 1929 (Goddard 2.656). But even if Lovecraft never read the novel, those he was acquainted with certainly did. In 1947, *Edison's Conquest of Mars* was republished in book form by a group of science fiction fans in Los Angeles who formed a publishing firm specifically for the venture. The firm was called Carcosa House, a reference to the works of Ambrose Bierce and Robert W. Chambers from which Lovecraft drew inspiration, and the effort was advised by William L. Crawford, one of Lovecraft's correspondents, commissioner of "Some Notes on Interplanetary Fiction," and publisher of the 1936 book version of "The Shadow over Innsmouth." However, due to poor sales of *Edison's Conquest of Mars,* Carcosa House folded. The novel would be resurrected next in 1969 by Forrest J Ackerman, the former youthful antagonistic correspondent to Lovecraft and Smith. Ackerman edited and severely abridged the novel, retitling it *Invasion of Mars* (Serviss and Ackerman).

Serviss may have been the first to posit an explicit connection between Martian visitors and ancient Earth cultures in fiction, but he was not the last. As already mentioned, both Moore's and Weinbaum's short stories included Martians forming the basis for Greek and Egyptian gods. Edmond Hamilton's first science fiction novella, *Across Space,* was published in three parts in *Weird Tales* from September to November 1926, the first issue of which also included Lovecraft's "He." The story features an ancient colony of Martians living beneath the moai statues of Easter Island. In *Across Space,* the moai statues were carved by ancient Martian visitors in resemblance of the aliens. The Martians had settled on an ancient Pacific continent; when it sank, Easter Island remained one of the only places above water (Hamilton 432), a plot point that perhaps influenced Lovecraft's later semi-credulous views of the moai as remnants of Lemuria (*CE* 4.51). The story includes a particularly Lovecraftian passage, as the protagonists attempt to foil the Martians' plan to destroy Earth:

More important far, what could we do to stop it, to hurl the planet back? What? For how could two men hope to strive against beings who could reach out and halt a rushing world, who concentrated their power and their craft into a mighty ray with which they stabbed out at the very stars themselves—across space! (Hamilton 321)

Martians build the Sphinx during their invasion of the Earth 9000 years earlier, from *Edison's Conquest of Mars* (public domain; Project Gutenberg).

9. At the Mountains of Mars

Another notable entry in this proto-ancient alien genre that Lovecraft probably read was "The Retreat to Mars" by Cecil B. White, the pseudonym of William Henry Christie (1896–1955). Similar to Serviss, Christie was primarily an astronomer who occasionally delved into science fiction. "The Retreat to Mars" was published in the August 1927 issue of *Amazing Stories,* alongside the first half of the magazine's reprint of *The War of the Worlds* (and one issue before the debut of "The Colour out of Space"). In the story, the narrator is an astronomer specializing in Mars. Both the narrator and Christie in a separate footnote endorse Lowell and his canal theory, long out of public favor by 1927. The astronomer is approached by a Smithsonian Institution archaeologist whose focus is on proving that humanity evolved in Central Africa rather than Central Asia, as the current theory was. While on a six-year expedition to Central Africa, the archaeologist excavates a mound that is revealed to have been built over an ancient structure with writings inside. Translating the records, the archaeologist discovers that it was built by ancient Martians, and that humans are the degenerate descendants of colonists artificially adapted for survival on Earth, before losing their alien civilization. Shown images of the past glories of Mars, the archaeologist notes that it resembles Babylonian architecture. Ultimately, the archaeologist discovers that the Martians left two other such libraries: one on what seems to be Atlantis, and one in Australia, which "may yet be found" (White 467).

A number of details from "The Retreat to Mars" appear in later Lovecraft works. Obviously, the creation of humans from aliens, and the decline of alien culture in their Earth colony, are central concepts of *At the Mountains of Madness,* while an ancient alien library in Australia describes Pnakotus from "The Shadow out of Time." Christie's association of a lost city, Babylonian culture, and Central Africa seems to indicate that White was at least partially inspired by contemporary theories of the construction of the medieval African city of Great Zimbabwe (Guimont, "Solomon" 156). Lovecraft was also interested in Great Zimbabwe, portraying it as a temple of the extraterrestrial Fishers from Outside in his 1930 poem "The Outpost" (*AT* 61–62) and the 1934 poem "Beyond Zimbabwe" (*AT* 79); his 1930 collaboration with Zealia Bishop, "Medusa's Coil" (*CF* 4.316); and even his notes to *At the Mountains of Madness* (*CE* 5.247) if not the finished story itself. The discovery of an alien civilization underneath an artificial mound is also featured in Lovecraft's additional Bishop collaboration, the 1929–30 novella "The

Mound." The titular mound of that story is a Native American mound, but legends of Mound Builders share colonial connections with the legends of Great Zimbabwe (Guimont, "Solomon" 137–38).

If not directly from *Edison's Conquest of Mars,* therefore, there were still a number of Martian-themed stories Lovecraft probably read that may have contributed to his ideas about ancient alien interaction with (or creation of) humanity. But beyond the perhaps circumstantial connections between Lovecraft and Serviss's spinoff of Wells, other authors have illustrated the ease with which Martian invasion created by Wells and the Cthulhu Mythos created by Lovecraft can be integrated. As of this writing, the most recent is the opening scene of the 2020 HBO TV show *Lovecraft Country,* depicting a dream where Cthulhu, Wells's Martian tripods, and Burroughs's Princess Dejah Thoris are all present together (Norris, "Cinema" 210). But perhaps the first was Brian Aldiss's *The Saliva Tree* (1965), explicitly a crossover of *The War of the Worlds* and "The Colour out of Space" in its depiction of the effects of a Victorian alien invasion on the life of a rural farm in East Anglia (Baxter, "Metaphor" 10–11; Nicholls, "Introduction" vi–viii). Dave Wolverton's 1996 short story "After a Lean Winter" tells Wells's Martian invasion from the viewpoint of Jack London. The fictional London discovers that some Martians survived in the more Mars-like climate of the Arctic after succumbing elsewhere on Earth, and may have built an underwater settlement beneath the Arctic ice cap to survive even longer—just as Dyer hypothesizes about Elder Things surviving in an underwater city beneath the Antarctic ice cap in *At the Mountains of Madness* (Wolverton 322–24; *CF* 3.116).

Stephen Baxter's 2017 sequel novel to Wells, *The Massacre of Mankind,* incorporates the idea from Wolverton and takes the Lovecraftian similarity closer by including a 1937 expedition by airship into the Arctic to locate the last redoubt of the Martian survivors (Baxter, *Massacre* 456–73, 486). The elderly narrator of Wells has been hospitalized due to his obsession with the symbols of the Martians—"more images I find it hard to get out of my mind"—and has come to believe that the ultimate Martian plan was eventually to establish themselves in the Antarctic (Baxter, *Massacre* 151–52). Baxter even has a character muse, Dyer-like, that "Some say the Martians were like us—once" (Baxter, *Massacre* 310). The Martian headquarters, dominated by the enormous cylindrical forms of their spacecraft sticking out of the ground, is even compared to suitably Lovecraftian ancient megaliths by the narrator, who sees it as a "Martian Stonehenge" (Baxter, *Massacre* 312). Notably, Baxter followed *The Massacre of Mankind* with "The Shadow over the Moon" (2018), an explicitly Lovecraftian pastiche.

There are also occasionally Lovecraftian pastiche authors whose characters themselves know of Wells's work. In his Dark Waters Trilogy, a tie-in to the Arkham Horror game, Graham McNeill has several references to the alien invasion tale. In *Ghouls of the Miskatonic* (2011), a professor at the eponymous university suggests to a colleague that humans can fight the Great Old Ones despite their insignificance, just as bacteria killed the Martians in *The War of the Worlds* (McNeill, *Ghouls* 167); while in *Dweller in the Deep* (2014), an imprisoned Irish smuggler compares the hot sunlight coming in through the jail windows to the heat-rays of Wells's Martians (McNeill, *Dweller* 45). Elizabeth Bear begins her Hugo-winning novella "Shoggoths in Bloom" (2008) with the main character, a Yale professor studying shoggoths, attempting to start a conversation with a Maine fisherman about the panic caused by Orson Welles's 1938 radio adaptation of the novel, which relocated the Martian invasion from London to New York City[18] (Bear 149). Ironically, in a letter to Donald A. Wollheim dated 9 July 1935, Lovecraft had speculated what a hypothetical Martian visitor might make of New York City (*RB* 307). This itself might have sprung from an idea suggested by Clark Ashton Smith, which Lovecraft included as entry 181 in his commonplace book: "Inhabitant of another world—face masked, perhaps with human skin or surgically alter'd human shape, but body alien beneath robes. Having reached earth, tries to mix with mankind. Hideous revelation" (*CE* 5.230). For his part, Wollheim and his fellow Futurians—a Brooklyn-based science fiction club that he had founded in September 1938—were thrilled with the Welles broadcast. In their first meeting after it, the Futurians hosted a debate on alien invasions, with Wollheim representing the Martians and Isaac Asimov representing humanity. Wollheim successfully carried the day for the Martian invaders (Nevala-Lee 104).

A less-obvious Lovecraftian *War of the Worlds* connection is Steven Spielberg's 2005 film adaptation. The Spielberg film follows the charac-

---

18. Welles' radio broadcast had the Martians landing in northern New Jersey and marching to destroy New York City; this had actually been the setup that Serviss used at the start of his own adaptation (Serviss, *ECM* 3).

ter of Ray Ferrier (Tom Cruise), who works in Brooklyn when the invasion of hostile aliens begins—shades of "The Horror at Red Hook." The film removes all references to Mars and Martians, save for a visual allusion at the start with a close-up shot of a red traffic light. Instead of arriving from space, the invaders' tripods are located underground, emerging when activated by coordinated lightning strikes. The character of Harlan Ogilvy (Tim Robbins) later claims that "They've been planning this for a million years." In his review of the movie, religious scholar and ufologist David J. Halperin noted that while Wells's Martians had clear motivation in trying to claim a new world to live in, the aliens of Spielberg lack any such justification. However, in being portrayed as aliens emerging from dormant sleep after millions of years, Halperin contrasted the film to "The Call of Cthulhu" and suggested, "Do Spielberg's aliens, in sharp contrast to Wells's Martians, belong in the Lovecraft tradition? If so, the question of their motivation becomes irrelevant."

But the most explicit link between Lovecraft and *The War of the Worlds* is Don Webb's 1996 short story "To Mars and Providence," published in the same anthology as Wolverton's story. "To Mars and Providence" depicts a young Lovecraft witnessing the Martian invasion, at the end learning in the manner of "The Shadow out of Time" that he is an advance psychic scout of the Martians inhabiting a human body, taking the real Lovecraft's sense of alienation to a literal extreme (261). It is possible that the story was inspired by an actual dream Lovecraft had—described in a letter to Rheinhart Kleiner (21 May 1920), wherein he witnessed some type of malignant meteoric object crashing to Providence as a prelude to an unspecific assault, including the destruction of the dome of the Central Congregational Church, imagery extremely similar to that used in *The War of the Worlds,* down to the Martians damaging the dome of St. Paul's Cathedral (*RK* 162; Wells, *WW* 286). Baxter read Webb's story (along with Wolverton's story, Serviss's novel, and Moore and O'Neill's comic) prior to writing *The Massacre of Mankind* (Baxter, *Massacre* 486; Baxter, "Metaphor" 7–8, 11–12). Webb had earlier written another Martian Mythos tale, the 1994 short story "The Comet Called Ithaqua." Its unnamed narrator is a starship crew member taken to a Martian colony, where he encounters Derleth's Great Old One Ithaqua, transposed from the frozen Arctic of Earth to the frozen surface of Mars—particularly appropriate given the similarities in later alien abduction lore to Derleth's story (Guimont, "Ithaqua" 76–78). On vaguely similar lines is Caitlín R. Kiernan's 2018 novella *Black Helicopters,* which ends with a vignette on a space station over the north pole of Mars, with agents of chaos planning on bringing a Lovecraftian apocalypse to the human Mars colonies (Kiernan, *BH* 191–96).

While not as explicit as "To Mars and Providence," the most thematically Lovecraftian follow-up to *The War of the Worlds,* one also involving a covert hybridization of Martian and human, was appropriately written by Wells himself: his final science fiction novel, *Star Begotten.* Its protagonist, historian Joseph Davis, conceives of a conspiracy by which Martians use cosmic rays to guide the evolution of select humans, with the goal of causing their descendants to evolve both physically and mentally toward the superior Martian form. Davis begins to suspect that he himself is one of those whom the Martians have selected for their influence—his suspicion partially fueled by a professor who had read *Last and First Men* and saw it as analogous to the Martian plan (Wells, *SB* 94). One of his confidants, the right-wing media baron Lord Thunderclap, transfers his anti-Semitism and anti-communism onto those who unknowingly carry the Martian blood, calling for "a vast sanitary concentration of all these people" with the Martian hybrids to be "arrested and secluded in protective isolation" to ensure "human race-purity" (Wells, *SB* 145–46).

Ultimately, however, *Star Begotten* is ambiguous as to whether Davis is correct, let alone whether Martians even exist; in this way, it is closer to Lovecraft and R. H. Barlow's 1936 collaboration "The Night Ocean" (*CF* 4.656–58). Whether or not the Martians of *Star Begotten* actually exist, the novel's approach of using them as a stand-in for interwar racism would be echoed in the 1988 short story "Famous Monsters" by Kim Newman, a frequent author of Lovecraftian pastiche. In Newman's story, following instability on Mars resulting from the Martian defeat in their first invasion of 1897, a number of Martian refugees flee the literal "Old World" for the United States, where they are subjected to anti-immigration sentiments. When the Martians launch a Second War of the Worlds in 1938 (analogous to the Welles broadcast), the Martian immigrants are labeled "enemy aliens" and placed in detention camps in Nevada, reminiscent of both Japanese internment and Area 51. After the war, they are smeared as "Reds" and the target of McCarthyism, and become associated with the Jewish community; the Martian thirst for blood means that Martian bars and kosher butchers make for good partnerships (Newman 527–34). One can only imagine the horror of an alternate Lovecraft encountering such a racial alliance in that universe.

Star Begotten has clear echoes of "The Shadow over Innsmouth," "The Whisperer in Darkness," and "The Shadow out of Time." Wells's earlier novel, *The Croquet Player* (1936), has also Lovecraftian undertones, given its theme of an evil pall coming to an English country village after the discovery of a cave of Neanderthal remains causes the town's inhabitants to suffer from the psychic anguish of contemplating the vast span of human history (Macdonald). Wells died in 1946, and it was only three years after *Star Begotten* that Arthur C. Clarke, a Wells enthusiast and future vice president of the H. G. Wells Society (a position that Stephen Baxter would also hold), wrote his own Lovecraft parody, as will be discussed in chapter 10. However, there is no evidence that Wells was influenced by Lovecraft or indeed ever knew of him. Lovecraft certainly never had the chance to read *Star Begotten,* it being published three months after his death in March 1937. He also may not have enjoyed it, given his low opinion of Wells's later works (*DS* 669–71).

Conclusion

While *At the Mountains of Madness* was not set on Mars, Lovecraft's details of its expedition anticipated the type of expedition authors after him would conceptualize for voyages to Mars, even while its theme of a lost alien civilization was more common among the Martian fiction of his own time. And while the Miskatonic Expedition was the predecessor of the types of realistic Mars missions that scientific advocates from Wernher von Braun to Robert Zubrin and Andy Weir would develop, the Lovecraftian concepts of alien civilizations, as well as the individual alienation of such expeditions, would influence his later adherents in their own Mars fiction. Even after the dawn of the Space Age, NASA uses Antarctica as a proving ground for equipment destined to be sent to Mars.

Bringing things full circle, it has even been proposed that archaeological sites on Earth can be used as the basis for studies of comparable locations on Mars for evidence of life, and comparisons of those equivalent locations can then be put to use for the study of potential remains of civilizations on extrasolar worlds (Sivier 417–25). After all, it was a 1984 Antarctic expedition that discovered a meteorite on the ice sheet. Named ALH84001, it was determined to have originated on Mars, and from 1996 on has been at the center of debate about whether or not it contains fossilized Martian bacteria from billions of years ago (McKay et al. 924–30; Grinspoon, *Lonely* 249–51). That same year, *The X-Files* aired the episode "Tunguska," in which the ALH84001 fossils were remains of a shape-changing, black extraterrestrial life form developed by ancient alien colonists of Earth, capable of assuming the form of and controlling humans, and which had also been brought to Earth in the eponymous 1908 Siberian meteorite impact. In 2000, the ALH84001 discovery was the basis for the video game *Martian Gothic: Unification*, which was set in a base established by a corporation attempting to find the origins of the meteorite's bacteria. The expedition from *Martian Gothic* perishes after discovering an ancient subterranean Martian city near Olympus Mons, leading to a relief expedition trying to uncover the cause of the first crew's deaths—like "The Vaults of Yoh-Vombis," a plot suspiciously similar to a Martian *At the Mountains of Madness*.

ALH84001 would not have surprised Lovecraft. After all, the colour out of space arrives on Earth in a meteorite. On a more scientific level, Lovecraft discussed the idea that meteorites could carry living bacteria to Earth in a letter to Willis Conover (20 January 1936; *RB* 410), and again in another to Nils Frome (8 February 1937), in which he argued that "primitive life-forms in meteorites, if such are ever found," would likely be the only alien life outside of Martian vegetation that could be discovered by humans (*FLB* 351). The idea of life being present in meteorites was discussed by Charles Fort in the fifth chapter of *The Book of the Damned* (56–57). In his nonfiction work *Curiosities of the Sky* (1909), Serviss also mentions the idea, citing Lord Kelvin, whom he included as a character in *Edison's Conquest of Mars* (Serviss, *Curiosities* 195–96; Serviss, *ECM* 5). Nineteenth-century newspapers were also replete with more exotic claims; for example, the supposed 1897 impact of a meteorite covered in Martian hieroglyphs in Binghamton, New York (Card 85–89). Less bombastically, recent radar data from Mars-orbiting probes suggests that there may still be lakes of liquid water underneath the Martian south polar ice cap (Khuller and Plaut 1–19). It does not require much extrapolation to imagine an Elder Thing settlement still active there, observing the decline of their terrestrial cousins in the same way as Wells's Martian astronomers in "The Star," and glad to see that it is now the turn of the descendants of the shambling primitive mammal food stock to deal with the shoggoths exiled from Mars on their meteoric prisons.

It was only by a few years that Lovecraft missed Clarke's and Bradbury's homages. Nevertheless, while he was not able to read those early works bridging his literary themes with Mars, and while he avoided Mars in his fiction, Lovecraft's interest in Mars was great and was the basis for some of his earliest writings. The influence of certain Mars-related authors—Wells, Burroughs, Serviss (even outside of *Edison's Conquest of Mars*)—is inarguable. The theories of Lowell, which influenced those authors, themselves show strong similarities to key aspects of Lovecraft's mythos: non-anthropological life, the unavoidable encroaching of a hostile environment, massive works of construction in lost cities, and a worldview where humanity is nothing more than a youthful upstart among the plurality of worlds. Therefore, while Webb might have been exaggerating in making Lovecraft into an actual Martian, Lovecraft himself undoubtedly had an interest in the Red Planet that caused his influence to sprawl over Mars' ruddy disc as much as any Cyclopean ruin witnessed by Randolph Carter.

Chapter 10
Yuggoth's Environs

Introduction

As mentioned in chapter 5, on 27 November 1933 Lovecraft described his thoughts on space travel to his correspondent Natalie H. Wooley. While he believed that a crewed flight to the moon and back via rocket would someday be attempted, he thought it very likely the voyagers would die in the attempt. He was also much less sanguine about the prospects of travel elsewhere in the universe, or of the likelihood that hypothetical human explorers would find any living being at their destination:

> Probably all current—& future—ideas of other celestial bodies are wholly wrong. . . . In the first place, the number of bodies inhabited by highly evolved organic beings at any one period of the cosmos is probably very small. It takes what amounts to a rare *accident* to produce a solar system, & still *another* rare accident, to produce the stream of biological modifications culminating (so far) on this planet as mankind. It is unlikely that any other planet of this system could have complexly evolved denizens—& other similar systems (if there are any) we can never know. Moreover—the results of complex evolution on other spheres would undoubtedly differ far more from anything we recognise as life than to any of the "Hul Jok" or "Korus Kan" of the indefatigable & repetitious Mr. Edmond Hamilton.[1] There is also the possibility that life is merely a temporary attribute of this one region & period—the complex structure of matter in other sections of space & time being totally alien to the anabolistic-katabolistic cell-pattern which we locally observe & embody. (*RB* 194–95)

From this extract, it is clear that, despite the plethora of cosmic entities in his fiction, Lovecraft believed the solar system, if not the entire

---

1. Hul Jok was actually a character in the stories of Nictzin Dyalhis (chapter 7). Korus Kan and his creator Hamilton are discussed in chapter 11.

universe, to be potentially barren. Of course, he also thought it possible that humans would never be able to confirm this fact. In a 19 December 1936 letter to Nils Frome, he wrote, "No—I don't think interplanetary travel will ever become a fact. The obstacles—thousands of separate ones—are vaster than most laymen can ever dream of, & no voyager would be likely to return alive. But it's a great theme for stories none the less" (*FLB* 348). He expanded on this in his letter to Frome of 20 January 1937:

> Regarding interplanetary travel—as I said, I'm not calling it *impossible*. I merely regard it as highly *improbable*. There are tremendous obstacles which no layman can grasp, & there are no good reasons for desperate attempts involving heavy sacrifice. Of course, pure intellectual curiosity is a powerful stimulus—but there are limits to it. Practically speaking, there is no reason why any species should try to get from an environment to which it *is* adapted to one in which it *is not* adapted. Fishes (or rather, amphibians) didn't take to the land because they wanted to, but because in certain times and places the sea went back on them & further marine existence became impossible. However—all this is purely academic matter. There may be *attempts* at interplanetary travel within the next few centuries if the present mechanical civilization persists with any degree of continuity. (*FLB* 348–49)

From the twenty-first-century vantage point, this is obviously far off. It is also somewhat surprising if we are to take at face value Lovecraft's purported longstanding interest in Robert Goddard's rocket research, as mentioned in chapter 5. But more interestingly, it indicates that Lovecraft's pessimism over the likelihood of interplanetary colonization stemmed from the same xenophobic views on habitability that colored his anti-immigration sentiment. To Lovecraft, just as ethnic groups should not attempt to emigrate to the nation-state of another ethnicity, whose institutions and environment were "foreign" to them—a sentiment he sometimes used to criticize terrestrial empires and colonization—there was no point for a species perfectly evolved for the environment of one world to migrate to a world for which it was manifestly unsuited (*RB* 157–58; *CE* 5.13–14).

Of course, aliens and humans coexisting, on either Earth or other planets, was a moot point of speculation for Lovecraft, given the views he expounded to Frome in his follow-up letter of 8 February 1937:

> Virtually all serious students—biologists, physicists, chemists, astronomers—agree in their estimate of *life* as a very minor phenomenon. It is,

10. Yuggoth's Environs

of course, the most *highly organised* form of matter & energy which we know; but it is probably of very rare occurrence in the cosmos (since it requires special conditions involving what we must regard as an accident in order to produce the sort of planetary system adapted to its appearance & growth), & we have certain knowledge that its development to complex forms like man & other mammals depends wholly on an intricate chain of accidents extending over hundreds of thousands of years & so utterly peculiar to the one planet in question that nothing similar could possibly occur anywhere else. That is not to say that *some* highly complex form of life could not grow on some other planet in some other galaxy; but merely to say that it is impossible for such an alien form of life to be anything like *our* terrestrial higher forms. (*FLB* 350)

Lovecraft's reference in the Frome letter to the "special conditions involving what we must regard as an accident in order to produce the sort of planetary system adapted" to life, and his statement in his 1933 Wooley letter that "It takes what amounts to a rare *accident* to produce a solar system," seem to indicate that until the end of his life Lovecraft maintained his 1929 conversion to the planetesimal hypothesis of solar system creation, as discussed in chapter 7. In this cosmological model, the material needed for planets to coalesce could only occur from the near-collision of two stars, an event that is extraordinarily rare given the distances of interstellar space. It is a model suitable for an adherent of cosmic indifference: life can only arise from an event that not only is all but impossible on the cosmic scale, but results in apocalyptic destruction for the two stars involved. While the modern conception of planet-building from planetesimals does not include the near-collision requirement, from the mid-twentieth century the apparent absence of the extraterrestrial intelligence, termed the Fermi Paradox or Great Silence, has been widely discussed (Brin 283–309; Grinspoon, *Lonely* 310–33; Clarke, *Astounding* 190–91). At the end of the twentieth century, the Rare Earth Hypothesis was proposed by a geologist and astronomer pair, proposing that even with modern cosmological assumptions, life (at least of the type that could survive on Earth) still might be rare in the universe (Ward and Brownlee 15–34; Grinspoon, *Lonely* 143–48).

Therefore, in Lovecraft's cosmology, even if extraterrestrial lifeforms existed, not only would the distances separating planets (let alone solar systems) doom any chance of communication with them, but they would also be just as inconsequential to the universe as humans. Lovecraft makes this view explicit in a letter to Helen V. Sully:

> The people on Mars will never know that any human race exists—the people on Neptune can never know that the earth exists—the people on the planets of Alpha Centauri can never know that the solar planets exist—the people of trans-galactic systems can never know that the sun exists—the people of the remotest nebulae can never know that our immediate stellar universe exists. A few trillion years hence there will be no consciousness in existence that can know of the former existence of such a thing as the human race. The universe will be just as it would have been had no earth existed. (5 March 1935; *WBT* 404)

Despite the fact that Lovecraft expressed such pessimistic views about the likelihood of extrasolar life existing, let alone reaching Earth, the notion of travel between the stars is at the heart of his fiction. Even with "Eryx" being the sole interplanetary story he (co)wrote, the theme was on his mind for almost the entire span of time he seriously devoted to fiction. Take for example Lovecraft's letter to Clark Ashton Smith dated 25 March 1923, in which he told his friend:

> It has always been my intention to write a set of tales involving other planets—both of this system & of other stars—but I keep deferring the project because of its magnitude. I want the things to be the fruit of a mind stored with all of the primordial, colourful, morbid, and grotesque lore of literature—and hitherto my reading has had some lamentable lacunae. I never got hold of "Vathek" until 1921, & all of Hoffman is still before me. (*DS* 49)

Beyond the moon, Mars, and even Venus, it is the outer worlds that are most relevant to Lovecraft—"Jupiter and beyond the infinite," to quote *2001: A Space Odyssey*. There are not only the unique circumstances that merged Lovecraft's Yuggoth into Pluto, but the fact that the majority of his entities come not only from other solar systems but other galaxies, and in some cases other universes entirely. Consequently, this chapter will focus on the asteroids, Jupiter, Saturn, Uranus, Neptune, Pluto, comets, and stars, and their role in both Lovecraft's fiction and the fiction which in turn influenced him.

The Asteroid Belt

Going outwards from Mars, one enters the asteroid belt. This belt, in the form of Ceres (originally believed to be a planet and now categorized as a dwarf planet), was discovered on New Year's Day 1801, making the asteroid belt's discovery one of the heralds of the nineteenth century. The discovery of Ceres was fortuitous, as it seemed to solve a problem from a hypothesis referred to as the Titius–Bode law. In the formula of the Titius–Bode law, each planet is about twice as far from the sun as the next-innermost planet.[2] In the late eighteenth century, this fit the distances of all known planets, with the exception of the space in between Mars and Jupiter. The discovery of Ceres fit approximately where a missing planet would have been predicted by the Titius–Bode law. However, the apparent solution was short-lived, as the next year another world, Pallas, was discovered in an orbit close to that of Ceres. Pallas was followed with Juno in 1804 and Vesta in 1807. Four "planets" were therefore found to be sharing the approximate location of the missing planet. The solution seemed clear: Ceres, Pallas, Juno, and Vesta were all the remnants of a larger "fifth planet" that had exploded at some point in the past. In 1823, the German linguist Johann Gottlieb Radlof (1775–1846) termed this hypothetical destroyed planet Phaeton.[3]

Beginning with Astraea in 1845, large numbers of additional objects began to be discovered in the asteroid belt, with nearly fifty being discovered in the decade of the 1850s. In 1846, the discovery of Neptune did not fit the predicted location stated by the Titius–Bode law, leading to the discarding of that model. Between these two developments, alternative models of asteroid development were developed that did not rely on their being the remnants of a destroyed planet. As such, the belief in Phaeton began to decline but retained strong pools of support into the twentieth century—and beyond, in the case of fringe pseudoscientists. Immanuel Velikovsky, mentioned in chapter 7, included Phaeton in his notions of celestial catastrophism inspiring ancient legends, arguing that Phaeton's destruction had been observed by humans a few thousand years ago (Velikovsky 151–53). Lovecraft obliquely mentions Phaeton in his 1915 astronomical article "Mars and the Asteroids." Unlike Vulcan, which he had entirely dismissed, he remains semi-credulous of Phaeton in this article, noting that "It was formerly believed that [the asteroid belt] are the fragments resulting from the explosion of a large planet; indeed, this theory has never been wholly disproved" (*CE* 3.293–94).

In terms of fiction Lovecraft may have read that features asteroids, mention must be made one last time of Garrett Serviss's novel *Edison's*

---

2. The Titius–Bode Law states: add 4 to the numbers in the sequence 0, 3, 6, 12, 24 . . . and divide by 10 to get the distances of the planets from the sun, in units of the Earth-Sun distance, giving 0.4, 0.7, 1.0, 1.6, 2.8, 5.2, 10.0 . . .

3. Not to be confused with the Apollo asteroid Phaethon, parent body of the Geminid meteor shower.

Conquest of Mars (1898). In the novel, the eponymous inventor's space fleet goes past an asteroid on its way to Mars, finding that the Martians have established a base on the asteroid's surface. The Martian fortress and the space fleet exchange fire as they fly past each other (Serviss, *ECM* 60–62). Not only does this make *Edison's Conquest of Mars* one of the first works of fiction to feature an asteroid, it has also been cited as the first example of a space battle in science fiction. As Lovecraft was an avid Sherlock Holmes fan as a youth, it should be pointed out that the seminal mathematical work of Holmes's archrival, Professor Moriarty, is a volume titled *The Dynamics of an Asteroid*. However, Sir Arthur Conan Doyle did not introduce this until his novel *The Valley of Fear*, published in 1914, years after Lovecraft had seemingly stopped reading Holmes stories (*IAP* 90–91).

In Lovecraft's own fiction, the sole reference to an asteroid can be found in "The Shadow out of Time." While in the Library of Pnakotus, Peaslee discovers a book written in

> queerly pigmented, brush-drawn letters of the text—symbols utterly unlike either the usual curved hieroglyphs or any alphabet known to human scholarship—with a haunting, half-aroused memory. It came to me that this was the language used by a captive mind I had known slightly in my dreams—a mind from a large asteroid on which had survived much of the archaic life and lore of the primal planet whereof it formed a fragment. At the same time I recalled that this level of the archives was devoted to volumes dealing with the non-terrestrial planets. (*CF* 3.435–36)

As can be seen, this one mention of asteroids, and from as late as 1935, is a reference to the Phaeton theory. Asteroids feature slightly more in Lovecraftian pastiches, particularly Colin Wilson's 1976 novel *The Space Vampires*. The titular creatures are found in suspended animation in an ancient spaceship in the asteroid belt by a mining expedition in the late twenty-first century. The aliens are eventually revealed to be the Ubbo-Sathla, taken from Clark Ashton Smith's story of the same name (*Weird Tales*, July 1933). In 1994, Peter F. Jeffery (as "Petal Jeffrey") published the short story "Princess of the Black Asteroid" in *Crypt of Cthulhu* No. 88, an in-universe story, originally called "Hasturoid," in a world where Derleth and not Lovecraft created Cthulhu. Leigh Kimmel's 2011 short story "The Damnable Asteroid" is the account of a Russian uranium-mining base on the asteroid Urtukansk unearthing a shoggoth-like entity that drives the crew mad, the last survivor warning the other mining settlements of the asteroid belt what their actions might also unearth (Kimmel 179–84). However, these examples seemingly constitute the bulk of asteroidal Lovecraftian fiction.

From the asteroid belt, going outwards, the prospective imitator of Randolph Carter would next encounter the king of the planets, Jupiter.

Jupiter and Its Moons

Jupiter is the largest of the solar system's planets. If all the other (non-solar) mass of the solar system were combined, Jupiter would still dwarf the accumulation. Outside of the sun, moon, and Venus, it is the brightest natural object in Earth's sky. As with the other outer system planets, Jupiter is what is known as a gas giant, a world with no solid surface; the term was invented in 1952 by science fiction writer James Blish (1921–1975), who had been a late correspondent of Lovecraft's. Jupiter has been known since prehistory, which made it an obvious target for the age of telescopic astronomy. In 1609, the Italian astronomer Galileo Galilei (1564–1642) built his own telescope and began looking at Jupiter. In either late 1609 or early 1610, he observed four moons of the planet, the first objects discovered via telescope as well as the first objects found to orbit a planet other than Earth. These four moons were eventually named (going outwards from Jupiter) Io, Europa, Ganymede, and Callisto, and are now known as the Galilean moons. These are among the largest non-planet bodies in the solar system; Ganymede is the largest moon in the solar system and is actually larger than the planet Mercury. As mentioned in chapter 1, Lovecraft himself frequently observed Jupiter with his small telescopes.

As of 2022, Jupiter has a remarkable eighty moons that have been discovered; more than half were first observed in the twenty-first century, the most recent in 2018.[4] However, the remaining seventy-six are all far smaller than the Galilean moons. They are so small that the fifth moon to be observed—called Jupiter V at the time, before the name Amalthea was adopted in 1976—was not discovered by American astronomer E. E. Barnard until 1892, nearly three hundred years after Galileo's discovery. Barnard's discovery of the fifth moon was the last visual find; photography would be the method by which the next moons were found. As mentioned in chapter 6, Lovecraft was interested in, but skeptical of, the idea that Jupiter V had been a comet captured by Jupiter

---

4. Accepting one candidate recently found on archived images of the planet.

in 1886. Indeed, Lovecraft's lifetime was an enormous wave of discovery of new moons of Jupiter, with five in total being discovered between 1892 and 1914, before the next two were discovered in 1938 (Lubnow, LSS 15–16). In his 1915 *Asheville Gazette-News* article "The Outer Planets," Lovecraft briefly discusses the discovery and nature of Amalthea and its relation to the larger Galilean moons (*CE* 3.295).

In terms of the scant works of fiction that Lovecraft owned and which may have contributed to his conception of Jupiter is John Jacob Astor IV's 1894 science fiction novel *A Journey in Other Worlds*, mentioned in earlier chapters. Nearing Jupiter in their spaceship, the *Callisto*, the crew of Astor's novel pass the moon of the same name, before landing on Jupiter—here depicted as having a rocky surface with large mountains, a breathable atmosphere, and springs and rivers of body-temperature water. The geological development of the world is identified as being at the equivalent of the Carboniferous period on Earth, approximately three hundred million years ago. Despite this, the fauna of Jupiter anachronistically include mastodons and dinosaurs, hunted by the crew. The entire novel serves as an allegory for American imperialism, assuring the readers that the closing of the American frontier is not the end of (literal) space for American power to expand (Fallon 103–10).

A less-sensational source of Jovian inspiration that young Lovecraft owned would have been Serviss's 1901 nonfiction book *Pleasures of the Telescope*. In it, Serviss notes that Jupiter's gravity probably makes it impossible "to become the abode of living beings of a high organization" (184–85). Lovecraft seemingly took this to heart, but reserved space in both his fiction and nonfiction for the Jovian system to be inhabited. Speaking of the Galilean moons in "The Outer Planets," he notes that "Conclusions respecting the habitability of these orbs would be baseless. If they do possess inhabitants, a thing by no means impossible, their astronomers must be fortunate indeed, for words cannot describe the grandeur with which Jupiter shines in their nocturnal skies" (*CE* 3.295). In his 1919 story "Beyond the Wall of Sleep," Lovecraft mentions "the insect-philosophers that crawl proudly over the fourth moon of Jupiter" (*CF* 1.83), an identification that at the time probably referred to Callisto. Presumably astronomy would have been one of the philosophies studied by the Callistan insects. In "The Shadow out of Time," Peaslee encounters "a mind . . . from an outer moon of Jupiter six million years in the past" (*CF* 3.398). Of the Jovian moons discovered as of 1935, Jupiter VIII (now called Pasiphae) and Jupiter IX (now called Sinope) are outermost, thus making them potential candidates for the Jovian guest of the Great Race.

Bridging the distance between nonfiction and fiction is British biologist J. B. S. Haldane's 1927 essay "The Last Judgment," mentioned in several previous chapters as being owned by Lovecraft. In the speculative future history of humanity that Haldane establishes, after the Earth is destroyed, humanity initially relocates to Venus. From Venus, the new race of humanity contemplates colonizing Jupiter, but finds it difficult due to the 130-degree Celsius temperature,[5] gravity three times that of Venus, and an atmosphere full of radioactive thoron gas. Haldane's errors can perhaps be forgiven due to his non-astronomical background. In any case, the Venusian humans selectively breed a dwarf-like offshoot of humanity through generations of centrifugal artificial gravity, resulting in beings one-tenth the height but far stockier than the average Venusian, and hopefully capable of settling Jupiter (Haldane, "Judgment" 308).

As mentioned in chapters 5 and 9, Nikola Tesla's fin de siècle claim to have received radio signals from Martians could possibly have been caused by his picking up signals from Jupiter's radiation belts, perhaps caused by the inner moon Io passing through them. Jupiter's gravity has caused Io to be a molten, volcanic world, but the other Galilean satellites are quite different. Europa, Ganymede, and Callisto have icy surfaces, and since the 1970s it has been suspected that each moon, particularly Europa, has a sub-surface ocean of liquid water (Hand 67–88; Grinspoon, *Lonely* 191–204). This, of course, opens the possibility of whether Y'ha-nthlei has any sister cities on the sub-ice ocean floors of Europa, Ganymede, and Callisto. On a more grounded level, the astronomer Jason T. Wright has argued that the moon, Mars, or one of the outer system moons are logical places to look for artifacts of ancient alien expeditions (Wright 96–100).

The importance of the ocean and its life to Lovecraft's themes has been noted by Kenneth Hite and Ralph Vaughan (Hite 37–42; Vaughan 3–7). Arthur C. Clarke, Carl Sagan, and diving pioneer Jacques-Yves Cousteau have likewise noted the similarities to exploring the oceans and space (Clarke, *Astounding* 123; Scharmen 122–24). The presence of oceans on

---

5. In his *Lessons in Astronomy* (1903), Young wrote that Jupiter was probably "hot, though not so hot as to be self-luminous." By the time of Haldane's 1927 essay, measurements indicated that its clouds were -140°C.

cosmic worlds is the perfect thematic blending. Independently, Robert M. Price has suggested that an adaptation of *At the Mountains of Madness* might best be set not on the ice sheet of Antarctica, but of the moon Europa (Price, "Episode 20"). If finding alien artifacts on the moons of Earth and Jupiter sounds like Arthur C. Clarke's 1968 novel *2001: A Space Odyssey* and its sequels, Price—as well as Joshi—have discussed the belief that *At the Mountains of Madness* was an inspiration for *2001,* as well as Clarke's 1953 novel *Childhood's End* (Price, "Episode 11"; *IAP* 1049).[6]

This is perhaps not as outlandish as it may seem. Clarke was an admirer of Lovecraft, and one of his first published stories was a 1940 parody titled "At the Mountains of Murkiness" (Derie, "Mountains"). The Antarctic explorers in Clarke's parody even compare the scenery they traverse to that of the moon (Clarke, "Murkiness" 96), the location where explorers found an ancient alien monolith in the more famous Clarke story. However, at the time Clarke's only exposure to Lovecraft was the versions of *At the Mountains of Madness* and "The Shadow out of Time" published in *Astounding Stories* in 1936; writing in 1990, Clarke would say the other works of Lovecraft he had read since included the letters collected in his friend Willis Conover's memoir of 1975 *Lovecraft at Last* (Clarke, *Astounding* 128–33; Joshi, *Recognition* 75n56).[7] But like Ray Bradbury, Clarke would continue to publish his early work in Lovecraftian waters. "The Sentinel," the short story that became the basis for *2001,* was first published in the Spring 1951 issue of the magazine *10 Story Fantasy,* alongside August Derleth's "The Other Side of the Wall" and Donald A. Wollheim's "Private World."

Another early story of Clarke's with Lovecraftian overtones is "Jupiter

---

6. Robert H. Waugh has discussed *Childhood's End* in the context of it being in the same continuum of tragic science fiction as *At the Mountains of Madness* (89–106). The novel was also praised by C. S. Lewis, who compared it to *The Time Machine* and *Last and First Men* (Lewis, "OSF" 104). Much like *At the Mountains of Madness, Childhood's End* had also been stranded in movie adaptation development hell for decades (Hughes 18–23; Barlowe, Summers, and Meacham 70–71).

7. Of further interest is that Clarke and HPL's idol Lord Dunsany carried on an extensive correspondence from 1944 to 1956. For several decades, Conover had possession of the letters and was editing them for publication; however, they would not be printed until 1998, two years after Conover's death, under the title *Arthur C. Clarke and Lord Dunsany: A Correspondence.*

Five" (1953), set on the moon of the same designation later named Amalthea. In Clarke's story, Amalthea is actually an immense spacecraft abandoned by aliens in the distant past, with the human crew exploring the artistic works left behind by its creators—in effect, *At the Mountains of Madness* if the titular mountains were flying through space. Clarke would expand this theme in his seminal 1973 novel, *Rendezvous with Rama*. However, as Amalthea orbits within the Galilean moons, rather than outside of their orbits, its crew cannot be the source of the Jovian mind encountered by Peaslee in Pnakotus. In his early drafts of *2001* Clarke incorporated the concept of "Jupiter Five," with the titular moon being an artificial construct where the human crew would enter the wormhole leading them to the builders of the monolith (Clarke, *Lost Worlds* 165–73).

Clarke was friends with the German émigré Willy Ley, who played a role in contributing a few ideas to the development of *2001* (Clarke, *Astounding* 171–72; Clarke, *Lost Worlds* 127). As mentioned in chapters 5 and 9, Ley himself had some potential indirect connections to Lovecraft and may have read a number of Lovecraft's stories in the magazines Ley inherited from Fritz Lang. Early drafts of the *2001* novel included scenes where the astronauts discuss the idea of aliens contacting ancient human civilizations (Clarke, *Lost Worlds* 112–13), and the crew being transported to an alien city whose architecture resembles that of Lovecraft's city of the Old Ones, including a statuary "line of cyclopean heads" (Clarke, *Lost Worlds* 195) and buildings consisting of "hemispherical domes . . . giant beehives . . . [some] plain and angular, being based on a few simple elements, others were as complex as Gothic cathedrals or Cambodian temples" (Clarke, *Lost Worlds* 207). Even the final *2001* novel names one of its early hominid characters contacted by the alien monolith as "the Old One" (Clarke, *2001* 3). The astronauts in Clarke's expedition hibernate during the voyage to their destination in the outer solar system; Fritz Leiber argued that Lovecraft's works were one of the pioneering uses of hibernation in science fiction, through the sleeping Cthulhu and the frozen Elder Things (Leiber, "Hyperspace" 168).[8]

Michael D. Miller has written an in-depth article illustrating the Lovecraftian traits of the *2001* film, and so it will not be recapitulated

---

8. In a similar vein, Jeff Rovin's 1987 novelization of the 1985 *Re-Animator* film has Dr. Carl Hill muse that Herbert West's reanimation technology could provide immortality to space travelers, allowing them to voyage to the stars and conquer the inhabitants of other worlds (Rovin 174).

here. However, Miller's article does not specifically address the novel or the contributions of Clarke, and its focus is on director Stanley Kubrick's approach (Miller, "2001"). It should be noted that, in a 1980 interview, Kubrick did speak admiringly of Lovecraft and of taking inspiration from "Supernatural Horror in Literature" (Foix). However, it was Clarke who was most involved in developing the core concepts of *2001*, and entirely responsible for the sequels. Clarke's three novel sequels to *2001*—*2010: Odyssey Two* (1982), *2061: Odyssey Three* (1987), and *3001: The Final Odyssey* (1997)—each prominently feature the Europa that Price favored, with an enormous alien artifact appearing on the moon's ice-covered surface. *2010* even features a first expedition to Europa to explore its alien life, landing in a feature termed the "Grand Canal" and compared to Percival Lowell's visions of Mars (Clarke, *2010* 55). Indeed, while less well known than his advocacy of Martian canals and Venusian spokes, Lowell also claimed to have observed linear features on the moons of Jupiter (Sheehan and Dobbins 58). However, Clarke's expedition ends in disaster, the last survivor broadcasting his testimony (Clarke, *2010* 59–69) before the HAL 9000 computer issues a Lovecraftian warning to humanity to "attempt no [further] landings there" (Clarke, *2010* 277). Clarke would later establish that the *Programming Manual for the HAL 9000 Computer: Revised Edition* would be printed by Miskatonic University Press in the year 2010, although he strangely locates the press in Oakland, California (Clarke, "Foreword" xvi). Perhaps by 2010, Miskatonic opened a Clark Ashton Smith Memorial California Satellite Campus to aid in Pacific exploration of R'lyeh.[9]

One of the most striking connections between *2010* and Lovecraft is certainly a coincidence, given the limited exposure to Lovecraft from Clarke. In an extended passage of Clarke's novel, the disembodied astronaut Dave Bowman—reborn as an incorporeal cosmic entity by the monolith—travels first through Europa, encountering the aquatic life on its seafloor, doomed to extinction as its lava vents slowly close (Clarke, *2010* 176–82), and then into the atmosphere of Jupiter, witnessing the balloon-like lifeforms floating in its clouds (Clarke, *2010* 186–90). The idea of balloon-like life in Jupiter's atmosphere goes back at least to a 1976 paper by Carl Sagan and E. E. Salpeter, with Sagan then popularizing it in his 1980 *Cosmos* (Sagan and Salpeter 747–52; Sagan, *Cosmos*

---

9. One might also draw a connection to John Carpenter's 1980 horror film *The Fog*, which places an "Arkham Reef" off the shore of California.

30). In Lovecraft and E. Hoffmann's Price's short story "Through the Gates of the Silver Key," a similarly disembodied Randolph Carter makes a similar voyage across the solar system, during which he "learned an untellable secret from the close-glimpsed mists of Jupiter and saw the horror on one of the satellites" (*CF* 3.315). It is not a giant leap to assume that the secret Carter glimpsed in the Jovian mists was the same as the creatures Bowman observed, or that the horror on the Jovian satellite was the knowledge of the approaching extinction of Europa's biosphere.

In 1984, *2010* received its own film adaptation, titled *2010: The Year We Make Contact*. The film largely eschews the novel's plotlines about the Jovian and Europan life, condensing the latter into the concluding scene. However, the *2010* novel's general storyline about an expedition accidentally being killed by life on Europa would come to fruition with the 2013 film *Europa Report*, which appears as a found footage entry recounting the destruction of the first crewed mission to Europa by a cephalopod drawn through the ice by the ship's light. Like the Elder Things, it kills the human explorers, but not through malice. The screenplay of *Europa Report* was written by Philip Gelatt, who in addition to serving as the director of the film schedule for NecronomiCon Providence, is a repeated guest of the H. P. Lovecraft Film Festival and co-host of the Clark Ashton Smith podcast *The Double Shadow*.

In the 1970s, early Lovecraft chronicler Lin Carter wrote a series of novels set on the moon Callisto, a deliberate homage to the Barsoom stories of Edgar Rice Burroughs. However, as there are scant (if any) Lovecraftian elements to them, they are beyond the scope of this work. Instead, this section on Jupiter will end with a brief mention of the story "Tidal Moon" by Stanley G. Weinbaum, who, as mentioned in chapter 9, was the rare author of interplanetary fiction whose work Lovecraft admired. "Tidal Moon" is set on Ganymede, which in Weinbaum's setting is covered in a mix of ice and frigid oceans, anticipating the conceptualizing of the Galilean moons by decades (although by the 1920s the low densities of Ganymede and Callisto had led to suggestions that they might be composed of ice or frozen carbon dioxide). Like Carter's series, there is little Lovecraftian in the content of "Tidal Moon," but something in its development. "Tidal Moon" was published in 1938—despite the fact that Weinbaum had died in 1935. Weinbaum left behind a page and a half of the story; the remaining ten pages were written by his sister

Helen, who would go on to write a number of other science fiction stories on her own. Not only did Weinbaum predict the surface of Ganymede ahead of mainstream astronomers, his sister pioneered the posthumous collaboration ahead of August Derleth.

Saturn, Uranus, and Neptune

If Lovecraft is to be believed, his only case of delirium was in 1903, when he was twelve years old and suffering from an "exaggerated cold" during which he "mumbled things about flying to Mars & Saturn" (*FLB* 185). As mentioned in chapter 1, 1903 was the year in which Lovecraft began his own telescopic observations of Saturn. But another possible inspiration for a dream flight to Saturn may have been *A Journey in Other Worlds,* as mentioned above. In the novel, after the crew of the *Callisto* leave Jupiter, they head to Saturn. Whereas Jupiter and its dinosaurs represent the continuation of American political expansion, Saturn represents the Anglo-Saxon race's spiritual development, the crew being informed by religious apparitions how the technological developments of American inventors will help hasten the evolution toward a more godlike height (Fallon 108–9). Such a notion may have had some interest as a speculative thought experiment for Lovecraft, even if he (especially as a young adult) may have disagreed with its validity.

Given the young Lovecraft's hallucinatory pairing of Mars and Saturn, it is apt that, just like Mars, Saturn is only mentioned once in Lovecraft's fiction. In *The Dream-Quest of Unknown Kadath,* Randolph Carter learns of "the one foe which earth's cats fear; the very large and peculiar cats from Saturn, who for some reason have not been oblivious of the charm of our moon's dark side. They are leagued by treaty with the evil toad-things, and are notoriously hostile to our earthly cats" (*CF* 2.119). The affiliation of the Saturnian cats with "evil toad-things" makes sense given that in the works of Clark Ashton Smith, Saturn is the home of his toad-like deity Tsathoggua, referenced extensively in Lovecraft's fiction. In Smith's fiction, Saturn is called Cykranosh and is described far differently from the Saturn of reality. Because of this, Fred S. Lubnow has proposed the intriguing retcon that Smith's Cykranosh is actually the Saturn of the Dreamlands, and that "our" Saturn would still be the Saturn of Carter's waking world and the larger Lovecraftian setting (Lubnow, LSS 18–19). In chapter 6, Lovecraft's denunciation of astrology is discussed, but Andrew Paul Wood's 2019 article "The Rings of Cthulhu" offers an analysis of the role of Saturn in astrology and how that may have influenced the development of "The Call of Cthulhu"

(Wood 58–60). It should also be noted that in the novel of *2001: A Space Odyssey,* the destination of the space expedition is not the Jupiter of the films (and novel sequels) but Saturn. Instead of the giant monolith Star Gate being in orbit of Jupiter, it is on the surface of Saturn's moon Iapetus (Clarke, *2001* 207). This was one of the ideas for which Clarke took inspiration from Willy Ley (Clarke, *Lost Worlds* 127).

Uranus is absent from Lovecraft's fiction, the only planet not even to be mentioned (Hite 146). Neptune does receive several mentions, most notably in "The Whisperer in Darkness" (1930), with the fake Akeley telling Wilmarth of his encounter with "two beings from Neptune (God! if you could see the body this type has on its own planet!)" (*CF* 2.523). In "Through the Gates of the Silver Key," the disembodied Randolph Carter "passed close to Neptune and glimpsed the hellish white fungi that spot it" (*CF* 3.315). In 1989, the *Voyager 2* space probe passed Neptune and observed white clouds in the world's atmosphere; Lubnow has proposed that these "clouds" were actually colonies of the hellish white fungi that Carter observed (Lubnow, LSS 23). It also stands to reason that Carter's fungi might be the same beings described by the fake Akeley, which might also be relatives of the fungi from nearby Yuggoth.

In terms of Neptunian fiction to which Lovecraft would have been exposed, one surprising source is Edgar Allan Poe's 1849 short story "Mellonta Tauta," as earlier discussed in chapter 5. The protagonist, Pundita, mentions having "a fine view of the five Neptunian asteroids" from her balloon vantage point (Poe, "MT" 1126). Neptune was discovered in 1846. Its largest moon, Triton—larger than Pluto, and believed to have originally also been a dwarf planet before being captured by Neptune's gravity—was first observed less than three weeks later. The second moon was not discovered until 1949, and the third in 1981, since Neptune's remaining moons are indeed asteroid-like. In 1989, *Voyager 2* discovered five more smaller inner moons of Neptune. Perhaps these are the moons Pundita observed. In any case, Poe's story is notable for being one of the first appearances of Neptune in a work of fiction, and apparently the first work of fiction to mention Neptune's moons.

Another work Lovecraft would have read was the poem "Planet Neptune to Mother Sun" in the September 1927 issue of *Amazing Stories*. This story was written by Leland S. Copeland (1886–1973) and reprinted from his 1921 volume *Whimsical Rimes*. Copeland was a poet and amateur astronomer; he was the first poet whose work was published by Hugo Gernsback in his magazines. The poem is written from the viewpoint of Neptune, recalling how it was born out of the sun (reflecting the planetesimal hypothesis) and jealous of the attention given to Earth and Mars by their mutual solar mother. A more substantive work in its appreciation by Lovecraft was Olaf Stapledon's *Last and First Men*. In it, Neptune serves as a refuge for the far-future Ninth Race of humanity after the inner worlds become no longer hospitable. Over the next several hundred million years, the human colonists of Neptune gradually evolve until they reach the Eighteenth Race, the Last Men of the title (Stapledon 273–83).

In finishing this section, it should be noted that, in addition to the better-known evidence for sub-ice oceans on Europa, Ganymede, and Callisto, Saturn's moons Titan and Enceladus, Uranus's moons Titania and Miranda, and Neptune's moon Triton may also have oceans beneath their icy surfaces (Hand 17). Much like the Galilean satellites of Jupiter, this establishes them as potential colonies of the Deep Ones. But beyond hypothetical settlements of Deep Ones, no discussion of the Lovecraftian outer solar system would be complete without a discussion of the haunt of the Mi-Go: the world known to them as Yuggoth and humanity as Pluto.

Yuggoth

In chapter 7, it was mentioned that Neptune was discovered by mathematically analyzing unexpected discrepancies in the orbit of Uranus. Within years, several astronomers believed that further observations of both Uranus and Neptune indicated that an additional planet beyond Neptune was possible. In the final decade of his life, Percival Lowell devoted Lowell Observatory to the search for what he termed "Planet X," hoping to rehabilitate his image after the Martian canal and Venusian spoke fiascos. Lowell's death in 1916 disrupted the search for Planet X for more than a decade, due to turmoil among the observatory's staff and a dispute over money with Lowell's widow. However, in 1929 the search resumed under the aegis of a twenty-three-year-old astronomer, Clyde Tombaugh (1906–1997). Tombaugh had been an amateur astronomer who had not even attended college before his appointment at Lowell. However, the observatory's astronomers were impressed by the drawings of Mars and Jupiter he made using his homemade telescope, offering an interesting contrast with Lovecraft's amateur astronomy days. A year after Tombaugh's appointment, on 13 March 1930 Lowell Observatory announced that he had discovered the planet in question, which was named Pluto on 1 May of that year. In comparison, Lovecraft wrote "Whisperer" from February to September 1930 (Hite 136–47; Lubnow, LSS 23–24).

It should be noted that Lowell's hopes that the search for Planet X would rehabilitate his observatory's reputation among professional astronomers would not quite come to pass, not least due to Tombaugh's own subsequent activities. On 27 August 1941, Tombaugh observed a flash of light on the surface of Mars. After World War II, Robert McLaughlin, commander of the White Sands missile test range, stated that Tombaugh had told him that he believed it to be Martians detonating an atomic bomb of their own.[10] Unlike Lowell, however, Tombaugh's observations of aliens, or at least possible alien artifacts, were not limited to Mars. Between 1949 and 1956, Tombaugh claimed to have experienced three different UFO sightings from his home in Las Cruces, New Mexico. In the mid-1950s it was rumored that he was part of a secret Air Force project searching for alien motherships in orbit over Earth, which probably stemmed from his search for small natural Earth satellites (Swords 688–92).[11] One wonders whether the Mi-Go were visiting the discoverer of their Yuggoth base.[12]

Lovecraft himself had suspected trans-Neptunian planets since his youth. His famous letter to *Scientific American* of 15 July 1906—identified by Joshi as "one of the most prominent publications of any work by Lovecraft for many decades"—was on that topic (*CE* 3.16–17; Joshi, "LOP" 5; Joshi, *Recognition* 11). In his article "Are There Undiscovered Planets?" for the *Pawtuxet Valley Gleaner* (5 October 1906), Lovecraft concludes by saying that "It is not likely that the limits of our solar system are yet found, and sooner or later Mercury and Neptune must lose the distinction that they now bear" (*CE* 3.30). Nor was Lovecraft alone among fiction writers in such speculation. Stapledon's *Last and First*

---

10. We have not, however, found any written account of this flare by Tombaugh himself.

11. Tombaugh's final report (1959) is available online.

12 Appropriately enough for the UFO sightings by the discoverer of icy Pluto, *At the Mountains of Madness* has been identified as playing a key role in the development of modern UFO conspiracy theory culture (Navroth 190–98).

Men, written just before Pluto's discovery, mentions three additional planets beyond Neptune. In discussing their lack of suitability for colonization, Stapledon describes how "The two outermost would remain glacial, and, moreover, lay beyond the range of the imperfect ether-ships of the Eighth Men. The innermost was practically a bald globe of iron, devoid not merely of atmosphere and water, but also of the normal covering of rock" (272). While very different from the Pluto of reality, one could also see why it would be an attractive mining destination for the Mi-Go.

However, Lovecraft's invention of Pluto predated the discovery of Pluto; as mentioned above, "The Whisperer in Darkness" was begun a month prior to the announcement of Lowell Observatory. But of course, "Whisperer" itself was not Yuggoth's origin. It first appears, appropriately enough, in the 1929–30 sonnet cycle *Fungi from Yuggoth*. In its original appearance, Yuggoth appears to be an extrasolar planet; it is only with "The Whisperer in Darkness" that it becomes associated with the newly discovered Pluto (Joshi, "LOP" 5–6; Hite 147).

In *Fungi from Yuggoth,* the titular world is initially described as a "strange, grey world . . . past the starry voids" (*AT* 82). There are seas and "lapping lakes of flame," with architecture consisting of miles-high marble towers and domes built upon domes, suggestive of Byzantium. The star Fomalhaut is mentioned, perhaps implying it is the sun that Yuggoth was originally meant to circle. Fomalhaut is also mentioned in *The Dream-Quest of Unknown Kadath* and Lovecraft's 1927 dream-snippet "The Very Old Folk" (*CF* 2.100; *CF* 3.500; Livesey, DPO 42–43). Derleth would later establish that his fire elemental Cthugha was from Fomalhaut (Derleth, *Trail* 26). In his seminal 1972 essay "The Derleth Mythos," Richard L. Tierney argued that Derleth chose Fomalhaut "presumably because Lovecraft once mentioned that star in one of his sonnets" (Tierney, "Mythos" 53). Of particular interest is that in 2008 an object orbiting Fomalhaut was discovered; initially believed to be a Jupiter-like planet, its precise characteristics are uncertain. Originally designated Fomalhaut b, in 2015 the mysterious object was given the formal, and very suggestive, name Dagon. Alas, there is now doubt as to whether Dagon exists as a planet; it may instead be an expanding gas and ice cloud.

Nithon, seemingly a companion world to Yuggoth, is also mentioned in *Fungi from Yuggoth*. The only details provided are that it has continents (implying seas as well) upon which scented flowers grow. Kenneth Hite suggests that Nithon may be a moon of Yuggoth (147).

If Yuggoth is indeed Pluto, then Nithon could be Charon, Pluto's largest moon, discovered in 1978. It should also be noted that in "Through the Gates of the Silver Key," there is a single reference to a triple star system named Nython (*CF* 3.314). The relation between Nithon and Nython is unclear; perhaps in the Dreamlands, Fomalhaut is a triple star system, one of which is Nython, around which orbit Nithon and Yuggoth.

In "The Whisperer in Darkness," the first reference of Yuggoth is on one of Akeley's recordings, where a Mi-Go collaborator declares that "Yuggoth is the youngest child, rolling alone in black aether at the rim" (*CF* 2.487)—establishing from the start that Yuggoth exists at the rim of the solar system. This is confirmed later when the Mi-Go are established as having come "from the dark planet Yuggoth, at the rim of the solar system; but this was itself merely the populous outpost of a frightful interstellar race whose ultimate source must lie far outside even the Einsteinian space-time continuum or greatest known cosmos" (*CF* 2.489). Notably, despite the name of the sonnet cycle, the Mi-Go are not fungi from Yuggoth, but merely fungi who settled Yuggoth.[13] However, despite the fungi's origin elsewhere, Yuggoth appears quite hospitable on the cosmic scene, and not only for the Mi-Go. As the fake Akeley states, "There are mighty cities on Yuggoth—great tiers of terraced towers built of black stone ... mysterious Cyclopean bridges—things built by some elder race extinct and forgotten before the things came to Yuggoth from the ultimate voids" (*CF* 2.518). Ramsey Campbell's 1964 story "The Mine on Yuggoth" features a 1924 voyage to one such city by the English occultist Edward Taylor (via Mi-Go teleportation, not brain cylinder). In Campbell's work, Yuggoth is a cosmopolitan planet "where dwell the denizens of many extraterrestrial realms" (Campbell, "Mine" 265).

A distinct aspect of the Mi-Go cities is that their buildings do not contain windows, as they not only do not need light to see, but light "hurts and hampers and confuses them" due to its absence in their transdimensional point of origin (*CF* 2.518). The Pennacook Algonquins, however, believe the Mi-Go originated from the Great Bear, not consistent with an origin beyond space and time (*CF* 2.471). However, a

---

13. However, in Fritz Leiber's influential 1966 pastiche "To Arkham and the Stars," set in the late 1950s, both Dyer and Wilmarth explicitly refer to the Mi-Go as "Plutonians" and "Yuggothians" (Leiber, "Arkham" 158–59, 162–63).

possible explanation is that the Mi-Go of Yuggoth simply traveled to our solar system from their previous destination, located somewhere in the direction of the Great Bear, which would also explain how their origin could be in a constellation whose shape is only visible from our solar system. It should also be noted that the stars Dubhe and Merak, which form one edge of the Great Bear, point toward Polaris, a star with particular resonance for Lovecraft's 1918 story of the same name. In it, the narrator describes Polaris as "winking hideously like an insane watching eye which strives to convey some strange message" (*CF* 1.65). Was the narrator receiving a psychic message from Mi-Go in the direction of Polaris? Further, both T. R. Livesey and Hite note that Lovecraft was aware that Polaris is a triple star system. As such, Polaris might be not only Nython, but the three-star system with "yellow, carmine, and indigo" suns located "infinitely north" that Gilman travels to in "The Dreams in the Witch House" (*CF* 3.249; Livesey, DPO 41; Hite 148n60).

Wherever the point of origin of the Mi-Go, Wilmarth is assured by the fake Akeley that "At the proper time, you know, the beings there will direct thought-currents toward us and cause it to be discovered—or perhaps let one of their human allies give the scientists a hint" (*CF* 2.503). This happens at the end of the novella, with Wilmarth associating it directly with Pluto—"and I shiver when I try to figure out the real reason *why* its monstrous denizens wish it to be known in this way at this especial time" (*CF* 2.530). Lovecraft could not have known it at the time, but his suggestion that Yuggoth would only be identified once its inhabitants wanted it to be fits in well with the fact that since 1909, Pluto had actually been unknowingly photographed sixteen times by astronomers, before Tombaugh identified it in 1930. For his part, Tombaugh had been systematically photographing the sky around the ecliptic. It is therefore not surprising that Pluto was eventually photographed. However, not until the photographic plates were examined with a blink comparator could Pluto actually be discovered. Dismayed by the huge number of stars on plates centered on eta and 36 Geminorum, Tombaugh jumped ahead to blink the delta Gem plates instead. It was then that he found Pluto (*Out of the Darkness: The Planet Pluto*). When Wilmarth's warning is taken into account, the evidence is clear: it was a telepathic signal from the Mi-Go that led Tombaugh to focus on the proper photographic plates.

Lovecraft next mentions Yuggoth in his 1932 revision story "The

Horror in the Museum." Museum owner George Rogers describes "lead-grey Yuggoth, where the cities are under the warm deep sea" (*CF* 4.443). It is those aquatic oceans that were the origin of the entity Rhan-Tegoth, which came to Alaska three million years ago, before being frozen in its citadel (*CF* 4.425). The final major reference of the world for Lovecraft is his 1933 revision work "Out of the Aeons," which mentions that the *Unaussprechlichen Kulten* of Friedrich von Junzt contains a passage on

> a kingdom or province called K'naa in a very ancient land where the first human people had found monstrous ruins left by those who had dwelt there before—vague waves of unknown entities which had filtered down from the stars and lived out their aeons on a forgotten, nascent world. K'naa was a sacred place, since from its midst the bleak basalt cliffs of Mount Yaddith-Gho soared starkly into the sky, topped by a gigantic fortress of Cyclopean stone, infinitely older than mankind and built by the alien spawn of the dark planet Yuggoth, which had colonised the earth before the birth of terrestrial life. The spawn of Yuggoth had perished aeons before, but had left behind them one monstrous and terrible living thing which could never die—their hellish god or patron daemon Ghatanothoa, which lowered and brooded eternally though unseen in the crypts beneath that fortress on Yaddith-Gho. (*CF* 4.460)

Among those early humans of K'naa, "There were always those who believed that sacrifices must be made to Ghatanothoa, lest it crawl out of its hidden abysses and waddle horribly through the world of men as it had once waddled through the primal world of the Yuggoth-spawn" (*CF* 4.461). Von Junzt further mentions "a carven cylinder of *lagh* metal—the metal brought by the Elder Ones from Yuggoth, and found in no mine of earth" (*CF* 4.463), which seems suggestive of the cylinders used by the Mi-Go. In Campbell's "The Mine on Yuggoth," the metal mined on Yuggoth for the Mi-Go cylinders is given the name "tok'l" (Campbell, "Mine" 261).

Jason Colavito identifies the first passage from "Out of the Aeons" as an early example of the ancient alien trope, to be described more extensively below (Colavito, *Cult* 89). Indeed, this description of terrestrial colonization from Yuggoth seems at odds with "The Whisperer in Darkness," where it is explicitly stated that the Mi-Go "did not live here . . . but merely maintained outposts and flew back with vast cargoes of stone to their own stars in the north" (*CF* 2.518). The answer seems to lie in the fact that the colonists who left ruins in K'naa were not the Mi-

Go, but the original inhabitants of Yuggoth. The predilection for Cyclopean stone architecture, while certainly widespread in Lovecraft's universe, seems to link the creatures of Yuggoth and K'naa. The mass relocation of the Yuggothians inwards to Earth further seems to reflect the nebular hypothesis and the migration of the Great Race, as described in chapter 7. Fleeing the encroaching cold of Yuggoth, they were then seemingly exterminated on Earth by Ghatanothoa. It is interesting that the Yuggothians are not cited as one of the other cosmic species inhabiting Earth encountered by the Elder Things in their Antarctic murals (*CF* 3.101).

On 24 August 2006, the International Astronomical Union developed a new definition of planet, one that controversially relegated Pluto from the status of planet to dwarf planet; the definitions of and reasons for this designation are beyond the scope of this book. The timing could not have been worse, as on 19 January of that year NASA launched the *New Horizons* spacecraft, the first probe aimed toward Pluto. Amidst its scientific instruments were the ashes of Clyde Tombaugh, potentially making him the first known human since Henry Akeley (whose voyage was preceded by that of Edward Taylor) to travel to Yuggoth (Lubnow, LSS 26). *New Horizons* passed by Pluto in 2015, resulting in an enormous amount of new data on the world and its moons, including images of surface features for the first time. Most notable of *New Horizons'* discoveries for the purposes of this book is a surface region that was given the name Cthulhu Macula. Adjacent to Cthulhu Macula is the Sputnik Macula region, which *New Horizons* data suggests may have a subsurface ocean (Hand 143–46). Perhaps this is the "warm deep sea" mentioned in "The Horror in the Museum." The reference to "warm" can perhaps be explained by its being relative in contrast to absolute zero. Lubnow has similarly proposed that evidence of methane cryovolcanism on Pluto might explain the references to "black rivers of pitch" on Yuggoth in "The Whisperer in Darkness" (*CF* 2.518; Lubnow, LSS 24–25). The passage of *New Horizons* by Pluto was also integrated into Caitlín R. Kiernan's 2017 novella *Agents of Dreamland,* which implies that Yuggoth is actually "a billion miles farther out than Pluto." Eris, the second-largest dwarf planet after Pluto (and with significantly higher mass), would average a little less than three billion miles further out, though its orbit is notably eccentric. At perihelion it can be closer than Pluto, although as of early 2022 Eris is not that far past aphelion. Despite *Agents of Dreamland*'s separation of Yuggoth and Pluto, the Mi-Go still send a probe to examine *New Horizons,* which is established as being responsible for a brief communications loss with *New Horizons* that happened ten days before its Pluto flyby (Kiernan, *Agents* 92).

While "The Whisperer in Darkness" was a very early appearance of Pluto in fiction, the new world's appeal to other authors is clear by how many others in the Lovecraft circle rushed to feature the ninth world. Kenneth Sterling published "The Brian-Eaters of Pluto" in *Wonder Stories* (March 1934); this was his first published story, prior to collaborating in his planetary fiction work with Lovecraft. "Report of the Plutonian Ambassador" (*Wonder Stories,* September 1935) was also the first published work by Robert A. W. Lowndes (1916–1998), a late Lovecraft correspondent who would go on to publish a number of other space operas. As mentioned in chapter 7, Clark Ashton Smith's "The Plutonian Drug" was featured in the September 1934 *Amazing Stories*. One of Lovecraft's favorite authors of space operas, Stanley G. Weinbaum, published his sole Pluto-set work, "The Red Peri," in the November 1935 *Astounding Stories*. This story included a scene where a character runs across one thousand feet of Pluto's surface between airlocks without wearing a protective suit. This scene was very influential for a young Arthur C. Clarke, who later used it as the inspiration for similar scenes in several of his works, including *2001* (Clarke, *Astounding* 122–24).

But while "The Whisperer in Darkness" states that Yuggoth is "alone in black aether at the rim" of the solar system, Lovecraft was not certain of Pluto having such finality. In a letter to Kenneth Sterling, he notes the possibility of "a couple of trans-Plutonians whose presence is suggested by the location of certain cometary aphelia" (20 November 1935; *RB* 255). This is reflected in "The Shadow out of Time," with Peaslee's mention of "a half-plastic denizen of the hollow interior of an unknown trans-Plutonian planet eighteen million years in the future" (*CF* 3.429). In this, as in his use of the Bering land-bridge and continental drift in *At the Mountains of Madness,* Lovecraft showed his ability to ride the scientific cutting edge. Almost from the start of Pluto's discovery, doubt was cast on whether it actually was the "Planet X" whose gravity could account for the suppose perturbations of Uranus and Neptune. Lovecraft would have been well aware of the Planet X predictions of William H. Pickering, the astronomer discussed in chapter 4. Pickering used comet aphelia as one element in some of his predictions. He published papers on this in *Popular Astronomy,* where Lovecraft might have seen them. Pickering was also not averse to newspaper publicity and touted his theories there (as well as claiming that he correctly predicted the existence of Pluto). The discovery of Charon in 1978 was the final nail in the coffin, as measuring the moon's orbit showed that Pluto's mass was far lower than originally believed in 1930.

At the same time observations of Pluto were being revised, much as with Mercury and Vulcan as described in chapter 7, improved observations of Uranus and Neptune eliminated the need for a "Planet X" in the first place. However, beginning in 2012 the idea of a massive planet far beyond Neptune was resurrected as a way of potentially explaining peculiarities in the orbits of a number of comets and dwarf planets in the outer solar system. In 2015, this hypothetical object was given the name Planet Nine, as the designation was no longer in use by Pluto. In "Through the Gates of the Silver Key," Randolph Carter "saw Kynarth and Yuggoth on the rim" (*CF* 3.315). Lubnow proposes that if Yuggoth is Pluto, then Kynarth may be Planet Nine (Lubnow, *JLS3* 51–52), although their grouping also allows for Kynarth to be Charon. In his 1982 article "Lovecraft's Other Planets," Joshi suggests that Shaggai from Lovecraft's 1935 short story "The Haunter of the Dark"—located "more distant" than Yuggoth (*CF* 3.476)—is the tenth planet of the solar system (Joshi, "LOP" 5). After Pluto's 2006 demotion, this would then mean that Shaggai could be Planet Nine. In his 1964 story "The Insects from Shaggai," Ramsey Campbell further develops the planet and its inhabitants, though he makes its status as an adjunct to our solar system impossible, as Shaggai is established as "a globe far beyond the reach of any earthly telescope, which orbited a double sun at the edge of the universe" (Campbell, *Inhabitants* 71).

In an inversion of the idea of Planet Nine as Kynarth or Shaggai is Richard A. Lupoff's 1977 story "Discovery of the Ghooric Zone—March 15, 2337," an early, seminal Lovecraftian space opera (Derie, "Discovery"). Lupoff's story establishes that the tenth planet is not only the Planet X of Lowell, but is the real Yuggoth. Yuggoth is discovered on the four hundredth anniversary of Lovecraft's death by an expedition that, ironically, was assembled and launched from Pluto. The Yuggoth of Lupoff has twice the mass of Jupiter, with an equatorial rotation of eighty thousand kilometers per hour. This Yuggoth has four moons: Nithon, Zaman, and the paired Thog and Thok (Lupoff, "Ghooric"); notably, the story was published a year before Pluto's first of five (known) moons was discovered. Nithon has already been documented, but Zaman seems to be an extrapolation of the setting of Zaman's Hill in *Fungi from Yuggoth*; Lupoff's use of it as a moon of Yuggoth is odd, as the sonnet makes it clear that it is a hill near Aylesbury (*AT* 83). Thog's only reference in Lovecraft is also in *Fungi from Yuggoth*, where it is the location whence the Pigeon-Flyers brought back something beneath their wings, although it is possibly one of the dark planets with crypts mentioned in the line earlier (*AT* 84). Thok was also mentioned in *Fungi from Yuggoth* as a world with jagged peaks, a fact derived from Randolph Carter's visit to it in *The Dream-Quest of Unknown Kadath* (*AT* 88; *CF* 2.131). Years after Lupoff's "Discovery of the Ghooric Zone," Kiernan's *Agents of Dreamland* also implies that Planet X/Planet Nine is the real Yuggoth and plausibly establishes that attempts to locate it have been frustrated by the same Mi-Go psychic clouding that they used to keep the false-flag Pluto hidden (Kiernan, *Agents* 91–92).

Whether or not Planet Nine exists, the outer solar system is far from empty. In particular, it is the home of the famous harbingers of doom throughout history, stars that were believed to bring doom when their appearance was right—stars that even left behind them tendrils evocative of the tentacles of some of Lovecraft's most famous cosmic terrors. However, these are not Cthulhu or his star-spawn, but rather comets.

Comets

As mentioned in chapter 1, the young Lovecraft made only one written account of the April–May 1910 passage of Halley's Comet, the only such return of that visitor during his lifetime. However, the shadow of the comet loomed large in the public. As mentioned in chapter 7, astronomers had identified trace amounts of cyanogen in the tail of the comet, which the Earth would pass through. This led to a large public fear over imminent cosmic death; obviously, this did not come to pass (Sagan and Druyan 149–50). As mentioned earlier, Lubnow proposed that the influence of this panic can be felt in the presence of cyanogen in the Venusian atmosphere in "Eryx" (Lubnow, LSS 12). Sir Arthur Conan Doyle's 1913 novel *The Poison Belt*, the first sequel to the previous year's *The Lost World*, draws upon the comet gas panic, although it proposes that the origin is not a comet but a deadly region of the interstellar luminiferous ether. As mentioned in chapters 6 and 7, the fear of cometary gas was merely the latest incarnation of an assumption that comets brought with them misfortune, a claim promoted by astrologers and at which Lovecraft took aim in his newspaper columns. Of particular note is his satirical 1914 letter "Delavan's Comet and Astrology," detailing the future destruction of Earth in the fiftieth century, but with the world's population being saved by "comet XY4"—a story that might potentially show the influence of the Phaeton claim, as mentioned above (*CE* 3.266–68).

In 1985, when Colin Wilson's novel *The Space Vampires* was adapted into the movie *Lifeforce*, the twenty-first-century asteroid locale as the discovery point for the titular aliens was replaced with Halley's Comet on its 1986 return. The 1993 videogame *Shadow of the Comet*, which draws inspiration from "The Dunwich Horror" and "The Shadow over Innsmouth," is set during the 1910 Halley's Comet visit, when a photographer visits the New England coast town of "Illsmouth" and comes to learn about strange events that occurred in the 1835 visit, and may happen again with the 1910 return. But as also mentioned in chapter 7, Halley's Comet was not the only comet of 1910, being preceded by Pons-Winnecke and, most spectacularly of all, the Great January Comet of 1910, which had a surprise appearance and could even be viewed in daylight at its brightest (although, as noted in chapter 1, Lovecraft reported that measles prevented him from seeing it). The media often confused these comets, and in retrospect a number of accounts of "Halley's Comet" are actually confusion with the brighter Great January Comet. However, one author who did not confuse the two was Mark Twain. Twain had been born on 30 November 1835, only a few weeks after the previous appearance of Halley's Comet, and throughout his life he believed he was destined to die when the comet returned. His prediction was borne out, as the author died in his Stormfield residence in Connecticut on 21 April 1910, a day after Halley's closest approach. Twain named his mansion after the last story published in his lifetime, the 1907 "Captain Stormfield's Visit to Heaven," in which comets are depicted as the spirits of the dead circling the afterlife. Due to its lateness in the author's oeuvre, it was not in any of the three Twain books that Lovecraft owned (*LL* 159). However, Don Webb's 1994 short story "The Comet Called Ithaqua" has a similar concept, where the Derlethian ice elemental is incorporated as a comet (Webb, "Ithaqua" 72).

Another nineteenth-century author admired by Lovecraft who wrote about a comet was Jules Verne, whose 1877 novel *Hector Servadac*—helpfully retitled *Off on a Comet* in English—features a fictional comet, Gallia, that has a near-impact with the western Mediterranean. As a result, a region of both the sea and coast are taken onto the comet, which itself has an oceanic surface. Using the *Dobryna,* the ship of a Russian explorer, the French characters are able to navigate around Gallia, encountering small pockets of other survivors taken up onto the comet. Two years after its initial brush with Earth, Gallia again nears the planet in its orbit. The human inhabitants of Gallia build a balloon out of the sails of the *Dobryna,* and as the comet touches Earth's atmosphere, they float down back to the mother planet, much like a reverse of Edgar Allan Poe's Hans Pfaall. Science fiction author Stephen Baxter has called *Off on a Comet* "a first vision of a human community surviving in a small, self-sustaining Earth-like environment far from the Earth itself" (Baxter, "From" 297). It is unknown if Lovecraft read *Off on a Comet* during his period of youthful Verne enthusiasm, but he certainly read it when it was serialized in the first two issues of *Amazing Stories,* for April and May 1926, which Lovecraft owned (*LL* 24). *Amazing Stories* would have another comet-focused story in its June 1927 issue, with "The Lost Comet" from the relatively obscure author Ronald M. Sherin. Sherin's story features a mathematician who predicts the arrival of a comet that will destroy the Earth. When the comet instead slightly misses the Earth, the world celebrates, while the mathematician is depressed at his errors in calculation.

The Oort cloud is the term given to a hypothetical area of the solar system first theorized in 1950, extending as far as three light years from the sun and marking the extreme end of the sun's gravitational dominance (Sagan, *Cosmos* 86–87; Sagan and Druyan 212–26). As such, the Oort cloud is believed to be a potential reservoir of trillions of comets, thus making a diffuse boundary with "true" interstellar space. In 1972, Anglo-American physicist Freeman Dyson (1923–2020) proposed the concept of a "Dyson tree," a plant (genetically engineered or naturally occurring) that might grow on the surface of Oort comets and live off starlight. Dyson trees as imagined could even have interior spaces habitable to terrestrial life, with other scientists following Dyson with their own concepts of arboreal cometary life (Sagan and Druyan 346–47; Brin 290). Kenneth Hite has written on the Lovecraftian concept of "the woods" and their presence as a liminal space where forces from outside of civilization (and sanity) can emerge, not only on their own but also through solicitation (Hite 6–12). Dyson trees transforming the Oort cloud into an interstellar forest is a particularly resonant take on Lovecraftian cosmic horror. Indeed, as mentioned in chapter 1, the book that introduced Lovecraft to astronomy, Charles Augustus Young's *Lessons in Astronomy,* analogizes the heavens to a forest, with stars and trees alike in all stages of life and death (Young 285). In his 2008 novel of the same name, Chinese science fiction author Liu Cixin coined the term "Dark Forest" as an explanation to the Fermi Paradox, suggesting that civilizations in the universe are common, but each stays hidden as it fears destruction if revealing itself to the others—the universe is therefore a dark forest, with civilizations like hunters simultaneously seeking to remain hidden while searching for rivals to destroy (Liu 484–86). It should also be noted that a Dyson tree—as a broad, many-branched, and dark holdout among even darker space—would be a good match for the tree-like Dark Young of Shub-Niggurath, developed by Robert Bloch in his story "Notebook Found in a Deserted House" (1951), based on the Mi-Go's mention of Shub-Niggurath's "thousand young" in "The Whisperer in Darkness" (*CF* 2.487; Bloch 238). Presumably, if any Lovecraftian species would know what dwells on Oort comets, it would be the Mi-Go.

In his 16 November 1906 *Pawtuxet Valley Gleaner* article on comets, Lovecraft presciently noted that "there are many which roam aimlessly through space, and are attracted to our sun by chance proximity. A comet of this kind never returns unless a large planet happens to keep it by gravitation" (*CE* 3.38). The idea was, of course, not new with Lovecraft; his Young's *Lessons in Astronomy* mentioned the possibility of comets being caught by the gravity of "some other sun" (Young, *Lessons in Astronomy* 213). The first such discovered interstellar comet was 1I/'Oumuamua in 2017, followed by 2I/Borisov in 2019. 'Oumuamua received widespread attention not only because of its status as the first such object, but because, despite a lack of persuasive evidence, Harvard University Department of Astronomy chair Avi Loeb advanced the idea that it is actually an enormous alien spacecraft. In 2021, thanks to media coverage of Loeb's proposal and the prestige of Harvard, Loeb was in line to run a new taxpayer-funded government office whose goal would be to study UFO reports in order to develop warp drive for the US Defense Department, although Loeb eventually lost the bid (Colavito, "Loeb"). Needless to say, the attempt to place Loeb into such an office had more to do with senators worried about their midterm re-elections than it did with real science, and one wonders what Lovecraft might have thought about this.

Recent modeling[14] indicates that water-covered planets between the sizes of Earth and Neptune may be very common in the universe, located around not only sun-like stars and dim red dwarfs, but even floating through interstellar space as sunless rogue planets, with heating provided by gravitational tides as on Jupiter's moons (Lingam and Loeb, 1–40; Nixon and Madhusudhan 1–19; Hand 146–47). Both scientific and science fictional works have addressed the difficulties that intelligent life would face in developing an advanced technological civilization in fully oceanic environments, especially ones with a kilometers-thick ice covering overhead (Clarke, *2010* 180–82; Hand 202–26; Brin 295). However, in the context of Lovecraftian fiction, a benefit is not having to address such real-world concerns. However it happened, in the context of the Lovecraftian universe we know that aquatic civilizations—the Deep Ones, the star-spawn, Elder Things, Father Dagon and Mother Hydra, even Cthulhu itself—*did* manage to evolve, and what is more, that they seem to be the dominant form of life (at least in the corporeal universe). This perhaps reflects a dominance of aquatic planets in the Lovecraftian cosmos.

As a final bridge between the solar system and interstellar space, we come—like Vulcan and Phaeton—to an idea that, while disproven, has an interesting Lovecraftian parallel. In 1984, paleontologists proposed that a seeming cycle of mass extinctions every 26 million years could be explained by a small, dim star in an elliptical orbit around the sun, which disrupted comets from the Oort cloud every time it drew near, showering the inner solar system with a cometary bombardment. They termed this star Nemesis. In 1989, Isaac Asimov used this theory as the basis for one of his last novels, simply titled *Nemesis*. By the early twenty-first century the idea of Nemesis had been disproven, as no star survey had managed to find any evidence of its existence (Melott and Bambach 1–10). However, the Nemesis theory does bring to mind Lovecraft's poem of the same name—already discussed in chapter 6, in relation to one of Lovecraft's articles in the Providence *Evening News*—written in the "sinister small hours of the black morning after Hallowe'en" in 1917 and first published in the June 1918 issue of *The Vagrant*. One need only look at one of the opening stanzas to see the connection:

---

14. Including by Loeb, on more scientifically grounded basis than his UFO advocacy.

> I have whirl'd with the earth at the dawning,
>   When the sky was a vaporous flame;
> I have seen the dark universe yawning,
>   Where the black planets roll without aim;
> Where they roll in their horror unheeded, without knowledge or lustre or name (*AT* 46; *RB* 249)

The poem almost works as a narration from the point of the view of Nemesis the star, much like Copeland's "Planet Neptune to Mother Sun." And indeed, a star causing mass death when it appears overhead—when the stars are right, in other words—with evidence for it being drawn up from analyzing its (literal) impact on prehistoric life is almost too good a fit for Lovecraft.

But from the borderlands of the solar system we now break free and voyage deep into interstellar space—to the stars themselves whose alignment is necessary for the impact of their denizens to be felt on Earth.

Churches of Starry Wisdom

In 2004, skeptic Jason Colavito wrote an article, expanded into book form the next year, arguing that the ancient alien theory that has since come to dominate the History Channel was directly inspired by Lovecraft. Colavito's argument is that the most important work in that field is Erich von Däniken's book *Chariots of the Gods?*, published in 1968 (the same year as *2001: A Space Odyssey*). Colavito charts how von Däniken was influenced by *The Morning of the Magicians* (1960) by French journalists Louis Pauwels and Jacques Bergier, and how Pauwels and Bergier were in turn avid readers of Lovecraft (Colavito, *Cult* 127–61; Hite 151–52). As illustrated in chapter 9, ideas of ancient aliens visiting Earth to inspire religions and build monuments predated Lovecraft; and Lovecraft, Pauwels, Bergier, and von Däniken in some cases all drew on those earlier sources independently. Along these lines, some of Colavito's arguments have since been challenged both inside and outside the Lovecraftian community (Joshi, *Recognition* 255–56). However, the significance of von Däniken on the genre cannot be underestimated, and Colavito's charting of how Lovecraft's work fed into von Däniken is sound. While some of his arguments may have been questionable, Colavito's basic thesis—that Lovecraft was a major, if indirect, contributor to the "modern" ancient alien idea that emerged in 1968—is now widely accepted. And beyond his influence on *Chariots of the Gods?*,

Lovecraft also played role in contributing to another foundational work in the modern ancient alien genre.

After the publication of *Chariots of the Gods?*, one of the most significant books on the ancient alien theme was *The Sirius Mystery* (1976) by Robert K. G. Temple (Colavito, *Cult* 185–203). The origin of *The Sirius Mystery* was a straightforward 1954 article by French anthropologists Marcel Griaule and Germaine Dieterlen on the cosmological views of the Dogon, a West African ethnic group located in what is now the country of Mali. In a small section of their article, Griaule and Dieterlen noted that the star Sirius played a major role in the Dogon religion, and that the Dogon religion appeared to incorporate knowledge of Sirius and its system that would have been impossible to know without modern telescopes (Griaule and Dieterlen 84–85). Since then, a number of critiques have been raised about their methodology, and proposals made about how the Dogon may have learned details of Sirius. For example, a team of French astronomers stayed in Dogon territory to observe the 16 April 1893 solar eclipse. However, Griaule and Dieterlen did not explicitly attempt to offer any hypotheses for how the Dogon came across their knowledge.

Temple came across Griaule and Dieterlen's article in 1965, when it was shown to him by the astrologer Alan M. Young. In 1967, Temple read unidentified "futuristic essays" by Arthur C. Clarke, which in turn inspired him to attempt to look further into the Dogon beliefs, including having other scholarship by Griaule and Dieterlen translated into English for the first time. Temple also reached out to Clarke on the subject. Over the next several years, Clarke helped Temple with his research, passing along information on Sirius B and discussing *Chariots of the Gods?*, which had not yet been widely read. Clarke also put Temple into contact with other researchers of "pet mysteries," such as Derek J. de Solla Price (who studied the Antikythera mechanism[15] and claimed that Babylonian mathematics could be found in New Guinea) and Alan Lindsay Mackay (who studied the Minoan Phaistos Disc). The end result of this collaboration with Clarke was what Temple called the Sirius Mystery (Temple, 2–4; Colavito, *Cult* 188–89). Griaule and Dieterlen

---

15. Clarke used the Antikythera mechanism elsewhere to discuss how artifacts from ancient aliens would be most likely to be discovered underwater (Scharmen 105), inverting the synthesis of cosmic life and ocean depths discussed above in relation to Europa and other icy moons.

had discussed the Nommo, amphibious ancestral spirits created by the Dogon sky god (Griaule and Dieterlen 85–87). Temple, in his book, argued that the Nommo were actually extraterrestrial visitors from Sirius, linking them not only to the development of Dogon culture, but to a wide range of Mesopotamian, Egyptian, and Greek beliefs (Temple 203–27).[16]

As mentioned earlier in the chapter, Clarke was a young Lovecraft admirer, and many of Lovecraft's proto-ancient alien ideas from *At the Mountains of Madness* and "The Shadow out of Time" colored the Space Odyssey series, among other works of Clarke. Within eight years of releasing *2001*—and six years before *2010*—Clarke played a direct role in developing another foundational work of the ancient alien genre, one that this time was ostensibly nonfictional. Further, the Sirius Mystery would prove to be fertile fields for future Lovecraftian pastiches. Indeed, Temple himself argued that the Mesopotamian god Dagon was one of the aliens from Sirius, a claim that has obvious crossover appeal for Lovecraft fans (Temple 201; Colavito, *Cult* 191). A more direct connection comes from the anthology *The Starry Wisdom Library* (2014), intended to be an 1877 auction catalogue for the library of the Church of Starry Wisdom from "The Haunter of the Dark" (*CF* 3.460). Jeffrey John Wells wrote the auction entry for Sir Wade Jermyn's *Observations on the Several Parts of Africa* from "Facts concerning the Late Arthur Jermyn and His Family."

In Wells's fictional entry, Sir Wade's work was a three-volume text published in 1762 by the Royal Geographic Society. While the second volume is stated as being about the lost white tribe of the Congo cited in the Lovecraft story, the first volume is established as being about Sir Wade's encounter with the Dogon in the upper Niger River in 1756 and learning about their culture (Wells 131). In the brief excerpt, the Nommo are implied to actually be Deep Ones, while their leader is given the name "Soth'Auk'Kua," the "Toad of Sothis" (Wells 133)—cleverly linking Tsathoggua with Sothis, the Greek name for Sirius. In this, Wells was perhaps building off of hints left by Lin Carter in his "Xothic Legend Cycle" of pastiches (1971–81). In Carter's works, Xoth is a binary star implied to be the system of Sirius A and B. It is Xoth/Sirius where

---

16. Interestingly, despite his ancient alien speculation, Temple did not believe that modern UFOs were extraterrestrial, instead attributing flying saucer sightings to hysteria, mistakes, or hoaxes (Temple 213–14).

Tsathoggua's Great Old One ancestors originated (Carter 38). Wendi Dunlap's story "The Sixth Vital Sign" (2017) serves as a sort of euhemeristic deconstruction of the Cthulhu Mythos in the same way that ancient alien theorists deconstructed actual ancient religions, by equating the Judeo-Christian deity Yahweh and the Muslim demon Shaitan with Cthulhu and Carter's Mythos deity Idh-yaa. Yahweh/Cthulhu and Shaitan/Idh-yaa are actually alien researchers working for the R'lyeh Scientific Council of Xoth, who create humanity and plant them on Earth to hide them from the other Xothians, causing the human race to be the actual star-spawn (Dunlap 414).

Nor are these the only times that Sirius and its Greek name would appear in pastiches. Will Murray's short story "The Sothis Radiant" (1996) is one of the few Lovecraftian pastiche works specifically dealing with Miskatonic University's Department of Astronomy. It establishes that Miskatonic is home to Sparhawk Observatory, the description of which is suspiciously reminiscent of Ladd Observatory. Murray's story involves the observatory's founding namesake, Professor Azor Sparhawk, having observed a cosmic tendril of Azathoth as it passed by Sirius in 1894, which he referred to as Sothis due to its being referenced as such in the Arabic translation of the *Necronomicon* (Murray, "Sothis" 290–92).

Outside of hypothetical depictions of the inhabitants of Sirius, a notable early interstellar work that was written in Lovecraft's time is the science-fantasy novel *A Voyage to Arcturus* (1920) by British author David Lindsay (1876–1945). Much like *The Worm Ouroboros*, written two years later by Lindsay's countryman E. R. Eddison, *A Voyage to Arcturus* takes an extremely liberal view of the star in question,[17] turning it into a binary sun (Branchspell and Alppain) and using it as a basis to tell a moral fable set on its fictional planet Tormance. The story involves the Earth characters discovering tentacles growing out of their bodies after undertaking the titular journey to Tormance. C. S. Lewis praised the novel and cited it as an inspiration for his *Space Trilogy*, the first two entries of which were discussed in chapters 7 and 9 (Lewis, "OSF" 112). Unlike *The Worm Ouroboros*, there is no evidence that Lovecraft read *A Voyage to Arcturus*, but Robert H. Waugh argues that Lindsay's novel and Lovecraft's fiction both represent a trend of "heroism, grandeur,

---

17. Arcturus may have once belonged to a dwarf galaxy, now merged into the Milky Way.

and tragedy among a number of science fiction writers in the middle of the twentieth century" (Waugh 7). However, it should be mentioned that Lovecraft does mention Arcturus in several stories, beginning with "Polaris" (1918; *CF* 1.65; Livesey, DPO 44–45). More substantively, "Beyond the Wall of Sleep" (1919) mentions "the worlds that reel about the red Arcturus" (*CF* 1.83) and "Through the Gates of the Silver Key" establishes "Kythanil, the double planet that once revolved around Arcturus" (*CF* 3.306). One wonders if Tormance was the paired world to Kythanil.

Outside of pastiches and novels with parallel themes, a number of stars, fictional and real, appear in Lovecraft's fiction. One of the most notable of these may have been inspired by a rare stellar event that came just before he turned his eyes skyward in 1903. On the morning of 22 February 1901, Thomas David Anderson, an astronomically minded clergyman in Edinburgh, was surprised to see that a new naked-eye star had appeared in the constellation Perseus. Nova Persei 1901, later known as GK Persei, rose to magnitude 0.2, rivaling such bright stars as Vega and Arcturus, and making it one of the most brilliant novae of the twentieth century. It did not linger long at that peak. By the summer of 1901, the nova had faded below the limit of naked eye visibility. By 1903 it had dropped below tenth magnitude, pushing the limit of visibility in Lovecraft's 2¼-inch telescope. This nova would figure in one of Lovecraft's first stories of weird fiction.

Lovecraft wrote "Beyond the Wall of Sleep" in 1919. In the tale, a being of light battles his foe, telepathically warning a psychiatric intern that he should "Watch me in the sky close by the Daemon-Star" (*CF* 1.84). The Daemon-Star was Algol, a bright eclipsing binary star in Perseus, known to Lovecraft since the first flourishing of his interest in astronomy. The nova of 1901 was the consequence of the celestial conflict. "Beyond the Wall of Sleep" begins with a quotation from Shakespeare, but it ends with a quote from Serviss's *Astronomy with the Naked Eye* (1908):

> On February 22, 1901, a marvelous new star was discovered by Dr. Anderson, of Edinburgh, not very far from Algol. No star had been visible at that point before. Within twenty-four hours the stranger had become so bright that it outshone Capella. In a week or two it had visibly faded, and in the course of a few months it was hardly discernible with the naked eye. (*CF* 1.85; Serviss, *Naked* 152)

10. Yuggoth's Environs

Nova Persei 1901 (now known as GK Persei) as it appeared more than a century after its outburst, combining X-ray, radio, and visual data. Courtesy of NASA and Wikimedia Commons.

Had the outburst happened two years later, as his enthusiasm for astronomy blossomed, Lovecraft would certainly have seen Nova Persei with his own eyes. In the *Asheville Gazette-News* for 23 March 1915, he wrote that the brilliant nova of 1901 "is still remembered by all who beheld it" (*CE* 3.306). Since he makes no mention of witnessing the event, it is likely that the ten-year-old Lovecraft missed its transient glory, a conclusion also drawn by Livesey (Livesey, DPO 37–38). Among those who carried out observations of the nova were Winslow Upton at Ladd; glass plate photographs taken by Upton of the nova are still extant at Ladd, although it is unknown whether young Lovecraft would have seen them.

It is worth noting one piece of star-related fiction Lovecraft did read, Sir Arthur Conan Doyle's short story "The Red Star" (1911). The story is told from the point of view of Manuel Ducas, a Byzantine trader in the Levant in the year 630. Urged by his companion merchants, Ducas tells a story of how he became fixated on a "great red star which burned in the south." On a journey to Saba in modern-day Yemen, Ducas's ship encounters

> dwarfish creatures—one could scarcely say if they were men or monkeys—who burrow for homes among the seaweed, drink the pools of brackish water, and eat what they can catch. These are the fish-eaters, the Ichthyophagi, of whom old Herodotus talks—surely the lowest of all the human race. Our Arabs shrank from them with horror, for it is well known that, should you die in the desert, these little people will settle on you like carrion crows, and leave not a bone unpicked. They gibbered and croaked and waved their skinny arms at us as we passed, knowing well that they could swim far out to sea if we attempted to pursue them; for it is said that even the sharks turn with disgust from their foul bodies.

Wandering in Arabia, Ducas comes across none other than the Prophet Muhammed and his entourage, then on the Hijrah prior to their return to Mecca. Muhammed tells a skeptical Ducas about his destiny of uniting Arabia for an eventual conquest of Constantinople, swearing upon "a dusky red star upon the horizon—the very one on which we are gazing now—'that is my star, which tells of wrath, of war, of a scourge upon sinners. And yet both are indeed stars, and each does as Allah may ordain.'"[18] "The Red Star" was included in the collection *Tales of Long Ago* (1922), which Lovecraft owned (*LL* 58). It is tempting to see in its depiction of Muhammed a template for the development of Abdul Alhazred in the "History of the 'Necronomicon'" (1927), as well as the Deep Ones in Doyle's description of the Ichthyophagi.

In terms of the other existing stars that Lovecraft merely mentions in his fiction, let alone nonfiction, a complete catalogue would take almost a full book. Indeed, the majority of *Collected Essays 3* by Hippocampus Press is Lovecraft's astronomical musings. A typical example would be the star Vega, which is offhandedly mentioned in "The Very Old Folk," "The Mound," *The Case of Charles Dexter Ward*, and *The Dream-Quest*

---

18. Despite its association with warfare, the titular red star is seemingly not Mars. Ducas contrasts the star with a bright planet, does not know its name, and says that it is always in the same position of the sky at the same time every year, which Mars would not be due to its orbit. However, to connect Martian fiction and Islam, H. G. Wells in *The War of the Worlds* has the Martians destroy the Shah Jahan Mosque, the first mosque in Britain (Wells, *WW* 61–62).

of Unknown Kadath. Aldebaran as well is mentioned in "The Festival" and *The Dream-Quest of Unknown Kadath* (Livesey, DPO 43). In his short story "The House on Curwen Street" (1944), Derleth would associate the star with the otherwise-unexplored "Lake of Hali" from "The Whisperer in Darkness" as a nearby "dark star" that is the realm of Hastur (Derleth, *Trail* 26, 54; Livesey, DPO 49).[19] But as the major narrative roles of existing stars have largely been detailed above, it perhaps would be more productive (and achievable) to end with a discussion of some of the invented worlds that Lovecraft placed around stars, fictional and real, which we have not yet discussed. Of relevance to this topic is the final chapter of Serviss's *Pleasures of the Telescope,* titled "Are There Planets among the Stars?" (183–92), which Lovecraft read. It includes the very Lovecraftian musing,

> If we grant that [our] solar system is the only one in which small planets exist revolving around their sun in nearly circular orbits, then indeed we seem to have closed all the outer universe against such beings as the inhabitants of the earth. Beyond the sun's domain only whirling stars, coupled in eccentric orbits, dark stars, some of them, but no planets—in short a wilderness, full of all energies except those of sentient life! This is not a pleasing picture, and I do not think we are driven to contemplate it. (Serviss, *Pleasures* 189)

Serviss's rejection of a scarcity of habitable planets in the universe would seem to be at odds with Lovecraft's own thoughts at the start of this chapter, but Lovecraft clearly did not let his astronomical idol interfere with authorial ideas of his own. For example, on that same page Serviss states that he does not believe that multi-star systems can have inhabitable planets around them. As described above, Lovecraft places an (if not *the*) world of the Elder Things in just such a system in "The Dreams in the Witch House." Both Livesey and Hite give reason to

---

19. It should be noted that HPL took the term "Lake of Hali" from Robert W. Chambers's short story "The Repairer of Reputations," the first in his collection *The King in Yellow* (1895). In Chambers's work, the Lake of Hali is an actual lake, over which twin suns set. While this does not fit with Derleth's depiction, Derleth does take the association of Hastur and Aldebaran from the Chambers story. Chambers in turn took the use of Hali and Aldebaran from Ambrose Bierce's 1886 short story "An Inhabitant of Carcosa."

suggest the planet to which Gilman travels there is meant to orbit Polaris, but there are two arguments against that identification. The first is that the colors of the triple suns of the Elder Thing world—"yellow, carmine, and indigo" (*CF* 3.251)—do not match the colors of the stars of the Polaris system. Its location, at "a point somewhere between [the constellations] Hydra and Argo Navis" (*CF* 3.249) from the perspective of our solar system, is also confounding. Not only would that vector exclude Polaris, but the north in general. A southern hemisphere location for the Elder Things' origin would mean that they could look out on their unattainable home star from their Antarctic redoubt as their civilization slowly collapsed, turning *At the Mountains of Madness* into something of an inversion of the story "Polaris."[20]

"Through the Gates of the Silver Key" is a veritable cosmography of Lovecraftian planets, in particular the world Yaddith, home of the wizard Zkauba, "bleached, viscous bholes in the primal tunnels that honeycombed the planet," and "libraries [with] the massed lore of ten thousand worlds living and dead"[21] (*CF* 3.311), and whose inhabitants live "ages longer than the brain of man could grasp, since the beings of Yaddith die only after prolonged cycles" (*CF* 3.312). However, Randolph Carter is able to ascertain that even the advanced wizards of the world will eventually fall prey to the bholes, the planet's destiny doomed to be a "black, dead Yaddith of the inconceivable future" (*CF* 3.314), again perhaps referencing the nebular hypothesis and its death by stellar cooling.

Like the similar-sounding Yuggoth, Yaddith is first referenced in *Fungi from Yuggoth*, where viewing it is associated with losing one's mind. Yaddith is also paired with the unsafe, but otherwise undescribed, Ghooric zone (*AT* 93). In Lupoff's "Discovery of the Ghooric Zone," the titular region is imagined as an area beneath the surface of Yuggoth's moon Thog, where "beside the oily, lapping sea [is] the foul lake where puffed shoggoths splash" (Lupoff, "Ghooric"). While Lupoff's story

---

20. In John W. Campbell's novella "Who Goes There?" (1938), largely seen as influenced by *At the Mountains of Madness* (Nevala-Lee 67–68), the aliens discovered in Antarctica from twenty million years ago are identified as being from a world surrounding a blue sun (Stuart 97). Perhaps this is the same star as Gilman's indigo sun, and Campbell's Thing is related to, or perhaps a colonial subject of, HPL's Elder Things?

21. Joshi has noted that history and libraries are a major focus of HPL's alien cultures (Joshi, "Civilizations" 10).

completely divorces the Ghooric zone from Yaddith, it does anticipate the later scientific suspicions of sub-surface oceans in the outer moons. In "The Diary of Alonzo Typer," the eponymous character makes a single prayer to the "Lords of Yaddith" (*CF* 4.593), an interesting pairing to its reference to the Lords of Venus. Similarly, there is a single invocation of Yaddith in "The Haunter of the Dark" (*CF* 3.476). The final semi-appearances of Yaddith in Lovecraft can be found in "Out of the Aeons." While the planet itself is not referenced, as mentioned above the land of K'naa includes a landmark named Mount Yaddith-Gho, atop which is the Cyclopean fortress of the ancient Yuggothian colonists. The connection between Mount Yaddith-Gho and Yaddith is unstated, but has to exist, particularly as the "-Gho" suffix is the first three words of the Ghooric zone which Yaddith originated alongside in *Fungi from Yuggoth*. A potential explanation is that the K'naaites read of Yaddith in some early version of the Pnakotic Manuscripts, Eltdown Shards, or some other lost eldritch text, and simply associated that cosmic civilization with the ruins of the Yuggothians—a primeval example of the ancient alien theory in action.

While Yaddith is doomed to eventual destruction from the dual threat of cold and bholes, there is hope for its denizens: they might flee to "Shonhi and Mthura and Kath, and other worlds in the twenty-eight galaxies accessible to the light-beam envelopes of the creatures of Yaddith" (*CF* 3.311). That Shonhi in particular is so accessible from Yaddith is somewhat surprising, given that Carter elsewhere identifies it as "still remoter [and] trans-galactic" (*CF* 3.306). Hite proposes that Lovecraft may have originally named Shonhi "Shalmali," the Theosophical name of Lemuria, and Price may have changed it out of opposition to simply "recycling" Theosophical names. Aside from the name-change, erroneous reprintings have led to the alternative name "Stronti" also being used in place of it (Hite 147n58).

"Through the Gates of the Silver Key" establishes one more world Randolph Carter visits, albeit without providing a name for it. It is

> a dim, fantastic world whose five multi-coloured suns, alien constellations, dizzy black crags, clawed, tapir-snouted denizens, bizarre metal towers, unexplained tunnels, and cryptical floating cylinders had intruded again and again upon his slumbers. That world, he felt vaguely, was in all the conceivable cosmos the one most freely in touch with others. (*CF* 3.307)

The reference to tapir-snouted residents with advanced technologies—including strange tunnels, construction materials, and relatively free contact with other worlds—brings to mind Kenton J. Stanfield's musing about an elder race on Venus. Did Carter encounter the homeworld of the man-lizards' ancestors, perhaps the Lords of Venus themselves who built the Venusian maze? It is intriguing conjecture, but it is nothing more than that with the data available.

Our discussion of Lovecraftian cosmography has two remaining worlds to cover: Yekub and Yith. But to discuss them, we must journey into the liminal boundaries of Lovecraft's authorship, toward two literary works we similarly have not landed upon yet. These short collaborations will be the basis for our next chapter.

Chapter 11
The Great Enveloping Cosmic Dark

Introduction

In 1981, the British author Roz Kaveney wrote an article analyzing the trends that had dominated the science fiction of the 1970s. Among her observations were that, particularly in the first half of the decade, a new trend had emerged, which she termed the "Big Dumb Object" or BDO. As described by science fiction scholar Christopher Palmer, BDOs

> seem to operate . . . by activating a complex of opposed qualities or possibilities: in this case, the cosmic and the domestic, the heroic and the bureaucratic [and] has the following qualities: it is artificial; it wasn't made by humans; its makers are absent so that it is or seems deserted; it is large enough to explore; indeed, it is usually very large, so that the human explorers are dwarfed; and very often the human explorers are swallowed up—they are enclosed, they are exploring an interior. . . . Because it is huge, alien and deserted the minds, intentions and technologies of those who built it seem superior to those of humans, but with an enigmatic twist, since the builders are gone, and this may be a sign of their failure or exhaustion, or, contrariwise, a sign that they exist or existed on a sublimely different plane to humans. The Big Dumb Object pre-empts easy human assumptions of superiority; it may well reduce humans to insignificance or simply puzzlement, yet it tantalises also, because it suggests there are or once were other minds in the universe, constructing, reasoning, acting with purpose. (Palmer 95–96)

Two of the best-known examples of the genre are Larry Niven's novel *Ringworld* (1970) and Arthur C. Clarke's novel *Rendezvous with Rama* (1973) (Kaveney 25; Nicholls, "Dumb" 11–23; Palmer 95–111). The connections between Clarke and Lovecraft have been documented in the previous chapter. For Niven, when MIT students responded to scientific inaccuracies in *Ringworld* with a protest at the World Science Fiction Convention in 1971, he wrote the short story "The Last Necronomicon," which imagined the form the 1960s student protest movement might take at Miskatonic University, as a playful rebuke. Niven would go on to write the far more influential fantasy novella "The Magic Goes Away" (1976), which incorporates Abdul Alhazred and Nyarlathotep. While Kaveney identified the BDO trend as being prominent in the early 1970s, others subsequently traced it back decades. An important predecessor to *Rama* was Clarke's short story "Jupiter Five" (1953), described in the previous chapter (Scharmen 99–100). Another early entry in the genre was the 1955–62 series *Cities in Flight,* one in which the BDO is an actual city (Nicholls, "Dumb" 14–15). *Cities in Flight* was written by James Blish, who had been a late correspondent of Lovecraft.

Of course, "Jupiter Five" and *Rendezvous with Rama* are not Clarke's only entries into the BDO genre. The monolith from *2001: A Space Odyssey* has also been retroactively added to the ranks of the Big Dumb Objects (Nicholls, "Dumb" 14–16). Clarke had a longstanding belief in artifacts of the "mysterious world" (to borrow the title of his 1980 television program) that appeared to be evidence of mysterious advanced civilizations that had vanished, such as the alleged crystal skull and the very real massive stone spheres of pre-Columbian Mesoamerica. Colonial-era racist assumptions, surviving well into the twentieth century, assumed that such achievements were beyond the skill of Aztecs or Maya, and therefore were evidence of Atlantis, or perhaps alien intervention. Clarke's monolith, and to an extent the BDO genre overall, are therefore directly connected to notions of ancient civilizations and alien visitation (Scharmen 102–4).

With these connections and descriptions of the genre, it is not difficult to trace it back to Lovecraft. Ringworld and Rama are megastructures built by aliens, and the human expeditions to them are successors of the Miskatonic Antarctic Expedition and Peaslee's Pnakotus expedition, more directly than Wernher von Braun's Mars mission plans. The builders of Ringworld are even revealed in the sequel, *The Ringworld Engineers* (1979), to have been the alien progenitors of humanity. Consider Palmer's description of how

> Arthur C. Clarke's Rama is mostly explored on foot and the explorers spend a great deal of time ascending and descending its giant staircases and worrying about breathlessness and tired muscles. They utilise a microlight plane at one point and a raft made from storage drums at another, but both vehicles are technologically simple and both are destroyed in the course of events. (Palmer 96)

11. The Great Enveloping Cosmic Dark

Consider also Kaveney's analysis of how for post-Niven space opera authors, "The Big Dumb Object becomes for them a peopled and moralised landscape" (Kaveney 31). These could be direct descriptions of the exploration and symbolic importance of the Elder Things' city in *At the Mountains of Madness* and Pnakotus in "The Shadow out of Time."

The early 1970s were a period when Lovecraft's revival was mainly among the fan presses (Joshi, *Recognition* 163–72). That makes it all the more significant that Lovecraft's DNA could be found in a space opera trope that emerged so dominantly at the same time—and indeed, that the trope in question owed so much to the ostensibly terrestrial *At the Mountains of Madness*. However, this is not as surprising as it seems, considering the exploration of that story's interplanetary fiction connections and influences in chapter 9. Lovecraft's literary legacy is often limited to horror or the weird, but his influence was felt from the start in science fiction, including its space opera subgenre. Previous chapters have covered Lovecraft's influence on space operas set on worlds in our solar system and around nearby stars, but the known universe is not the boundary of his influence. Not only does Lovecraft's work influence interstellar fiction, he continues to have a profound impact on foundational tropes of the space opera genre as well. The best examples of this are two of Lovecraft's shortest works.

Collaborations and Commonplace

In chapter 7 it was mentioned that "In the Walls of Eryx" is one of Lovecraft's very few purely space opera works. Those qualifiers were well merited, as "Eryx" is not his only "pure" space opera. However, it is perhaps notable that, just like "Eryx," the remaining contenders are either collaborations, unfinished ideas, or both. And the two most prominent examples, "The Challenge from Beyond" and "Collapsing Cosmoses," border on parody before fully crossing over. Before the collaborations, however, come the ideas: the unused entries from Lovecraft's commonplace book that touch on what might be considered space opera themes.

These are present from the start, with entry 2: "Inhabitants of Zinge, over whom the star Canopus rises every night, are always gay and without sorrow" (*CE* 5.219). The premise of a story about an always-happy society is certainly a rare development for Lovecraft. Entries 35 and 36, show the theme must have been on his mind:

Special beings with special senses from remote universes. Advent of an external universe to view.

Disintegration of all matter to electrons and finally empty space assured, just as devolution of energy to radiant heat is known. Case of acceleration—man passes into space. (*CE* 5.221)

Entry 113 proposes "Biological-hereditary memories of other worlds and universes" (*CE* 5.226)—something of an early seed for "The Shadow out of Time," perhaps? The final entry of note is 221: "Insects or other entities from space attack and penetrate a man's head and cause him to remember alien and exotic things—possible displacement of personality" (*CE* 5.233). As Kenneth W. Faig, Jr. notes, this also seems to be something of a setup for "The Shadow out of Time," but was also the basis for Colin Wilson's novel *The Mind Parasites* (1967), whose titular creatures are named the "Tsathogguans," and which was eventually followed by *The Space Vampires* (Faig, *Voyages* 126).

There is one further commonplace book entry to be discussed below, but for now we will turn from incomplete ideas to an incomplete collaboration: "Collapsing Cosmoses," Lovecraft and R. H. Barlow's parody of the space operas of Edmond Hamilton (1904–1977) and E. E. "Doc" Smith (1890–1965). Hamilton's 1928–30 series *Interstellar Patrol* was seemingly the first space opera set outside the Milky Way; one of the main characters was Korus Kan, criticized by Lovecraft in his 1933 letter to Natalie H. Wooley quoted at the start of chapter ten. Lovecraft typically dismissed Hamilton as "Single-Plot Hamilton" (*RB* 47) but admitted that he "escapes his formula fairly well" and could write good stories when he did so (*EHP* 426). For his part, Hamilton appreciated Lovecraft's work (Joshi, *Recognition* 44). Hamilton himself was married to another author of space opera, Leigh Brackett (1915–1978). Brackett was a member of the Mañana Literary Society formed by Robert A. Heinlein, among whom were a number of Lovecraft's correspondents, as described in chapter 7 (Nevala-Lee 123–24). Brackett herself wrote a series of planetary tales around the character Eric John Stark, intended as an anti-colonialist satire of Burroughs's John Carter. Brackett's Stark stories would particularly influence Lin Carter's Callisto fiction. Outside of pulp magazines, Brackett was also a Hollywood screenwriter; notably, she wrote or co-wrote the screenplays for *The Big Sleep* (1946), *Rio Bravo* (1959), *Hatari!* (1962), *Man's Favorite Sport?* (1964), *El Dorado* (1966), and *Rio Lobo* (1970) for director Howard Hawks, along with *The Long Goodbye* (1973) for Robert Altman. Hawks

11. The Great Enveloping Cosmic Dark 309

and *Rio Bravo* in particular would become major influences on filmmaker and Lovecraft aficionado John Carpenter, whose *The Thing* (1982) is a remake of Hawks's *The Thing from Another World* (1951). However, Brackett is probably best remembered for the last script she wrote, the first draft of the screenplay for what would eventually be titled *Star Wars Episode V: The Empire Strikes Back* (1980).

During his visit to Florida in 1934, Lovecraft and Barlow came close to meeting Hamilton, who was visiting Florida with another early space opera pioneer, Jack Williamson (1908–2006). Williamson is now remembered for inventing the terms "terraforming" and "genetic engineering." At the same time, another author of interplanetary fiction, Ray Cummings (mentioned in chapter 7), was separately in Florida, and Barlow attempted to sound him out as well. Ultimately, Lovecraft and Barlow were unable to meet any of the three space opera authors (*FLB* 84; *OFF* 114, 127, 134, 136). One wonders whether, if the meeting had occurred, some off-the-cuff collaboration in the vein of "Collapsing Cosmoses" or "The Challenge from Beyond" might have been the result.

Doc Smith was another notable figure in the field. *The Skylark of Space* (1928), the first work of interstellar space opera, made him arguably the most prominent of the early magazine science fiction authors (Ashley and Lowndes 73; Nevala-Lee 30; Clarke, *Astounding* 101–6). Willis Conover urged Lovecraft to read *The Skylark of Space*, despite Lovecraft's own reservations (*RB* 390). For all Lovecraft's dismissal of Smith's works, Cyril M. Kornbluth, a member of the Brooklyn-based Futurians group of science fiction fans, argued that the politics of the *Skylark* series were close to those espoused by Lovecraft via the Great Race in "The Shadow out of Time" (Kornbluth 60; Joshi, "Civilizations" 10–11; *CF* 3.404–5). The Futurians were formed in 1938 by Lovecraft correspondent Donald A. Wollheim (who would go on to establish a major science fiction press, DAW Books, in 1971), and its members included James Blish and Robert A. W. Lowndes, who were also Lovecraft's correspondents. However, undoubtedly the most famous Futurian was Isaac Asimov (Nevala-Lee 99–105). In 1974 Asimov published *Before the Golden Age,* an anthology of twenty-five science fiction stories that influenced him as a youth in the 1930s; it included Donald Wandrei's "Colossus" (1934) along with stories by Stanley G. Weinbaum, Hamilton, and Williamson. His collection *100 Great Fantasy Short Stories* (1984) included Lovecraft's "Ex Oblivione," an interesting choice from the Lovecraft canon. Hamilton, Smith, and the

Futurians were the figures whom Barlow and Lovecraft parodied in "Collapsing Cosmoses," which was co-written during Lovecraft's visit to Barlow in Florida in 1935 and published by Barlow in 1938 (*IAP* 950–51; *OFF* xv). The two alternated paragraphs in the existing snippet, with the opening paragraph being Lovecraft's:

> Dam Bor glued each of his six eyes to the lenses of the cosmoscope. His nasal tentacles were orange with fear, and his antennae buzzed hoarsely as he dictated his report to the operator behind him. "It has come!" he cried. "That blur in the ether can be nothing less than a fleet from outside the space-time continuum we know. Nothing like this has ever appeared before. It must be an enemy. Give the alarm to the Inter-Cosmic Chamber of Commerce. There's no time to lose—at this rate they'll be upon us in less than six centuries. Hak Ni must have a chance to get the fleet in action at once." (*CF* 4.548)

Barlow then introduces the character of Oll Stof, President of the Chamber and representative of the Milliner's Soviet, whom Lovecraft then describes as a "a highly developed protozoan organism from Nov-Kas, [who] . . . spoke by emitting alternate waves of heat and cold" (*CF* 4.549). The short story draft ends with Barlow having Hak Ni hearing the challenge being raised by the enemy fleet, a half-million light years across; Lovecraft's final entry being "Hak Ni too raised his snout in defiance, radiating a masterful order to the captains of the fleet. Instantly the huge space-ships swung into battle formation, with only a hundred or two of them many light-years out of line" (*CF* 4.550).

That this is a comedic work is obvious; the same type of parodic names (damn bore, hackneyed) used in "Eryx" are evident, for example. But even with the layers of jokes and satire piled on top, there is still a stunning maximalist science fiction story at the base. Creatures communicate by color and heat, rather than though humanlike sound. There is an invasion from outside space and time; planning on the scale of centuries; and fleets hundreds of thousands of light years long; all these are aspects of space opera a thousandfold more ambitious than most works in the genre. As novels like Harry Harrison's *Star-Smashers of the Galaxy Rangers* (1973) and Douglas Adams's *The Hitchhiker's Guide to the Galaxy* (1979) show, a work can be both comedic and a large-scale space opera worthy of the name.

While less outwardly humorous—though humor (perhaps inadvertent) is certainly present through its hyperbolic exaggeration and incongruity, particularly in the middle two segments—"The Challenge from

11. The Great Enveloping Cosmic Dark

Beyond" is at least more complete. A round-robin entry in five parts, it was written by C. L. Moore, A. Merritt, Lovecraft, Robert E. Howard, and Frank Belknap Long, and published in the September 1935 issue of *Fantasy Magazine* (*IAP* 952–53). Moore opens the story by introducing George Campbell, a geology professor enjoying a camping trip in the Canadian woods, where he discovers a quartz cube with a cuneiform-inscribed disc visible inside (*CF* 4.551–53). Merritt's section has Campbell become obsessed with the embedded disc, seeing it glow and hearing voices coming from it. Determining it to be of alien origin, Campbell is suddenly sucked into the disc, which has turned into a three-dimensional sphere—a planet in space (*CF* 4.554–56).

Lovecraft's section begins with establishing that the planet is surrounded by "sapphire suns." He provides some additional information in his notes on the story:

> Orb is one of a cluster of a dozen sapphire suns. Always faces to star, but others perpetually lighten dark side. Atmosphere dense with CO_2 and water vapour—lush vegetation—violent storms. Beings inhabit boxlike houses of concrete in clusters—rooms high but doorways low. Every sort of strange flora and fauna present. (*CE* 5.259)

The color of the stars indicate bright, young suns, perhaps intended to be the actual Pleiades cluster.[1] Such stars are probably too young for habitable worlds to have developed around them, but perhaps the planet in question is the result of cosmic engineering by an elder race. Certainly, the fact that it is tidally locked would help protect the far side from the radiation of its nearest neighbor. Lovecraft mentions the Pleiades in his 1926 short story "The Silver Key" (*CF* 2.83) and indirectly mentions one of the cluster's stars, Celaeno (in its origin as a Greek mythological character), in the epigraph to "The Dunwich Horror" (*CF* 2.417), which is a quotation from "Witches and Other Night-Fears" (1821) by English essayist Charles Lamb (1775–1834).

On the basis of this mention, Derleth would establish in "The House on Curwen Street" that the fourth planet around the star is the location of "that great library of ancient monolithic stones with their books and

---

1. HPL was of course familiar with the actual appearance of the Pleiades in the night sky. He included a drawing of the group in the 17 January 1904 *Rhode Island Journal of Astronomy* and quoted Tennyson's poetic mention of them in his 31 August 1917 column for the Providence *Evening News* (*CE* 3.233).

hieroglyphs stolen from the Elder Gods" (Derleth, *Trail* 51). After twenty years on Celaeno, Derleth's Dr. Laban Shrewsbury returns to Miskatonic University to write the *Celaeno Fragments* based on his memories of the library's contents. Bringing the trope full circle is Graham McNeill's pastiche novel *Dweller in the Deep* (2014). In it, the character Oliver Grayson conducts a séance to reach Celaeno via the Dreamlands and appropriately quotes the astronaut Dave Bowman's famous line from Clarke's *2001* novel: "My God, it's full of stars . . ." (McNeill, *Dweller* 238).

Whether the planet Campbell found himself on is in the Pleiades or not, its presence in a star cluster opens up another interesting similarity. The mention that even the "dark" side is lightened by the other suns in the cluster is suggestive of Isaac Asimov's famous short story "Nightfall" (1941), written at the urging of John W. Campbell. "Nightfall" is set on the planet Lagash in a six-sun system, where every thousand years the fall of night during a total eclipse causes the collapse of civilization in panic. Closer to home, Lovecraft's mention of the dense carbon dioxide and water-rich atmosphere and its population by varied flora and fauna is also suggestive of contemporary depictions of Venus, as outlined in chapter 7. One wonders if these notes for "The Challenge from Beyond" became incorporated into Lovecraft's Venus when he turned to working on "Eryx" the next year.

Lovecraft next has Campbell lapse into unconsciousness (as Lovecraftian protagonists are wont to do). When Campbell wakes, he begins to associate the cube with what he had read about "those debatable and disquieting clay fragments called the Eltdown Shards, dug up from pre-carboniferous strata in southern England thirty years before" and translated in 1912 by the Sussex clergyman Arthur Brooke Winters-Hall (*CF* 4.557–58). In doing so, Lovecraft incorporates the Eltdown Shards invented by Richard F. Searight in 1934, though not the lore on the Shards that Searight developed independently (*EHP* 13; Stanley 19–20; Price, "Notes" 34–37). In Winters-Hall's translation, the Shards told of how

> there dwelt on a world—and eventually on countless other worlds—of outer space a mighty order of worm-like beings whose attainments and whose control of nature surpassed anything within the range of terrestrial imagination. They had mastered the art of interstellar travel early in their career, and had peopled every habitable planet in their own galaxy—killing off the races they found. Beyond the limits of their own

galaxy—which was not ours—they could not navigate in person; but in their quest for knowledge of all space and time they discovered a means of spanning certain transgalactic gulfs with their minds. They devised peculiar objects—strangely energized cubes of a curious crystal containing hypnotic talismans and enclosed in space-resisting spherical envelopes of an unknown substance—which could be forcibly expelled beyond the limits of their universe, and which would respond to the attraction of cool solid matter only. These, of which a few would necessarily land on various inhabited worlds in outside universes, formed the ether-bridges needed for mental communication. Atmospheric friction burned away the protecting envelope, leaving the cube exposed and subject to discovery by the intelligent minds of the world where it fell. (*CF* 4.558–59)

When the cubes found a race capable of spaceflight, and therefore of potentially challenging the worms' dominance, the possessed individuals would act as a fifth column, leading to the destruction of the native population (*CF* 4.559–60).[2] However, this was presumably rare, given that

Only three, ran the story, had ever landed on peopled worlds in our own particular universe. Of these one had struck a planet near the galactic rim two thousand billion years ago, whilst another had lodged three billion years ago on a world near the centre of the galaxy. The third—and the only one ever known to have invaded the solar system—had reached our own earth a hundred and fifty million years ago. (*CF* 4.560)

The worm-like beings who had emerged from the Earthbound cube had done so during the reign of the Great Race in their rugose cone form. The Great Race, perhaps from experience, could tell when one of their own was taken over, and quickly moved to murder their possessed members; as a result, Earth became a point of hatred for the worms (*CF* 4.560–61). Lovecraft does not use the term Great Race in the story itself, although he does in his story notes (*CE* 5.258), but this is still their first appearance in published fiction. However, there are some inconsistencies with "The Shadow out of Time" (Price, "History" 22–23). For example, Lovecraft here states that the

cone-shaped terrestrial beings kept the one existing cube in a special shrine as a relique and basis for experiments, till after aeons it was lost

---

2. The worms' aggressively genocidal policies would seemingly indicate they are not in fact celestial neighbors to the Great Library of Celaeno. But there have been stranger pairings in the history of HPL's work.

amidst the chaos of war and the destruction of the great polar city where it was guarded. When, fifty million years ago, the beings sent their minds ahead into the infinite future to avoid a nameless peril of inner earth, the whereabouts of the sinister cube from space were unknown. (*CF* 4.561)

The polar city can be explained as a reasonably distant location to store a dangerous artifact from Pnakotus, or perhaps be attributed to either Campbell misremembering or Winters-Hall mistranslating the Eltdown Shards. Lovecraft's part of the story ends with Campbell coming to the horrified realization that his mind has been transported into one of the "great centipedes" themselves (*CF* 4.563–64).

Chad Fifer and Chris Lackey, the hosts of the H. P. Lovecraft Literary Podcast, while also noting similarities to the premise of *Invasion of the Body Snatchers*, suggest that Lovecraft reused the concept of "The Shadow out of Time" because he didn't think it would get published at that point. He had initially written it from November 1934 to February 1935, and it would not be published until June 1936. Joshi argues slightly differently, believing that Lovecraft was fine with recycling the plot of "Shadow" because "Challenge" was merely "a sporting venture of no conceivable literary consequence" (*IAP* 953). Michael D. Miller splits the difference, placing "Challenge" as a sort of expansion or spinoff of "Shadow" (Miller, "Look" 6–7).

The use of a collaboration to introduce the Great Race is also apt, as the Great Race itself has elements of collaboration in its conception. In "The Shadow out of Time," the Great Race is stated as being originally from the planet Yith, described in terms reminiscent of Douglas Adams as an "obscure trans-galactic world" (*CF* 3.407). Yith itself originated in Duane W. Rimel's poem "Dreams of Yith" (July 1934), which describes the world in detail. It is distant, with ragged peaks and islands dotting dried seabeds. While there are dead cities and "age-old tombs," the world's current inhabitants are "Dread batlike beasts," poison mosses, and towering fungus. However, amid distant caves, survivors of Yith's calamity exist, waiting for a savior named Sotho to return (*FLB* 380–82). Rimel's original name for the planet was "Yid," which in a letter dated 13 May 1934 Lovecraft suggested he change to "Yith" due to Yid having "a slang connotation" (*FLB* 174). Yith's one mention in "Shadow" is Lovecraft's sole reference to the planet in his works. This is somewhat ironic given how the Great Race has become better known as the Great Race of Yith in pastiche works such as the game *Call of Cthulhu* (*FLB* 177n7).

With Lovecraft's segment ended, Robert E. Howard immediately begins his section by subverting the typical Lovecraftian ending, with Campbell instead realizing the mental and physical superiority of the worm form. Through accessing the memory of his host body, Tothe, Campbell learns that the worms' home planet is named Yekub. In a feat worthy of Conan, Tothe/Campbell assassinates Yukth, the Supreme Lord of Science, and becomes king of Yekub (*CF* 5.16–19). Long's conclusion has Campbell's mindless body back in Canada die from stumbling into a stream and drowning, as the "round red god" of Yekub explains to Campbell that Yekubians cannot possess a human. Campbell, now trapped in Tothe's body, "sat on a throne and ruled an empire of worms more wisely, kindly, and benevolently than any man of earth had ever ruled an empire of men" (*CF* 4.567–69).

There were actually two "Challenges from Beyond." The one with Lovecraft was the weird fiction one, while a speculative fiction one consisted of entries by Weinbaum, Wandrei, Doc Smith, Harl Vincent, and Murray Leinster. However, the science fiction counterpart is more lackluster than the weird one, which itself contains a large science fiction presence (Miller, "Look" 3–4). Fritz Leiber noted that it was Lovecraft, and not any of the other more science-fiction-oriented authors, who provided the "scientifically plausible" plot device of the "small encapsulated send-receive telepathy stations" in the collaboration (Leiber, "Hyperspace" 169–70). That Lovecraft would be the most science fictional of a group of collaborators that included science fiction authors writing a space opera segment says all that needs to be said about Lovecraft's science fiction credentials.

But the nature of the Yekubian mental teleportation devices is not the most significant contribution by Lovecraft to the fictional technologies of space opera authors. That is to be found, if unnamed, in a work that Lovecraft had already written by this point—at least from the viewpoint of a reader existing in our current of the space-time continuum. But as we know from the calculations of Walter Gilman, time and space can inadvertently become tangled up easier than it might be thought.

Through Hyperspace with Walter Gilman

As noted, one of the landmark works exploring the influence of Lovecraft in science fiction was Fritz Leiber's essay "Through Hyperspace with Brown Jenkin" (1966). Among other arguments Leiber makes about the debt of the science fiction genre to Lovecraft is that

"The Dreams in the Witch House" (as well as "The Dunwich Horror") was an early pioneer in the concept of trans-dimensional hyperspace and its use to travel interstellar distances, a stock space opera trope (Leiber, "Hyperspace" 170–73; Hite 134–35). Leiber's claim has longevity; in Kenneth Hite's *Tour de Lovecraft: The Destinations* (2020), hyperspace gets its own chapter as one of the Lovecraftian settings (Hite 129–36). Lovecraft wrote "The Dreams in the Witch House" in early 1932, less a year after John W. Campbell introduced the term "hyperspace" to science fiction (from mathematics) in his short story "Islands of Space," published in the spring 1931 *Amazing Stories Quarterly*. Despite this, Lovecraft never uses the term "hyperspace," although the concept was arguably one of the cores of Lovecraft's fiction for years by that point (Hite 129). "The Jaunt" by Stephen King and "Hinterlands" by William Gibson, both short stories published in 1981, explore the themes of travels through hyperspace driving humans insane from exposure to the inherent outsideness of the other dimension. King's debt to Lovecraft has been documented, but Gibson's own relation to Lovecraft, via the tragic thread of his novel *Neuromancer* (1984), has been explored by Robert H. Waugh (Waugh 133–43).

But outside of travel through alternate dimensions, there is also a recurring Lovecraftian element of using the curvature of space as a "shortcut," in very modern terms. In "The Whisperer in Darkness," the Mi-Go travel "outside the curved cosmos of space and time" (*CF* 2.525). While in "The Dreams in the Witch House,"

> One afternoon there was a discussion of possible freakish curvatures in space, and of theoretical points of approach or even contact between our part of the cosmos and various other regions as distant as the farthest stars or the trans-galactic gulfs themselves—or even as fabulously remote as the tentatively conceivable cosmic units beyond the whole Einsteinian space-time continuum. (*CF* 3.240)

Later in the story, there is a mention of an "ultimate black vortex" (*CF* 3.264), a description that immediately brings to mind a black hole. An object whose gravity was so intense that light could not escape had been hypothesized since the late eighteenth century, but the mathematical development of the concept only began with Albert Einstein's development of general relativity in 1915, continuing into the late 1950s. The related concept of a wormhole, a hypothetical traversable "tunnel" combining two distant areas of the universe, was proposed by Einstein

11. The Great Enveloping Cosmic Dark

and American physicist Nathan Rosen (1909–1995) in 1935. One wonders whether *De Vermis Mysteriis* is actually a guide to the mysteries of worm*holes*, not of worms, and hence how Robert Blake was able to summon a star vampire to Earth through reading it.

While wormholes remain (and probably always will remain) in the realm of speculation and fiction, the first candidate for a black hole, Cygnus X-1, was observed in 1964. Cygnus was mentioned in "The Very Old Folk" (*CF* 3.500) as well as "The Colour out of Space" (*CF* 2.396)—where it was the destination of the colour after it left the Gardner farm to return to space. Was Cygnus X-1 its destination? Does the indescribable color of the colour perhaps indicate it is a radiation that lives in, or at least can traverse, the event horizon of a black hole? Black holes have been fruitful locations for blending of space opera and horror, given the deformities they impose on space and time. The film *The Black Hole* (1979)—Disney's *2001*-infused *Star Wars* ripoff—and *Event Horizon* (1997)—starring Sam Neill, fresh from John Carpenter's 1994 Lovecraft pastiche *In the Mouth of Madness*—both featured black holes as gateways to hell. Michael Crichton's 1987 novel *Sphere* (adapted to film in 1997) features the US Navy discovering what is initially believed to be an immense alien ship that crashed onto the seafloor centuries ago. When explored, it is discovered to be an American starship from the future that was sent back in time after recovering the titular alien artifact during a mission into a black hole. The artifact causes the projection of nightmares, including a giant squid summoned from Jules Verne's *20,000 Leagues under the Sea*.[3] Despite *Sphere*'s agglomeration of themes onto the topic of black holes, Lovecraft might have been most interested in Carl Sagan's more scientifically minded novel *Contact* (1985) (and its 1997 film adaptation) and particularly Christopher Nolan's *Interstellar* (2014), with its blending of terrestrial apocalypse, time dilation, the effects of black holes and wormholes, and communication with higher-dimensional beings.[4]

---

3. Of potential significance is that from Crichton's previous novels, *Eaters of the Dead* (1976) directly references both HPL and the *Necronomicon* as entries in its bibliography, and *Congo* (1980) has several parallel plot points to "Arthur Jermyn" (Guimont, "Arctic" 158n10).

4. Nolan's previous movie, *Inception* (2010), might also have been of interest to HPL as a sort of alternate exploration of the Dreamlands. And of course, Nolan's *Batman Begins* (2005) prominently featured the DC Comics asylum named after Arkham.

That *Contact* and *Interstellar*'s exploration of relativity and time dilation would have intrigued Lovecraft is evident from the fact that, as Hite has argued, "Polaris" and "The Quest for Iranon" explore those concepts, while "Beyond the Wall of Sleep" establishes the unity of time and space (Hite 130). One can also look to the commonplace book entry 34: "Moving away from earth more swiftly than light—past gradually unfolded—horrible revelation" (*CE* 5.221). This seems to show a remarkably solid grasp of relativity: were one actually to move faster than light, the past would presumably unfold as time moved backwards, although obviously this is a complicated hypothetical scenario, with lots of causality questions.

A potential influence, however unintentional, on Lovecraft's emerging melding of the distorting effects that space travel could have on time was the novel *The Star Rover* (1915) by American adventure writer Jack London (1876–1916), which Lovecraft owned (*LL* 103).[5] The novel's narrator, Darrell Standing, even has a somewhat Lovecraftian backstory, being a former professor of agronomics at the University of California, imprisoned for life in San Quentin State Prison for the murder of a fellow professor (London 5). While in prison, he is tortured by a guard, leading him to develop the ability to transmit his consciousness into space, going on time-bending interstellar voyages while only fractions of a second pass on Earth:

> And now, to give some comprehension of the extension of time and space that I was experiencing. Many days afterwards I asked [fellow prisoner] Morrell what he had tried to convey to me. It was a simple message, namely: "Standing, are you there?" He had tapped it rapidly, while the guard was at the far end of the corridor into which the solitary cells opened. As I say, he had tapped the message very rapidly. And now behold! Between the first tap and the second I was off and away among the stars, clad in fleecy garments, touching each star as I passed in my pursuit of the formulæ that would explain the last mystery of life. And, as before, I pursued the quest for centuries. Then came the summons, the stamp of the hoof of doom, the exquisite disruptive agony, and again I was back in my cell in San Quentin. It was the second tap of Ed Morrell's knuckle. The interval between it and the first tap could have been no more than a fifth of a second. And yet, so unthinkably enormous was

---

5. HPL's friend James F. Morton had been a youthful correspondent with London (Long 52).

the extension of time to me, that in the course of that fifth of a second I had been away star-roving for long ages. (London 69)

Obviously, this is not a scientific depiction of relativity, where the shorter perspective of time would be experienced by the high-speed voyager. But it does demonstrate that interstellar voyagers would experience *an* effect of changing time. The incorporeal star voyaging of Standing would seemingly influence the writing of "Through the Gates of the Silver Key" years later (Guimont, "Arctic" 156–57).[6]

Another work that explores the tangle of time and space is the film *Arrival* (2016), directed by Denis Villeneuve[7] and written by Eric Heisserer, based on Ted Chiang's short story "Story of Your Life" (1998). Duncan Norris has written on the Lovecraftian themes of the film, which depicts tentacled aliens who perceive time non-linearly, coming to Earth to save humans from a crisis because in thousands of years the descendants of humanity will help save their own species. Heisserer, a Lovecraft fan who had previously written the 2011 prequel to John Carpenter's *The Thing*, was responsible for most of the Lovecraftian elements in *Arrival*, but there is no need to recapitulate them all here when Norris has done them extensively in his own work (Norris, "Arrival" 110–17).

But the related effects of time dilation and interstellar travel are most starkly brought to mind by Lovecraft's letter to Clark Ashton Smith:

> As for your idea of shifted senses in an interstellar voyager, & the painful strangeness of the earth on his return—really it is a *tremendous* thing! It vividly shews up the whole matter of relativity & subjectivity in our notions of the external world, and gives an opportunity of unlimited phantasy in description, atmosphere, and plot-weaving. The specimen details you cite seem to me admirable in every way—& if I were you I would have the victim *not recognize the earth at all* until the very last. Let him think that he has landed, through a miscalculation, on the wrong planet; & let the few approximations to familiarity be only of the vaguest, most grotesque, & most disquieting sort. (7 November 1930; *DS* 264–65)

---

6. The use of San Quentin prison by HPL in his 1928 revision work "The Last Test" (*CF* 4.105) may also be a legacy of *The Star Rover*.

7. As of 2022, Villeneuve is also set to direct an adaptation of Clarke's *Rendezvous with Rama*.

It is almost as if Lovecraft predicted the plot, and the infamous ending twist, of the film *Planet of the Apes* (1968)—a twist that also has some echoes of "Arthur Jermyn." It should be noted that the screenplay of *Planet of the Apes* was written by famed *Twilight Zone* host Rod Serling (1924–1975), a reader of *Weird Tales*. Robert Bloch would write for *The Twilight Zone,* and Serling's subsequent show *Night Gallery* would include adaptations of "Cool Air" (written by Serling) and "Pickman's Model," along with adaptations of Clark Ashton Smith, Donald Wandrei, August Derleth, and Fritz Leiber (*IAP* 1045). One of the last things Serling worked on was serving as narrator for the TV special *In Search of Ancient Astronauts* (1973), based on *Chariots of the Gods?* and including such figures as Wernher von Braun and Carl Sagan (Scharmen 124–25).

More pedestrian than four-dimensional travel, but no less important to actual voyagers—including Randolph Carter, Walter Gilman, George Campbell, much less the Elder Things on their solar wings—is the problem of relativistic interstellar navigation (Bailer-Jones). But even Lovecraft anticipated this, writing in a letter to Kenneth Sterling on the problem of "directional notions in ultimate space" (3 August 1935, *RB* 250). Which leads us, in suitably retrograde format, from a discussion of trans-dimensional and reverse-time travel to travel through conventional space—and Lovecraft's influence on more traditional spaceship-set space opera.

Beyond the Infinite

S. T. Joshi has pointed out that Lovecraft's use of aliens "would alone suffice to give him a place as a forerunner of interplanetary or science fiction" (Joshi, "LOP" 3). Despite this, the science fiction community of the 1960s and 1970s was seemingly prejudiced against Lovecraft, perhaps due to the fact that his works focused on gods and dreams over hard science fiction, or avoided the social themes of the New Wave that was prominent at the time (*IAP* 1049; Joshi, *Recognition* 187). Of course, Lovecraft was in good company. For example, during the 1970s, the Science Fiction Writers of America were also hostile to Polish author Stanisław Lem, now considered a genre giant (Kaveney 5). Even after the Lovecraftian renaissance of the early twenty-first century, explicitly Lovecraftian space operas exist—the *Future Lovecraft* (2012) and *Ride the Star Wind: Cthulhu, Space Opera, and the Cosmic Weird* (2017) are

11. The Great Enveloping Cosmic Dark

two anthology examples—but are less common than, for example, Lovecraftian Sherlock Holmes pastiches.[8]

However, even in the 1960s and 1970s Lovecraft's influence on science fiction, let alone space opera, was not negligible. Even beyond giants such as Clarke as detailed above—or Heinlein, whose probable influence from Lovecraft was recounted in chapter 7—a number of authors in the field had direct connections to Lovecraft, particularly as correspondents in the last few years of his life, as Lovecraft turned more toward science fiction. In particular, his influence could be felt in nonliterary space opera—albeit to varying degrees—as television and film emerged into the dominant media forms of the genre.

Perhaps most notable of these space opera influences was Robert Bloch. While most famous as a horror author, Bloch also wrote three episodes of arguably one of the two most influential American space operas of the twentieth century, *Star Trek: The Original Series*.[9] All three of his episodes have traces, however faint, of the Old Gentleman in them. Bloch's first episode, "What Are Little Girls Made Of?" (1966), featured an archaeologist whose expedition had been lost underground on an ice planet years earlier. Bloch's second episode, "Catspaw" (1967), featured a planet where small aliens protect themselves by using telepathy to project imagery of Earth witchcraft iconography. Notably, both of those episodes also refer to ancient alien entities called the Old Ones. Bloch's final episode was "Wolf in the Fold" (1967), which revealed that Jack the Ripper was actually an incorporeal being who hopped from planet to planet across the galaxy, possessing local entities in order to carry out murders. Bloch's script for "Wolf in the Fold" drew inspiration from Guy de Maupassant's short story "The Horla" (1887), which Lovecraft had praised in "Supernatural Horror in Literature," and which has been seen as an influence on "The Call of Cthulhu" (*CE* 2.99; Joshi and Schultz 28).

Another *Star Trek* writer with a connection to Lovecraft was one of his late correspondents, James Blish (Joshi, *Recognition* 83–84; *IAP* 993). From 1967 to 1977, Blish novelized almost all the episodes of *Star Trek: The Original Series*, as well as writing the first original *Star*

---

8. *All-Consuming Fire* (1994) by Andy Lane is a rare example of all three, crossing over the Cthulhu Mythos, the Holmes canon, and *Doctor Who*.

9. Duncan Norris has written more substantively of the Lovecraftian themes in both *Star Trek* and *Star Wars* in his article "The Reverberation of Echoes: Lovecraft in Twenty-First-Century Cinema" (205–09).

Trek novel. However, Blish was not merely a tie-in author. As mentioned above, he is most famous for his *Cities in Flight* series, won the Hugo Award for Best Novel in 1959, and was inventor of the planetary science term "gas giant." Blish also co-wrote two stories with late Lovecraft correspondent Robert A. W. Lowndes, who himself wrote the novel *The Puzzle Planet* (1961), an early SF murder mystery set on an extrasolar planet. Nor were Lovecraft connections in *Star Trek* limited to writers who had known the man himself. John M. Ford's tie-in novel *How Much for Just the Planet?* (1987) establishes that Miskatonic University continues to exist in the twenty-third century, and the *Star Trek: Enterprise* episode "Regeneration" (2003) shows its descent from *At the Mountains of Madness*, with the cybernetic Borg taking the place of shoggoths (Guimont, "Arctic" 159). The actor Jeffrey Combs—Dr. Herbert West himself—is one of the most prolific guest stars across the *Star Trek* franchise. The connections between the two franchises perhaps reached an apotheosis with Leslie Thomas's 2008 fan chapbook *Cthulhu Trek* (Derie, "Trek").

Of course, *Star Trek* is not the only major American space opera "Star" franchise to have the influence of Lovecraft sneak in. In Graham McNeill's pastiche *Dweller in the Deep* (2014), the characters visit the Markham-Hyde Library located Marin County, California. The library is a sprawling white colonial-style villa with shuttered windows and columns in front, and of course contains many forbidden books, including the *Necronomicon* (McNeill, *Dweller* 158–61). From the location and description, this seems to be the Skywalker Ranch property of George Lucas (b. 1944). There is of course no indication that Lucas owes the success of *Star Wars* to an invocation from the *Necronomicon*, although it may seem like that at times. If anything, the *Necronomicon* is more likely to be used by Lucas's successor as *Star Wars'* owner, Disney. But for all its immediate success, the first sequel to *Star Wars* was not *The Empire Strikes Back* (with its Leigh Brackett script), but rather a tie-in novel, *Splinter of the Mind's Eye* (1978) by prolific novelization author Alan Dean Foster, who had earlier written the novelization of *Star Wars* and would go on to write those of *The Black Hole*, *Alien* (and its sequels), and *The Thing*. *Splinter*'s plot centers around Luke Skywalker and Princess Leia recovering a powerful Force artifact from the ancient Temple of Pomojema. When Dark Horse Comics[10] adapted *Splinter of the Mind's*

---

10. Also publishers of the Lovecraftian-infused comic *Hellboy*.

Eye to the comic book format in 1995, Pomojema was explicitly depicted as what had by then become the widely accepted form of Cthulhu.

Splinter of the Mind's Eye was one of the older *Star Wars* works that inspired the development of the spinoff movie *Solo: A Star Wars Story* (2018). The film includes a scene with an enormous tentacled space monster that lives around a black hole; the script identifies it as a "summa-verminoth." According to the scriptwriter Jon Kasdan (b. 1979), he and director Ron Howard (b. 1954) are Lovecraft fans and named the entity after Robert Bloch's *De Vermis Mysteriis*. Another reference to Lovecraft can be found in the movie's climax, when Han Solo succeeds in defeating his enemies on a sandy coast; the script identifies the location as the Pnakotic Dunes, in reference to the Great Race's own desert redoubt (Kasdan). The reference to Pnakotus is apt, as with its collection of aliens of all types from across the galaxy, the infamous Mos Eisley Cantina is in its own way a working-class equivalent to the Great Library.[11]

On the heels of the success of *Star Wars,* a number of space-set films were rushed into production, one of the most significant being Ridley Scott's *Alien* (1979). The script to *Alien* was co-written by Dan O'Bannon (1946–2009), who had previously done animation work on *Star Wars*. O'Bannon was a Lovecraft fan who infused the themes of the author into the film script. While some of O'Bannon's original ideas were removed in subsequent rewrites, much of the atmosphere remains. For example, when the crew first awakens from hibernation, it is "Antarctica Traffic Control" they attempt to contact to understand why they are being diverted to the mysterious planet LV-426. O'Bannon's idea was that LV-426 was either the world or a fragment of the world where the Old Ones had originated, and he was pleased when one early reviewer believed that LV-426 was meant to be Yuggoth. O'Bannon also believed that the titular Xenomorph creature was related to Yog-Sothoth (Kulcsar; Migliore and Strysik 95–99; Joshi, *Recognition* 259). Given the joking family tree that Lovecraft sketched out in his letter to James F. Morton of 27 April 1933 (*JFM* 317), in which both Lovecraft and Yog-Sothoth were descended from Azathoth, this would make Lovecraft and the Xenomorph distant cousins. Nor was O'Bannon the only Lovecraft-influenced crewmember on *Alien;* the design of the Xenomorph came from Swiss artist H. R. Giger (1940–2014), who based it

---

11. With thanks to Justin Mullis for the comparison.

on a piece of art he had done in 1976, suggestively titled *Necronom IV* (Joshi, *Recognition* 189).

O'Bannon would go on to direct *The Resurrected* (1991), an adaptation of *The Case of Charles Dexter Ward*. He would return to the *Alien* universe only once more, helping develop the story to the crossover prequel *Alien vs. Predator* (2004). Involving the discovery of an ancient alien pyramid in Antarctica, under which sleeping Xenomorphs are resurrected by a scientific expedition, O'Bannon explicitly drew from *At the Mountains of Madness*. Ridley Scott's return to the franchise with the film *Prometheus* (2012) instead took the format of *At the Mountains of Madness* and placed it on another planet; the similarity was obvious enough that director Guillermo del Toro was dissuaded from continuing with his attempt to film a more direct adaptation of Lovecraft's novella (Lambie; Norris, "Cinema" 187–88; Joshi, *Recognition* 259, 298).

Stephen Walker has argued that while Lovecraft's greatest contribution was to the horror genre, his "second greatest influence has been on humor" (162). In that light, it is perhaps worth examining the extent to which one of the most popular space-related comedy films, the comic adaptation *Men in Black* (1997), reflects Lovecraftian elements. Despite the comedic context, it is hard to ignore the parallel to the famous opening lines of "The Call of Cthulhu" when Agent K, one of the titular agents, tells his new partner, "There's always an Arquillian Battle Cruiser, or a Corillian Death Ray, or an intergalactic plague that is about to wipe out all life on this miserable little planet, and the only way these people can get on with their happy lives is that they do not know about it!"[12] Or the cosmicism of Agent K's revelation that "Human thought is so primitive it's looked upon as an infectious disease in some of the better galaxies." Then there is the film's villain, an enormous dimensionally folded intelligent insect (perhaps from the fourth moon of Jupiter?) that judges Earth: "Nothing but undeveloped, unevolved, barely conscious pond scum, totally convinced of their own superiority as they scurry about their short, pointless lives." And of course, the end of the movie reveals that our galaxy is merely a marble being used in a game by an intelligent being whose dimensions cannot even be guessed at, reducing us all to alien playthings in the manner of Charles Fort's speculation (Fort, *Damned* 154).

---

12. One wonders if the film's titular organization was involved in any sort of activities off the coast of Massachusetts in February 1928.

11. The Great Enveloping Cosmic Dark

The expansion of the video game industry in the 1990s also opened the door for "Lovecraft in space" games. *Shadow of the Comet* (1993) and *Martian Gothic: Unification* (2000) have been mentioned previously, but the most significant entry of the decade was *Quake* (1996), a massive hit and defining early entry in the first-person shooter genre. In *Quake,* the player is a soldier sent through a teleportation system to various planets to fight enemies who take their names (if little else) from Lovecraftian entities such as Tsathoggua and Shub-Niggurath. The *Dead Space* series (2008–13) takes stock Lovecraftian themes like tentacles, evil cults, madness, relics of ancient alien civilizations, and even a character named Howard Philips, placing them on spaceships and mining colonies, both extrasolar and on Saturn's moon Titan (Norris, "Cinema" 217).

The *Mass Effect* series (2007–17) perhaps comes closest to Lovecraftian themes, with the main enemies of the series being enormous, unstoppable cephalopod entities who sleep in the intergalactic void, awakening in cycles of hundreds of thousands of years to destroy galactic civilization for reasons that are inscrutable to the lesser species impacted by their return when the stars are right (Norris, "Cinema" 208–9). *Mass Effect 3* (2012) even allows the player to visit the aquatic homeworld of the creatures, where they evolved underwater more than a billion years ago. As part of the games' backstory, humanity gains the technology to join the interstellar community by the discovery of an enormous alien research base under the south polar ice cap on Mars, built by aliens tens of thousands of years ago to study to evolution of humanity and abandoned as its creators went extinct. As part of humanity's expansion into the galaxy, they next discover that Pluto's moon Charon is actually a frozen-over interstellar transportation device linking the solar system with the next "mass relay" orbiting Arcturus.

Another world that can be visited in *Mass Effect 3* is Carcosa, where a crumbling palace is located on the shores of a dead lake. Peter Rawlik's short story "In the Hall of the Yellow King" (2011) similarly turns Carcosa into a planet that is the destination of the starship *Armitage,* its population a mix of Tcho-Tcho, Yithians, Aihais, shoggoths, and others with whom the human ambassadors must negotiate (Rawlik 13–14). "In the Hall of the Yellow King" is a sort of Lovecraftian parody of *Star Trek*—a mix of strange aeons and strange new worlds.

The space operas *Star Trek, Star Wars, Alien*, *Dead Space,* and *Mass Effect* share a common interest in developing the settings of their stories. The history of how and why those settings came to be, and how they connect to the readers' present, are very loosely developed, if at all. In contrast, the development of elaborate timelines linking the earthbound present to the interstellar future were key aspects of the space operas of Heinlein, Asimov, and the authors who followed them. As Peter Cannon showed in his *The Chronology out of Time* (1986), Lovecraft, too, paid close attention to the dates in his fiction, including how they would interconnect, linking them into both deep time and the distant future. As a conclusion to the chapter, we turn from an exploration of the spatial aspect of Lovecraft's space opera fiction to its temporal framework.

The History of the Future

At the conclusion of his Providence *Evening News* article of 2 October 1917, Lovecraft painted a vivid picture of the distant future. Contemplating a remote time when stars and nebulae have ceased to produce significant light, he imagined a "vast sepulchral universe of unbroken midnight gloom and perpetual arctic frigidity, through which will roll dark, cold suns with their hordes of dead, frozen planets, on which will lie the dust of those unhappy mortals who will have perished as their dominant stars faded from the skies" (*CE* 3.238; see also chapter 6). Even before Lovecraft turned toward his major period of fiction writing, conceptions of the far future and the evolution of life into that period were on his mind. See for example his above-referenced satire of Comet XY4 in the fiftieth century.

Lovecraft was certainly not the first author of speculative fiction to include details on how future settings linked to the present. Early examples include Poe's "Mellonta Tauta," in which the (literal) medium for linking the story's twenty-ninth-century setting to the present is a psychic, and Edgar Rice Burroughs's serialized novel *The Moon Maid* (1923), spanning from the immediate aftermath of World War I to the post-apocalyptic struggle over North America in the mid-twenty-first century. Also mentioned before are J. B. S. Haldane's speculative nonfiction essay "The Last Judgment" (1927), recounting the destruction of the Earth and colonization of Venus millions of years into the future; and H. G. Wells's novel *The Shape of Things to Come* (1933) and its movie adaptation *Things to Come* (1936), both of which chart the development of international political and social development from the immediate present through the following century. Indeed, the twentieth-century trope of a future history charting the economic, political, and cultural transformation of the present into a science fictional future probably borrowed from the notion of "universal history," a genre that looks at human history as a unified totality, outside of any national perspective or cultural context and often incorporating geological timescales as an important component to the historical record. One of the most significant universal histories of the twentieth century in terms of its influences was Wells's *The Outline of History* (1920), which Lovecraft owned and recommended (*LL* 164–65).

Olaf Stapledon's *Last and First Men* (1930) is an example of an early future history that Lovecraft certainly read and from which he took inspiration. The novel spans hundreds of millions of years into the future, but it begins its coverage of human development with a summary of World War I (Stapledon 21–22).[13] That Stapledon influenced Lovecraft's view of how spans of time could be depicted in fiction is evident from Lovecraft's letter to Donald A. Wollheim of 7 October 1935, in which he discussed Robert E. Howard's approach to fictional history:

> Howard has the most magnificent sense of the drama of "history" of anyone I know. He possesses a panoramic vision which takes in the evolution & interaction of races & nations over vast periods of time, & gives one the same large-scale excitement which (with even vaster scope) is furnished by things like Stapledon's "Last & First Men". (*RB* 319)

However, *Last and First Men* differs from later future histories in that it was conceived of and written as a single novel, which allowed Stapledon to plot out the entire vast scope of his human history in one piece. Most subsequent future histories, particularly those that developed in the science fiction magazines of the 1930s and 1940s, were more like Lovecraft's own works: short stories that were loosely connected in a unified setting, the relationship often being worked out by the author in a post-hoc form. The works of Isaac Asimov, particularly those comprising his *Robot* and *Foundation* settings, are notable examples. Asimov began writing the first short story in 1939; the final novel was published posthumously in 1993. During that span, Asimov further amalgamated the two series in their 1980s entries. The combined setting begins with exploring the development of commercial household robotics in the 1980s United States and ends with the development of a telepathic, galaxy-spanning hive mind more than thirty thousand years in the future.

---

13. Interestingly, Stapledon then predicts that by the start of the twenty-first century, the world's two superpowers will be the United States and China, while European countries outside of Russia will join a political confederacy (Stapledon 42–55).

However, the ur-example of pulp-era future histories is Robert A. Heinlein's eponymous "Future History." As mentioned in chapter 7, Heinlein's Future History originated with his first published work, "Life-Line" (1939), and included the Venus-set "Logic of Empire." Much like August Derleth and the "Cthulhu Mythos," the name and initial systematization of the Future History did not come from Heinlein, but from John W. Campbell (Nevala-Lee 113–14). Heinlein would continue to publish entries in the Future History until 1987, the year before his death; chronologically and spatially, they spanned from the late nineteenth century to the late forty-third century, and from being set entirely in Sacramento to spanning the galaxy. Heinlein's planned but unwritten Future History stories included "Fire Down Below," set in Antarctica; and "Eclipse," about independence movements on the Venusian and Martian colonies (Heinlein, "Concerning" 261–66).

Does Lovecraft's fiction count as a future history? Certainly, he has stories spanning huge reaches of time. Both Leiber and Hite have explored how Lovecraft's use of geological deep time serves as a mirror of a future history (Leiber, "Hyperspace" 174–76; Hite 201). With few exceptions, Lovecraft typically set his stories in times roughly contemporary to his own era. Even the exploration of the deep past is generally done through the lens of contemporary academics uncovering records or remains. One of the few exceptions is "Eryx," set at some indeterminate point in the (relatively) near future, seventy-two years after the first landing on Venus—an event that, given Lovecraft's spaceflight musings in chapter 5, he probably thought was at least a century ahead (and he was optimistic in that regard, something that can rarely be said for him). "'Till A' the Seas'" also serves as a condensed historical narrative of the death of humanity, in the mold of both Stapledon and William Hope Hodgson's 1912 "dying Earth" novel *The Night Land* (OFF 317). But it is the psychic time travel aspects of "Beyond the Wall of Sleep" and particularly "The Shadow out of Time"—with their references to events such as the rise of the cruel empire of Tsan-Chan in the year 5000 and the dark conquest of the year 16,000—that allow for the argument that Lovecraft created an outline of a future timeline predating the more famous ones begun later in the 1930s by Heinlein and Asimov. In his short story "To Arkham and the Stars" (1966), Fritz Leiber draws a further connection between Lovecraft's cosmic focus and his use of immense historical timeframes, a connection appropriate given the theory

11. The Great Enveloping Cosmic Dark 329

of relativity's linking of time and space. In the story, Leiber has an elderly Nathaniel Peaslee reflect on the Anglo-Australian rocket range established in 1946, "Let the young spacemen at Woomera . . . fire their rockets over our old diggins, I say . . . and blow the sand more thickly there. It is better so" (Leiber, "Arkham" 159).

Perhaps ironically given that the majority of stated dates in Lovecraft's fiction are in the 1662–1935 range (Cannon, *Chronology* 12–36), it is the outlying dates prior to and after that span whose continuity has proved contentious. In his article "Lovecraft's Cosmic History" (1986) Robert M. Price firmly argues that Lovecraft's internal timeline "cannot be harmonized" (18). The same year, in *The Chronology out of Time* Cannon notes Lovecraft's attention to detail when it came to plotting the dates of his stories. But in charting them, Cannon deliberately ignored both the deep past and distant future elements that might have allowed for a better evaluation of Lovecraft's work as a future history, and which are particularly the aspects that Price finds in contradiction (Cannon, *Chronology* 6–7). However, one of Price's claims is that Lovecraft's deep history dates do not align because Lovecraft was writing the stories as he went, with no overarching plan (Price, "History" 24). This was the same as Heinlein and Asimov, who often edited the dates of their stories on republishing to fit better into the emerging context of the fictional setting. It is obviously impossible to say that Lovecraft would have done the same had he lived longer, particularly given his attitude toward editing manuscripts, but he showed a strong commitment to editing errors in his printed works. Had a collection of his stories been published during his lifetime, it is not inconceivable that Lovecraft would have edited them further for cohesion. Of course, it is also evident that evaluating the span of deep time and distant future in Lovecraft's work requires doing so from a human vantage point—a point of view that is not only not the primary one, but one entirely at odds with the themes of Lovecraft's cosmic horror. As Leiber argued,

> In both *At the Mountains of Madness* and *The Shadow Out of Time*[14] it is clear that Lovecraft has become deeply interested in picturing in detail the careers of galactic races and the future history of mankind; that, although still holding onto the supernatural-horror pattern in his stories, he was trending more and more in the direction of creativity like Olaf

---

14. The stories appeared in *Astounding*, the magazine published in and read by Asimov and Heinlein.

Stapledon's. The extra-terrestrials are the real heroes of these long stories. Their unending struggles for survival and to increase their store of knowledge, their wise, rational, enlightened, and even "humane" cultures, are Lovecraft's finest vision of mind embattled against space and time . . . . By collating these two short novels, one can discover an imagined history of the earth, not altogether unlike Robert Heinlein's "future history," though on a much vaster scale and concerned mostly with the past. (Leiber, "Hyperspace" 174)

Ultimately, the extent to which Lovecraft's works can be seen as a future history depend on the extent to which one accepts them as a relatively unified setting—a related but distinct question from whether one accepts Derleth's concept of the Cthulhu Mythos or the various alternative nomenclatures offered since (Price, "Mythology" 247). But it was exactly that undefined aspect of Lovecraft's work, deliberately left open for the contributions of his friends and fans, through which Lovecraft was responsible for creating one of the first modern examples of a type of genre fiction even more dominant than the future history: the "shared universe," the cornerstone of modern SF blockbuster franchises such as *Star Wars* and the Marvel Cinematic Universe (Leiber, "Hyperspace" 176–77; Price, "Mythology" 252–56; Canote). It was this openness and willingness to share and collaborate—a spirit, it must be said, that was far less apparent in Derleth and his efforts to systematize and canonize Lovecraft's setting—that resulted in the flowering of Lovecraftian fiction from the late twentieth century on, allowing it to be used, modified, and adopted by authors whom Lovecraft himself probably would have found personally unpleasant to interact with.

In the end, whether Lovecraft's fiction is a future history or not is up to personal debate. But if the reason it is not seen as such is because of its lack of precise coherence and singular focus to notions of continuity and canon, it is exactly those elements that have allowed it to thrive in a way that corporate-controlled media universes, by their very nature, cannot achieve.

Conclusion

After its encounter with Neptune in 1989, the *Voyager 2* probe began its journey out of the solar system and into interstellar space. Its primary mission achieved, in 1990 NASA directed the spacecraft to turn around and take one final photograph of home. The resulting image, termed the Pale Blue Dot, showed the Earth reduced to the size of a few pixels of blue in a sunbeam. The photograph was the brainchild of the astronomer Carl Sagan (1934–1996), who upon viewing the image was inspired to write:

> The Earth is a very small stage in a vast cosmic arena. Think of the rivers of blood spilled by all those generals and emperors so that, in glory and triumph, they could become the momentary masters of a fraction of a dot. Think of the endless cruelties visited by the inhabitants of one corner of this pixel on the scarcely distinguishable inhabitants of some other corner, how frequent their misunderstandings, how eager they are to kill one another, how fervent their hatreds. Our posturings, our imagined self-importance, the delusion that we have some privileged position in the Universe, are challenged by this point of pale light. Our planet is a lonely speck in the great enveloping cosmic dark. In our obscurity, in all this vastness, there is no hint that help will come from elsewhere to save us from ourselves. The Earth is the only world known so far to harbor life. (Sagan, *Dot* 6–7)

Sagan meant this optimistically, a call to action for humans to treat both themselves and their world better. If the Earth is merely "a lonely speck in the great enveloping cosmic dark," then cruelty and selfishness make no sense. But it is also easy to imagine Lovecraft reading that quotation, agreeing with all Sagan's written sentiments completely, yet going one step further to arrive at a very different conclusion, one that justifies his worldview of cosmic indifference. If the Earth is merely a speck, then hope and kindness make no sense either.

But at the same time, one can also imagine a different Lovecraft, or perhaps a different aspect of him, reading Sagan's words and feeling *relief*. For if the Earth truly is unique in the universe in harboring life, then it means the beliefs of the Cthulhu cultists, the warnings of Dyer and Peaslee, the evidence gathered by Federal agents at Innsmouth can all be safely discounted. If "there is no hint that help will come from elsewhere to save us from ourselves," then there is also no hint that entities of another sort will arrive when the stars are right to end us. In light of this, it is worth considering the Mi-Go colonization of Yuggoth and the Yuggothian colonization of Earth—not to mention the subsequent waves of settlement of Earth by Deep Ones, Yithians, Elder Things, and starspawn. All this seems to fly in the face of Lovecraft's own thoughts on the likelihood (or lack thereof) of interplanetary settlement, as mentioned at the start of the chapter. In doing so, Lovecraft's fictional predilection for successful colonization not only counteracts his personal scientific views when it comes to space, but also his pseudoscientific views on race and inherent suitability to areas of supposed national origins.

This might seem like a contradiction, if not outright hypocrisy given Lovecraft's encouragement of authors of interplanetary fiction to follow the latest science. But it shows the difference between Lovecraft the scientific thinker and Lovecraft the fiction writer, and demonstrates that Lovecraft was flexible enough to compartmentalize the two. He might never believe that extraterrestrials exist, let alone that they settled (or even would be capable of settling) on Earth. But as an author, he was not about to let those scientific certainties get in the way of writing a good story. One might as well complain that Robert E. Howard wrote about historical Cimmeria despite knowing it had never existed in actual history. And, indeed, in many cases Lovecraft the fiction writer and Lovecraft the scientific-minded rationalist could find a happy, if inadvertent, common ground. Take the proposals of some astronomers that in the past 500 million years the region of the Milky Way in which the Earth lies is the best suited for the emergence of intelligent life; previously, it would have been exposed to too many supernovae, as the outer edge of the galaxy now might be (Brin 300–302; Spinelli et al 1–10). Consider that proposal in the context of "The Call of Cthulhu," where life on Earth can thrive when the stars are wrong; for when the stars are right, their emissaries come to Earth to end life. Cthulhu as a supernova is less outlandish when one further considers the association of Joe Slater's psychic visitor and GK Persei in "Beyond the Wall of Sleep."

Or take the famous opening of "The Call of Cthulhu," that "We live on a placid island of ignorance in the midst of black seas of infinity, and it was not meant that we should voyage far" (*CF* 2.21). Compare that to another famous opening, that of Sagan's book version of *Cosmos* (1980):

> The surface of the Earth is the shore of the cosmic ocean. From it we have learned most of what we know. Recently, we have waded a little out to sea, enough to dampen our toes or, at most, wet our ankles. The water seems inviting. The ocean calls. Some part of our being knows this is from where we came. We long to return. These aspirations are not, I think, irrelevant, although they may trouble whatever gods may be. (Sagan, *Cosmos* 2)

Compare it also to a line in the opening of "The Last Judgment," where Haldane discusses his difficulty in believing that God would end all of creation simply due to the humans of Earth: "At worst our earth is only a very small septic area in the universe, which could be sterilized without very great trouble, and conceivably is not even worth sterilizing" (288).

Consider as well that Haldane's essay also features new lands emerging from the central Pacific (299), and Antarctica as the last redoubt of the humans of Earth (306)—a logical comparison given that Dyer himself relates the Elder Things to humanity. Haldane wrote the essay in 1927, showing that while it did not serve as an influence on "Cthulhu," Lovecraft's cosmicism was parallel to the evolutionary speculation of the British biologist, as it was to the humanist musing of the American astronomer.

In the introduction to their anthology *Future Lovecraft* (2012), editors Silvia Moreno-Garcia and Paula R. Stiles note that "H. P. Lovecraft is not generally considered a writer of science fiction, even though he had a personal interest in the sciences (astronomy, of course). . . . [But] his realistic view of the tiny human position in the cosmos, and his espousal of a very long view of human history, [has] had as large an influence on science fiction as on horror" (9). This chapter and the previous have had an expansive focus, from a tour of the outer solar system, through interstellar space, and ultimately through genre conventions. In each case, Lovecraft's use of existing science, in some cases his prediction of scientific discoveries yet to come, and his influence on not only future authors but those future discoveries themselves have been highlighted. If nothing else, this chapter has cemented Lovecraft's position as an author not just of science fiction, but of interplanetary fiction; his commitment to and use of astronomy; and how the former was intricately informed, while not being constrained, by the latter.

Chapter 12
Astronomy at the End

"When the stars were right, They could plunge from world to world through the sky; but when the stars were wrong, They could not live."—"The Call of Cthulhu" (1926)

In the last summer of his short life, Lovecraft made his way back to the Ladd Observatory, the scene of his youthful encounter with the world of academic astronomy. His purpose was to see a comet that had been discovered by amateur astronomer Leslie Peltier.[1] It was not a comet of extraordinary brilliance, but it did become bright enough to be seen with the unaided eye. Lovecraft wrote: "Last night I had an interesting view of Peltier's comet through the 12″ telescope of Ladd Observatory (of Brown U) a mile north of here. I used to haunt this observatory 30 years ago" (letter to R. H. Barlow, 23 July 1936; *OFF* 356). At the time that Lovecraft saw Comet Peltier, he was unaware that he had less than a year to live. Death would find him on 15 March 1937.

When the not-quite forty-six-year-old Lovecraft climbed to the Ladd Observatory, his writing of weird fiction was over, with the exception of "The Night Ocean," mostly the creation of R. H. Barlow with light revisions by Lovecraft.[2] He had written his last major work, "The Shadow out of Time," in late 1934 and early 1935, a story of vast scope that exhibits the cosmicism that Joshi considered Lovecraft's "one distinctive contribution to literature" (*IAP* 1054). "The Haunter of the Dark," entertaining but usually regarded as a lesser tale, was written in November 1935 in response to Robert Bloch's "The Shambler from the

---

1. Peltier (1900–1980) has been called "the world's greatest non-professional astronomer." His autobiographical book, *Starlight Nights,* is charming.
2. Some of HPL's fiction did not, however, see print until years after it was written. An apparent minor revision to a story by Duane W. Rimel early in 1937 is lost (*IAP* 1007).

334

12. Astronomy at the End

Stars," in which a character inspired by Lovecraft meets a terrible demise. Early in 1936 he collaborated with Kenneth Sterling on their Venus-set tale, "In the Walls of Eryx," as discussed in chapter 7. Revisions for others and ghostwriting occupied most of his working hours in his final year.

In chapter 1 we considered the first years of Lovecraft's love of astronomy. We now consider the role of astronomy in the final years of his abbreviated life. Our emphasis is not on Lovecraft's fiction, which we discussed in prior chapters. Instead, we turn to Lovecraft himself in the final decade of his life, when youthful dreams of astronomy as a profession were long vanished, but the stars remained. To what degree did astronomy linger in these later years?

Comet Peltier 1936, the last comet that Lovecraft would see. Astronomical Society of the Pacific.

Still Gazing Upward

In the 1930s, Lovecraft no longer ventured out to observe night after night, as he had in his teens. That was especially true in winter, when a sensitivity to cold weather often left him trapped indoors (*IAP* 1006). Nevertheless, even a brief perusal of his letters shows that astronomy was not forgotten. In his correspondence, the mature Lovecraft often addresses astronomical topics in a matter-of-fact manner, but on occasion he could wax picturesque and philosophical. Eight years before his death, he wrote a long letter (25 February–1 March 1929) to revision client Woodburn Harris,[3] explaining that he could simultaneously see the heavens through two very different intellectual filters:

---

3. David Haden presents Randy Everts's study of Woodburn Harris in the

> I am, as I may have told you, rather an astronomical devotee; yet these evenings when I tread the narrow ancient streets on the brow of the hill and look westward over the outspread roofs and spires and domes of the lower town to where the distant hills of the countryside stand out against the fading sky, I do not scan that sky as a measurer or an analyst. Resplendent Venus and Jupiter shine close together, hanging over the great beacon-tower of the terraced Industrial Trust Building as they used to hang 2000 years ago over the towering Pharos in Alexandria's crowded harbour; and as I watch them and compare them with the great red beacon and the mystic twinkling lights of the dusk-shadowed city below, I surely hold no thoughts of their objective nature and position. I do not say to myself that Jupiter is a cloudy belted sphere 1300 times larger than the earth and situate some 480,000,000 miles from the sun, or that Venus is a globe slightly smaller than the earth, perpetually veiled by a cloudy atmosphere, and about 66,000,000 miles from the sun. I do not reflect that Jupiter's orbit is outside the earth's while Venus's is inside, and that this circumstance determines the vastly different apparent motions they display in the terrestrial sky. The fact is, I do not say or reflect anything—I merely watch and dream . . . As I watch them, I feel that they watch me, and that the beauty they cast upon the thickening night and the candle-pierced, crepuscular town is a symbol of primal glories older than man, older than earth, older than Nature, older even than the gods, and designed for my mystic soul alone. This, indeed, is feeling—but when I approach the same objects as an astronomical student I do so very differently. Then I leave my dreams behind and take along my telescope; and instead of glancing at the lighted town below, I curse it for the smoke and heat-vapours it sends up to obscure telescopic definition. I note the phase of Venus and the curve of the terminator, and reflect how far past greatest elongation it is; and when I turn the glass on Jupiter I regret its long distance past opposition. I don't couple the two planets at all now—the pattern vanishes with the aesthetic mood—and would much rather have Jupiter over in the east, where it is on the evenings when it is nearest the earth. (*WH* 134–35)

Lovecraft was middle-aged at his death and few would deem a man of forty-six a senior citizen. However, in letters to friends, he had long advertised himself as old, often in a jocular and familiar tone, but not, perhaps, without in some sense believing it himself. Though he may rarely have ventured to the eyepiece in his later years, the self-proclaimed "Old Gentleman" had not forgotten the observing skills learned so well

---

Tentaclii blog for 10 July 2014. See also *Tentaclii* for 23 April 2013.

in his adolescence. In 1933 he used his telescope to examine a very close conjunction of Mars and Jupiter, seeing both planets within the same field of view at 150 power (letter to August Derleth, 5 June 1933; *ES* 580). Two years later we find Lovecraft again shaking the dust from the 3-inch Bardou telescope to show celestial sights to young Kenneth Sterling. Lovecraft recounted this episode to his friend James F. Morton: "The archaick wreck (not me—the telescope) will do pretty well under a power of forty-five, but with one hundred it ain't so hot." (letter of 29 December 1935; *JFM* 371). Given his aversion to cold, it is notable that Lovecraft was willing and able to step outside on a late December evening to show Sterling the planet Saturn and the crescent moon. Historical weather data indicate that the day was cold in Providence, with a high temperature in the low 20s F, falling into the teens at night—not at all what Lovecraft preferred. He elaborated upon the less-than-perfect condition of his telescope in a letter to August Derleth dated 9 July 1936: "I have a 3" telescope which was never very good, & which the years (no doubt disturbing the alignment of the lenses through the denting of the brass) have done nothing to improve" (*ES* 739).[4] There can be no doubt that, from his thirteenth year until he drew his last breath, Lovecraft could rightly be called an amateur astronomer—and a good one at that.

Until 1928, Lovecraft's journeys were limited to the northeastern United States, but after that he ranged more widely despite an ever-slender wallet, going to Quebec, Charleston, New Orleans, and Florida. His excursions appear to have been planned with history, friends, his pocketbook, and sometimes warm weather in mind, but not with any particular astronomical goal. Never did he venture to Arizona's Lowell Observatory or to the mountain observatories of California. That, of course, is entirely understandable given the damage such a trip would have inflicted on Lovecraft's meager bank account. A trip to Wisconsin's Yerkes Observatory might have been more feasible, especially given his extensive correspondence with native Wisconsinites such as August Derleth, Alfred Galpin, and Maurice W. Moe. However, Lovecraft never ventured to Wisconsin, nor do his letters disclose any unfulfilled desire to see for himself George Ellery Hale's first major telescope. Had Lovecraft

---

4. The brass tube today retains a dent toward the eyepiece end of the optical tube. In 1926, HPL had written to James F. Morton of his not-entirely-successful efforts to clean the brass tube (*JFM* 125).

taken up science journalism, visits to observatories might have been justified as inspiration for articles, but, as we have seen, Lovecraft never returned to science-writing after 1918.

This postcard from the early 1900s depicts the Maria Mitchell Observatory and the historic Mitchell house. H. Smith collection.

Two years before Comet Peltier lured him back to Ladd Observatory, a shorter journey took Lovecraft to another observatory. Lovecraft spent a week on the island of Nantucket as August turned to September in 1934, touring the island by foot and bicycle (*IAP* 886–87) and delighting in its antique buildings. Amidst its historic structures, he came across the modest Maria Mitchell Observatory. Named for the native of Nantucket who discovered a comet in 1847 before going on to become professor of astronomy at Vassar, the observatory conducted observing sessions for the public during the summer tourist season. Lovecraft took advantage of the opportunity and was repaid by a fine view of Saturn through the observatory's 5-inch telescope (letter to J. Vernon Shea, 10 February 1935; *JVS* 248).

Home from Nantucket, Lovecraft was astonished to read a statement in Donald Wollheim's fanzine, *The Phantagraph*, that claimed that Lovecraft had at one time been in the position of observatory director! His response appeared in the next issue (November–December 1934): "Your statement that I was once director of the Providence Observatory

12. Astronomy at the End

flabbergasted me a bit, inasmuch as there has never been any 'Providence Observatory.'" Lovecraft eventually realized that Wollheim must have somehow come across one of his juvenile hectographed publications. "Thus do the exaggerations of youth bear misleading fruit in old age."

His visits to Florida allowed Lovecraft to see a swath of the southern sky never visible from Providence, but that does not appear to have been a motivation for the trips. However, it was from Florida in 1935 that Lovecraft was able to admire a rare spectacle he had not seen before, a lunar rainbow, which appeared as

> a clear, complete bow in the northwestern sky opposite the rising full moon. Bob [Robert Barlow] claimed he could detect colours in it—especially red on the outer edge—though to me it appear'd of an uniform greyness—faint tho' distinct. Having beheld two total solar eclipses & now a lunar rainbow, I feel myself quite a connoisseur of odd phenomena! (Letter to James F. Morton, 19 August 1935; *JFM* 367)

The year 1935 brought another opportunity for Lovecraft to indulge his interest in astronomy. In October, the Hayden Planetarium of the American Museum of Natural History opened its doors. When Lovecraft visited New York City at the end of the year, staying through the start of 1936, visits to the planetarium were not omitted. The first projection planetarium in the United States, Chicago's Adler Planetarium, had opened only five years previously, and Lovecraft had not seen such a device before. He was enthusiastic about the new tool for public education. In January, he wrote to Alfred Galpin:

> On two occasions—once with Sonny [Frank Belknap Long] & once with Sonny & [Donald] Wandrei—I visited the new Hayden Planetarium of the Am. Museum, & found it a highly impressive device . . . Altogether, it is the most complete & active popular astronomical centre imaginable. It seems to be crowded at all hours—attracting a publick interest in astronomy which did not exist when I was young. (Letter to Alfred Galpin, 17 January 1936; *AG* 328–29)

As noted in chapter 9, the planetarium projector reminded Lovecraft of the armored Martians in *The War of the Worlds* or a spaceship from Edmond Hamilton (*EHP* 219).

Getting the Stars Right

Livesey (DPO 31–36) noted that Lovecraft was meticulous in matching the skies of his stories to what an observer of that specified time and place would actually have seen. If, on a particular day, a full moon was noted as restraining the Mi-Go from attacking Henry Akeley ("The Whisperer in Darkness"), the reader may be assured not only of the accuracy of the lunar phase on that date, but also that all other mentions of lunar phase would be consistent. To Lovecraft's dismay, other writers were not always as fastidious in that respect as he was.[5]

Lovecraft bought inexpensive planispheres for Frank Belknap Long and Donald Wandrei "so that those young rascals won't get the constellations wrong in their future stories, as they have in the past!" (letter to August Derleth, 16 January 1936; *ES* 724). The last full year of his life saw Lovecraft schooling August Derleth on how the constellations visible at night changed with time, so that Derleth might better incorporate the night sky into his own fiction. He recommended Garret P. Serviss's book *Astronomy with an Opera Glass,* suggested that Derleth buy a planisphere, and gave him various tips on star gazing and on maintaining the accuracy of celestial imagery in his fiction (letters to August Derleth, 7 May, 5 June, 20 June, 23 September, and 24 October 1936; all in *ES*). Lovecraft's letters to Derleth included several instructive sketches of stars and constellations—the didactic tendency apparent thirty years before in Lovecraft's hectographed science journals had not departed. His tutoring had only limited success. Although Derleth acquired Lovecraft's Barritt-Serviss Star and Planet Finder after his death, his depictions of fictional skies were not always completely correct (DPO 48–49, Howard 55). Joshi ("Time" *LA* 4.177) regarded Lovecraft's insistence on accuracy in descriptions of the sky to be "amusingly trivial." Lovecraft, on the other hand, would have been mortified were his accounts of the moon or the stars found to be wanting. He was never satisfied unless the stars were right!

In the spring of 1936, Lovecraft was able to rejoice in a genealogical discovery—his apparent descent on his mother's side from the astronomer who had introduced Copernican astronomy to Elizabethan England. That astronomer was John Field (about 1520–1587). To make it even better, Field was acquainted with Dr. John Dee (1527–1608/9), whom Lovecraft credited with a nearly lost English translation of the *Necronomicon*. The supposed line of descent ran back through the Whipples, eventually arriving at a John Field (1616?–1686), who was an early

---

5. Such carelessness also annoyed writer Ambrose Bierce, who wrote a sarcastic piece on the subject, "The Moon in Letters."

12. Astronomy at the End

The title page of John Field's 1557 ephemeris mentions both Copernicus and John Dee, who wrote an introduction to the text.

settler of Providence. So far, so good. However, some authorities went on to state that this John Field of Providence, from whom Lovecraft was actually descended, was the grandson of the Tudor astronomer John Field. A visitor brought Lovecraft word of this illustrious (to him) ancestor.

This discovery thrilled Lovecraft so much that it merited mention in letters to several of his regular correspondents (to James F. Morton, 12 May [*JFM* 383–86]; to R. H. Barlow, 14 May [*OFF* 332]; to Kenneth Sterling, 25 May [*RB* 277–8]; to August Derleth, 5 June [*ES* 733–34]; to J. Vernon Shea, 19 May [*JVS* 290–91]). His letter to Barlow exclaimed: "For one who has always had an eye for the heavens himself, this sure is quite a find!" Lovecraft hoped that the lineage would withstand scrutiny, but, unbeknownst to Lovecraft, the genealogist Osgood Field had already thrown cold water on the connection (Field 1868): "As for the assertion . . . that William and John Field, the early settlers of Rhode Island, were the . . . grandsons of the astronomer, they are not entitled to the slightest credence, not being supported by a shadow of evidence." Lovecraft would have been terribly disappointed had he known that, but instead he seems to have died in the happy belief that the sixteenth century Copernican was a distant ancestor.

On 4 May 1936, Lovecraft attended a lecture at Brown University by physicist Dayton C. Miller. Miller (1866–1941) believed that his experiments contradicted the results of the Michelson-Morley experiment.

The Michelson-Morley experiment had found no evidence for the existence of a luminiferous ether, the medium imagined to be the carrier of electromagnetic radiation. It was a result consistent with Einstein's theory of special relativity. As discussed by Livesey (DPO 52–54), Lovecraft was slow to dismiss the concept of ether. After Miller's talk, Lovecraft's doubts were raised anew: "Is our view of the universe due for another jolt?" (letter to Kenneth Sterling, 25 May 1936; *RB* 277). It wasn't, at least not from Miller's experiments, which are today regarded as erroneous, and which even in the 1930s were regarded skeptically by most physicists. Lovecraft's attendance at the lecture demonstrates his continued interest in the validity of Einstein's theories and in the ether, topics touched upon in chapters 5 and 11.

As the year 1936 entered autumn, and as Lovecraft entered the final half year of his life, astronomy could still capture his attention. Sufficiently memorable to be recalled in letters to more than one correspondent was Lovecraft's visit to a meeting of Providence's Skyscrapers astronomy club:

> October 9th I attended a meeting of the local organisation of amateur astronomers—'The Skyscrapers', which functions more or less under the auspices of Brown University—and was astonished at its degree of development. Some of the members are really serious scientific observers, and the society has recently purchased a well-known private observatory (that of the late F.E. Seagrave—whom Charles A. A. Parker once knew—with an 8″ refracting telescope[6]) in the western part of the state. It has separate meteor, variable star, planet, etc. sections, which hold meetings of their own and report as units, and enjoys the use of the college observatory. At the recent meeting there was an address on early Rhode-Island astronomy, and the reflecting telescope of Joseph Brown—used to observe the transit of Venus here on June 3, 1769 and owned by the college since 1780—was exhibited. (Unfinished letter to James F. Morton; *JFM* 392)

Charles Hugh Smiley (1903–1977), founder of the Skyscrapers, had come to Brown University in 1930 as an assistant professor of mathematics, but astronomy was his chief interest. In 1938 he would formally be made associate professor of astronomy and named director of Ladd Observatory. He had not waited, however, to form the Skyscrapers, which held its first meeting in May 1932. After his attendance at the

---

6. Seagrave Memorial Observatory, with its 8¼-inch telescope, is now operated by the Skyscrapers astronomy club.

12. Astronomy at the End

October meeting, Lovecraft wrote to Derleth (24 October 1936; *ES* 754): "It brings back my early astronomical interests so vividly that I am half-tempted to apply for membership!" Subsequent letters would instead carry increasing intimations of mortality.

Early Interests Crop Up Again

Considering that he was only forty-six years old at the time of his death, there is pathos in the lines within a letter to Morton, unfinished when Lovecraft died on 15 March 1937 (*JFM* 393): "Curious how one's early interests crop up again in one's sunset years." This sentiment had also been expressed in a letter to August Derleth: "Funny how early interests crop up again toward the end of one's life" (17 February 1937; *ES* 769). The early interest particularly in his mind was astronomy.

As 1937 arrived, Lovecraft's life was rushing toward its painful end. As his cancer progressed and he felt increasingly ill, the letter-writing essential to his social interactions became increasingly difficult. Nevertheless, in his final letters we find hopes for the future jumbled with remembrances of times past. Lovecraft began his letter to August Derleth of 17 February by noting that his handwriting had become so poor that he was forced to resort to the "hated clicker"—the typewriter—to be readable. Despite his dire condition, he wrote of his need to brush up on modern astronomy, so as to be able to update his early columns for a new series of newspaper articles on astronomy. The series would never be written (see chapter 6), but even at this late date Lovecraft was writing to Derleth as though it might be. He mentioned that he had begun to freshen his knowledge of astronomy, the progress of which had left him "absurdly behind." He expressed continued admiration for the Barritt-Serviss Star and Planet Finder that would eventually come into Derleth's hands, as would Lovecraft's Bardou telescope (*CE* 3.14). That Lovecraft still could look to the future as his life ebbed is conveyed by his remark that he would probably spend $1.50 on an annual subscription to Leon Barritt's *Monthly Evening Star Map* (*ES* 768–69). Writing his final letter to Derleth may have taken the ailing Lovecraft some time, so that the ideas expressed within may have had their origin some days before its date of 17 February. A specialist who saw Lovecraft on 16 February reportedly realized that Lovecraft's illness was terminal, something he told his patient during a visit on 27 February (*IAP* 1007).

Books introduced Lovecraft to astronomy, and it is fitting that books also appear in his last mentions of the subject. As he attempted to catch up with the progress of astronomy for the proposed newspaper series, a necessarily frugal Lovecraft patronized his local library rather than bookstores. John Charles Duncan's *Astronomy: A Text Book* (3rd ed. 1935) won especially favorable mention (*ES* 768; *JFM* 392).[7] Comparing Duncan's text to the one by Young that so thrilled him on his 1903 trolley ride, Lovecraft would have discovered notable changes in emphasis. Duncan's book devoted significant space to nebulae, the structure of the Milky Way, and galaxies beyond our own—topics given scant treatment in Young's book, indicative of the profound scientific ignorance of those subjects in 1903.

Edgar Allan Poe, Lovecraft's nineteenth-century predecessor in the development of the weird tale, is credited with genuine, if eccentrically presented, contributions to the science of astronomy (Tresch 306–7). No such advancement of the science can be associated with Lovecraft. Indeed, by the twentieth century progress in astronomy was increasingly, if not yet entirely, the work of professional researchers. However, if Lovecraft's name is not written with Hubble's or Leavitt's, his literary contributions were profoundly shaped by astronomy.

Astronomical influences on Lovecraft's writing range from nineteenth-century concepts that would have been familiar to Poe, such as ether and the nebular theory; to fin de siècle notions of planetary evolution and canal-building Martians; to early skepticism over the (mis)identification of unknown lights in the sky as intelligently piloted craft; to very twentieth-century notions, such as relativity and higher-dimensional ordering. While the last pushed the envelope of what was, by 1937, both a limited and an outdated formal education, Lovecraft's imagination was not subject to such constraints. His fiction, informed by astronomical knowledge, would influence both his contemporaries and those who came after him, and not only in the realm of fiction. As explored in prior chapters, Lovecraft's influence potentially extended to rocket scientists, such as Wernher von Braun and Jack Parsons, and to science popularizers, such as Willy Ley and Arthur C. Clarke. Together, their efforts helped humans begin to explore those celestial bodies that were important to Lovecraft throughout his life.

It is easy to regard the painful conclusion of Lovecraft's life with sympathy and sadness. Rather than ending this chapter with his agonizing death, instead let us back up five months to conclude with a stroll at

---

7. HPL also thought well of two "layman's manuals," Walter Bartky's *Highlights of Astronomy* (1935) and Thomas Stokley's *Stars and Telescopes* (1936).

dusk. On 28 October 1936, Lovecraft visited Neutaconkanut hill on the western edge of Providence. He gazed back at the city as the sun set:

> The upper windows of some of the taller towers held the fire of the sun after I had lost it, affording a spectacle of cryptic & curious glamour. Then I saw the great yellow disc of the Hunter's Moon (two days before full) floating above the belfries & minarets, while in the orange-glowing west Venus & Jupiter commenced to twinkle . . . The outspread city was rapidly lighting up, & lay like a constellation in the deepening dusk. The moon poured down increasing floods of pale gold, & the glow of Venus & Jupiter in the fading west grew intense. Then down the steep hillside to the car line (too cold for enjoyable walking without scenery to compensate for shivers) & back to the prosaic haunts of man. (Unfinished letter to James F, Morton; *JFM* 394)

Readers of this book who are themselves addicted to star-gazing may spare a thought for Lovecraft on some clear night when the stars twinkle and meteors fly—or could it be a Mi-Go flitting above?

The sky from Neutaconkanut hill as twilight darkened on 28 October 1936. Simulated with Stellarium planetarium software.

Appendix I
A Partial Timeline of Lovecraft and Astronomy

20 August 1890	Lovecraft is born
21 October 1891	Ladd Observatory is dedicated
1894	Lowell Observatory is established in Flagstaff, Arizona
April 1897	H. G. Wells begins to serialize *The War of the Worlds*
21 October 1897	Yerkes Observatory is dedicated
12 January–10 February 1898	Garrett P. Serviss serializes *Edison's Conquest of Mars*
22 February 1901	Thomas Anderson discovers the nova in "Beyond the Wall of Sleep"
12 February 1903	Lovecraft buys Young's *Lessons in Astronomy*
February 1903	Lovecraft acquires an Excelsior spyglass
July 1903	Lovecraft acquires his 2¼-inch telescope
2 August 1903	The first issue of Lovecraft's *Rhode Island Journal of Astronomy*
December 1903	Lovecraft gives his first astronomy lecture
December 1903	Lovecraft begins his study of the lunar crater Eratosthenes
September 1905	Einstein's Special Theory of Relativity is published
27 April 1906	Lovecraft begins astrophotography

3 June 1906	Lovecraft's letter criticizing astrology appears in the *Providence Sunday Journal*
27 July 1906	Lovecraft's first astronomy article in the *Pawtuxet Valley Gleaner*
1 August 1906	Lovecraft's first astronomy article for the Providence *Tribune*
14 September 1906	Lovecraft acquires a 3-inch Bardou telescope
28 December 1906	Last article by Lovecraft in the *Pawtuxet Valley Gleaner* known to survive
7 January 1907	Lovecraft is introduced to Percival Lowell
1 June 1908	Lovecraft's final astronomy article in the Providence *Tribune*
February 1909	Date of the last, incomplete issue of the *Rhode Island Journal of Astronomy*
1909	Lovecraft begins his personal *Astronomical Notebook*
26 December 1909	Lovecraft's letter to the *Providence Sunday Journal* tells of the public mistaking Venus for a mysterious airship
January 1910	An ill Lovecraft misses seeing a great comet
26 May 1910	Lovecraft sketches Halley's Comet in his *Astronomical Notebook*
1908–1912	Henrietta Leavitt discovers the Cepheid period-luminosity relation
1905–1913	The distinction between giant and dwarf stars is established
1 January 1914	Lovecraft's first astronomy article for the Providence *Evening News*
8 January 1914	Death of Winslow Upton, director of the Ladd Observatory
9 September 1914	Lovecraft begins criticism of astrologer Hartmann

A Partial Timeline of Lovecraft and Astronomy 349

17 September 1914	Last entry in Lovecraft's *Astronomical Notebook*
16 February 1915–17 May 1915	Lovecraft's astronomy articles for the *Asheville Gazette-News*
1915	John Edwards joins the staff of the Van Vleck Observatory
November 1915	Einstein presents the core of the General Theory of Relativity
1917	The 100-inch (2.5 m) telescope goes into operation at the Mount Wilson Observatory
1915–1919	Harlow Shapley shows that the sun is not near the center of our galaxy
24 April 1918	John Edwards dies
2 May 1918	Lovecraft's last astronomy article in the Providence *Evening News*
29 May 1919	Solar eclipse leading to the confirmation of the Theory of General Relativity
October 1919	"Beyond the Wall of Sleep" is published
December 1920	"Polaris" is published
1924	Edwin Hubble proves that the Milky Way is not the only galaxy
24 January 1925	Lovecraft's first total solar eclipse
16 March 1926	Robert Goddard launches his first liquid-fueled rocket
September 1927	"The Colour out of Space" is published
1927–1929	Edwin Hubble and George Lemaître discover the expanding universe
February 1928	"The Call of Cthulhu" is published
April 1929	"The Dunwich Horror" is published
13 March 1930	Discovery of Pluto (Yuggoth?) is announced
August 1931	"The Whisperer in Darkness" is published
5 May 1932	Organizational meeting of the Skyscrapers, Providence's amateur astronomy association

31 August 1932	Lovecraft's second total solar eclipse
July 1933	"The Dreams in the Witch House" is published
3 September 1934	Lovecraft visits Maria Mitchell Observatory on Nantucket
August 1935	"Collapsing Cosmoses" is written
September 1935	"The Challenge from Beyond" is published
December 1935–January 1936	Lovecraft visits Hayden Planetarium in New York City
January 1936	"In the Walls of Eryx" is written
February–April 1936	*At the Mountains of Madness* is published
November 1936	The "Shadow over Innsmouth" is published
22 July 1936	Lovecraft sees Peltier's Comet at Ladd Observatory
9 October 1936	Lovecraft visits the Skyscrapers astronomy club
15 March 1937	Lovecraft dies
4 December 1944	Frederick Slocum dies
3 June 1948	The 200-inch (5-m) Palomar telescope is dedicated
4 October 1957	Sputnik is launched

Appendix II
Lovecraft Dabbles in Astrophotography

We have become rather blasé about seeing fabulous astronomical images. Newspapers, television, and the Internet showcase colorful space telescope depictions of star clusters, galaxies, and nebulae. Robotic space probes detail the clouds of Jupiter and the valleys of Mars. Even amateur astronomers, equipped with electronic light detectors, now produce thrilling full-color views of celestial sights that go far beyond those produced by the best-instrumented observatories of Lovecraft's youth.

By 1906, fifteen-year-old H. P. Lovecraft had become a skilled visual observer of the night sky, adept at identifying constellations and the brighter stars visible to the naked eye (chapter 1). At the telescope, he could point out by name craters on the moon or show the rings of Saturn and the belts of Jupiter. Among professional astronomers, however, the switch from the eye to the photographic plate was well under way.

In the early 1900s, astronomical photography was still relatively new, having flourished for scarcely three decades. The sun and moon had been successfully photographed beginning in the 1840s. However, the sun and the moon are bright objects. Fainter objects proved a challenge to daguerreotypes or the insensitive wet-collodion plates of the Civil War era. Widespread application of photography to astronomy awaited the introduction of more sensitive and convenient dry photographic plates in the 1870s. During the 1880s and 1890s, photography with these new plates became one of the major tools—for many purposes *the* major tool—of the astronomer. In 1903, Lovecraft began to visit Brown University's Ladd Observatory (chapter 2). Winslow Upton, first director of that observatory, was well aware of the uses of astronomical photography. He had begun to apply it to various projects soon after the observatory opened.

By the turn of the twentieth century, celestial photography was not solely the preserve of professional astronomers. The very first issue of *Popular Astronomy* (September 1893) included an article titled "Astronomy with a Small Camera" (as well as an article on constellations by

Ladd Observatory director Winslow Upton). Through his reading, and probably through his acquaintance with the Ladd Observatory staff, Lovecraft would have become familiar with the growing utility of astronomical photography. It is natural that he would want to try his hand at it. However, Lovecraft first turned to photography to further another of his enthusiasms, meteorology. At some point he began photographing different types of clouds. When his cloud photography began is unclear, but the May 1906 hectographed issue of his *Rhode Island Journal of Astronomy* announced that his efforts in that field had been resumed. Lovecraft does not tell us what camera he used for his initial foray into cloud photography. A simple box camera of the sort used at the time for popular photography may have sufficed. However, when his cloud photography resumed in 1906, he employed a new camera, one that he could use for stars as well as clouds.

Information about this camera is divided between Lovecraft's meteorological and astronomical writings. In his usual editorial style, he wrote in the June 1906 issue of the *Rhode Island Journal of Astronomy:* "The R. I. Journal has now begun the work of celestial photography. We have procured a camera with a 3" Darlot Lens of 22" focus." More information is found in the *Third Annual Report of the Providence Meteorological Station*, which Lovecraft published 16 January 1907 (*CE* 3.84–87). He writes of

Total solar eclipse of 28 May 1900. Excerpted from a photograph taken with a Darlot lens of 22 inches focal length during the Ladd Observatory expedition to Centreville, Virginia. Brown Digital Repository. Brown University Library.

his cloud photography that "This work was performed with a new 6.5 × 8.5 camera . . . Celestial views were also taken. The camera lens is by Darlot, body by Edwards, and back by Blair Optical Co."

That description calls for a little expansion. Darlot was a well-known French manufacturer of quality lenses for photography and other purposes. Edwards is presumably John Edwards, the longtime assistant at the

Ladd Observatory who helped young Lovecraft with a number of his astronomical endeavors (chapter 2). The Blair Optical Company was a Boston camera firm, later acquired by Kodak. Assuming that 6.5 × 8.5 is a size in inches, it would be "full plate" size in the terminology of early photography, although by 1906 sheet film could be used instead of photographic plates.

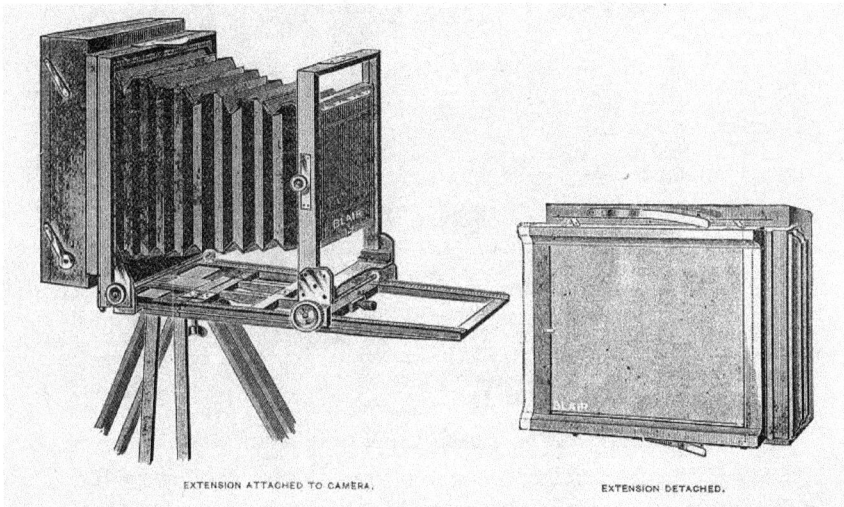

The 1898 catalog of the Blair Company shows an extension box that could be added to a camera to hold 6.5 × 8.5-inch photographic plates. In the picture it is shown attached to a folding camera. The back of Lovecraft's camera might have been made from something of its sort. Collection of the California Museum of Photography, University of California, Riverside, gift of Larry Pierce and Sharon Moore.

The involvement of Edwards is confirmed by a letter that Lovecraft wrote to Jonquil Leiber on 29 November 1936 (*CLM* 290). In that letter he mentioned that Ladd Observatory assistant John Edwards had helped him secure "a long-focus celestial camera," which sounds very much like the camera with the Darlot lens. Edwards would have been familiar with Darlot lenses. A Darlot lens of 22 inches focal length had been used on Brown University's successful expedition to observe the total eclipse of the sun from Centreville, Virginia, in 1900. Edwards was a member of the expedition. For several years around the turn of the century, he was also involved with attempts to photograph Leonid meteors from the Ladd Observatory grounds using cameras on simple mountings. A photograph showing the Ladd observers ready to go on

14 November 1898, shows a camera similar in appearance to the one Lovecraft used eight years later.

This cropped image from a photograph from 1898 of the Ladd Observatory's equipment for photographing meteors shows a long-focus camera (the lower one on the tripod) similar to that used by Lovecraft in 1906. Ladd Observatory astronomer Frederick Slocum stands nearby. Courtesy of Brown University Library.

A 3-inch lens would have enough light-gathering power to be well suited for amateur astrophotography. Such a large camera would not have been attached to Lovecraft's relatively small 2¼-inch and 3-inch aperture telescopes. It would be used on its own, fixed to some sort of mounting by which it could be pointed and held steady during an exposure. It might have been used wide open, at full aperture, to take full advantage of its light gathering power, but images across a large field of view might have been sharper if the lens were diaphragmed to a somewhat smaller diameter (giving a higher f-ratio).

What sort of photographs would Lovecraft's long focus camera produce? Its photographs would not seem spectacular to those acquainted with modern digital imaging. If 22 inches is indeed the effective focal length, then the image scale of the camera was 2.6 degrees per inch (1 degree per centimeter). At that scale, the full moon would be about a fifth of an inch (half a centimeter) in size on photographic negatives. That would serve to show the phases of the moon and the lunar seas (maria), but not its craters. Lovecraft noted that when he photographed Venus, presumably with this camera, it appeared only as a star would, which is consistent with the expected resolution of the camera. Even when Venus is at its nearest, its crescent is only about 1 arcminute in size. That would correspond to a very small image on Lovecraft's photographic plates, about 0.006 inch in size. Other planets would have similarly starlike images.

Lovecraft's drawing of his camera in the August 1906 issue of the *Rhode Island Journal of Astronomy*. It is depicted on a simple equatorial mounting. Howard P. Lovecraft Collection, Ms. Lovecraft, Brown University Library.

Lovecraft does not specify the film or film size he used for his astronomical photographs, or even whether he used flexible film or the then still common glass plates. For his renewed work on clouds, he used a "3¼ × 4¼ quarter plate" camera. That may just mean that he used 3¼ × 4¼-inch film in his long-focus camera. If the same "quarter plate" size were used for astrophotography, each exposure would cover an 8.4 × 11-degree field of view. The distance between the two pointer stars at the end of the bowl of the Big Dipper is about 5 degrees. A single photograph would be about the size of the Big Dipper's bowl. If full-plate, and more costly, 6.5 × 8.5-inch film were employed, then the field of view would be about 17 × 22 degrees, almost but not quite large enough to cover the entire Big Dipper. We do not know whether Lovecraft developed and printed his own photographs, but it is possible that he did so.

Most photographic emulsions of the early 1900s were more sensitive to blue light than to red, and film sensitivity was low compared to the high-speed photographic films developed later. Thus, long exposure photographs of the sky would not show stars as faint as could have been secured in later years with the same camera and exposure time. On the plus side, Providence skies in 1906 were less brightened by light pollution than would be the case in subsequent decades. Still, dazzling images of the star clouds of the Milky Way were probably beyond Lovecraft's methods.

The bright stars of the constellation Cassiopeia might have looked something like this on one of Lovecraft's photographs. Astronomers often worked with the original photographic negatives rather than making a positive print. Too long an exposure with an unmoving camera would produce trailed star images rather than points. H. Smith photograph.

Lovecraft described the targets of his first efforts in astrophotography in the June 1906 *Rhode Island Journal of Astronomy:*

> The first photo. was taken April 27, 1906, of the 4^d moon, and since then we have photographed the horizontal sun or moon (for distortion) also the moon in various phases, and diff't sky regions. The latter we give 1^m exposure, which makes short trails. This is a great advance, for we have never before applied photography beyond the clouds. In negatives and prints of the full moon we can easily see the spots.

The spots are presumably the lunar maria, the dark areas that allow us to imagine the man in the moon.

Lovecraft's one-minute exposures of stars produced trails because of the rotation of the earth. Such trails would be short for stars located near Polaris, close to the north celestial pole, but longer for stars near the celestial equator. At the celestial equator, a one-minute exposure with his camera fixed in position would produce a star trail a tenth of an inch long. But what were his "horizontal" sun and moon photographs?

Lovecraft drew this view of the Moon in 1903. Photographs with his long-focus camera would have revealed the lunar maria, but with less detail than shown in the drawing. Howard P. Lovecraft Collection, Ms. Lovecraft, Brown University Library.

In this case, "horizontal" refers to the sun and moon when they were located low in the sky, close to the horizon, a phenomenon Lovecraft would have seen mentioned in his copy of Burritt's *Geography of the Heavens*. Lovecraft had become intrigued by the distortion of images of the sun and moon caused by atmospheric refraction when they were low in the sky. In the October 1906 *Rhode Island Journal of Astronomy*, he noted that "The photographs of Professor Prinz, of the Brussels Observatory, show a great distortion of the sun's disc when on the horizon. The ratio is 75 to 84. The R.I. Journal is doing the same work although results are not yet out." A drawing of the flattened horizontal moon was included in the December 1906 issue of the *Journal*.

Lovecraft's drawing of the horizontal moon in the December 1906 issue of the *Rhode Island Journal of Astronomy*. The stars of the Hyades cluster are above the Moon. Howard P. Lovecraft Collection, Ms. Lovecraft, Brown University Library.

Lovecraft Dabbles in Astrophotography 359

How did Lovecraft learn of Professor Prinz's work? Professor Wilhelm Prinz (1857–1910), who, like Lovecraft, had some interest in William Pickering's studies of changes on the moon, had published a paper on the subject: "Photographies du soleil couchant" (Prinz 1898). It is possible that Lovecraft came across Prinz's paper, or one of his later notes on the subject, in the Ladd Observatory library. Alas, the *Rhode Island Journal of Astronomy* would cease publication before the results of his horizontal moon photography were written up.

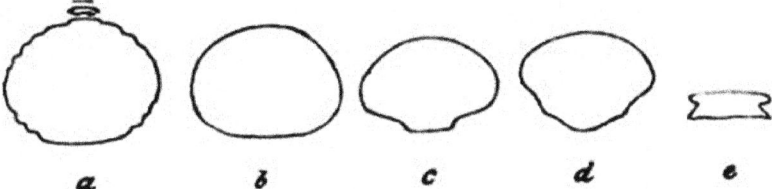

Fig. 8. — Aspects du soleil conchant, ou levant, d'après des observations et des photographies.

Drawings of the distorted Sun near the horizon, from Prinz's 1898 paper.

Sometimes, as in the November 1906 *Rhode Island Journal of Astronomy,* Lovecraft appears to use the term "horizontal moon" in another sense, to refer to what is now frequently called the "moon illusion." This is the apparent enlargement of the moon when it is seen near the horizon with the naked eye. This is an optical illusion, as the moon's image is not really larger near the horizon. By contrast, the atmospheric distortion of the moon is a genuine change in its apparent dimensions. Livesey (DPO 22–23) criticized Lovecraft's use of the term "horizontal moon" in this sense, arguing that Burritt's *Geography of the Heavens* ought to have set him straight on the terminology. However, perhaps we can exonerate Lovecraft on this point. The term "horizontal moon" is not mentioned in the original edition of *Geography of the Heavens* (1833) and, when it does appear in later editions, the term is not used consistently through different revisions of Burritt.[1]

The June 1906 issue of the *Rhode Island Journal of Astronomy* noted that he had "acquired an equatorial motion for telescope and camera." The August issue of the *Journal* included a drawing of the camera upon

---

1. The term is used in Burritt's 1836 edition in the sense of the illusory enlargement of the moon near the horizon. The 1856 edition, revised by Hiram Mattison, uses the term "horizontal moon" in connection with the apparent flattening of the moon when it is near the horizon.

its equatorial mounting. There are many variants of such a mounting, and Lovecraft's drawing does not make the details of his arrangement clear. An equatorial mounting would have an axis that can be pointed toward the celestial pole. The camera or telescope can then be rotated with one motion around the polar axis. Because that axis is parallel to the rotational axis of the earth, motion of a camera around such an axis at the right rate of speed can compensate for the rotation of the Earth, so that star images remain point-like rather than trailing on long exposures. The motion can be supplied by a mechanism, as was the case with the weight-driven clock-drive that moved the Ladd Observatory 12-inch telescope. There is, however, no evidence that such an expensive clock-drive was fitted to Lovecraft's equatorial mounting. Nonetheless, if the rotational motion can be carefully provided by hand, such a mounting will still follow the apparent motion of the stars, at least for modest intervals of time, until the person adjusting the mounting tires. Lovecraft may have attempted long-exposure photographs with his equatorial mounting, but, if he did, he did not provide an account of his efforts in the *Rhode Island Journal of Astronomy*.

As mentioned, Lovecraft's long focus camera did not provide a scale large enough to show the craters of the moon. Had Lovecraft wanted to capture lunar craters on his photographs, he would have needed a different sort of camera. He might, for example, have placed a small box camera behind the eyepiece of his 3-inch refracting telescope. In that way it might have been possible to take a snapshot that would satisfactorily expose the moon, a relatively bright target, and show its surface detail. However, we have not found evidence that he made this attempt.

We suspect that Lovecraft's dabbling in astrophotography was not long sustained, but our access to his daily astronomical endeavors recedes with the ending of regular publication of the *Rhode Island Journal of Astronomy* early in 1907. The *Astronomical Notebook* Lovecraft kept intermittently between 1909 and 1914 makes no mention at all of photography. Perhaps writing his newspaper articles on astronomy began to occupy much of the time that could otherwise have been devoted to photographic experiments. Or perhaps he found photographic work not to his taste. To get any scientific results from his photographs would have required tedious measurements of images, something that Livesey (DPO 76–78) thought would not have been to Lovecraft's taste. Lovecraft's breakdown in 1908, which ended his high school attendance, may have made such photographic measurements particularly uncongenial.

In his letter to Jonquil Leiber of 29 November 1936, Lovecraft noted that he still retained the astronomical photographs he had taken in his youth. We have not discovered what happened to his astronomical and cloud photographs after his death in 1937. Someone unfamiliar with astronomy who came across his negatives might have dismissed them as unimportant, if their nature were recognized at all. Nonetheless, perhaps they exist unremarked in some private collection. They would not have shown anything new about Providence skies, but it would be pleasant nonetheless to see some of the fruits of Lovecraft's brief excursion into celestial photography.

Appendix III
Astronomy with Lovecraft's First Telescope

I bought Lovecraft's first telescope. Well, not Lovecraft's actual first telescope, but an antique telescope of the type that Lovecraft acquired in February 1903. Howard Phillips Lovecraft's enthusiasm for astronomy burgeoned as 1902 turned into 1903. It was natural that the twelve-year-old should want to observe the heavens through a telescope as well as with the eye alone. His first telescope was, however, hardly a splurge. It was an Excelsior spyglass, sold by the New York mail-order firm of Kirtland Brothers & Company for the grand sum of 99 cents.

A advertisement for the Excelsior from 1901. The Man in the Moon apparently objects to being spied upon.

Excelsior telescopes, made in Germany, were widely advertised at the end of the nineteenth and start of the twentieth centuries by a variety of vendors, with slight variations in construction over time. Astronomy was by no means their only selling point. As one advertisement from 1901 stated: "Every sojourner in the country or at seaside resorts should

---

Originally published by H. A. Smith in *Lovecraft Annual* No. 15 (2021).

certainly secure one of these instruments, and no farmer should be without one." However, that ad also touted the line: "Face to face with the man in the moon!" I even came across an advertisement from 1913 that implied that the *Titanic* might have been saved had it been equipped with a telescope like the Excelsior. Although Excelsior telescopes were sold for decades, after World War I the price increased, usually to between $1.50 and $2.50.

To my knowledge, Lovecraft never explicitly states that his first telescope was an Excelsior, so why do I think it was? He wrote that he bought his first telescope for 99 cents from Kirtland Brothers early in 1903. In the August 1903 issue of his juvenile scientific magazine, the *Scientific Gazette,* Lovecraft wrote that the 99-cent telescope sold by Kirtland Brothers is "a big bargain worth $10.00 named 'Excelsior.'" In the second issue of the *Rhode Island Journal of Astronomy,* dated 9 August 1903, Lovecraft offered to sell a second-hand Excelsior for the reduced price of 50 cents. So, putting two and two together, I think we can have confidence that the Excelsior was the one.

A Kirtland Brothers & Company ad for the Excelsior in 1906, with the price jumped to $1.00 from 99 cents.

In July 1903, Lovecraft (or his mother) purchased a larger telescope from Kirtland Brothers for $16.50. It boasted an objective lens 2¼ inches in diameter, and for the next few years most of the astronomical observations in Lovecraft's self-published science magazines were made with its aid. He did not, however, despise his inexpensive starter telescope. The 21 May 1905 issue of the *Rhode Island Journal of Astronomy* carried an article titled "The Cheap Telescope." It begins with the narration of an advertisement for a 99-cent telescope that reads very much like one of the advertisements for the Excelsior. However, Lovecraft continued: "The average reader pays no attention to these ads., thinking such cheapness below his notice. Such, however, is not the case." He went on to note that he owned three cheap telescopes, the cheapest of them being his 99-cent instrument. Despite their price, he found that the views of celestial objects his cheap telescopes provided were surprisingly good. This led to the question, what could I see through a telescope like the Excelsior? What better way to answer than to acquire my own Excelsior and give it a try?

Fortunately, since they were widely sold for years, antique Excelsiors can still be purchased today. Mine came via eBay. I didn't need a pristine example, untouched by time or human hand, with a perfect original box and a correspondingly high price tag. Mine does have its original box, but both it and the telescope itself have obvious dings and wear, hence its $20 price. However, my Excelsior is still fully functional. In fact, my $20 in 2019 is not very different from the value of 99 cents in 1903, at least according to some inflation calculators.

My Excelsior telescope with its now somewhat battered original box. The draw tubes are at much less than their full extension. The box features a cap with solar filter that allows direct viewing of solar eclipses and sunspots. That solar cap is detached in the photograph.

What did I get for my $20? As I mentioned, the telescope came in a battered but original Kirtland Brothers & Company cardboard box. The label glued to the box featured the "solar eyepiece," to which it gave a 24 April 1906 patent date. Alas, my Excelsior was therefore made a few years after the one Lovecraft purchased—so much for fantasies of having the same Excelsior Lovecraft once owned. The label is headlined "'The Excelsior' Telescope and Microscope Combined"—more about that microscope a bit later. Kirtland Brothers were apparently jealous of their product, because the label on the box claims that unscrupulous vendors were stealing their advertising pictures to sell inferior telescopes.

Astronomy with Lovecraft's First Telescope

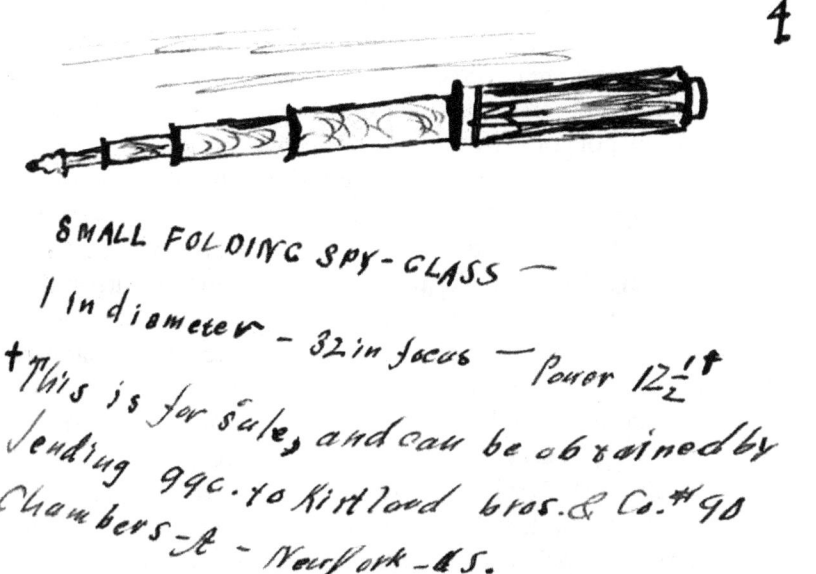

Lovecraft's drawing of a spyglass in his *Science Library* matches my Excelsior very well. The science magazines that Lovecraft "published" in his youth are now online at the Brown Digital Repository.

Somewhat oddly, to me at least, the label does not specify the magnifying power of the telescope. Almost all Excelsior advertisements are also silent on that subject. Lovecraft in the *Scientific Gazette* and in the *Science Library* gave the Excelsior a magnifying power of 12½. However, in his "Cheap Telescope" article, he stated that his 99-cent telescope magnified 10 times. To complicate the issue further, I came across one advertisement for the Excelsior that claimed a magnifying power of 16. It is possible, I suppose, that not all Excelsiors were built with exactly the same optics, and that not all had the same magnifying power. I measured the magnification of my Excelsior to be about 10, in good agreement with the Cheap Telescope article.

My Excelsior looks very much like the drawing of the 99-cent Kirtland Brothers telescope that Lovecraft included in the *Science Library*. Inside its cardboard box I found a telescope about a foot long with its drawtubes closed. That grows to three feet when all four pull tubes are extended to full length from the tube holding the objective. Brass caps hold the objective lens and the eyepiece, but the tubes themselves appear to be made of what looks like stiff cardboard, although the label on the box calls them "drawn paper" and Lovecraft stated that his cheap telescopes were papier-mâché. The draw tubes are secured with brass fastenings and are covered with decorative and water-resistant paper. A small cap that can be slid over the eyepiece holds a dark solar filter for viewing sunspots or solar eclipses. The objective lens of my Excelsior is about one inch across, with a focal length of about 32 inches. However, a diaphragm behind it limits the effective aperture to ¾ of an inch. The eyepiece is a three-lens terrestrial one. That is, an extra lens is added to a two-lens eyepiece to make the image right-side-up rather than inverted, as is usual with eyepieces made for purely astronomical use.

Simple single lenses do not focus light of all colors to the same point. This chromatic aberration can produce images that are not sharp in all colors and which appear to have colored fringes. That fault can be partially remedied by using an achromatic objective lens, composed of two different types of glass. My Kirtland Brothers Excelsior label does not claim it to have an achromatic lens, and Lovecraft's writings signify that he believed "cheap telescope" objective lenses to be non-achromatic. However, some, but by no means all, advertisements of the 1899–1910 period call the Excelsior an achromatic telescope. I have not attempted to disassemble the lens mounting of my Excelsior, but the objective looks to me as though it might be a single lens. Nevertheless, as Lovecraft noted, if a small non-achromatic lens has a long focal length compared to its size (a high focal ratio), then chromatic aberration can be reduced so as to be unimportant. That is the case with the Excelsior.

On inspection, my eBay Excelsior appeared to have safely survived shipping, but what kind of images did it actually produce? I took the telescope outside and removed its solar filter. I began by pointing it at some distant trees. I slid the tubes back and forth until I achieved focus. The images of the trees were sharp, and showed little distortion until very near the edge of the field of view. But would I see what Lovecraft wrote that a "cheap telescope" should reveal when I turned the Excelsior on the heavens?

Lovecraft wrote that his 99-cent telescope provided "excellent views of the moon." The moon was in the waning gibbous phase when I first turned my Excelsior toward it. The image of the moon was sharp and revealed only slight chromatic aberration. The gray lunar maria that make up the Man in the Moon were clearly defined. White rays diverged from the bright crater Tycho. Toward the terminator, where shadows were long, many of the larger craters could be recognized. Like Galileo,

I could see that the moon was a world rather than just a light in the sky—a promising beginning. On other nights with different phases, I again turned the Excelsior toward the moon. The views were similarly pleasing. Excellent views of the moon? For a telescope of its size, I would check "yes."

This figure illustrates the detail that can be seen when the Excelsior is pointed at the moon (but it is not actually a photograph taken through the Excelsior).

On to the sun. I slid the solar filter into place, and it dimmed the sun's image enough to provide a comfortable view. I kept my views brief at first, because I was not sure how well the filter was keeping out the sun's infrared light. I have not experienced any signs of retinal burning, so the solar cap is probably safe enough in that regard. It should be mentioned, however, that eyepiece solar filters can be dangerous. Even if they adequately block light, they heat up as they absorb the sun's radiation. Sometimes that heat can cause them to crack suddenly, letting the solar blaze through and risking the eye. That is less of a risk with so small a telescope as the Excelsior, but I still do not recommend solar observation with an eyepiece filter.

It was approaching minimum in the eleven-year solar cycle when I turned my Excelsior to the sun, and I had to wait a few weeks before any sizable sunspot appeared. When one did, I was able to see it as a well-defined dot on the sun's disk. When sunspots are more plentiful, the Excelsior should do a good job of revealing the larger spots—although I think I will project the sun's image onto paper to look for spots rather than trust the solar filter.

So far so good. However, holding a three-foot telescope steady by hand is difficult. The field of view is small, only about 1⅓ degrees (less than three moon diameters), and unless I prop the tube against a tree or post, the sun and moon are difficult to keep fixed in view. The Excelsior is much more difficult to use than the much shorter modern prism binoculars, which also have a wider field of view (typically around 6 degrees for a 10-power instrument). I soon concluded that I would not have been a good lookout in olden days, trying to scout out lurking pirates through my hand-held spyglass from the crow's nest atop a tossing sailing vessel. Lovecraft eventually made a table stand to hold his cheap telescope, and I could certainly see why. Attaching my Excelsior to a sturdy camera tripod helped considerably.

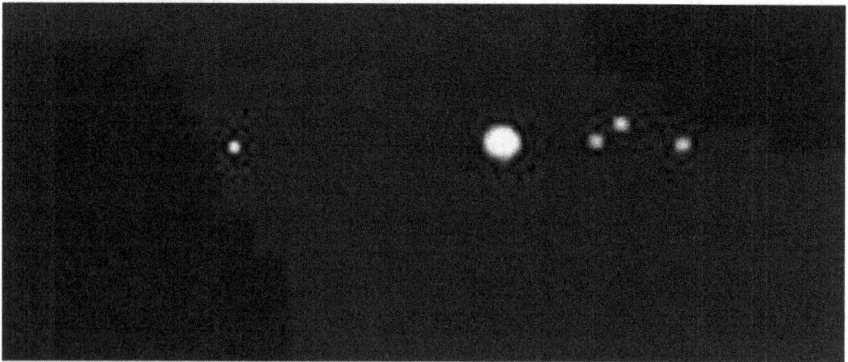

This illustrates the amount of detail that the Excelsior reveals when turned toward Jupiter. The four Galilean moons are visible unless they are close to the brilliant disk of the planet, which shines with greater glare than the figure might suggest.

Astronomy with Lovecraft's First Telescope

Jupiter was celestial target number three. The image again was sharp. Even at only 10 power, I could see that Jupiter had a tiny disk rather than the point-like appearance of a star. No details on the planet itself could be discerned. However, all four of the Galilean moons of Jupiter could be seen when they were not positioned too near the much brighter planet. A patient Galileo could have eventually measured the orbital periods of the Jovian moons with an Excelsior, but I did not target Jupiter often enough to attempt that feat.

Galileo's drawing of the Pleiades, with additional stars revealed by his telescope, from the Sidereus Nuncius. My view was not too dissimilar.

When the Excelsior was pointed toward Saturn, I could tell that the planet was extended in size along the direction of the long-axis of the rings, but I could not tell that the extension was due to a ring system. By contrast, when Venus was almost between the earth and the sun, I could clearly see its crescent form. As Venus became more distant from the earth, smaller in apparent size, and closer to being full, it became hard to tell what its phase was using the Excelsior.

Lovecraft would have observed from areas around his Providence homes, but urban light pollution has become much worse since 1903. I sought a location with a dark sky for my next trials. When I turned the Excelsior on the stars, I found that its narrow field of view and relatively small aperture limited what I could see. A few double-stars separated by more than about 20 arc seconds (an arc second is 1/3600 of a degree) could be recognized as double. Albireo (blue and yellow stars separated by 35 seconds of arc) could just be seen as two stars, but the blue color of the fainter star was not well shown. Mizar, a double star with components of unequal brightness separated by 14 arc seconds, was not resolved.

The Pleiades star cluster made a pretty target, as the Excelsior brought into view many more stars than could be seen with my eye alone. In seeing these additional members of the Pleiades, I again duplicated a discovery of Galileo. Pleiades stars of the sixth and seventh magnitude were easily seen. None of the nebulosity surrounding the stars of the Pleiades was visible, but I would not have expected it to be with such a small telescope.

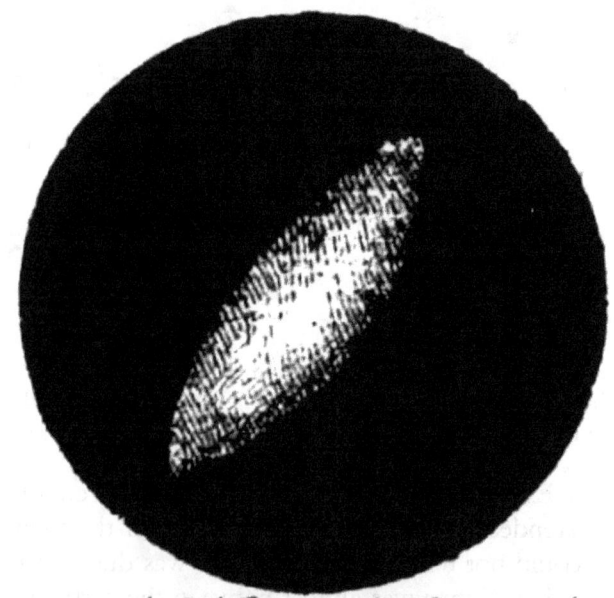

The drawing of the Andromeda Nebula in R. A. Proctor's *Half-Hours with the Telescope* (1878 edition) resembles my view with the Excelsior, although in my case the nebula stretched across the entire field of view.

The Great Nebula (M42) within Orion's Sword was a bit disappointing. It was visible, and more stars could be seen around it than the eye alone revealed, but the gaseous nebula itself was not bright or detailed. Galileo also saw additional stars around M42, but he made no note of its nebulosity in the *Sidereus Nuncius*. The brighter globular star clusters, such as M3 and M13, were fuzzy spots in the sky— nothing to write home about. The Andromeda Nebula (not yet confirmed as a galaxy separate from the Milky Way when Lovecraft first observed) was an elongated glow, brighter toward the center, that stretched across the entire width of the field of view. Overall, I would not recommend the Excelsior to today's deep sky observers, who want to tease out the faintest glows of distant galaxies, but it performed as well as one would expect given its small aperture.

Now what about that statement on the label that the Excelsior was both a "telescope and microscope"? If the final drawtube of the Excelsior, holding the optics for the terrestrial eyepiece, is removed, it can be used as a low-power microscope. One looks through the end of the tube as usual, and moves the tube toward or away from the subject until a magnified image comes into focus. Voilà, microscope as well as telescope.

Overall, I saw through the Excelsior enough to confirm Lovecraft's conclusion that such instruments are not to be despised. However, will I continue to use my Excelsior? I must admit that the answer is: not often. Its small field of view and unwieldy length make it too inconvenient compared to modern binoculars, especially those capable of image stabilization. However, in 1903 the Excelsior was much cheaper than a good pair of binoculars. Lovecraft wrote of spending the fabulous sum of $55 around 1907 on a pair of Bausch & Lomb prism binoculars. That would be the equivalent of more than a thousand dollars in 2019. Opera glasses or field glasses lacking prisms were cheaper, but still cost several dollars and typically had magnifying powers a third or a half that of the Excelsior. One can see why the inexpensive Excelsior successfully sold for decades.

The opportunity has not yet arisen for me to make all possible tests of my Excelsior. I have, for example, not yet ventured to Dunwich to confirm the Excelsior's effectiveness in delineating the features of any unearthly Whateley who happens to be momentarily puffed into view while climbing Sentinel Hill. The stars haven't yet been right for such an experiment. Maybe next year.

Bibliography

Adams, Mark B. "Last Judgment: The Visionary Biology of J. B. S. Haldane." *Journal of the History of Biology* 33 (Winter 2000): 457–91.

Aldiss, Brian W. *The Saliva Tree and Other Strange Growths*. Boston: Gregg Press, 1981.

Arnold, Edwin Lester. *Lieut. Gullivar Jones: His Vacation*. 1905. New York: Arno Press, 1975.

Ashley, Mike, and Robert A. W. Lowndes. *The Gernsback Days: A Study of the Evolution of Modern Science Fiction from 1911 to 1936*. Holicong, PA: Wildside Press, 2004.

Asimov, Isaac. "What Truck?" *Magazine of Fantasy & Science Fiction* 65 (August 1983): 119–28.

Astor IV, John Jacob. *A Journey in Other Worlds: A Romance of the Future*. London: Longmans, Green, 1894.

Bailer-Jones, Coryn A. L. "Lost in Space? Relativistic Interstellar Navigation Using an Astrometric Star Catalogue." *arXiv,* 02 June 2021. arxiv.org/abs/2103.10389

Barlowe, Wayne Douglas; Summers, Ian; and Meacham, Beth. *Barlowe's Guide to Extraterrestrials*. 1979. New York: Workman, 1987.

Barnard, Edward Emerson. Review of W. H. Pickering's *The Moon*. *Astrophysical Journal,* 20 (December 1904): 359–64.

Baxter, Stephen. "From the Brick Moon to Island One: Space Habitats in Science Fiction Before O'Neill's *High Frontier*." *Journal of the British Interplanetary Society* 72 (2019): 296–301. ["From"]

———. "H. G. Wells's *The War of the Worlds* as a Controlling Metaphor for the Twentieth Century." *The Wellsian: Journal of the H. G. Wells Society* 32 (2009): 3–16. ["Metaphor"]

———. *The Massacre of Mankind*. New York: Crown, 2017. [*Massacre*]

———. "The Shadow over the Moon." In Stephen Jones, ed. *The Lovecraft Squad: Dreaming*. New York: Pegasus, 2018. 171–206. ["Shadow"]

Bear, Elizabeth. "Shoggoths in Bloom." 2008. In Ross E. Lockhart, ed. *The Book of Cthulhu: Tales Inspired by H. P. Lovecraft*. New York: Night Shade, 2011. 149–68.

Beatty, J. Kelly. "Case for 'Ashen Light' Weakens." *Sky & Telescope* 101 (May 2001): 27.

Beer, Gillian. "'The Death of the Sun': Victorian Solar Physics and Solar Myth." In J. D. Bullen, ed. *The Sun Is God: Painting, Literature and Mythology in the Nineteenth Century*. Oxford: Clarendon Press, 1989. 159–80.

Benford, Gregory, and David Brin. "Paris Conquers All." In Kevin J. Anderson, ed. *War of the Worlds: Global Dispatches*. New York: Bantam Spectra, 1996. 231–50.

Bennett, Chris. "H. P. Lovecraft and the Origins of 420." *Cannabis Culture,* 19 April 2010. www.cannabisculture.com/content/2010/04/19/hp-lovecraft-and-origins-420/

Bergerac, Cyrano de. "Voyage to the Moon." 1657. In Sam Moskowitz, ed. *Masterpieces of Science Fiction*. Westport, CT: Hyperion Press, 1974. 27–43.

Bergonzi, Bernard. *The Early H. G. Wells: A Study of the Scientific Romances*. Manchester: Manchester University Press, 1961.

Bleiler, Richard, "H. P. Lovecraft's First Appearance in Print." *Lovecraft Annual* No. 14 (2020): 26–36.

Bloch, Robert. "Notebook Found in a Deserted House." 1951. In August Derleth, ed. *Tales of the Cthulhu Mythos*. Sauk City, WI: Arkham House, 1969. 222–41.

Bogdanov, Alexander. *Red Star: The First Bolshevik Utopia*. 1908. Bloomington: Indiana University Press, 1984.

Bradbury, Ray. *The Martian Chronicles*. 1950. New York: Bantam Spectra, 1979.

Braun, Wernher von. *The Mars Project*. Urbana: University of Illinois Press, 1953.

Brin, Glen David. "The 'Great Silence': The Controversy concerning Extraterrestrial Intelligent Life." *Quarterly Journal of the Royal Astronomical Society* 24 (September 1983): 283–309.

Brunner, Bernd. *Moon: A Brief History*. New Haven: Yale University Press, 2010.

Burritt, Elijah Hinsdale. *Geography of the Heavens*, Boston: Allen & Ticknor, 1833.

Burritt, Elijah Hinsdale. *The Geography of the Heavens and Class Book of Astronomy: Accompanied by a Celestial Atlas*. Rev. Hiram Mattison. New York: F. J. Huntington, 1853.

Burroughs, Edgar Rice. *The Gods of Mars*. 1913. Chicago: A. C. McClurg, 1918. [*Gods*]

———. *A Princess of Mars*. 1912. New York: Grosset & Dunlap, 1917. [*Princess*]

———. *The Warlord of Mars*. 1914. Chicago: A. C. Clurg, 1919. [*Warlord*]

Caidin, Martin; Barbree, Jay; and Wright, Susan. *Destination Mars: In Art, Myth, and Science*. New York: Penguin Studio, 1997.

Callaghan, Gavin. "A Reprehensible Habit: H. P. Lovecraft and the Munsey Magazines." In Robert H. Waugh, ed. *Lovecraft and Influence: His Predecessors and Successors*. Lanham, MD: Scarecrow Press, 2013. 69–82.

Campbell, Ramsey. *The Inhabitant of the Lake and Less Welcome Tenants*. Sauk City, WI: Arkham House, 1964. [*Inhabitant*]

———. "The Mine on Yuggoth." 1964. In Lin Carter, ed. *The Spawn of Cthulhu*. New York: Ballantine, 1971. 260–74. ["Mine"]

Cannon, Peter. *The Chronology out of Time: Dates in the Fiction of H. P. Lovecraft*. 1986. West Warwick, RI: Necronomicon Press, 2019.

———. *The Lovecraft Chronicles*. Poplar Bluff, MO: Mythos, 2004. [*Chronicles*]

Canote, Terence Towles. "Shared Universes Before the Marvel Cinematic Universe." *A Shroud of Thoughts,* 22 August 2014. mercurie.blogspot.com/2014/08/shared-universes-before-marvel.html

Card, Jeb J. *Spooky Archaeology: Myth and the Science of the Past*. Albuquerque: University of New Mexico Press, 2018.

Carter, John. *Sex and Rockets: The Occult World of Jack Parsons*. 1999. Rev. ed. Port Townsend, WA: Feral House, 2005.

Carter, Lin. "Out of the Ages." 1975. In Robert M. Price, ed. *The Xothic Legend Cycle: The Complete Mythos Fiction of Lin Carter*. Hayward, CA: Chaosium, 1997. 28–48.

Cassutt, Michael. "The Sunset of Time." In George R. R. Martin and Gardner Dozois, ed. *Old Venus*. New York: Bantam, 2015. 358–95.

Catalogue of Brown University 1909–1910. Providence, RI: Brown University, 1909.

Chambers, George F. *A Handbook of Descriptive and Practical Astronomy*. 4th ed. Oxford: Clarendon Press, 1889.

Clark, Jerome. "The Extraterrestrial Hypothesis in the Early UFO Age." In David M. Jacobs, ed. *UFOs and Abductions: Challenging the Borders of Knowledge*. Lawrence: University Press of Kansas, 2000. 122–40.

Clarke, Arthur C. *Astounding Days: A Science Fictional Autobiography*. New York: Bantam, 1990. [*Astounding*]

———. "At the Mountains of Murkiness." 1940. In George Locke, ed. *At the Mountains of Murkiness and Other Parodies*. London: Ferret Fantasy, 1973. 94–111. ["Murkiness"]

———. "Foreword." In David G. Stork, ed. *HAL's Legacy: 2001's Computer as Dream and Reality*. Cambridge, MA: MIT Press, 1996. xi–xvi.

———. "Jupiter Five." 1953. In *Reach for Tomorrow*. New York: Ballantine, 1956. 128–60. ["JF"]

———. *The Lost Worlds of 2001*. New York: Signet, 1972. [*Lost*]

———. *2001: A Space Odyssey*. 1968. New York: New American Library, 1999. [*2001*]

———. *2010: Odyssey Two*. New York: Ballantine, 1982. [*2010*]

Cockell, C. S. "The Polar Exploration of Mars." *Journal of the British Interplanetary Society* 48 (August 1995): 355–64.

Colavito, Jason. *The Cult of Alien Gods: H. P. Lovecraft and Extraterrestrial Pop Culture*. Amherst, NY: Prometheus, 2005. [*Cult*]

———. "Kirsten Gillibrand Offers Legislation to Bring Avi Loeb into Government UFO Office." JasonColavito.com, 5 November 2021. www.jasoncolavito.com/blog/kirsten-gillibrand-offers-legislation-to-bring-avi-loeb-into-government-ufo-office ["Loeb"]

———. "Mystery Solved: Why H. P. Lovecraft and Erich von Däniken Thought Aliens Wrote the 'Stanzas of Dzyan.'"

JasonColavito.com, 30 May 2016. www.jasoncolavito.com/blog/mystery-solved-why-h-p-lovecraft-and-erich-von-daniken-thought-aliens-wrote-the-stanzas-of-dzyan ["Dzyan"]

Croker, Thomas Crofton. *Daniel O'Rourke*. London: Ainsworth, 1828.

Crossley, Robert. *Imagining Mars: A Literary History*. Middletown, CT: Wesleyan University Press, 2011. [*Imagining*]

———. "Mars as Cultural Mirror: Martian Fictions in the Early Space Age." In Howard V. Hendrix, George Slusser, and Eric S. Rabkin, ed. *Visions of Mars: Essays on the Red Planet in Fiction and Science*. Jefferson, NC: McFarland, 2011. 165–74. ["Cultural"]

Crowe, Michael J. *The Extraterrestrial Life Debate 1750–1900: The Idea of a Plurality of Worlds from Kant to Lowell*. Cambridge: Cambridge University Press, 1986.

de Camp, L. Sprague. *Lovecraft: A Biography*. Garden City, NY: Doubleday, 1975.

"Death of Professor Upton." *Brown Alumni Momthly* 14, No. 7 (February 1914): 169–71.

Deischer, Jeff. "Antarctica and Mars in Early Genre Fiction Part II: Mars." *ERBZine,* 2009. www.erbzine.com/mag50/5019.html

Derie, Bobby. "'At the Mountains of Murkiness, or From Lovecraft to Leacock' (1940) by Arthur C. Clarke." *Deep Cuts in a Lovecraftian Vein,* 21 December 2019. deepcuts.blog/2019/12/21/at-the-mountains-of-murkiness-or-from-lovecraft-to-leacock-1940-by-arthur-c-clarke/ ["Mountains"]

———. "Cthulhu Trek (2008) by Leslie Thomas." *Deep Cuts in a Lovecraftian Vein,* 9 February 2022. deepcuts.blog/2022/02/09/cthulhu-trek-2008-by-leslie-thomas/ ["Trek"]

———. "'The Discovery of the Ghooric Zone' (1977) by Richard Lupoff & 'In the Yaddith Time' (2007) by Ann K. Schwader." *Deep Cuts in a Lovecraftian Vein*, 7 September 2019. deepcuts. blog/2019/09/07/the-discovery-of-the-ghooric-zone-1977-by-richard-lupoff-in-the-yaddith-time-2007-by-ann-k-schwader/ ["Discovery"]

———. "'Shambleau' (1933) by C. L. Moore." *Deep Cuts in a Lovecraftian Vein,* 22 May 2021. deepcuts.blog/2021/05/22/shambleau-1933-by-c-l-moore/ ["Shambleau"]

Derie, Bobby, and Joe Linton. "Providence 8." *Facts in the Case of Alan Moore's Providence,* 18 April 2016. factsprovidence.wordpress.com/moore-lovecraft-comics-annotation-index/providence-8/

Derleth, August. "The Snow-Thing." 1933. In Robert M. Price, ed. *The Ithaqua Cycle: The Wind-Walker of the Icy Wastes.* Hayward, CA: Chaosium, 2006. 69–79. ["Ithaqua"]

———. *The Trail of Cthulhu.* Sauk City, WI: Arkham House, 1962. [*Trail*]

———. *The Watchers out of Time and Others.* Sauk City, WI: Arkham House, 1974. [*Watchers*]

Dobbins, Thomas, and Richard Baum. "Observing a Fictional Moon." *Sky and Telescope* 95, No. 6 (June 1998): 105–9.

Dodge, Ernest Green. "Can Men Visit the Moon?" *Munsey's Magazine* 30 (October 1903): 29–32.

Dorr, James S. "Dark of the Moon." 2002. In Silvia Moreno-Garcia and Paula R. Stiles, ed. *Future Lovecraft.* Germantown, MD: Prime, 2012. 195–205.

Duncan, John Charles. *Astronomy: A Textbook.* 3rd ed. New York: Harper & Brothers, 1935.

———. "The Bright Aurora of 1918, March 7." *Popular Astronomy* 26 (April–May 1918): 350.

Dunglison, Robley. "Voyage to the Moon." *American Quarterly Review* 3, No. 5 (March 1828): 61–88.

Dunlap, Wendi. "The Sixth Vital Sign." In Scott Gable & C. Dombrowski, ed. *Ride the Star Wind: Cthulhu, Space Opera, and the Cosmic Weird.* n.p.: Broken Eye Books, 2017. 403–15.

Eckhardt, Jason C. "Behind the Mountains of Madness: Lovecraft and the Antarctic in 1930." *Lovecraft Studies* No. 14 (Spring 1987): 31–38.

Emrys, Ruthanna, and Anne M. Pillsworth. "Successful Pulp Heroes Need to Be More Genre Savvy: 'In the Walls of Eryx.'" *The Lovecraft Reread,* 13 October 2015. www.tor.com/2015/10/13/lovecraft-reread- in-the-walls-of-eryx/

Faig, Jr., Kenneth W. "Lovecraft's Travelogues of Foster, Rhode Island." *Lovecraft Annual* No. 9 (2015): 75–135.

———. *Lovecraftian Voyages.* New York: Hippocampus Press, 2017. [*Voyages*]

———. *The Parents of Howard Phillips Lovecraft*. West Warwick, RI: Necronomicon Press, 1990. [*Parents*]

Fallon, Richard. *Reimagining Dinosaurs in Late Victorian and Edwardian Literature: How the 'Terrible Lizard' Became a Transatlantic Cultural Icon*. Cambridge: Cambridge University Press, 2021.

Faunce, William Herbert Perry. *Annual Report of the President to the Corporation of Brown University*. Providence, RI: Brown University, 1907.

Field, Osgood. "Notes on the Field Family." *New England Historical & Genealogical Register* [22] (April 1868): 166–73.

Foix, Vicente Molina. "An Interview with Kubrick by Vicente Molina Foix." 1980. *Cinephilia & Beyond*, 2017. cinephiliabeyond.org/interview-stanley-kubrick-vicente-molina-foix/

Fort, Charles. *The Book of the Damned*. New York: Boni & Liveright, 1919. [*Damned*]

———. *New Lands*. New York: Boni & Liveright, 1923. [*NL*]

Fulwiler, William. "E. R. B. and H. P. L." 1989. In Robert M. Price, ed. *Black Forbidden Things: Cryptical Secrets from the "Crypt of Cthulhu."* San Bernardino, CA: Borgo Press, 1992. 60–65.

Garofalo, Charles. "A 'Lovecraftian' Scene in *Perelandra*." *Crypt of Cthulhu* No. 13 (Roodmas 1983): 37.

Gelatt, Philip, and Tim Mucci. "Episode #39: "The Vaults of Yoh-Vombis." *The Double Shadow*, 11 March 2014. player.fm/series/the-double-shadow/episode-39–the-vaults-of-yoh-vombis

Goddard, Robert. *The Papers of Robert H. Goddard*. New York: McGraw-Hill Education, 1970. 2 vols.

Gold, H. L. "Of All Things." *Galaxy* 18 (December 1959): 6–7.

Graham, Loren R. *The Ghost of the Executed Engineer: Technology and the Fall of the Soviet Union*. Cambridge, MA: Harvard University Press, 1993.

Grinspoon, David. *Lonely Planets: The Natural Philosophy of Alien Life*. New York: Ecco Press, 2003. [*Lonely*]

———. *Venus Revealed: A New Look Below the Clouds of Our Mysterious Twin Planet*. New York: Perseus, 1998. [*Venus*]

Gordin, Michael D. *The Pseudoscience Wars: Immanuel Velikovsky and the Birth of the Modern Fringe*. Chicago: University of Chicago Press, 2012.

Guimont, Edward. "An Arctic Mystery: The Lovecraftian North Pole." *Lovecraft Annual* No. 14 (2020): 138–65. ["Arctic"]

———. "At the Mountains of Mars: Viewing the Red Planet through a Lovecraftian Lens." In Dennis P. Quinn, ed. *Lovecraftian Proceedings No. 3*. New York: Hippocampus Press, 2019. 52–69. ["Mountains"]

———. "From King Solomon to Ian Smith: Rhodesian Alternate Histories of Zimbabwe." Ph.D. diss.: University of Connecticut, 2019.

———. "An Historical and Environmental Reading of August Derleth's 'Ithaqua.'" *Dead Reckonings* No. 27 (Spring 2020): 71–81. ["Ithaqua"]

Griaule, Marcel, and Germaine Dieterlen. "The Dogon of the French Sudan." 1954. In Daryll Forde, ed. *African Worlds: Studies in the Cosmological Ideas and Social Values of African Peoples*. Oxford: James Currey Publishers, 1999. 83–110.

Haden, David. "'Angling in Time': Some Possible Inspirations for H. P. Lovecraft's 'The Shadow out of Time.'" 2020. www.patreon.com/posts/10-000-word-on-37657545 ["Angling"]

———. "Friday 'Picture Postals' from Lovecraft: Stars and Time in Providence." *TENTACLII*, 17 December 2021, jurn.link/tentaclii/index.php/2021/12/17/friday-picture-postals-from-lovecraft-stars-and-time-in-providence/ ["Stars and Time"]

———. "Lovecraft and Fritz Lang's *Siegfried*." *TENTACLII*, 27 March 2019. www.jurn.org/tentaclii/2019/03/27/fritz-langs-siegfried/ ["Siegfried"]

———. "Lovecraft and Websters." *TENTACLII*, 13 August 2020. jurn.link/tentaclii/index.php/2020/08/13/lovecraft-and-websters/

———. *Lovecraft in Historical Context: Essays*. Morrisville, NC: Lulu Press, 2010. [*LH*]

———. *Lovecraft in Historical Context: The Fourth Collection of Essays and Notes*. Morrisville, NC: Lulu Press, 2013. [*LH4*]

———. "Man-Gods from Beyond the Stars (1975)." *TENTACLII*, 12 November 2018. www.jurn.org/tentaclii/2018/11/12/man-gods-from-beyond-the-stars-1975/ ["Man-Gods"]

———. "'Picture Postals' from Lovecraft: The Almanacs." *TENTACLII*, 7 January 2022, jurn.link/tentaclii/index.php/2022/01/07/picture-postals-from-lovecraft-the-almanacs/ ["Almanacs"]

———. "Volcanoes on the Moon." *TENTACLII*, 14 January 2022. jurn.link/tentaclii/index.php/2022/01/14/picture-postals-from-lovecraft-volcanoes-on-the-moon/

Hale, Edward Everett. "The Brick Moon." 1872. In Sam Moskowitz, ed. *Masterpieces of Science Fiction*. Westport, CT: Hyperion Press, 1974. 207–75.

Haldane, J. B. S. *Daedalus; or, Science and the Future*. 1923. *Marxists.org*, May 2002. www.marxists.org/archive/haldane/works/1920s/daedalus.htm [*Daedalus*]

———. "The Last Judgment." 1927. In *Possible Worlds*. Abingdon: Routledge, 2002. 287–312. ["Judgment"]

Halperin, David J. "'War of the Worlds'—Steven Spielberg's Version." *David Halperin*, 29 September 2020. www.davidhalperin.net/war-of-the-worlds-steven-spielbergs-version/

Hamilton, Edmond. "Across Space [Part 1]." *Weird Tales* 8 (September 1926): 307–22, 430–32.

Hand, Kevin Peter. *Alien Oceans: The Search for Life in the Depths of Space*. Princeton: Princeton University Press, 2020.

Hanley, Terence E. "Artists & Writers in The Unique Magazine." *Tellers of Weird Tales*, 14 November 2015. tellersofweirdtales.blogspot.com /2015/11/before-star-trek-and-star-wars.html

Hannay, Margaret. "The Mythology of *Out of the Silent Planet*." *Mythlore* 1, No. 4 (October 1969): 11–14.

Harms, Daniel, and John Wisdom Gonce III. *The Necronomicon Files: The Truth Behind Lovecraft's Legend*. Boston: Weiser, 2003.

Harpold, Terry. "Where Is Verne's Mars?" In Howard V. Hendrix, George Slusser, and Eric S. Rabkin, ed. *Visions of Mars: Essays on the Red Planet in Fiction and Science*. Jefferson, NC: McFarland, 2011. 29–35.

Hawley, Russell J. "Dinosaurs on Venus!" *Prehistoric Times* No. 116 (Winter 2016): 46–47.

Heinlein, Robert. "Concerning Stories Never Written." 1952. In *Revolt in 2100 & Methuselah's Children*. New York: Baen, 1999. 261–66. ["Concerning"]

———. "Logic of Empire." 1941. In *The Past through Tomorrow*. New York: Putnam, 1967. 304–40. ["Logic"]

———. "Science Fiction: Its Nature, Faults and Virtues." In Basil Davenport, ed. *The Science Fiction Novel: Imagination and Social Criticism*. Chicago: Advent: Publishers, 1959. 14–48. ["Virtues"]

———. *Stranger in a Strange Land*. 1961. New York: Ace, 1987. [*Stranger*]

Hester, Jessica Leigh. "Everybody Shut Up! We're Listening to Mars." *Atlas Obscura*, 3 August 2018. www.atlasobscura.com/articles/radio-signals-from-mars

Hite, Kenneth. *Tour de Lovecraft: The Destinations*. Alexandria, VA: Atomic Overmind Press, 2020.

Hoff, Darrel B. "History of the Teaching of Astronomy in American High Schools." In J. M. Pasachoff and J. R. Percy, ed. *The Teaching of Astronomy, Proceedings of IAU Colloq. 105*. Cambridge: Cambridge University Press, 1990. 249–53.

Howard, John. "Somebody Pointed Earth: August Derleth's Science Fiction." In James P. Roberts, ed. *Return to Derleth: Selected Essays, Volume Two*. Madison, WI: White Hawk Press, 1995. 53–59.

Hughes, David. *The Greatest Sci-Fi Movies Never Made*. Rev. and expanded ed. London: Titan, 2008.

Huntington, John W. "The (In)Significance of Mars in the 1930s." In Howard V. Hendrix, George Slusser, and Eric S. Rabkin, ed. *Visions of Mars: Essays on the Red Planet in Fiction and Science*. Jefferson, NC: McFarland, 2011. 80–85.

Jacobs, David Michael. "The Controversy over Unidentified Flying Objects in America: 1896–1973." Ph.D. diss.: University of Wisconsin–Madison, 1973.

Jones, Bessie Zaban, and Lyle Gifford Boyd. *Harvard College Observatory: The First Four Directorships*. Cambridge, MA: Belknap Press, 1971.

Joshi, S. T. *I Am Providence: The Life and Times of H. P. Lovecraft*. New York: Hippocampus Press, 2 volumes, 2010. [*IAP*]

———. *Lovecraft and a World in Transition.* New York: Hippocampus Press, 2014.

———. "Lovecraft's Alien Civilizations: A Political Interpretation." *Crypt of Cthulhu* No. 32 (St. John's Eve 1985): 8–24, 31. ["Civilizations"]

———. "Lovecraft's Other Planets." *Crypt of Cthulhu* No. 4 (Eastertide 1982): 3–11. ["LOP"]

———. "The Political and Economic Thought of H. P. Lovecraft." *Miskatonic* 6, No. 4 (February 1979): 20–24. ["Thought"]

———. *The Recognition of H. P. Lovecraft.* New York: Hippocampus Press, 2021. [*Recognition*]

———. "Time, Space, and Natural Law: Science and Pseudo-Science in Lovecraft." *Lovecraft Annual* No. 4 (2010): 171–201. ["Time"]

Joshi, S. T., and David E. Schultz. *An H. P. Lovecraft Encyclopedia.* New York: Hippocampus Press, 2004.

———. *Lovecraft's Library: A Catalogue.* 4th ed. New York: Hippocampus Press, 2017. [*LL*]

Jordan, Stephen J. "H. P. Lovecraft in Florida." *Lovecraft Studies* Nos. 42–43 (Autumn 2001): 32–45.

Kaempffert, Waldemar. "Life on the Moon." *Munsey's Magazine* 33 (July 1905): 588–92.

Kasdan, Jon. "Continued." Twitter, 24 September 2018. twitter.com/JonKasdan/status/1040529511513616385

Kaveney, Roz. "Science Fiction in the 1970s: Some Dominant Themes and Personalities." *Foundation* 22 (June 1981): 5–35.

Keen, Antony. "Mr. Lucian in Suburbia: Links Between *The True History* and *The First Men in the Moon*." In Brett M. Rogers and Benjamin Eldon Stevens, ed. *Classical Traditions in Science Fiction.* Oxford: Oxford University Press, 2015. 105–20.

Khuller, Aditya R., and Jeffrey J. Plaut. "Characteristics of the Basal Interface of the Martian South Polar Layered Deposits." *Geophysical Research Letters* 48 (June 2021): 1–19.

Kiernan, Caitlín R. *Agents of Dreamland.* New York: Tor, 2017. [*Agents*]

———. *Black Helicopters.* New York: Tor, 2018. [*BH*]

Kimmel, Leigh. "The Damnable Asteroid." 2011. In Silvia Moreno-Garcia and Paula R. Stiles, ed. *Future Lovecraft*. Germantown, MD: Prime, 2012. 179–84.

King, Stephen. "I Am the Doorway." 1971. In *Night Shift*. Garden City, NY: Doubleday, 1978. 63–75.

Kirby, Jack, and Joe Simon. "The Face on Mars." *Race for the Moon* 2 (September 1958): 1–5.

Knight, Damon. *Charles Fort: Prophet of the Unexplained*. Garden City, NY: Doubleday, 1970.

Koenigs, Thomas. *Founded in Fiction: The Uses of Fiction in the Early United States*. Princeton: Princeton University Press, 2021.

Koren, Marina. "The Most Overhyped Planet in the Galaxy." *The Atlantic*, 11 August 2020. www.theatlantic.com/science/archive/2020/08/mars-solar-system-exploration/615163/

Kornbluth, C. M. "The Failure of the Science Fiction Novel as Social Criticism." In Basil Davenport, ed. *The Science Fiction Novel: Imagination and Social Criticism*. Chicago: Advent, 1959. 49–78.

Kulcsar, Dominic. "Alien: Dan O'Bannon's Admiration for Lovecraft." *Alien Explorations*, 4 April 2020. alienexplorations.blogspot.com/1979/09/dan-obannons-admiration-for-lovecraft.html

Lake, David. "Mr Bedford's Brush with God: Fantastic Tradition and Mysticism in *The First Men in the Moon*." *The Wellsian: The Journal of the H. G. Wells Society* 13 (1990): 2–17.

Lambie, Ryan. "HP Lovecraft and His Lasting Impact on Cinema." *Den of Geek*, 14 October 2011. www.denofgeek.com/movies/hp-lovecraft-and-his-lasting-impact-on-cinema/

Lane, K. Maria D. *Geographies of Mars: Seeing and Knowing the Red Planet*. Chicago: University of Chicago Press, 2011.

Langan, John. "Nature's Other, Ghastly Face: H. P. Lovecraft and the Animal Sublime in Stephen King." In Robert H. Waugh, ed. *Lovecraft and Influence: His Predecessors and Successors*. Lanham, MD: Scarecrow Press, 2013. 155–64.

Lee, Oliver Justin. "Frederick Slocum 1873–1944." *Popular Astronomy* 53 (June 1945): 276–79.

Leiber, Fritz. "Through Hyperspace with Brown Jenkin: Lovecraft's Contribution to Speculative Fiction." In August Derleth, ed. *The

Dark Brotherhood and Other Pieces. Sauk City, WI: 1966. 164–78. ["Hyperspace"]

———. "To Arkham and the Stars." In August Derleth, ed. *The Dark Brotherhood and Other Pieces*. Sauk City, WI: 1966. 153–63. ["Arkham"]

Letson, Russell. "Russell Letson Reviews Old Venus." *Lotus*, 22 February 2015. locusmag.com/2015/02/russell-letson-reviews-old-venus/

Levenson, Thomas. *The Hunt for Vulcan: . . . And How Albert Einstein Destroyed a Planet, Discovered Relativity, and Deciphered the Universe*. New York: Random House, 2015.

Levine, Joel S. "The Ashen Light: An Auroral Phenomenon on Venus." *Planetary and Space Science* 1 (June 1969): 1081–87.

Lewis, C. S. "On Science Fiction." 1955. In *Of Other Worlds: Essays and Stories*. New York: HarperCollins, 2017. 93–115. ["OSF"]

———. *Out of the Silent Planet*. 1938. Quebec City: Samizdat, 2015. [*Silent*]

———. *Perelandra*. 1943. Quebec City: Samizdat, 2015.

———. "Will We Lose God in Outer Space?" *Christian Herald* 81 (April 1958): 19, 74–76. ["God"]

Ley, Willy, and Wernher von Braun. *The Exploration of Mars*. New York: Viking Press, 1956.

Ligner, Meddy. "Trajectory of a Cursed Spirit." In Silvia Moreno-Garcia and Paula R. Stiles, ed. *Future Lovecraft*. Germantown, MD: Prime, 2012. 207–20.

Lingam, Manasvi, and Abraham Loeb. "Characteristics of Aquatic Biospheres on Temperate Planets around Sun-like Stars and M-dwarfs." *arXiv*, 26 February 2021. arxiv.org/abs/2005.14387

Livesey, T. R. "Dispatches from the Providence Observatory: Astronomical Motifs and Sources in the Writings of H. P. Lovecraft." *Lovecraft Annual* No. 2 (2008): 3–87. [DPO]

———. "Green Storm Rising: Lovecraft's Roots in Invasion Literature." In Robert H. Waugh, ed. *Lovecraft and Influence: His Predecessors and Successors*. Lanham, MD: Scarecrow Press, 2013. 83–94. ["Green"]

Locke, Richard Adams. "The Moon Hoax." 1835. *Amazing Stories* 6 (September 1926): 556–75.

London, Jack. *The Star Rover*. 1915. New York: Modern Library, 2003.

Long, Frank Belknap. *Howard Phillips Lovecraft: Dreamer on the Nightside*. Sauk City, WI: Arkham House, 1975.

Lovecraft, H. P. *Collected Essays*. Ed. S. T. Joshi. New York: Hippocampus Press, 2004–06. 5 volumes. [*CE*]

———. *Letters to Alfred Galpin and Others*. Ed. S. T. Joshi and David E. Schultz. New York: Hippocampus Press, 2020. [*AG*]

———. *Letters to C. L. Moore and Others*. Ed. David E. Schultz and S. T. Joshi. New York: Hippocampus Press, 2017. [*CLM*]

———. *Letters to E. Hoffmann Price and Richard F. Searight*. Ed. S. T. Joshi and David E. Schulz. New York: Hippocampus Press, 2021. [*EHP*]

———. *Letters to Elizabeth Toldridge and Anne Tillery Renshaw*. Ed. David E. Schultz and S. T. Joshi. New York: Hippocampus Press, 2014. [*ET*]

———. *Letters to F. Lee Baldwin, Duane W. Rimel, and Nils Frome*. Ed. S. T. Joshi and David E. Schultz. New York: Hippocampus Press, 2016. [*FLB*]

———. *Letters to Family and Family Friends*. Ed. S. T. Joshi and David E. Schultz. New York: Hippocampus Press, 2 volumes, 2020. [*LFF*]

———. *Letters to J. Vernon Shea, Carl F. Strauch, and Lee McBride White*. Ed. S. T. Joshi and David E. Schultz. New York: Hippocampus Press, 2016. [*JVM*]

———. *Letters to James F. Morton*. Ed. David E. Schultz and S. T. Joshi. New York: Hippocampus Press, 2014. [*JFM*]

———. *Letters to Maurice W. Moe and Others*. Ed. David E. Schultz and S. T. Joshi. New York: Hippocampus Press, 2018. [*MWM*]

———. *Letters to Rheinhart Kleiner and Others*. Ed. S. T. Joshi and David E. Schultz. New York: Hippocampus Press, 2020. [*RK*]

———. *Letters to Robert Bloch and Others*. Ed. S. T. Joshi and David E. Schultz. New York: Hippocampus Press, 2015. [*RB*]

———. *Letters to Wilfred B. Talman and Helen V. and Genevieve Sully*. Ed. S. T. Joshi and David E. Schultz. New York: Hippocampus Press, 2019. [*WBT*]

———. *Letters to Woodburn Harris and Others*. Ed. S. T. Joshi and David E. Schultz. New York: Hippocampus Press, 2022. [*WH*]

———. *Miscellaneous Letters*. Ed. David E. Schultz and S. T. Joshi. New York: Hippocampus Press, 2022. [*Misc*]

———. *O Fortunate Floridian: H. P. Lovecraft's Letters to R. H. Barlow*. Ed. S. T. Joshi and David E. Schultz. Tampa, FL: University of Tampa Press, 2016. [*OFF*]

Lovecraft, H. P., and August Derleth. *Essential Solitude: The Letters of H. P. Lovecraft and August Derleth*. Ed. David E. Schultz and S. T. Joshi. New York: Hippocampus Press, 2008. 2 vols. [*ES*]

Lovecraft, H. P., and Clark Ashton Smith. *Dawnward Spire, Lonely Hill: The Letters of H. P. Lovecraft and Clark Ashton Smith*. Ed. David E. Schultz and S. T. Joshi. New York: Hippocampus Press, 2017. [*DS*]

Lovecraft, H. P., and Robert E. Howard. *A Means to Freedom: The Letters of H. P. Lovecraft and Robert E. Howard*. Ed. S. T. Joshi, David E. Schultz, and Rusty Burke. New York: Hippocampus Press, 2 volumes, 2017. [*MF*]

Lowell, Percival. *Mars as the Abode of Life*. 1908. New York: Macmillan, 1910.

Lubnow, Fred S. *Essays from Beyond the Wall of Eryx*. n.p.: Lovecraftian Science Press, 2021. [*Essays*]

———. *Journal of Lovecraftian Science, Volume 3*. n.p. Lovecraftian Science Press, 2021. [*JLS3*]

———. "The Lovecraftian Solar System." *Lovecraft Annual* No. 13 (2019): 3–26. [LSS]

Lucibella, Michael. "March 9, 1611: Dutch Astronomer Johannes Fabricius Observes Sunspots." *APS News* 24, No. 3 (March 2015): 2–3.

Lupoff, Richard A. "Discovery of the Ghooric Zone—March 15, 2337." 1977. *Infinity Plus,* 2001. www.infinityplus.co.uk/stories/ghooric.htm ["Ghooric"]

———. *Master of Adventure: The Worlds of Edgar Rice Burroughs*. 1965. Lincoln: University of Nebraska Press, 2005. [*ERB*]

MacColl, Hugh. *Mr. Stranger's Sealed Packet*. London: Chatto & Windus, 1889.

Macdonald, Kate. "H G Wells Does Lovecraft." *Kate Macdonald,* 24 July 2017. katemacdonald.net/2017/07/24/h-g-wells-does-lovecraft/

Mariconda, Steven J. "Some Antecedents of the Shining Trapezohedron." *Etchings & Odysseys* 3 (1983): 14–20.

Mars, Kelli. "Antarctic Stations (NSF)." NASA, 11 June 2018. www.nasa. gov/analogs/nsf

McKay, David S., et al. "Search for Past Life on Mars: Possible Relic Biogenic Activity in Martian Meteorite ALH84001." *Science* 273 (Spring 1996): 924–30.

McGiveron, Rafeeq O. "Heinlein's Inhabited Solar System, 1940–1952." *Science Fiction Studies* 23, No. 2 (July 1996): 245–52.

McInnis III, John Lawson. "H. P. Lovecraft: The Maze and the Minotaur." Ph.D. diss.: Louisiana State University, 1975.

McNeill, Graham. *Dweller in the Deep.* Roseville, MN: Fantasy Flight, 2014. [*Dweller*]

———. *Ghouls of the Miskatonic.* Roseville, MN: Fantasy Flight, 2011. [*Ghouls*]

Melott Adrian L., and Richard K. Bambach. "Nemesis Reconsidered." *arXiv,* 02 July 2010. arxiv.org/abs/1007.0437

Merritt, Abraham. "The Moon Pool." *All-Story Weekly* (22 June 1918).

Migliore, Andrew, and John Strysik. *The Lurker in the Lobby: A Guide to the Cinema of H. P. Lovecraft.* San Francisco: Night Shade, 2006.

Miller, Michael D. "A Look Behind 'The Challenge from Beyond.'" *Dead Reckonings* No. 25 (Fall 2019): 3–11. ["Look"]

———. "2001: A Lovecraftian Odyssey." *Lovecraft Annual* No. 12 (2018) 75–89. ["2001"]

Miller, Thomas Kent. *Mars in the Movies: A History.* Jefferson, NC: McFarland, 2016.

Moore, Alan, and Jacen Burrows. *Providence Act 2.* Rantoul, IL: Avatar Press, 2017.

Moore, Alan, and Kevin O'Neill. *The League of Extraordinary Gentlemen, Volume I.* La Jolla, CA: America's Best Comics, 2000.

Moore, C. L. "Shambleau." *Weird Tales* 22 (November 1933): 531–50.

Moreno-Garcia, Silvia, and Paula R. Stiles. "Introduction: The Future is Lovecraft." In Silvia Moreno-Garcia and Paula R. Stiles, ed. *Future Lovecraft*. Germantown, MD: Prime, 2012. 9.

Moskowitz, Sam. "H. P. Lovecraft and the Munsey magazines." In Sam Moskowitz, ed. *Under the Moons of Mars: A History and Anthology of "The Scientific Romance" in the Munsey Magazines, 1912–1920*. New York: Holt, Rinehart & Winston, 1970. 373–79.

Murray, Will. "Clark Ashton Smith of Mars." *Crypt of Cthulhu* No. 113 (Lammas 2019): 11–14. ["Mars"]

———. "The Sothis Radiant." In Martin H. Greenberg and Robert Weinberg, ed. *Miskatonic University*. New York: DAW, 1996. 271–99. ["Sothis"]

Nakamura, Remy. "The Children of Leng." In Scott Gable and C. Dombrowski, ed. *Ride the Star Wind: Cthulhu, Space Opera, and the Cosmic Weird*. n.p.: Broken Eye, 2017. 5–17.

Navroth, John M. "Lovecraft and the Polar Myth." *Lovecraft Annual* No. 3 (2009): 190–98.

Nevala-Lee, Alec. *Astounding: John W. Campbell, Isaac Asimov, Robert A. Heinlein, L. Ron Hubbard, and the Golden Age of Science Fiction*. New York: HarperCollins, 2018.

New England College Entrance Certificate Board. *Fifth Annual Report of the New England College Entrance Certificate Board*. Providence, sRI: Snow & Farnham, 1907.

Newcomb, Simon. *Astronomy for Everybody*. New York: McClure, Phillips, 1902.

Newman, Kim. "Famous Monsters." 1988. In Gardner Dozois, ed. *The Year's Best Science Fiction: Sixth Annual Collection*. New York: St. Martin's Press, 1989. 527–34.

Nicholls, Peter. "Big Dumb Objects and Cosmic Enigmas: The Love Affair Between Space Fiction and the Transcendental." In Gary Westfahl, ed. *Space and Beyond: The Frontier Theme in Science Fiction*. Westport, CT: Greenwood Press, 2000. 11–23. ["Dumb"]

———. "Introduction." In *The Saliva Tree and Other Strange Growths*. Boston: Gregg Press, 1981. v–xii. ["Introduction"]

Nixon, Matthew C., and Nikku Madhusudhan. "How Deep Is the Ocean? Exploring the Phase Structure of Water-Rich Sub-Neptunes." *arXiv*, 03 June 2021. arxiv.org/abs/2106.02061

Norris, Duncan. "Lovecraft and *Arrival*: The Quiet Apocalypse." *Lovecraft Annual* No. 11 (2017): 110–17. ["Arrival"]

———. "The Reverberation of Echoes: Lovecraft in Twenty-First-Century Cinema." *Lovecraft Annual* No. 15 (2021): 183–243. ["Cinema"]

Orton, Vrest. "Recollections of H. P. Lovecraft." 1982. In Peter H. Cannon, ed. *Lovecraft Remembered*. Sauk City, WI: Arkham House, 1998. 339–46.

Palmer, Christopher. "Big Dumb Objects in Science Fiction: Sublimity, Banality, and Modernity." *Extrapolation* 47 (Spring 2006): 95–111.

Pedersen, Nate, ed. *The Starry Wisdom Library: The Catalogue of the Greatest Occult Book Auction of All Time*. Hornsea, UK: PS, 2014.

Perridas, Chris. "The Aurora Borealis in 'Polaris.'" *H. P. Lovecraft and His Legacy*, 4 April 2011. chrisperridas.blogspot.com/2011/04/aurora-borealis-in-polaris.html

———. "Ray Bradbury's circa 1950 Parody of HP Lovecraft." *H. P. Lovecraft and His Legacy*, 1 February 2008. chrisperridas.blogspot.com/2008/02/ray-bradburys-circa-1950-parody-of-hp.html

Pickering, William. H. "The Canals in the Moon." *Century Magazine* 64 (June 1902): 189–195.

———. "Eratosthenes No. 1." *Popular Astronomy* 27 (November 1919): 579–583.

———. "Eratosthenes No. 4." *Popular Astronomy* 32 (February 1924): 69–78.

———. "Is the Moon a Dead Planet?" *Century Magazine* 64 (May 1902): 90–99.

———. "Meteorology of the Moon." *Popular Astronomy* 23 (March 1915): 129–140.

———. *The Moon*. New York: Doubleday, Page, & Co., 1903.

———. "Visual Observations of the Moon and Planets." *Annals of the Harvard College Observatory* 32 (1895): 116–317.

Plotkin, Howard. "William H. Pickering at Jamaica: The Founding of Woodlawn and Studies of Mars." *Journal for the History of Astronomy* 24 (May 1992): 101–22.

Poe, Edgar Allan. "The Balloon-Hoax." 1844. In *The Unabridged Edgar Allan Poe*. Ed. Tam Mossman. Philadelphia: Running Press, 1983. 884–95. ["Balloon"]

———. "Hans Phaall—A Tale." 1835. In Sam Moskowitz, ed. *Masterpieces of Science Fiction*. Westport, CT: Hyperion Press, 1974. 60–109. ["Phaall"]

———. "Mellonta Tauta." 1849. In *The Unabridged Edgar Allan Poe*. Ed. Tam Mossman. Philadelphia: Running Press, 1983. 1117–29. ["MT"]

———. "The Murders in the Rue Morgue." 1841. In *The Unabridged Edgar Allan Poe*. Ed. Tam Mossman. Philadelphia: Running Press, 1983. 655–84. ["Morgue"]

———. "Note on 'Hans Phaall.'" 1840. In Sam Moskowitz, ed. *Masterpieces of Science Fiction*. Westport, CT: Hyperion Press, 1974. 110–18. ["Note"]

———. "Richard Adams Locke." 1850. In Sam Moskowitz, ed. *Masterpieces of Science Fiction*. Westport, CT: Hyperion Press, 1974. 118–27. ["Locke"]

Pope, Gustavus W. *Journey to Mars. The Wonderful World: Its Beauty and Splendor; Its Mighty Races and Kingdoms; Its Final Doom*. New York: G. W. Dillingham, 1894. [*Mars*]

———. *Journey to Venus the Primeval World; Its Wonderful Creations and Gigantic Monsters*. Boston: Arena, 1895. [*Venus*]

Portree, David S. F. *Humans to Mars: Fifty Years of Mission Planning, 1950–2000*. Washington, DC: NASA History Division, 2001.

Price, Robert M. "Episode 9." *The Lovecraft Geek*, 17 March 2014. www.talkshoe.com/episode/4887700

———. "Episode 11." *The Lovecraft Geek*, 25 April 2014. www.talkshoe.com/episode/4887757

———. "Episode 20." *The Lovecraft Geek*, 16 October 2015. www.talkshoe.com/episode/4731995

———. "Lovecraft's 'Artificial Mythology'." In David E. Schultz and S. T. Joshi, ed. *An Epicure in the Terrible: A Centennial Anthology of Essays in Honor of H. P. Lovecraft*. Madison, NJ: Fairleigh Dickinson University Press, 1991. 247–56. ["Mythology"]

———. "Lovecraft's Cosmic History." *Crypt of Cthulhu* No. 37 (Candlemas 1986): 18–24. ["History"]

———. "Randolph Carter, Warlord of Mars." 1991. In Robert M. Price, ed. *Black Forbidden Things: Cryptical Secrets from the "Crypt of Cthulhu."* San Bernardino, CA: Borgo Press, 1992. 66–68. ["Warlord"]

———. "Some Notes on the Eltdown Shards." *Crypt of Cthulhu* No. 23 (St. John's Eve 1984): 34–37. ["Notes"]

Prinz, Wilhelm. "Photographie des Deformations du Soleil Couchant." In *XXV Album Jubilaire: Anniversaire de la Fondation, 1874–1898*. Association Belge de Photographie. Bruxelles: E. Bruylant, 1898. 111–19.

Proctor, Richard A. *Half-Hours with the Telescope*. London: Longman, Greens, 1902.

Rawlik, Peter. "In the Hall of the Yellow King." 2011. In Silvia Moreno-Garcia and Paula R. Stiles, ed. *Future Lovecraft*. Germantown, MD: Prime, 2012. 13–19.

Report of the Eclipse Expedition to Caroline Island May 1883. Washington, DC: Government Printing Office, 1884.

Rieder, John. *Colonialism and the Emergence of Science Fiction*. Middletown, CT: Wesleyan University Press, 2008.

Rovin, Jeff. *Re-Animator*. New York: Pocket, 1987.

Ruff, Matt. "Old Venus." *Kirkus Reviews*, 22 December 2014. www.kirkusreviews.com/book-reviews/george-rr-martin/old-venus/

Russell, H. N.; Dugan, R. S.; and Stewart, J. Q. *Astronomy: A Revision of Young's Manual of Astronomy*. Volume 1. Boston: Ginn, 1926.

Sagan, Carl. *Cosmos*. 1980. New York: Ballantine, 2013.

———. *Pale Blue Dot: A Vision of the Human Future in Space*. 1994. New York: Ballantine, 1997. [*Dot*]

Sagan, Carl, and Ann Druyan. *Comet*. 1985. New York: Ballantine, 1997.

Sagan, Carl, and E. E. Salpeter. "Particles, Environments, and Possible Ecologies in the Jovian Atmosphere." *Astrophysical Journal Supplement Series* 32 (October 1976): 737–55.

Schaffer, Simon. "The Nebular Hypothesis and the Science of Progress." In James R. Moore, ed. *History, Humanity, and Evolution: Essays for John C. Greene*. Cambridge: Cambridge University Press, 1989. 142–53.

Scharmen, Fred. *Space Forces: A Critical History of Life in Outer Space*. New York: Verso, 2021.

Schroeder, David. "A Message from Mars: Astronomy and Late-Victorian Culture." Ph.D. diss.: Indiana University, 2002.

Schwaiger, Thomas, "A Lover of Past Phantoms: Lovecraftian Reflections in R. H. Barlow's Life and Work." In Dennis P. Quinn and Elena Tchougounova-Paulson, ed. *Lovecraftian Proceedings No. 4*. New York: Hippocampus Press, 2022. 126–48.

Sconce, Jeffrey. *Haunted Media: Electronic Presence from Telegraphy to Television*. Durham, NC: Duke University Press, 2000.

Serviss, Garrett P. *Astronomy with an Opera-Glass*. 1888. New York: Appleton, 1890. [*Opera*]

———. *Astronomy with the Naked Eye*. New York: Harper & Brothers, 1908. [*Naked*]

———. *A Columbus of Space*. New York: Appleton, 1911. [*ACS*]

———. *Curiosities of the Sky*. New York: Harper & Brothers, 1909. [*Curiosities*]

———. *Edison's Conquest of Mars*. 1898. Burlington, ON: Collector's Guide Publishing, 2010. [*ECM*]

———. "The Moon Metal." 1900. *Amazing Stories* 1 (July 1926): 322–45, 381. [*TMM*]

———. *Pleasures of the Telescope*. New York: Appleton, 1901. [*Pleasures*]

Serviss, Garrett P. *Invasion of Mars*. Ed. Forrest J Ackerman. Reseda, CA: Powell, 1969.

Sivier, David J. "Extraterrestrial Hissarlik: Mars as Model for Planetary Archaeology." *Journal of the British Interplanetary Society* 56 (November 2003): 417–25.

Sheehan, William. P. *Planets and Perception*. Tucson: University of Arizona Press, 1988.

Sheehan, William. P., and Thomas A. Dobson. *Epic Moon: A History of Lunar Exploration in the Age of the Telescope*. Richmond, VA: Willmann-Bell, 2001.

———. "The Spokes of Venus: An Illusion Explained." *Journal for the History of Astronomy* 34 (February 2003): 53–63.

Smith, Clark Ashton. "The Vaults of Yoh-Vombis." 1931. In *The Dark Eidolon and Other Fantasies*. Ed. S. T. Joshi. New York: Penguin Classics, 2014. 91–111.

Smith, Horace A. "Lovecraft Seeks the Garden of Eratosthenes." *Lovecraft Annual* No. 13 (2019): 53–174 [*LA* 13]

———. "Astronomy with Lovecraft's First Telescope." *Lovecraft Annual* No. 15 (2021): 6–16. [*LA* 15]

———. "Guest Post: 'John Edwards of the Ladd Observatory at Brown—Cockney or Cornishman?'" *TENTACLII*, 31 May 2019, jurn.link/tentaclii/index.php/2019/05/31/guest-post-john-edwards-of-the-ladd-observatory-at-brown-cockney-or-cornishman/

———. *Willimantic Skies*. n.p.: Kindle Direct Publishing, 2021.

Smith, Robert, *The Expanding Universe: Astronomy's Great Debate*. Cambridge: Cambridge University Press, 1982.

Sobel, Dava. *The Glass Universe*. New York: Viking Press, 2016.

Špaček, Jan. "Organic Carbon Cycle in the Atmosphere of Venus." *arXiv*, 4 August 2021. arxiv.org/ftp/arxiv/papers/2108/2108.02286.pdf

Spinelli, R., et al. "The Best Place and Time to Live in the Milky Way." *arXiv*, 26 January 2021. arxiv.org/abs/2009.13539

St. John, Charles E., and Seth B. Nicholson. "On the Absence of Selective Absorption in the Atmosphere of Venus." *Publications of the Astronomical Society of the Pacific* No. 194 (August 1921): 208–9.

Stanley, Joan L. *Ex Libris Miskatonici: A Catalogue of Selected Items from the Special Collections in the Miskatonic University Library*. 1993. West Warwick, RI: Necronomicon Press, 2019.

Stapledon, Olaf. *Last and First Men*. 1930. n.p.: Distributed Proofreaders Canada, 2020.

Sterling, Kenneth. "Lovecraft and Science." 1944. In Peter H. Cannon, ed. *Lovecraft Remembered*. Sauk City, WI: Arkham House, 1998. 423–25.

Stross, Charles. "A Colder War." 2000. In Ross E. Lockhart, ed. *The Book of Cthulhu: Tales Inspired by H. P. Lovecraft*. San Francisco: Night Shade, 2011. 51–80.

Stuart, Don A. "Who Goes There?" *Astounding Science-Fiction* 21 (August 1938): 60–97.

Swords, Michael D. "Clyde Tombaugh, Mars, and UFOs." *Journal of Scientific Exploration* 13 (Winter 1999): 685–94.

Temple, Robert K. G. *The Sirius Mystery*. New York: St. Martin's Press, 1976.
The Blue and White. Providence, RI: Hope Street High School, 1903.
Tice, John H. "The Supposed Planet Vulcan." *Scientific American* 35 (December 1876): 389.
Tierney, Richard L. "The Derleth Mythos." In Meade Frierson and Penny Frierson, ed. *HPL*. Birmingham, AL: Meade & Penny Frierson, 1972. 53. ["Mythos"]
———. "Lovecraft and the Cosmic Quality in Fiction." In S. T. Joshi, ed. *H. P. Lovecraft: Four Decades of Criticism*. Athens: Ohio State University Press, 1980. 191–95. ["Cosmic"]
Tidhar, Lavie. "The Drowned Celestial." In George R. R. Martin and Gardner Dozois, ed. *Old Venus*. New York: Bantam, 2015. 38–69.
Titelman, Carol. *The Art of Star Wars*. New York: Ballantine, 1979.
Tombaugh, C. W. *The Search for Small Natural Earth Satellites: Final Technical Report*. New Mexico State University—Physical Science Laboratory (10 June 1959). nmsu.contentdm.oclc.org/digital/collection/Ms0407/id/16556
Tresch, John. *The Reason for the Darkness of the Night: Edgar Allan Poe and the Forging of American Science*. New York: Farrar, Straus & Giroux, 2021.
"Trip to the Moon." *FTIA: Film & Television Industry Alliance*, 24 August 2020. productionlist.com/production/trip-to-the-moon/
Upton, Winslow. "The Ladd Observatory." *Sidereal Messenger* 10 (December 1891): 502–5.
———. *Star Atlas*. Boston: Ginn, 1896.
———. "The Use of the Spectroscope in Meteorological Observations." *Memorie della Società degli Spettroscopisti Italiani* 13 (1885): 113–18.
Valdron, Den. "Aelita: Princess of Barsoom." *ERBzine*, 2010. www.erbzine.com/mag17/1742.html ["Aelita"]
———. "Tama, Princess of Mercury." *ERBzine*, 2010. www.erbzine.com/mag17/1743.html ["Tama"]
Vaughan, Ralph E. "The Old Man and the Sea: The Ocean and Life as Viewed by H. P. Lovecraft." *Lovecraft Studies* No. 7 (Fall 1982): 3–7.

Velikovsky, Immanuel. *Worlds in Collision*. 1950. London: Paradigma, 2009.

Verne, Jules. "Commentary." 1904. In H. G. Wells. *The War of the Worlds*. New York: Modern Library, 2002. 185–86.

———. *From the Earth to the Moon*. 1865. New York: Hurst, 1909. [*FEM*]

Walker, Stephen. "The Shadow of His Smile: Humor in H. P. Lovecraft's Fiction." In John Michael Sefel and Niels-Viggo S. Hobbs, and Robyn Hill, ed. *Lovecraftian Proceedings No. 1*. New York: Hippocampus Press, 2015. 151–64.

Ward, Peter D., and Donald Brownlee. *Rare Earth: Why Complex Life is Uncommon in the Universe*. 2000. New York: Copernicus, 2003.

Watt-Evans, Lawrence. "Just Who Were Those Martians, Anyways?" In Glenn Yeffeth, ed. *The War of the Worlds: Fresh Perspectives on the H. G. Wells Classic*. Dallas: BenBella, 2005. 165–72.

Waugh, Robert H. *The Tragic Thread in Science Fiction*. New York: Hippocampus Press, 2019.

Webb, Don. "The Comet Called Ithaqua." 1994. In Silvia Moreno-Garcia and Paula R. Stiles, ed. *Future Lovecraft*. Germantown, MD: Prime, 2012. 67–72. ["Ithaqua"]

———. "To Mars and Providence." In Kevin J. Anderson ed. *War of the Worlds: Global Dispatches*. New York: Bantam Spectra, 1996. 251–61. ["Mars"]

Webb, T. W. *Celestial Objects for Common Telescopes*. Revised and greatly enlarged by Rev. T. E. Espin. Volume 1. London: Longman, Greens, 1904.

Weinbaum, Stanley G. *The Martian Odyssey and Other SF*. Los Angeles: Aegypan, 2008.

Wells, H. G. *The Croquet Player*. 1936. Lincoln, NE: Bison, 2004. [*Croquet*]

———. *The First Men in the Moon*. 1901. New York: Airmont, 1965. [*FM*]

———. *Star-Begotten: A Biological Fantasia*. New York: Viking Press, 1937. [*SB*]

———. *The Time Machine*. New York: Henry Holt, 1895. [*TM*]

———. *The War of the Worlds*. 1897. London: William Heinemann, 1898. [*WW*]

Wells, Jeffrey John. "Observations on the Several Parts of Africa." In Nate Pedersen, ed. *The Starry Wisdom Library: The Catalogue of the Greatest Occult Book Auction of All Time*. Hornsea, UK: PS, 2014. 131–33.

Whalen, Stephen, and Robert E. Bartholomew. "The Great New England Airship Hoax of 1909." *New England Quarterly* 75 (September 2002): 466–76.

White, Cecil B. "The Retreat to Mars." *Amazing Stories* 2, No. 5 (August 1927): 460–68.

Whyte, Brandan. "H. P. Lovecraft's First Appearance in Print Reconsidered." *Lovecraft Annual* No. 15 (2020): 94–99 [*LA 15*]

Williams, I. P., and A. W. Cremin. "A Survey of Theories Relating to the Origin of the Solar System." *Quarterly Journal of the Royal Astronomical Society* 9 (March 1968): 40–62.

Williams, T. R., and M. Saladyga. *Advancing Variable Star Astronomy*. Cambridge: Cambridge University Press, 2011.

Williamson, Jack. "The Evolution of the Martians." In Glenn Yeffeth, ed. *The War of the Worlds: Fresh Perspectives on the H. G. Wells Classic*. Dallas: BenBella, 2005. 189–98.

Winsor, George McLeod. *Station X*. Philadelphia: Lippincott, 1919.

Wood, Andrew Paul. "The Rings of Cthulhu: Lovecraft, Dürer, Saturn, and Melancholy." *Lovecraft Annual* (2019): 53–68.

Wolverton, Dave. "After a Lean Winter." In Kevin J. Anderson, ed. *War of the Worlds: Global Dispatches*. New York: Bantam Spectra, 1996. 299–324.

Wright, Jason T. "Prior Indigenous Technological Species." *International Journal of Astrobiology* 17, No. 1 (June 2018): 96–100.

Young, Charles Augustus. *Elements of Astronomy: A Textbook*. Rev. ed. Boston: Ginn, 1903.

———. *Lessons in Astronomy: Including Uranography*. Boston: Ginn, 1903.

Yudina, Ekaterina. "Dibs on the Red Planet: The Bolsheviks and Mars in the Russian Literature of the Early Twentieth Century." In Howard V. Hendrix, George Slusser, and Eric S. Rabkin, ed. *Visions of Mars: Essays on the Red Planet in Fiction and Science*. Jefferson, NC: McFarland, 2011. 51–55.

Ziegler, Charles A. "Mythogenesis: Historical Development of the Roswell Narratives." In Benson Saler, Charles A. Ziegler, and Charles B. Moore, ed. *UFO Crash at Roswell: The Genesis of a Modern Myth*. Washington, DC: Smithsonian Institution Press, 1997. 1–29.

Index

ALH84001 262-63
Ackerman, Forrest J 196, 202, 246-47, 255
"Across Space" (Hamilton) 255-56
Aelita (Tolstoi) 231, 117-18
aether 117-18, 283, 287
Africa 123, 129, 196, 243, 250, 254, 255, 257-58, 295-97
"After a Lean Winter" (Wolverton) 258
Agents of Dreamland (Kiernan) 286-87, 289
Aldiss, Brian 258
Alhazred, Abdul 300, 306
Alien (film) 323-24
All-Story 116, 137, 141-42, 185, 247-48
Allen, Leah Brown 72-74
Allen, Reuben L. 23, 28, 84, 95
Antikythera mechanism 295
Amalthea 271-72, 275
American Association of Variable Star Observers 21, 73
American Astronomical Society 21n8
ancient aliens 191, 254, 257-58, 273, 285, 294-97, 303, 324, 325
Andromeda galaxy 20, 152, 370, 371
Annals of the Providence Observatory (Lovecraft) 15, 17n6, 26, 84, 95, 98
Antarctica 65, 141, 142, 145, 190, 239, 242-44, 246, 250, 258, 262-63, 274, 286, 302, 306, 323, 324, 328, 333
Anthea 234
Apollo 18 (film) 136-37
Arcturus 25, 297-98, 325

"Are There Undiscovered Planets?" (Lovecraft) 174-75, 241, 281
Arkham, Mass. 57, 65, 116n3, 119, 142, 197, 317n14
Arkham House 200, 234
Arrakis 234
Arrival (film) 319
ashen light 179-81, 186
Asheville Gazette-News 24, 152, 155, 159, 160, 167, 176, 180, 272, 299, 349
Asimov, Isaac 116, 119, 202, 204, 209, 245, 250n18, 259, 293, 309, 312, 326, 327, 328, 329
asteroids 268-71, 279, 290
Astor IV, John Jacob 132-33, 184, 237, 272
Astounding Stories 143-44, 205, 209, 245, 274, 287, 329n14
astrology 147, 155-56, 158-61, 209-10, 228, 278, 289-90, 295, 348
Astronomy with the Naked Eye (Serviss) 139, 298
Astronomy with an Opera-Glass (Serviss) 30, 118, 124, 130, 139, 167, 168, 170, 185, 340
astrophotography 18-19, 20, 48, 90, 235, 271, 299, 347, 351-361
Atlantis 190, 209, 245, 257, 306
At the Mountains of Madness (Lovecraft) 65, 111, 123n12, 126, 139, 144, 145, 173, 178, 197, 207, 230, 241-47, 248, 252-53, 257, 258, 262-63, 274-75, 281n12, 287, 302, 307, 324, 329-30, 350
"At the Mountains of Murkiness" (Clarke) 274
Auburn, Mass. 119
Aurora, Tex. 163-65

399

Australia 257, 329
Aylesbury 289

"Balloon-Hoax, The" (Poe) 126-27
Bardou & Son 23, 29, 49, 78-80, 106, 337, 343, 348
Barlow, R. H. 12, 48, 49n28, 57, 128, 130, 136n15, 143-44, 157-58, 173, 177, 185, 189, 196, 202n15, 253, 261, 308-10, 334, 339, 341, 387, 393
Barnard, Edward Emerson 105, 271, 373
Barsoom (Burroughs) 189, 232, 247-49, 258, 277, 308
"Battle That Ended the Century, The" (Lovecraft-Barlow) 196
Baudoin, Jean 121-22, 126, 128-29, 134, 136
Baxter, Stephen 136, 258-59, 260, 262, 291
Beer, Wilhelm 132
Bergerac, Cyrano de 126, 128, 135, 374
"Beyond the Wall of Sleep" (Lovecraft) 60n8, 139, 144, 161, 229, 240-41, 272, 298-99, 318, 328, 332, 347, 349
bholes 302-03
Big Dumb Object 305-07
Bishop, Zealia 144, 257-58
Black Helicopters (Kiernan) 260-61
Black Hole, The (film) 317, 322
black holes 316-17, 323
"Black Thirst" (Moore) 190
Blish, James 306, 309, 321-22
Bloch, Robert 11, 31, 145, 150, 202, 250, 292, 320-21, 323, 334-35, 374, 386
Bogdanov, Aleksandr 231
Book of the Damned, The (Fort) 166, 181, 263, 324
Boston, Mass. 70, 136, 159, 165, 221-22, 228, 254, 255
Bova, Ben 209
Brackett, Leigh 308-09, 322
Bradbury, Ray 234, 254, 263, 274
"Brian-Eaters of Pluto, The" (Sterling) 287

Braun, Wernher von 143, 244-47, 262, 306, 320, 344, 374, 385
"Brick Moon, The" (Hale) 136
British Astronomical Association 21-22, 33
Brooks, William 153
Brown University 9, 18, 22, 23-25, 33, 35-36, 38, 43-47, 52-53, 55, 57-59, 61-64, 66, 68-75, 72n15, 77, 81, 83, 88, 97, 101, 104-5, 119n6, 119n7, 148, 152, 161, 170, 212, 222n7, 228, 237n9, 238, 253, 334, 341-42, 351-55, 358, 376-77, 379, 394
bulbous vegetable entities 178
Burritt, Elijah H. 14-17, 30, 40-41, 85, 117, 138, 161, 358-59, 375
Burroughs, Edgar Rice 116, 137, 188-89, 195, 230, 232-233, 242, 244-45, 247-50, 254, 258, 264, 277, 308, 326, 375, 387
Butler, Howard Russell 218
Byrd, Mary 31
Byrd, Richard 244, 246

Callaghan, Gavin 10, 116, 121, 137, 139, 142, 244, 247, 375
California 9, 18, 54, 67, 72, 200, 205, 233n8, 276, 318-19, 322, 337, 353
California Museum of Photography 9, 353
"Call of Cthulhu, The" (Lovecraft) 64, 75, 124-25, 144, 183, 185, 201, 208, 220, 224, 241n14, 252, 253, 260, 278, 321, 324, 332-34, 349
Callisto 132, 271-73, 277-78, 280, 308
Campbell, John W., Jr. 209, 302n20, 312, 316, 328, 389
Campbell, Ramsey 283, 288, 375
Campbell, Thomas 170
"Can Men Visit the Moon?" (Dodge) 114-16, 119, 121, 140
"Can the Moon be Reached by Man?" (Lovecraft) 113-14, 116-17, 121-22, 124, 127-28, 132-33, 135, 140, 146, 186

Index

Cannon, Annie Jump 19, 73
Cannon, Peter 146, 191n12, 195, 198, 329, 375, 390, 394
"Captain Stormfield's Visit to Heaven" (Twain) 290
Carcosa 167, 301n19, 325
Carcosa House 255
Caroline Island 64-65, 392
Carpenter, John 231, 276n9, 309, 317, 319
Carter, John 188-89, 247-49, 308
Carter, Lin 245, 249n17, 277, 296-97, 308, 375-376
Carter, Randolph 239, 248-49, 264, 271, 277, 278, 279, 288, 289, 302, 303, 320
Case of Charles Dexter Ward, The (Lovecraft) 67, 128, 144, 161, 167, 191, 249, 300, 324
Cast a Deadly Spell (film) 136n16
Celaeno 311-12
celestial globe 76, 82
Century Magazine 94, 98, 103, 107, 390
Charon 283, 288, 325
"Challenge from Beyond, The" (Lovecraft et al.) 195, 307, 309-12, 314-15, 350, 388
Chariots of the Gods? (Däniken) 294-95, 320
Christie, William Henry 257
Chronology out of Time, The (Cannon) 191n12, 195, 198, 326, 329, 375
Clark, Alvan 54, 54n1, 78
Clark, Franklin Chase 47, 60,
Clark, Lillian D. 17, 29, 47, 60, 212, 216
Clarke, Arthur C. 136, 145, 202, 204, 208, 245, 250n18, 262, 263, 273-76, 279, 287, 295-96, 305-6, 312, 319n7, 321, 344
Colavito, Jason 143, 145, 163, 183, 191, 231, 239, 285, 292, 294-96, 376-77
"Collapsing Cosmoses" (Lovecraft-Barlow) 307-10, 350
colonialism 198, 204, 232, 254, 258, 302n20, 308, 392

"Colour out of Space, The" (Lovecraft) 38, 120-21, 136-37, 142, 162, 207, 220, 237n10, 252, 257-58, 317, 349
Columbus of Space, A (Serviss) 185-87, 195
Combs, Jeffrey 322
"Comet Called Ithaqua, The" (Webb) 260, 290
comets 20, 21, 27, 34, 49, 51, 57, 74, 96, 132, 140, 153, 160, 166, 195, 209-10, 228n3, 260, 268, 271, 287, 288, 289-93, 325, 326, 334-35, 338, 348, 350
Comical History of the States and Empires of the Moon (Bergerac) 126
Commonplace Book (Lovecraft) 135n13, 171, 187, 196-97, 201, 259, 307-8, 318
"Confession of Unfaith, A" (Lovecraft) 39
Conover, Willis 250, 263, 274, 309
Contact (Sagan) 317-18
Cook, W. Paul 221-22
cosmicism 39-41, 170-71, 252, 267-68, 324, 328-34, 395
Cosmos (Sagan) 121, 245, 276, 291, 332, 392
"Crawling Chaos, The" (Lovecraft-Jackson) 142
Crichton, Michael 317
Croker, Thomas Crofton 126, 377
Crypt of Cthulhu 12, 192, 207, 270, 379, 383, 389, 391-92
"Crystal Egg, The" (Wells) 250-51
Cthulhu 13, 64, 75, 124-25, 141-42, 144, 183, 185, 192, 197-98, 201, 208, 220, 224, 230, 233, 241n14, 247, 252-54, 258, 260, 270, 275, 278, 286, 289, 293, 297, 314, 320-24, 328, 330-34, 349, 374-75, 377-79, 383, 389, 394, 397
Cthulhu Macula 286
Cummings, Ray 177, 241, 248, 309
cyanogen 195, 289

Dagon 64, 144, 200, 282, 296

"Damnable Asteroid, The" (Kimmel) 270-71
Daniel O'Rourke (Croker) 126
Däniken, Erich von 294, 376
Dark Forest hypothesis 292
"Dark of the Moon" (Dorr) 137, 378
Darrow, Jack 196
Darwin, Charles 137, 139, 237
Darwin, George 139
de Camp, L. Sprague 16, 50, 245, 377
De Vermis Mysteriis 317, 323
Dead Space (video game) 325
Dee, John 340-41
Deep Ones 188, 198, 221n4, 280, 293, 296, 300, 331
"Delavan's Comet and Astrology" (Lovecraft) 160, 290
Dench, Ernest A. 213, 215
Derleth, August 11, 106n3, 157n6, 172, 173n7, 175, 178, 192, 196-97, 202, 208, 233-34, 246, 249, 260, 270, 274, 278, 282, 290, 301, 311-12, 320, 328, 330, 337, 340-41, 343, 374, 378, 380, 382, 384-85, 387, 395
"Derleth Mythos, The" (Tierney) 282
"Diary of Alonzo Typer, The" (Lovecraft-Lumley) 191, 303
Dick, Thomas 16, 40
Dieterlen, Germaine 295
dinosaurs 184, 189, 193, 272, 278
"Discovery of the Ghooric Zone—March 15, 2337" (Lupoff) 288-89, 302-3
Dodge, Ernest Green 114-16, 119, 121, 140, 378
Dogon 295-96, 380
"Doom That Came to Sarnath, The" (Lovecraft) 111, 144
Dorr, James S. 137, 378
Doyle, Arthur Conan 270, 289, 299-300
Dream-Quest of Unknown Kadath, The (Lovecraft) 111, 144, 278, 282, 289, 300-301
"Dreams in the Witch House, The" (Lovecraft) 65, 130, 206, 284, 301-2, 315-16

"Dreams of Yith" (Rimel) 314
Duncan, John Charles 29, 344, 378
Dune (Herbert) 199, 234-35
Dunglison, Robley 126, 378
Dunsany, Lord 135n13, 274n7
Dunwich, Mass. 13, 119, 201, 220, 240, 290, 311, 316, 349, 371
"Dweller in the Gulf, The" (Smith) 246-47
Dyson, Freeman 291-92

Easter Island 255
eclipses 18, 29, 34, 49n27, 58, 64-65, 69, 71, 170n5, 174, 176, 211-25, 228n3, 228n4, 240, 295, 312, 328, 339, 349-50, 352-53, 364, 366, 392
Eddison, E. R. 177-78, 297
Edison, Thomas 139-42, 165, 167, 177, 185, 231, 254-56, 258, 263-64, 270, 347, 393
Edison's Conquest of Mars (Serviss) 12, 139-41, 165, 254-56, 258, 263-64, 269-70, 347, 393
Edwards, Alban 70, 72
Edwards, John 34, 52, 55, 57, 70-72, 74, 349, 352-53, 394
Egypt 14, 140, 243, 250, 254-55, 296
Einstein, Albert 176, 211, 316, 342, 347, 349, 385
Elder Things 111, 125, 141, 198, 239, 242, 246, 258, 275, 286, 293, 301-2, 307, 320, 331, 333
Elements of Astronomy (Young) 37, 397
Eltdown Shards 303, 312-14
Epicurus 169
Eratosthenes (crater) 62, 65, 90, 92, 94, 97-106, 108, 110, 111, 347, 390, 394
Event Horizon (film) 317
Europa 271, 273-74, 276-77, 280
Europa Report (film) 277
extinction 174, 197, 276-77, 283, 293, 325

Fabricius, David 128-29
face on Mars 329

"Facts concerning the Late Arthur Jermyn and His Family" (Lovecraft) 144, 204, 296, 317n3, 320
Falvey Memorial Library 48
"Famous Monsters" (Newman) 261-62
Fermi Paradox 267, 292
Field, John 340-34, 379
First Men in the Moon, The (Wells) 92-3, 110, 133-35, 137-38, 144, 207, 233, 383-84, 396
Fleming, Williamina 31
Florida 128, 157, 177, 309-10, 337, 339, 383
Fomalhaut 282-83
Fontenelle, Bernard Le Bovier de 128-29
Fort, Charles 165-166, 166n2, 181, 243, 263, 324, 379
From the Earth to the Moon (Verne) 121, 124, 127-32, 396
Frome, Nils 11, 263, 266-67, 386
Fungi from Yuggoth (Lovecraft) 111, 241, 279, 282-83, 289, 302-3
future history 138, 188, 202-3, 205-6, 273, 326-30
Futurians 259, 309-10

Gallomo 76n1, 87, 120
Galpin, Alfred 11, 16, 28n16, 38-39, 45, 47, 87n8, 96-97, 154, 181, 217, 337, 339, 386
Gauss, Carl Friedrich 130
Gelatt, Philip 277
Geography of the Heavens (Burritt) 14-15, 17, 30, 40-41, 85, 117, 161, 358-59, 375
Gernsback, Hugo 132, 196, 237n10, 280, 373
Ghatanothoa 285-86
Ghooric zone 288-289, 302-3, 377, 387
Ghosts of Mars (film) 231
Gibson, William 316
Gillis, Andrew "Bossy" 222
globular clusters 156, 370-71
Goddard, Robert H. 119-21, 250n18, 255, 266, 349, 379
Godwin, Francis 122, 134

Great Moon Hoax 122-26, 139, 385
Great Race 114, 136, 172, 178, 186n11, 189, 200, 205n17, 210, 249, 252, 254, 273, 286, 313-14, 323
Great Silence 267
Great Zimbabwe 257-58, 380
Greene, Sonia H. 146, 212, 217, 220
Griaule, Marcel 295
Gruithuisen, Franz von Paula 109, 130-32, 179

Haden, David 9, 16, 37, 50n29, 54, 70, 91, 139, 142, 144, 185, 213n1, 214, 215n2, 224, 234, 240-41, 255, 335, 380-81
Haldane, J. B. S. 137-39, 188, 207, 210, 239-40, 273, 326, 332-33, 373, 381
Hale, Edward Everett 136, 381
Hale, George Ellery 18, 67, 337
Hale (200-inch) telescope 18, 112, 350
Hali, Lake of 301
Halperin, David J. 9, 227n1, 260
Hamilton, Edmond 196, 242, 248, 252, 255-56, 265, 265n1, 308-10, 339, 381
Hansen, Peter Andreas 111, 112n1, 143
Harris, Woodburn 11, 173, 335, 387
Harvard College Observatory 19, 32, 58, 65, 70, 73, 90, 94, 99-100, 382, 390
Hartmann, Joachim F. 159-61, 210, 348
Hastur 270, 301
"Haunter of the Dark, The" (Lovecraft) 128, 134, 144, 198, 251, 288, 296, 303, 334
Heald, Hazel 64, 144, 204
Heinlein, Robert A. 202-9, 234, 308, 321, 326-30, 382
Herschel, John 123, 125, 129,
Herschel, William 156
Hess, Clara 32, 34, 36
"Hinterlands" (Gibson) 316

"History of the 'Necronomicon'" (Lovecraft) 300
Hite, Kenneth 111-12, 116n3, 135, 139, 161, 183, 187, 191, 197, 273, 279, 281-82, 284, 291, 294, 301-3, 316, 318, 328, 382
Hollow Earth 122-23n12, 243
Hope Street High School 39, 43-45, 72, 395
Howard, Robert E. 11, 44, 164, 198, 226, 311, 315, 327, 332, 387
Hubbard, L. Ron 202, 389
Hubble, Edwin 20, 157, 344, 349
human evolution 137, 139, 188, 207n19, 237, 239-40, 261, 265, 278, 325-27, 333
Huxley, Thomas Henry 137
Hyperspace 315-16

"I Am the Doorway" (King) 201
"Immeasurable Horror, The" (Smith) 190
"Impressions of the Planets—Venus" (Searight) 190
"In the Hall of the Yellow King" (Rawlik) 167, 325
"In the Walls of Eryx" (Lovecraft-Sterling) 117, 144, 168, 182-83, 186-87, 189, 191-202, 204-5, 207-9, 228n2, 247, 250, 268, 289, 307, 310, 312, 328, 335, 350, 378, 387
Invaders from Mars (film) 145
"Insects from Shaggai, The" (Campbell) 288
Interstellar (film) 317-18
"Is There Life on the Moon?" (Lovecraft) 90, 103, 108, 130
Islam 13, 128, 297, 299-300
"Islands of Space" (Campbell) 316
Ithaqua 197, 260, 290, 378, 380, 396
"Jaunt, The" (King) 316
Jeffery, Peter F. 270
Johnston, Charles 157-58
Joshi, S. T. 9, 11, 12, 15, 17, 28, 31, 34, 36, 40n21, 42-44, 47-48, 50, 60, 74, 107, 112, 116-18, 120n10, 122, 151-52, 154n4, 155n5, 159, 168n4, 169, 175, 177, 182, 192, 196, 200, 204, 213, 230, 232n7, 248-49, 274, 281-82, 288, 294, 302n12, 307-9, 314, 320-21, 323-24, 334, 340, 382-83, 386-87, 391, 394-95
Journey in Other Worlds, A (Astor) 132-33, 184, 237, 272, 373
"Julhi" (Moore) 190
Jupiter 20, 27, 29, 33-34, 58, 81-82, 88, 96, 104, 153, 172, 195, 209, 216, 223, 229, 238, 268-69, 271-80, 282, 288, 293, 306, 324, 336-337, 345-46, 351, 368-369
"Jupiter Five" (Clarke) 275, 306, 376
Just Imagine (film) 231-232

K'naa 285-86, 303
Kelvin, Lord 239, 263
Kiernan, Caitlín R. 260-61, 286-87, 289
Kimmel, Leigh 270
Kirk, George 213, 215, 217
King, Stephen 201, 316, 384
Kirtland Brothers & Co. 95, 362-66
Kleiner, Rheinhart 11, 23, 42, 55, 62, 74, 104, 109, 229, 231n6, 235, 247-48, 260, 386
Kline, Otis Adelbert 189
Klumpke, Dorothea 31
Kornbluth, Cyril M. 309
Kubrick, Stanley 276
Kuttner, Henry 177-78, 202
Kynarth 288

Ladd, Herbert W. 52
Ladd Observatory 9, 18, 22, 25-27, 27n15, 31, 34, 38, 43, 47, 52-75, 81-83, 85, 88-89, 99, 104-6, 108, 111, 119n7, 148, 170n5, 191, 218, 227n2, 228, 236, 237n9, 240n13, 297, 299, 334, 338, 342, 347-48, 350-54, 359-60, 394-95
Lagh metal 285. *See also* tok'l
Lang, Fritz 143-44, 245, 275, 380
Last and First Men (Stapledon) 138, 188, 198, 207, 233, 253, 274n6, 280-82, 327, 394

"Last Judgment, The" (Haldane) 137–39, 171, 188, 207, 273, 326, 332, 381
"Last Man, The" (Campbell) 170
League of Extraordinary Gentlemen, The (Moore-O'Neill) 135n14, 249, 388
Leavitt, Henrietta 31–32, 73, 157, 344, 348
Leeds, Arthur 213, 215
Leiber, Fritz 10, 118, 233, 249, 275, 283n13, 315–16, 320, 328–30, 384–85
Leiber, Jonquil 57, 70, 105, 353, 360
Lemuria 255, 303
Lessons in Astronomy (Young) 16–20, 17n6, 37, 85, 93–94, 96, 147n1, 169, 273, 292, 347, 397
Lewis, C. S. 177, 190, 202, 206–9, 233–34, 247, 274n6, 297, 385
Ley, Willy 143, 245, 275, 279, 344, 385
Lick Observatory 18, 18n7, 54, 72
light pollution 25, 54n1, 97, 369
Lifeforce (film) 290
Lindbergh, Charles 120, 250n18
Lindsay, David 297
Livesey, T. R. 10, 11, 17, 47, 74, 94, 100, 109–11, 113, 118, 140, 154, 161, 211, 254, 282, 284, 298–99, 301, 339, 342, 359, 360, 385
Locke, Richard Adams 122–25, 129, 136, 385
"Logic of Empire" (Heinlein) 202–6, 208, 328, 382
López-Gallego, Gonzalo 136–37
Lords of Venus 183–84, 191, 197, 303–04
Lovecraft at Last (Conover) 274
Lovecraft Country (TV series) 258
Lovecraft (crater) 178
Lovecraft, H. P.: and almanacs, 23, 381; and astrology, 156–61, 210, 228, 278, 290, 348; *Astronomical Notebook* of, 48–49, 51, 78n3, 348–49, 360; astronomical research of, 27–28, 90–111, 181–82, 344; and astronomy books, 14–17, 24, 30–31, 38, 40, 42, 59, 62, 73, 85, 110, 118, 139, 157, 161, 167, 227n2, 251, 343–44; and astrophotography, 347, 351–61; and aurora borealis, 29–30, 390; breakdown of 1908, 43, 47–50, 74, 108, 151, 158, 360; and a career in astronomy, 37, 43–50, 52, 61, 72, 74, 89, 106, 110, 150, 152, 335; and chemistry, 16–17, 26, 35, 38, 42–43, 45n23, 46–47; final illness of, 158, 343–45; genealogy of, 340–41; juvenile science publications of, 26–31, 33, 34, 39, 48, 61, 65–66, 76, 80, 84, 95–97, 100–108, 113–16, 149–51, 168, 175, 182, 212, 235, 238, 311n1, 339–40, 347, 348, 352, 355, 357–60, 363, 365; lectures of, 34–36, 56; and mathematics, 30, 37, 43–47, 85, 89, 108; and meteorology, 38, 61, 147, 352; and misogyny, 31; newspaper columns of, 28, 34–35, 37, 43, 48–49, 63, 95, 147–63, 175, 211, 290, 343, 360; and planispheres, 22–23, 49, 340; racism of, 13–14, 204; sensitivity to cold, 100, 110, 213, 215, 217, 223, 230, 335, 37, 345; school grades of, 43–45; and solar eclipses, 29, 65, 176, 211–26, 339, 349–50; spectroscopes of, 38–39, 62; telescopes of, 23–24, 26–27, 29, 32–33, 49, 55, 57, 78–80, 78n4, 83–84, 87, 89, 95–96, 100, 106, 106n3, 181–82, 298, 337, 337n4, 343, 347–48, 354, 362–66; xenophobia of, 204, 266
Lovecraft, Sarah Susan (Phillips) 14, 23–24, 35, 38, 46–47, 55, 60, 76, 84, 100, 340, 363
Lovecraft, Winfield Scott 14
Loveman, Samuel 143, 206n18, 215
Lowell Observatory 153, 157, 179, 235–36, 245, 247, 280–82, 337, 347
Lowell, Percival 20, 62–63, 92, 121, 139, 153, 156, 168, 170, 176, 179–81, 228–30, 233, 235–37, 241, 244–45, 247–48, 254, 257, 264, 276, 280–81, 288, 348, 377, 387

Lowndes, Robert A. W. 237, 244, 287, 309, 322, 373
Lubnow, Fred S. 11, 113, 139, 167-68, 173n7, 178, 193, 195-96, 198-99, 230, 235, 239, 241, 272, 278-79, 281, 286, 288-89, 387
Lucian of Samosata 134, 383
Lupoff, Richard A. 189, 244, 247, 288-89, 302, 377, 387

Mädler, Johann Heinrich von 132
Man in the Moone, The (Godwin) 122
man-lizards 187, 189, 192-94, 196-98, 200, 304
Mañana Literary Society 202, 308
Marconi, Guglielmo 239
Maria Mitchell Observatory 338, 350
marijuana 199-200
Mariconda, Steven J. 134, 251, 388
Mars 12, 27, 34, 49, 62-64, 81-82, 98, 109, 114, 120, 132, 134, 137-41, 149-51, 156, 158, 165, 167n3, 168-69, 171, 176-77, 182-85, 188-90, 195, 206-7, 227-64, 268-70, 273, 276, 278, 280-81, 300n18, 306, 325, 337, 347, 351, 374-77, 380-82, 384-85, 387-93, 395-98
Martian Chronicles, The (Bradbury) 234, 374
Martian Gothic: Unification (video game) 263, 325
"Martian Odyssey, A" (Weinbaum) 250
Mass Effect (video game) 325
Massacre of Mankind, The (Baxter) 258-60
McNeill, Graham 259, 312, 322, 388
Melbourne telescope 18n7
Méliès, Georges 143, 145
"Mellonta Tauta" (Poe) 126-27, 279, 326, 391
Men in Black (film) 324
Menzies, William Cameron 145
Mercury 104, 111, 138, 168, 170, 172, 174, 176-78, 182, 216, 229, 271, 281, 288, 395

Method of Reaching Extreme Altitudes, A (Goddard) 119
Mi-Go 41, 197-98, 241, 280-86, 289, 292, 316, 331, 340, 345
Michelson-Morley experiment 118, 341-42
Milky Way 19-20, 152, 156, 297n17, 308, 332, 344, 349, 356, 371, 394
Miller, Dayton 118, 341-42
Miller, Michael D. 275-76, 314
Mind Parasites, The (Wilson) 308
"Mine on Yuggoth, The" (Campbell) 283, 285, 375
Miskatonic University 65, 75, 163n1, 186, 191, 205, 244, 259, 262, 276, 297, 306, 312, 322, 383, 388-89, 394
Moe, Maurice W. 11, 14, 26, 30, 87, 159, 239, 337, 386
"Monster God of Mamurth, The" (Hamilton) 196
Moon (Earth's) 16, 20-21, 27, 29-31, 33-35, 42, 49, 60, 64, 66, 81, 85, 88, 90-146, 149-51, 162, 170, 172, 176-77, 179, 181-82, 184, 186, 188, 190, 195, 207, 211-13, 215, 220-21, 223-25, 233, 240, 242, 251, 259, 265, 268, 274, 278, 337, 339-40, 345, 351, 355, 357-60, 362-63, 366-68, 373-75, 378, 381, 383-84, 390, 393, 396
"Moon-Bog, The" (Lovecraft) 135
Moon Maid, The (Burroughs) 137, 326
Moon Metal, The (Serviss) 141-42, 393
Moore, Alan 135n14, 167, 249, 260, 378, 388
Moore, C. L. 11, 168, 190, 202, 249, 311, 377, 386
Morton, James F. 11, 30, 74, 111, 157, 211, 213, 217, 222, 318n5, 323, 337, 337n4, 339, 341-43, 345
Mound, The (Lovecraft-Bishop) 144, 186n10, 300
Mount Wilson Observatory 67, 349

Index 407

"MS. Found in a Bottle" (Poe) 122n12
Muhammed 300
Munroe, Chester 28, 36, 155
Munroe, Harold 36
Munsey, Frank 108-9, 114-16
Munsey's Magazine 108-9, 114-16, 375, 378, 383, 389
"Murders in the Rue Morgue, The" (Poe) 169-70
Murray, Will 246-47, 297, 389
"My Opinion as to the Lunar Canals" (Lovecraft) 106-7, 130

Napier, Carson 188-89
Nantucket 122n12, 126, 225, 338, 350
Narrative of Arthur Gordon Pym of Nantucket, The (Poe) 122n12, 126
NASA 114, 235, 246, 262, 286, 299, 330, 388, 391
nebular hypothesis 155, 169-74, 178-79, 195, 207, 228-29, 237, 286, 302, 344, 392
Necronomicon (Alhazred) 201, 242, 297, 317n3, 322, 340
Neith 181
Nemesis (solar companion) 293-94
"Nemesis" (Lovecraft) 154, 293-94
Neptune 20, 120n9, 147n1, 174, 241, 268-69, 278-82, 287-88, 293, 294, 330, 389
Neutaconkanut hill 345
New Jersey 165, 185, 259n19
New Lands (Fort) 165-66, 379
New York City 23, 132, 142-44, 165-67, 206n18, 211-13, 215, 220, 224, 239n12, 243, 245, 250, 252, 259-60, 309, 339, 362
Newburyport, Mass. 211, 220-24
Newman, Kim 261, 389
Nichol, John Pringle 169-70
"Night Ocean, The" (Lovecraft-Barlow) 130, 173, 334
"Nightfall" (Asimov) 312
Nithon 282-283, 288
Niven, Larry 305-6, 307
"Nyarlathotep" (Lovecraft) 142

O'Bannon, Dan 323, 384
Off on a Comet (Verne) 290-91
Olympus Mons 239, 263
O'Neill, Kevin 135n14, 249, 260, 388,
orrery 76, 80-82, 80n5, 87
"Other Gods, The" (Lovecraft) 135, 144, 224
"Out of the Aeons" (Lovecraft-Heald) 64, 144, 171, 285, 303
Out of the Silent Planet (Lewis) 206-07, 233, 381, 385

Pacific Ocean 64, 65, 139, 240, 241n14, 255, 276, 333, 335
Pale Blue Dot (Sagan) 330, 392
Palomar Observatory 18, 112, 350
Parsons, Jack 121, 202n16, 245, 344, 375
Pastorff, Johann Wilhelm 131-32
Pawtuxet Valley Gleaner 37, 64, 89-90, 107-8, 113, 148-52, 156, 174-75, 227, 281, 292, 348
Peltier, Leslie C. 57, 74, 334-35, 338, 350
Perelandra (Lewis) 202, 206-8, 233, 379, 385
Petaja, Emil 202
Phaeton 269-70, 290, 293
Phaistos Disc 295
Phantagraph 338
Phillips, Robie 14-16, 41, 85
Phillips, Whipple 46, 60, 84, 100
Pickering, Edward Charles 90, 92
Pickering, William Henry 62, 66, 90-92, 94, 98-100, 102-4, 105-11, 156, 227-28, 287-88, 359, 373, 390
"Planet Neptune to Mother Sun" (Copeland) 279-80
Planet Nine 288-89
Planet of the Apes (film) 319-20
Planet X 241, 281, 287-89
Planetarium 21, 80, 252, 339, 350
planetesimal hypothesis 173-74, 267, 280
planisphere 22-23, 49, 340
Pleasures of the Telescope (Serviss) 86, 139, 272, 301, 393

Pleiades 311-12, 311n1, 369-70
Pluto 157, 200n14, 229, 241, 268, 279-89, 325, 349
"Plutonian Drug, The" (Smith) 200n14, 287
Pnakotus 186, 191, 239, 257, 270, 275, 303, 306-7, 314, 323,
Poe, Edgar Allan 42, 122-27, 395
Poison Belt, The (Doyle) 289
Polaris (star) 284, 302, 357
"Polaris" (Lovecraft) 29-30, 29n17, 50, 144, 161, 298, 302, 318, 349, 390
Pope, Gustavus 184, 189, 243-44, 391
Popular Astronomy 57n6, 94, 109, 109n4, 161-62, 175, 287, 351-52, 378, 384, 390
Port of Peril, The (Kline) 189-90
Porter, Russell W. 24
Price, E. Hoffmann 11, 128, 177, 183, 191, 224, 229, 251, 277, 386
Price, Robert M. 145, 244, 249, 252, 274, 276, 312-13, 329-30, 376, 378-79, 386, 391-92
"Princess of the Black Asteroid" (Jeffrey) 270
Proctor, Richard A. 24, 86, 370, 392
Prometheus (film) 324
Providence, R.I. 5, 9, 14, 21-25, 27-28, 34-37, 46, 49, 53-56, 63, 67, 72, 75, 83-84, 87, 97, 111, 114n2, 145, 147-49, 152-55, 158-59, 166-67, 191-92, 200, 210, 211, 220, 224, 225, 227n1, 249, 260-61, 277, 337-39, 341-42, 345, 349, 356, 361, 370
Providence (Moore-Burrows) 167, 378, 388
Providence Astronomical Society 34, 36
Providence Journal 63, 147, 149, 175, 348
Providence Tribune 37, 62-63, 71, 89, 148-53, 166, 175, 348

Quake (video game) 325
Quebec 126, 225, 337

"Quest of Iranon, The" (Lovecraft) 144, 318

R'lyeh 64, 141, 224, 239, 276, 297
racism 13-14, 204, 232, 258, 261, 266, 306
radiation 186, 273, 311, 317, 342, 368
Rare Earth Hypothesis 267
Rawlik, Peter 128, 167, 325, 392
"Red Peri, The" (Weinbaum) 287
"Red Star, The" (Doyle) 299-300
Rendezvous with Rama (Clarke) 275, 305-6, 319n7
"Retreat to Mars, The" (Christie) 257
Rhode Island Journal of Astronomy 14, 23, 26-37, 48, 65-66, 76-77, 82, 84-85, 87-89, 95-98, 100-101, 103-8, 113-16, 149-51, 168, 175, 182, 212, 235, 238, 311n1, 347-48, 352, 355, 357-60, 363
Richardson, Roland 71
Rimel, Duane W. 11, 56, 105, 144-45, 314, 334n2, 386
Ringworld (Niven) 305-06
R'lyeh 64, 141, 224, 239, 276, 297
rockets 116-17, 119-21, 126, 143, 177, 202n16, 244, 250n18, 255, 265, 329, 344, 349, 375
Roerich, Nicholas 178
Roswell, N.M. 120, 163, 165, 398
Royal Astrophysical Observatory 67
Russia 119, 137, 178, 183, 270, 291, 327n13, 397. *See also* Siberia, Soviet Union

Sagan, Carl 121, 195, 245, 273, 276, 289, 291, 317, 320, 331-32, 392
Saliva Tree, The (Aldiss) 258
Saturn 27, 29, 34, 55, 61, 81, 91, 96, 104, 155, 228n3, 268, 278-80, 325, 337-38, 351, 369, 397
Schiaparelli, Giovanni 62, 176, 180-181, 186, 227-28
Schmidt, Johann Friedrich Julius 131-32
Science Fiction League 196

Science Library (Lovecraft) 66, 84, 365
Scientific Gazette (Lovecraft) 26, 31, 33, 95, 363, 365
Seagrave, Frank 25, 54, 240, 342
Searight, Richard F. 11, 78, 145, 190, 230, 251, 312, 386
"Sentinel, The" (Clarke) 274
Serling, Rod 320
Serviss, Garrett P. 12, 22, 30, 49, 85, 116, 118, 121, 124, 130, 139–43, 162, 165, 167–68, 170, 185–87, 195, 206n18, 230, 249, 251, 254–55, 257–60, 263–64, 269–70, 272, 298, 301, 340, 343, 347, 393
Shaggai 288
Shadow of the Comet (video game) 290, 325
"Shadow out of Space, The" (Derleth) 172–73
"Shadow out of Time, The" (Lovecraft) 111, 127, 140, 144, 172–73, 178, 186n11, 191, 205, 229, 234, 240, 249, 257, 260, 262, 270, 272, 287, 296, 307–9, 313–14, 328–29, 334, 380
"Shadow over Innsmouth, The" (Lovecraft) 64, 67, 144, 188, 198, 221, 255, 262, 290, 331, 350
"Shadow over the Moon, The" (Baxter) 136
"Shambleau" (Moore) 190, 249
"Shambler from the Stars, The" (Bloch) 334–35
Shapley, Harlow 20, 156–57, 349
Shepperson, Claude Allin 93
Shining Trapezohedron 134, 251
shoggoths 190, 201, 259, 263, 270, 302, 322, 325
"Shoggoths in Bloom" (Bear) 259
Shonhi 303
Shub-Niggurath 292, 325
Siberia 129, 231, 263. *See also* Russia, Soviet Union
Sinclair, Upton 205
Sirius 295–97, 395
Sirius Mystery, The (Temple) 295–96, 395

skyscrapers 21, 54, 111, 342, 349–50
Slocum, Frederick 52, 57, 58n6, 65–71, 74, 104, 218, 350, 354, 384
Smiley, Charles Hugh 221–22, 342
Smith, Clark Ashton 11, 17, 29, 168, 177, 187, 190, 197, 200n14, 205, 231n5, 242, 246–48, 254–55, 259, 268, 270, 276–78, 287, 319, 320, 387, 389, 394
Smith, E. E. 308–9, 315
Smithsonian Institution 119, 158, 257
"Some Notes on Interplanetary Fiction" 135, 187–88, 197, 205, 207, 232, 240, 249, 255
"Sothis Radiant, The" (Murray) 297, 389
South Africa 123
Soviet Union 114, 119n6, 137, 183, 230–31. *See also* Russia, Siberia
space opera 168, 177, 192, 244, 250n18, 287–88, 307–10, 315–17, 320–23, 325–26
Space Vampires, The (Wilson) 270, 290, 308
spectroscopy 19, 38–39, 62, 68, 90, 395
Sphere (Crichton) 317
Spielberg, Steven 259–60
Stapledon, Olaf 138–39, 188, 198, 207, 210, 233, 253–54, 280–82, 327–30, 394
"Star, The" (Wells) 252
Star Begotten (Wells) 261–62
Star Rover, The (London) 233n8, 318–19
Star Trek (TV series) 187, 199, 321–22, 325
Star Wars (film) 234–35, 309, 317, 321–23, 325, 330, 395
star-spawn 198, 289, 293, 297
Starry Wisdom Library, The (Pedersen) 128, 296–97
Station X (Winsor) 187, 240–41
stellar evolution. *See* nebular hypothesis, planetesimal hypothesis
Sterling, Kenneth J. 112, 117, 118, 120, 168, 176, 189, 192, 194–96,

198-99, 200, 207, 250, 287, 320, 335, 337, 341-42
Stetson, Harlan True 72-74
Stetson University 157-158
Stranger in a Strange Land (Heinlein) 234
Stross, Charles 208, 394
Sully, Helen V. 11, 267, 386
"Supernatural Horror in Literature" (Lovecraft) 171, 183, 276, 321

Talman, Wilfrid 11, 223, 243, 386
Temple, Robert K. G. 295-96, 395
Tesla, Nikola 134, 239, 273
Theosophy 183, 191, 231
Thing, The (film) 231, 309, 319, 322
Things to Come (film) 144-45, 326
Thog 288-89, 302
Thok 288-89
"Through the Gates of the Silver Key" (Lovecraft-Price) 186n10, 229-30, 239, 248, 279, 288, 298, 302-4, 319
"Through Hyperspace with Brown Jenkin" (Leiber) 118, 233, 275, 315-16, 328-30
"Tidal Moon" (Weinbaum) 277-78
Tierney, Richard L. 118, 252, 282, 395
"'Till A' the Seas'" (Lovecraft-Barlow) 328
Tillinghast, Wallace 157, 165-67
Time Machine, The (Wells) 134, 171, 185, 208, 252, 274n6, 396
Titan 280, 325
Titius-Bode law 268-269, 269n2
"To Arkham and the Stars" (Leiber) 283n13, 328-29
"To Mars and Providence" (Webb) 260-61
Todd, David Peck 240
tok'l 285. *See also* lagh metal
Toldridge, Elizabeth 11, 42, 220, 386
Tolstoi, Alexei 231
Tombaugh, Clyde 157, 241, 280-81, 284, 286, 395
Tormance 297-98
transit telescope 53-54, 76, 83-84

Triton 279-80
Tsathoggua 278, 296-97, 308, 325
Tucker, Bob 196
Tucker, George 126
Trip from the Earth to the Moon, A (Baudoin) 121-22, 126
Trip to the Moon, A (film) 143, 145, 395
True History (Lucian) 134
Tsan-Chan 328
Twain, Mark 290
2001: A Space Odyssey (Clarke) 145, 268, 274-76, 279, 287, 294, 296, 306, 312, 317
2010: Odyssey Two (Clarke) 276-77, 296

"Ubbo-Sathla" (Smith) 270
Unidentified Flying Objects (UFOs) 30, 163-167, 281, 292, 293n14, 296n16, 376, 382, 395, 398
Umbricht, Michael 9, 26n14, 54n4, 61n10, 81
"Unparalleled Adventure of One Hans Pfaall, The" (Poe) 122-24, fa127
Upton, Winslow 38, 47, 52-55, 57-68, 70-72, 74, 85-86, 99, 104-6, 148-51, 170, 173-74, 228-29, 240, 299, 348, 351-52, 377, 395
Uranus 174, 182, 241, 268, 278-80, 287-88

"Valley of Dreams" (Weinbaum) 250
Van Vleck Observatory 67, 69-72, 218, 349
"Vaults of Yoh-Vombis, The" (Smith) 246, 263
Velikovsky, Immanuel 209-10, 269, 380, 396
Venus 20, 27, 30, 34, 96-98, 104, 106, 108, 110-11, 113, 117, 120, 137-38, 147, 159-60, 163-210, 228n2, 229, 242, 244, 247, 249, 253, 268, 271, 273, 276, 289, 303-4, 312, 326, 328, 335-36, 342, 345, 348, 355, 369, 376, 379, 381, 385, 391-95

Index 411

Verne, Jules 42, 121-22, 124, 126-33, 136, 138, 143, 145-46, 185-86, 208, 230, 246, 251, 290-91, 317, 381, 396
Voyage to Arcturus, A (Lindsay) 297-98
Voyage to the Moon, A (Tucker) 126
"Voyage to Sfanomoë, A" (Smith) 190
Vulcan 174-76, 269, 288, 293, 385, 395
"Vulthoom" (Smith) 247

Wandrei, Donald A. 11, 309, 315, 320, 339, 340
War of the Worlds, The (Wells) 134-35, 137-38, 139, 184-85, 187, 207, 230, 232-33, 251-54, 258-60, 261, 300n18, 339, 347
War of the Worlds (film) 259-60
Waugh, Robert H. 191-92, 197, 198, 207, 274n6, 297-98, 316
Webb, Don 260, 264, 290
Webster's International Dictionary 16
Weinbaum, Stanley G. 250, 255, 277-78, 287, 309, 315
Wells, H. G. 42, 92, 110, 121, 122, 133-36, 137, 138, 143, 144-45, 171, 184-85, 207, 210, 230, 231, 233, 249, 250-54, 258-62, 263, 264, 300n18, 326-27, 347
Wesleyan University 57, 67, 68, 71-72
West, Herbert 143, 144, 275n8, 322
"When the Green Star Waned" (Dyalhis) 187-88, 265n1
"Whisperer in Darkness, The" (Lovecraft) 144, 220, 229, 241, 262, 279, 281, 282, 283, 285-87, 292, 301, 316, 340, 349

White, Cecil B. *See* William Henry Christie
"Who Goes There?" (Campbell) 302n20
Williamson, Jack 309
Wilson, Colin 270, 290, 308
Wollheim, Donald 189, 259, 274, 327, 338-39
Wolverton, Dave 258
Woman in the Moon (film) 143
Wooley, Natalie H. 117, 130, 188, 202n15, 265, 267
Woomera 329
Worcester, Mass. 23, 119, 165
Worm Ouroboros, The (Eddison) 177-78, 207, 208, 297
wormholes 275, 316-17
Wright, Farnsworth 196, 200

X-Files, The (TV series) 263
Xoth 296-97

Yaddith 302-3
Yaddith-Gho 285, 303
Yekub 195, 304, 315
Yerkes Observatory 67, 96, 181, 337, 347
Y'ha-nthlei 273
Yith 304, 314, 325, 331
Yog-Sothoth 201, 323
Young, Charles Augustus 16-20, 37, 85, 93-94, 96, 147n1, 169, 273n5, 292, 344, 347
Yuggoth 41, 111, 178n9, 241, 268, 279, 280-89, 302-3, 323, 331, 349
Yuggothians 283n13, 285-86, 303, 331

Zaman 288-89
Zkauba 302

www.ingramcontent.com/pod-product-compliance
Lightning Source LLC
Chambersburg PA
CBHW060105170426
43198CB00010B/773